OXFORD IB DIPLOMA PROGRAMME

2014 EDITION

BUSINESS MANAGEMENT

COURSE COMPANION

Loykie Lominé
Martin Muchena
Robert A. Pierce

OXFORD
UNIVERSITY PRESS

OXFORD
UNIVERSITY PRESS

Great Clarendon Street, Oxford, OX2 6DP, United Kingdom

Oxford University Press is a department of the University of Oxford. It furthers the University's objective of excellence in research, scholarship, and education by publishing worldwide. Oxford is a registered trade mark of Oxford University Press in the UK and in certain other countries

British Library Cataloguing in Publication Data

Data available

978-0-19-839281-1

13

MIX
Paper from
responsible sources
FSC® C007785
www.fsc.org

Paper used in the production of this book is a natural, recyclable product made from wood grown in sustainable forests. The manufacturing process conforms to the environmental regulations of the country of origin.

Printed in Great Britain by Bell and Bain Ltd, Glasgow

Acknowledgements

The publishers would like to thank the following for permissions to use their photographs:

Cover: MJ Prototype/Shutterstock **p1:** ChristineGonsalves/Shutterstock; **p5:** iStock; **p10:** iStock; **p19:** iStock; **p23:** Ken Wolter/Shutterstock; **p34:** iStock; **p41:** razihusin/Shutterstock; **p45:** UIG/Getty Images; **p52:** iStock; **p69:** Greg Epperson/Shutterstock; **p72:** AFP/Getty Images; **p74:** iStock; **p94:** aerogondo2/Shutterstock; **p97:** tab62/Shutterstock; **p101:** iStock; **p111:** © Imaginechina/Corbis; **p122:** iStock; **p159:** Mazzzur/Shutterstock; **p162:** (a) © James Leynse/Corbis, (b) © Michael S. Yamashita/Corbis; **p165:** (a) Thomas Mukoya/Reuters, (b) Bloomberg/Getty Images; **p169:** Mike Hutchings/Reuters; **p173:** (a) © Alex Robinson/JAI/Corbis, (b) © Michael Hanson/National Geographic Society/Corbis; **p174:** © Julian Eales/Alamy; **p180:** © Krista Rossow/National Geographic Society/Corbis; **p182:** Vitaly Titov & Maria Sidelnikova/Shutterstock; **p198:** David Becker/Stringer/Getty Images; **p210:** M. Unal Ozmen/Shutterstock; **p215:** (a) © Rodach, Johannes/the food passionates/Corbis, (b) © Michele Eve/Splash News/Corbis; **p222:** © Yuri Arcurs/Tetra Images/Corbis; **p241:** (a) © Neil Farrin/JAI/Corbis, (b) © Danny Lehman/Corbis; **p247:** Curioso/Shutterstock; **p250:** iStock; **p252:** Gil C/Shutterstock; **p253:** Bloomberg/Getty Images; **p256:** eans/Shutterstock; **p267:** (a) U. Baumgarten/Getty Images, (b) Annette Shaff/Shutterstock; **p270:** Iraidka/Shutterstock; **p281:** © Samantha Craddock / Alamy; **p300:** Bloomberg/Getty Images; **p301:** iStock; **p311:** © Cienpies Design / Alamy; **p318:** (a) jo Crebbin/Shutterstock, (b) Richard Kuhlmann/www.qdrum.co.za; **p329:** Bocman1973/Shutterstock; **p332:** Tupungato/Shutterstock;

p334: iStock; **p338:** pick/Shutterstock; **p340:** bikeriderlondon/Shutterstock; **p344:** Jason Mintzer/Shutterstock; **p347:** iStock; **p355:** Manufactus.com; **p357:** Oxford University Press; **p364:** Oxford University Press; **p366:** Mesut Dogan/Shutterstock; **p374:** (a) © Frederic Neema/Sygma/Corbis, (b) © Corbis; **p376:** Oxford University Press

Artwork by Six Red Marbles and Oxford University Press

The authors and the publisher are grateful to the following for permission to reprint the copyright material listed:

The Association of Chartered Certified Accountants (ACCA) for the five fundamental principles from *Code of Ethics and Conduct* (January, 2011), www.accaglobal.com.

Acorn Systems for case study on Coca-Cola Turkey Icecek, from www.acornsys.com.

Bennett, Coleman & Co, Ltd (BCCL) for 'Pepsico targeting mass marketing, will cater to different segments of consumers: Manu Anand' by Ratna Bhushan, 6 June 2011, *Economic Times*, Times of India Group, copyright © BCCL 2011. All Rights Reserved.

Pearson Education for 'The Power Interest Model', original model by A L Mendelow published in the *Proceedings of the Second International Conference on Information Systems*, Cambridge MA, 1991, this version from G Johnson & K Scholes: *Exploring Corporate Strategy* (5e, Prentice Hall, 1999).

UNDP for Summary from 'Vodafone and Safaricom: Extending Financial Services to the Poor in Rural Kenya' by Winifred N Karugu and Triza Mwendwa, copyright © 2007 United National Development Programme, published at www.growinginclusivemarkets.org. All rights reserved.

Although we have made every effort to trace and contact all copyright holders before publication this has not been possible in all cases. If notified, the publisher will rectify any errors or omissions at the earliest opportunity.

Course book definition

The IB Diploma Programme course books are resource materials designed to support students throughout their two-year Diploma Programme course of study in a particular subject. They will help students gain an understanding of what is expected from the study of an IB Diploma Programme subject while presenting content in a way that illustrates the purpose and aims of the IB. They reflect the philosophy and approach of the IB and encourage a deep understanding of each subject by making connections to wider issues and providing opportunities for critical thinking.

The books mirror the IB philosophy of viewing the curriculum in terms of a whole-course approach; the use of a wide range of resources, international mindedness, the IB learner profile and the IB Diploma Programme core requirements, theory of knowledge, the extended essay, and creativity, action, service (CAS).

Each book can be used in conjunction with other materials and indeed, students of the IB are required and encouraged to draw conclusions from a variety of resources. Suggestions for additional and further reading are given in each book and suggestions for how to extend research are provided.

In addition, the course companions provide advice and guidance on the specific course assessment requirements and on academic honesty protocol. They are distinctive and authoritative without being prescriptive.

IB mission statement

The International Baccalaureate aims to develop inquiring, knowledgeable and caring young people who help to create a better and more peaceful world through intercultural understanding and respect.

To this end the organization works with schools, governments and international organizations to develop challenging programmes of international education and rigorous assessment.

These programmes encourage students across the world to become active, compassionate and lifelong learners who understand that other people, with their differences, can also be right.

The IB Learner Profile

The aim of all IB programmes to develop internationally minded people who work to create a better and more peaceful world. The aim of the programme is to develop this person through ten learner attributes, as described below.

Inquirers: They develop their natural curiosity. They acquire the skills necessary to conduct inquiry and research and show independence in learning. They actively enjoy learning and this love of learning will be sustained throughout their lives.

Knowledgeable: They explore concepts, ideas, and issues that have local and global significance. In so doing, they acquire in-depth knowledge and develop understanding across a broad and balanced range of disciplines.

Thinkers: They exercise initiative in applying thinking skills critically and creatively to recognize and approach complex problems, and make reasoned, ethical decisions.

Communicators: They understand and express ideas and information confidently and creatively in more than one language and in a variety of modes of communication. They work effectively and willingly in collaboration with others.

Principled: They act with integrity and honesty, with a strong sense of fairness, justice and respect for the dignity of the individual, groups and communities. They take responsibility for their own action and the consequences that accompany them.

Open-minded: They understand and appreciate their own cultures and personal histories, and are open to the perspectives, values and traditions of other individuals and communities. They are accustomed to seeking and evaluating a range of points of view, and are willing to grow from the experience.

Caring: They show empathy, compassion and respect towards the needs and feelings of others. They have a personal commitment to service, and to act to make a positive difference to the lives of others and to the environment.

Risk-takers: They approach unfamiliar situations and uncertainty with courage and forethought, and have the independence of spirit to explore new roles, ideas, and strategies. They are brave and articulate in defending their beliefs.

Balanced: They understand the importance of intellectual, physical and emotional ballance to achieve personal well-being for themselves and others.

Reflective: They give thoughtful consideration to their own learning and experience. They are able to assess and understand their strengths and limitations in order to support their learning and personal development.

A note on academic honesty

It is of vital importance to acknowledge and appropriately credit the owners of information when that information is used in your work. After all, owners of ideas (intellectual property) have property rights. To have an authentic piece of work, it must be based on your individual and original ideas with the work of others fully acknowledged. Therefore, all assignments, written or oral, completed for assessment must use your own language and expression. Where sources are used or referred to, whether in the form of direct quotation or paraphrase, such sources must be appropriately acknowledged.

How do I acknowledge the work of others?

The way that you acknowledge that you have used the ideas of other people is through the use of footnotes and bibliographies.

Footnotes (placed at the bottom of a page) or endnotes (placed at the end of a document) are to be provided when you quote or paraphrase from another document, or closely summarize the information provided in another document. You do not need to provide a footnote for information that is part of a 'body of knowledge'. That is, definitions do not need to be footnoted as they are part of the assumed knowledge.

Bibliographies should include a formal list of the resources that you used in your work. 'Formal' means that you should use one of the several accepted forms of presentation. This usually involves separating the resources that you use into different categories (e.g. books, magazines, newspaper articles, internet-based resources, Cds and works of art) and providing full information as to how a reader or viewer of your work can find the same information. A bibliography is compulsory in the Extended Essay.

What constitutes malpractice?

Malpractice is behaviour that results in, or may result in, you or any student gaining an unfair advantage in one or more assessment component. Malpractice includes plagiarism and collusion.

Plagiarism is defined as the representation of the ideas or work of another person as your own. The following are some of the ways to avoid plagiarism:

- words and ideas of another person to support one's arguments must be acknowledged
- passages that are quoted verbatim must be enclosed within quotation marks and acknowledged
- CD-Roms, email messages, web sites on the Internet and any other electronic media must be treated in the same way as books and journals
- the sources of all photographs, maps, illustrations, computer programs, data, graphs, audio-visual and similar material must be acknowledged if they are not your own work
- works of art, whether music, film dance, theatre arts or visual arts and where the creative use of a part of a work takes place, the original artist must be acknowledged.

Collusion is defined as supporting malpractice by another student. This includes:

- allowing your work to be copied or submitted for assessment by another student
- duplicating work for different assessment components and/or diploma requirements.

Other forms of malpractice include any action that gives you an unfair advantage or affects the results of another student. Examples include, taking unauthorized material into an examination room, misconduct during an examination and falsifying a CAS record.

Contents

Introduction

This book is a companion for students of Business Management in the International Baccalaureate Diploma Programme. IB Business Management is a component of an exciting education that seeks to "develop inquiring, knowledgeable and caring young people who help to create a better and more peaceful world through intercultural understanding and respect."

During the two years of your IB Diploma Programme Business Management Course you will study a diverse range of business organizations, allowing you to develop a robust understanding of the core principles of modern business activity, as well as the skills needed to manage businesses successfully.

The structure of our book is closely based on the programme in the Subject Guide and covers both Standard and Higher Level material. As well as covering all the syllabus content, this book aims to capture the spirit of the IB learner profile (see page iii), allowing you to make links to your other subjects, to TOK, and to the wider world. Throughout the book, you will find the following features:

Contexts and concepts

Contexts and concepts are essential features of the Diploma Programme Business Management course. By considering concepts and contexts, as well as content (lots of 'c's!), you should develop a wide-reaching, holistic understanding of business management and its place in the world.

Contexts are the case studies and examples that you will encounter throughout your course - in this book, in other resources, and in your own research. By looking at these examples, you will find real-world context for the ideas and principles you learn about. You are encouraged to analyse and evaluate these examples, and think carefully about the issues they raise.

The Subject Guide has identified six key concepts which underpin all of the content in the course. They are:

- change
- culture
- ethics
- globalization
- innovation
- strategy

Throughout this book, we have aimed to integrate all six concepts. Sometimes, this is simply as part of the discussion of the content, but we have also included some extra 'concept boxes' which identify additional links to the concepts and suggest research and activities for you to take forward in class or as part of your assessment. These are just some of our thoughts – the concepts can be applied to all areas of the course and you should keep them in mind from the very beginning.

Student workpoints

These activities encourage you to reflect on what you've learned and apply new skills. Many encourage you to do your own research, which can be a great opportunity to find new case studies which you could use in assessment.

Exam practice

Throughout the book, you'll find exam and exam-style questions to help you prepare for your assessment. Many of these follow on from case studies, encouraging you to think critically about solutions to real-world problems. We've also included dedicated chapters on the examination and the internal assessment.

Theory of knowledge

We've included lots of links to TOK in the book and encourage you to find more! In common with the other subjects in its group, Business Management is concerned with the activities and attitudes of individuals and societies, and the relationships between them

We hope that this book is useful to you in your studies. The authors, as well as being experts in IB Business Management, are truly international, and have tried to reflect this in the examples and case studies used. It is not expected that this book will be your only resource. The business world is ever-changing and the more research you do, the more case studies you find, and the more questions you ask, the more you will get out of this course.

We wish you the best of luck in your studies and assessment!

1 BUSINESS ORGANIZATION AND ENVIRONMENT

1.1 An introduction to business management

By the end of this chapter, you should be able to:

→ Explain the role of businesses in combining human, physical and financial resources to create goods and services

→ Understand the main business functions and their roles (human resources, finance and accounts, marketing, and operations)

→ Define primary, secondary, tertiary and quaternary sectors

→ Outline the nature of business activity in each sector and the impact of sectoral change on business activity

→ Explain the role of entrepreneurship (and entrepreneur) and intrapreneurship (and intrapreneur) in overall business activity

→ Identify reasons for starting up a business or an enterprise

→ Outline common steps in the process of starting up a business or an enterprise

→ Examine problems that a new business or enterprise may face

→ Outline the elements of a business plan

The role of business

A business aims to meet the needs and wants of individuals or organizations through any of the following activities:

● producing crops or extracting raw materials from the earth

● creating a product

● providing a service.

Some businesses focus on one activity. A business may grow olives or manufacture transistors. Other businesses engage in multiple activities. A farm that grows olives may convert the olives into olive oil for sale under its own label. Sometimes a business will cluster several related activities or sometimes even engage in activities that are generally distinct. Regardless, a business inputs resources and processes them to generate the desired output. In this fashion, the business adds value (sometimes referred to as "added value") to the inputs and is rewarded for doing so either by gaining revenue (sales) for satisfying what is wanted or by gaining recognition for satisfying what is needed.

Many activities or organizations that most people would not consider "a business" nonetheless operate under many business principles. All organizations must have human, physical, and financial resources. Thus, many religious organizations (churches, mosques, synagogues, etc.), charities, and other types of organizations such as clubs are in a certain sense a business. Needs and wants are different: to live we all need the basics – food and water, clothing and shelter – and many businesses provide for our needs. Other businesses provide for our wants. Religious organizations, charities, clubs, etc. all provide services or products that people need or want and in that sense they are businesses.

Business activity can be summarized in the flow chart shown in Figure 1.1.1.

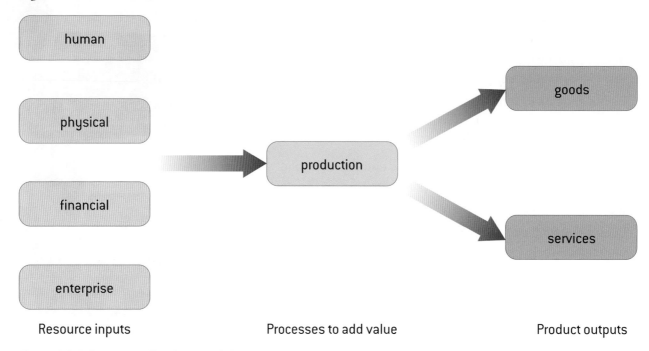

Figure 1.1.1. Summary of business activity

The resource inputs can be categorized as follows:

- **Human** – the right quality and quantity of people required to make the product or provide the service. All businesses, even highly automated ones, still require human input – even if only one person. Others require many individuals, often with different skill sets.

- **Physical** – the right quality and quantity of materials, machinery, and land space required to make the product or service. Even Internet businesses require some office space and a computer.

- **Financial** – the right quality and quantity of cash and other forms of money required to make the product or service.

- **Enterprise** – the least tangible input but crucially important for business. It is the business idea and the will to see the other elements become a functioning and, ideally, thriving business. Enterprise is sometimes referred to as "entrepreneurship", which today often has the connotation of high-tech and cutting-edge businesses: computers, telephones, social media. Enterprise, though, exists in all types of business, including the everyday (lawn-mowing services, institutional laundry services, brick manufacturing, etc.)

Production processes can take many forms:

- **Capital intensive** processes use a large proportion of land or machinery relative to other inputs, especially labour. Sometimes the land or machinery may have proprietary or special qualities (land rich in a resource or specialized equipment with unique features), or the land and the machinery simply cost a great deal due to the scale of the operation (an automobile factory, for example).

- **Labour-intensive** processes use a large proportion of labour relative to other inputs, especially in relation to land or machinery. Labour-intensive operations may involve fairly low-skilled workers but can also involve highly skilled employees.

Product outputs can be categorized as follows:

- **Goods** – these are tangible products that we can physically take home. They might include items produced in the primary sector, such as agricultural products or other items extracted from the environment, or they might include items made in the secondary (manufacturing) sector, such as an iPad or a car.

- **Services** – these are intangible and the buyer does not physically take them home. They include, for example, a karate class, a medical examination, and the international delivery of a package. Retail sales are a service: the retailers provides the service of having an array of products for consumers to purchase.

Business functions

All businesses, from small start-ups to huge conglomerates, are organized on the same lines, by function – what is to be done. There are four key functions:

- human resources (HR)
- marketing
- finance and accounts
- operations management or production

A small business

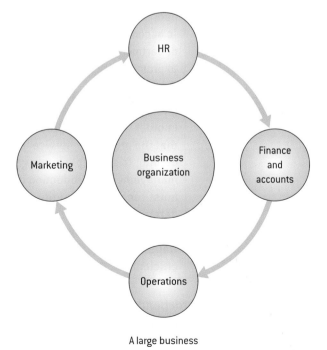

A large business

Figure 1.1.2. Business functions in a small business and a large business

The only difference between the two types of business is that the owner or owners of a smaller business have to deal with these functions themselves and a larger business can afford to hire **specialized** managers to do the same jobs organized in separate departments.

The role of business departments

In larger businesses these managers will focus on their function and in doing so help the business achieve its overall objectives. Some examples are set out below.

Table 1.1.1. Business functions

Function	Role
HR	Ensuring that appropriate people are employed to make the product or service and that the people are suitably rewarded for doing so. To accomplish these goals, the HR department must recruit people, train them, at times dismiss them, and determine appropriate compensation.
Finance and accounts	Ensuring that appropriate funds are made available to make the product or service. To accomplish this goal, the finance and accounts department must forecast requirements, keep accurate records, procure financial resources from various providers, and ensure proper payment for goods and services acquired to operate the business.
Marketing	Ensuring that the business offers a product or service that is desired by a sufficient number of people or businesses for profitable operations. To accomplish this goal, the marketing department must use appropriate strategies to promote, price, package, and distribute the product or service.
Operations management or production	Ensuring that appropriate processes are used in order to make the product or service and that the product or service is of the desired quality. To accomplish this goal, the operations management or production department must control the quantity and flow of stock, determine appropriate methods of production, and, in today's competitive world, look for ways to produce the good or service more efficiently.

All these functions are interdependent. For example, if the marketing department determines that a product needs to be made differently as a result of changes in consumer taste, the operations management or production function must redesign its processes, at least to some degree. That redesign may require financial resources, which the finance department must procure. The redesign may influence the number and type of people working in the business, which would have to be coordinated with the HR function.

The character of the interdependence can change over time. Initially, businesses typically focus on survival, with HR, finance and accounts, marketing, and operations management or production all geared toward that end. Once a business is established in the marketplace, its priorities may change. For example, a business may plan to diversify (produce other goods or services), which places new requirements on each of the four business departments. If a business is very successful, then growth and even control of the market might become a priority, which could require significant modifications to the different business departments.

The strength of a particular business depends upon how successfully aligned the four functions are. Is the business producing a desired good or service for the market it aims at? Are the right people producing the good or service, and are those people rewarded appropriately (financially and non-financially)? Small businesses often have an advantage in that they can respond quickly to changes in the marketplace. On the other hand, large businesses generally have greater resources, wider reach, and more name recognition. However, even a business dominating a market must remain vigilant. Large businesses, when they become complacent, can fail.

Case study

Kodak

For most of the 20th century, Kodak dominated the US photographic film market. However, because of the introduction of digital photography (the technology for which Kodak itself actually developed), the business began to see sales of its photographic film decline. By the late 1990s, the company was starting to struggle financially. The last year in which the company made a profit was 2007 and in 2012 Kodak filed for bankruptcy. Since then, the company has made several attempts to revitalize the business through redirection of operations and sale of assets. Although the business emerged from bankruptcy in September 2013, its health prospects for the future are uncertain.

Kodak's early cameras made home photography possible for many people. The company continues to dominate the market throughout much of the 20th century.

Sectors of business activity

Business activity takes place in a number of different areas: in the local community, in a country, or even within the global community. Traditionally, economists have grouped business activity into different sectors, as set out in Table 1.1.2.

Table 1.1.2. Sectors of business activity

Goods	Primary	All raw materials are acquired in the primary sector. This can be by extraction, mining, farming, fishing, hunting, or even trapping. Today, because of the scarce nature of many resources in the primary sector or because of the potential to damage fragile environments, governments closely monitor activities in the primary sector.
	Secondary	In the secondary sector raw materials are processed, usually by manufacturing. Goods from the secondary sector can take many forms, such as consumer durables, non-durable consumer goods, and capital goods. For most of the 19th and 20th centuries, much secondary sector production occurred in what are referred to today as "developed countries". Since the 1970s, however, manufacturers in developed countries have been facing increasing competition from manufacturing firms located in "developing nations" and "emerging markets".
Services	Tertiary	All services are provided in the tertiary sector, sometimes using manufactured products. These services can be financial, leisure, healthcare, education, transport, security, and many others. As manufacturing (the secondary sector) has shifted to developing countries, the tertiary sector has grown in importance in developed countries. Services such as banking, insurance, transportation, retail and wholesale, and consultancy have become especially important.
	Quaternary	This sector, a subgroup of the tertiary sector, provides services that are especially focused on knowledge. Generally speaking, various types of e-services and those involving IT, the media, and web-based services are considered quaternary. This sector is typical of "post-industrial" economies and, thus, many businesses in the developed world engage in quaternary activities.

These sectors are typically linked in what is referred to as the **production chain** or **chain of production**. A chain of production is the steps through the different sectors that must be made to turn raw materials into a consumer good that is marketed. For example, many types of raw material (metals, rubber, materials to make plastic and glass, etc.) are extracted (primary sector) and processed into the materials (secondary sector) that automobile parts manufacturers and automobile manufacturers turn into automobile parts (secondary sector). The automobile parts are then used on an assembly line to make automobiles (secondary sector). The cars are shipped (tertiary sector) to automobile dealerships, which sell the cars to consumers (tertiary sector). Automobile dealers also typically provide after-sale service (oil changes, tune-ups, and even major repairs), also in the tertiary sector. Sometimes, before consumers purchase cars, they read magazine or online reports about automobile features and service records. Sometimes this information is free and provided by the government, but in other cases this type of information is produced by for-profit companies that sell information. This type of business is in the quaternary sector.

Student workpoint 1.1

Be a thinker

Think of some everyday products that you use and imagine their production chain. Consider:

- a cherry pie you purchase
- a skateboard
- a cellphone.

What primary, secondary, tertiary, and quaternary business are involved in the production, distribution, and marketing of these products?

As businesses grow, they often acquire other businesses. Sometimes this is "horizontal" growth, which refers to a business acquiring or merging with another business engaged in more or less the same activity, for example, when two airlines merge or when one chain of grocery stores purchases another. When horizontal integration occurs, the new business (the combination of the two that merged or were involved in the acquisition) will have increased market share.

At other times, businesses grow "vertically" by acquiring other businesses involved in earlier or later stages in the chain of production or by beginning operations in an earlier stage through internal growth. If the activity of the business acquired or entered is earlier in the chain, such as a lumber company purchasing forest reserves to harvest its own trees, this process is called **backwards vertical integration**. When a business purchases another business or enters another business, the process is called **forward vertical integration**. For example, a farm producing organic crops and meats might open a retail store or a restaurant that sells the organic food and meats produced on the farm.

Horizontal integration is usually intended to increase market share and market power and to take advantage of economies of scale. Vertical integration occurs for varied reasons:

- Lowering transaction costs – transactions between businesses typically have transaction costs. These are eliminated.
- Ensuring reliable supply – if the vertical integration is backward (or "upstream"), the upstream stage can treat the "downstream" stage as a preferred customer in terms of quantity, availability, and price.
- Avoiding government regulation – such as price controls, taxes, or explicit regulation of various stages through integration.
- Increasing market power – if integration is successful (that is, if it lowers costs), the business has greater flexibility in setting its prices to others and can use various pricing strategies to increase its market power.
- Eliminating or weakening the market power of other businesses.[1]

---

[1] Carlton, Dennis W., and Perloff, Jeffrey M. 2005, *Modern Industrial Organization*, 4th ed. Addison-Wesley, Boston, MA

Common to all these purposes is the aim of becoming more profitable. Not always does vertical (or horizontal) integration lead to greater profits, as it can introduce proportionally greater complexity (costs) than savings. Also, the profitability of integration can change over time: sometimes a business will integrate vertically only to divest upstream and downstream stages at another time.

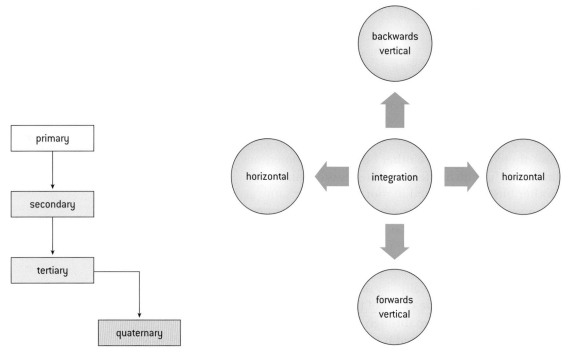

Figure 1.1.3. Business sectors and types of integration

Sectoral change

The size of each sector of the economy may change because, just as individuals or businesses grow and develop, so too will countries. Economists usually measure the size of each sector in terms of the number of people employed by the industries in that sector. The traditional pattern is set out in Figure 1.1.4.

Closely related to changing economies are what some scholars have termed "social technologies". The more advanced a sector is, the more complex are the needed social contexts for businesses to thrive. Thus, whereas raw material extraction is often possible with relatively few skilled workers and large numbers of low-skilled workers, the quaternary sector relies both on highly skilled workers (producers and managers of information) and consumers – people and businesses that want and have the ability to make use of advanced information. Thus, more developed economies typically see social technologies and economies advance in tandem: as the economy develops, social technologies improve; as social technologies improve, economies develop.

Developments are not, however, linear. Technological innovation in one area (for example computerized word processors) and its related workers (individuals knowledgeable about operating word processors) can make other technologies and occupations obsolete, such as typewriters and typists. Thus, while some occupations become obsolete, new ones emerge (which are often perceived as "high skill").

TOK discussion

Are business sectors "timeless"?

Have they always existed, or are they specific to certain historic periods?

Businesses that can anticipate or adapt to the changing environment can do well, even in industries that are perceived as "in decline". In general, developed economies have moved away from the primary sector. In both Canada and Australia, however, two primary sector industries have done remarkably well: organic farming in Canada and wine production in Australia. Another example is Germany: as one of the most developed economies of the world, it has a strong quaternary sector. However, German businesses have retained two of its long-standing strengths: high-quality engineering and a strong secondary sector.

The process of shifting from one proportional weighting of sectors in an economy to a different weighting (shifting from an economy based on the primary sector to an economy based on the secondary sector, for example) can produce strains on resources, such as human resources. Secondary sector businesses may require specialist skills that may be in short supply. Financial resources, too, will be diverted from one sector to another. Finally, an economy mostly based in the tertiary or quaternary sectors will require fewer physical resources (as these will not be needed as much in the production of intangible services as for tangible goods). Other strains can occur as well. As an economy shifts to the secondary sector, legislation and other protections against environmental damage are often weak, and manufacturing firms in developing countries often do more damage to the environment than manufacturing in developed economies.

Entrepreneurship and intrapreneurship

Both **entrepreneurs** and **intrapreneurs** are vital to business activity as they provide the impetus for innovative products and new business opportunities. Entrepreneurs are typically self-employed (or were central to the start-up of a business for which they work). Intrapreneurs are employed by large organizations and develop new products or services for the benefit of their employers (which usually benefit them, the intrapreneurs, as well). Both entrepreneurs and intrapreneurs must balance the risk of failure against the likelihood of success for new business ventures. They are both types of people who want to create a start-up, either for a new product or for a whole new business.

Innovation is central to what entrepreneurs and intrapreneurs do. This typically comes in one of three forms[2]:

- market reading: observing customers and competitors and then making small changes to existing products

- need seeking: communicating with current and potential customers to determine their needs

- technology driving: investing in research and development and following opportunities offered by technological capabilities.

Sometimes people imagine that "innovation" always involves new technologies (computers, telephones, electronics, etc.), but need-seeking innovation often occurs simply because someone understands that a need exists for otherwise ordinary products or services. For example, in

---

[2] Robert M. Price, "Infusing Innovation into Corporate Culture," *Organizational Dynamics* (2007), vol. 36, issue 3, pages 320-328.

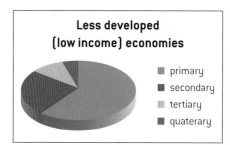

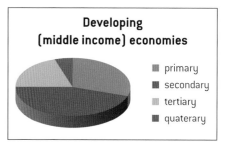

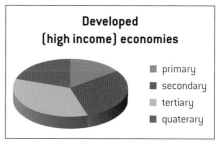

Figure 1.1.4. Size of sectors

the United States social changes and changes in homeowning patterns in the last 30 years have increased the demand for lawn and garden services. Although some innovations have occurred in the equipment and the processes involved, mostly the demand has been met by an increase in the number of workers providing these services. Some entrepreneurs who understood these social changes successfully built large, profitable businesses in this industry.

Other social changes have prompted other industries. As the percentage of women in the workforce increased in the United States, for example, one new business emerged: the dog-walking business. Now that fewer women are home all or most of the day, the family pet often has nine or ten hours alone in the house. Some businesses go to the homes in which both partners work and, for a fee, take the family pet on a 30-minute walk in the middle of the day. Dog-walking services are now common in many US cities.

Professional dog-walkers have made the most of changes to families' working habits

Reasons for starting up a business

People start business for many reasons, as summarized in Table 1.1.3.

Table 1.1.3. Reasons to start up a business

Rewards	Working for someone else means that you do not get to keep all the rewards yourself. Although some criticize this aspect of capitalism, one central element is that those who put their capital at risk (the business owners) get the rewards, whereas those who do not put their capital at risk (employees) receive wages or salaries that are typically less than the return on capital is to the owners. Many millionaires own "boring" small businesses.
Independence	Working for yourself means that you are your own boss and not following someone else's rules. Individuals with an entrepreneurial spirit sometimes feel constrained by bosses, policies, and procedures in large organizations. Starting your own business means that you can set and change the policies and procedures as you see fit.
Necessity	Sometimes businesses are started by individuals whose positions were made redundant or who could not find work. The necessity of having an income led them to starting a small business.
Challenge	Some people just want to see whether they can "make it" themselves. Starting a small business typically requires one person to perform all functions of the business (HR, marketing, accounts and finance, and operations management or production). Over time, if the business is a success, the business owner then has to learn new skills as his or her role changes to accommodate a larger and more complex operation.
Interest	Many interesting businesses are set up by people with a passion for something who want to just keep doing what they enjoy doing. The business producing Hawaiian Tropic suntan lotion was begun by a high-school chemistry teacher who liked spending time at the beach. Many specialty shops – guitar stores, lamp stores, ballet clothing stores, rare books stores, and many others – allow their owners to work in an area for which they have a passion.
Finding a gap	Businesses may see or find an untapped opportunity in order to achieve "first mover advantage". Sometimes businesses, large or small, stumble into opportunities for which they were not looking. The idea of Post-its®, one of the most successful products of the 3-M Corporation and which revolutionized interoffice communications, was stumbled across by accident by Dr Spender Silver, a scientist working at 3-M.
Sharing an idea	If you really believe in something, you may want to sell the idea to others. Yoga studios, for example, are typically owned by people who themselves do yoga and want to spread the idea that yoga enhances quality of life. Marketing the idea helps their business, but often the original motivation to open a yoga studio is to spread the idea.

The process of starting up a business

The time it takes to register a business might vary, for example, from 15 minutes in Singapore to up to 4 weeks in Argentina. Two features are common to all successful start-ups:

- the business idea

- planning.

The business idea refers to the fundamental activity that the business will do, whether it is something basic, such as a house-cleaning service, or something more sophisticated, for example manufacturing. The business idea can be market-driven – that is, determined by the needs of the market or product – or service-driven, which means that in some sense the entrepreneur or business must convince others that the product or service is worth purchasing. Regardless of whether the new business is basic or sophisticated, market- or product-driven, the entrepreneur must have a basic business idea. Then the entrepreneur should carefully plan the business in order to reduce the many risks associated with starting up a business.

Figure 1.1.5. Steps for start-ups

1. **Organizing the basics**. The entrepreneur starting a new business must address several basic questions: Where is the business going to be based? How will the entrepreneur name the business? What will be its legal structure? What will be its operational structure? Is there a sufficient business infrastructure to make the business feasible – suppliers, potential customers, and government services?

2. **Refining the business idea through market research.** Once the entrepreneur has determined that, in broad outline, the business concept is feasible, he or she should do market research to determine how the business will distinguish itself from others in the market. Rarely is a gap in the market obvious. Were that the case, starting a successful business would be easy. However, new businesses have very high failure rates. While precise rates of failure are difficult to determine, as many business are so small and so short-lived that they elude detection in surveys, failure rates in the United States, for example, are between 50 and 80 per cent in the first four years of operation; 25 per cent fail in the first year alone.[3] In Europe, another developed economy, failure rates are also high. Thus, once the basic business idea is determined, the business must then do market research to determine the precise market segment it will target, and the entrepreneur must answer some basic questions: How will he or she conduct market research? Who will be the target market? Can the new business test its concept? What will

---

[3] http://www.statisticbrain.com/startup-failure-by-industry/

be its "unique selling proposition (USP)"? How will the business communicate with the market?

Let's consider the example of the entrepreneur who wants to enter the grocery business. The idea is very attractive. After all, food is one of the basic necessities of human existence. However, market research may be very revealing. A market may have too many competitors, or a segment of the grocery market (high volume, low cost, for example) may be saturated. Market research might reveal that a small niche market (such as for organic products or specialized meats) is where there is a gap in the market. Thus, researching the market has refined the basic business idea (a grocery store) and narrowed and refined it to a significantly more precise idea: a speciality grocery store that offers either organic products and/or specialized meats.

3. **Planning the business.** Once the concept has been narrowed, the entrepreneur should write a business plan, which is a document that addresses all the issues that need to be planned before operations begin. The elements of the business plan are detailed below. The business plan will serve multiple stakeholders, especially potential owners of the business and financial institutions (banks, lending companies) that may provide capital. The composition of the business plan requires the entrepreneur or people starting the business to think through most of the specific elements of how the business will operate. For investors and financiers, the business plan can provide some confidence, as it indicates that the business has foreseen potential issues and is trying to address them.

4. **Establishing legal requirements.** All businesses operate in countries that have laws that can influence the legal organization of the business, its labour practices, and its operational practices, as well as determine tax obligations. In most countries, all businesses must be registered, even if a sole trader (which is not a legally separate entity from the operator of the business). Other types of business – corporations, for example – are legal entities that must be established in accordance with the laws of the host country. In many countries businesses must have specific licences and/or pass certain inspections before they can operate. These legal requirements can be extensive and costly. Finally, the business must investigate the tax requirements of the country. These taxes would include not only income taxes, but also various sorts of payroll taxes that must be paid, such as for employees' pensions from the government, unemployment and sickness benefits, or even medical insurance.

5. **Raising the finance.** Once the basic business idea has been refined, a business plan written, and legal requirements met, the business must then raise finance – money – to get the business started and to support the business until it can sustain operations from profits, which can often take years (even if the business is profitable from the beginning, its cash requirements may be greater than the profits). Any investor or lender must have confidence in the accounting and auditing procedures of the business. Who will prepare accounts in the business and who, external to the business,

Student workpoint 1.2

Be a thinker

Choose one of the following businesses:

- local delicatessen and café

- manufacturer of a new energy drink

- travelling hairdresser and beautician

- after-school sports club

Work in groups to create a business plan for your new business. Divide the steps between you and write down at least five bullet points for each step will verify that they are accurate? Then, the business must attract start-up monies. Some or all may come from the entrepreneur, or other investors may be required. When someone provides equity capital, it means that person is a partial owner of the business. Most entrepreneurs who start up a business do not want to lose control of the business, so some of the capital will be in the form of investment – selling shares – but some of the capital may be loans to the business. Who will be the lenders? What kind of terms will they want?

Table 1.1.4. Possible problems for a start-up

Problems a new business may face	
Organization	• The location of the business is inappropriate. • The name does not register. • The structure does not work. • Supplies are unreliable.
Market research	• The research was poor. • The target market wasn't appropriate. • The test was too optimistic. • Channels of communication were weak.
Business plan	• The business plan did not convince. • Goals were too vague or contradictory.
Legal requirements	• Labour laws were not addressed. • Registration was too difficult. • Tax obligations were not addressed.
Finance	• The accounts were not kept properly – cash flow, in particular, was a problem. • Raising start-up capital was too difficult. • Raising medium-term to long-term finance was difficult.
The market	• The launch failed. • The pilot was inconclusive. • Success was limited – the product failed to inspire.

6. **Testing the market.** The final stage is the launch of the business. How will that occur? Will the business begin on a small scale (a "pilot") to test consumer reaction? What will the criteria for success of the pilot be? In some types of business, especially capital-intensive manufacturing, the initial launch is extremely expensive and the firm can respond to market reactions in only a limited and slow way. Other types of business – restaurants, for example – can often respond quickly and easily, by changing the menu, changing recipes, or changing other aspects of the business. The purpose of testing the market is to verify that the business idea will be well enough received by consumers to suggest that the business has a reasonable chance of success.

Problems a new business may face

Even when all these steps are followed, start-ups still have a high probability of failure. Businesses that fail often do so because of what they did before the business ever opened: the business had problems in basic organization, its products or services were based upon insufficient or poor-quality market research, planning was poor or unconvincing to investors or lenders, legal requirements were not properly satisfied, accounts were poorly kept and/or the business had insufficient funds to operate, or the launch was unsuccessful and sales did not materialize. All of these problems can cause a business to fail.

Even if a start-up has a good business idea and develops a strong business plan, the business may still fail. Sometimes failure results from lack of name recognition in the marketplace. Other times failure stems from the inability to recruit labour with the right skills. In other cases it is because businesses cannot always accurately anticipate the reactions of competitors and certainly a start-up cannot *control* the actions of its competitors. New businesses generally have less capital to rely upon if the economy weakens, and a strained business often brings out problems between managers or executives which would not be present if the business were operating successfully. Therefore many things outside a business's control can cause it to fail.

The elements of a business plan

A business plan sets out how the organization will meet its business objectives. It involves stepping back from day-to-day operations and asking where the business is heading and what its priorities should be. The plan applies to a specific period, potentially over several years, and is a detailed statement of the short-term and long-term objectives of the business with an analysis of the resources needed to achieve these objectives. It should be regularly reviewed and, if necessary, updated.

Responsibility for delivering all the elements of the business plan will be allocated to key individuals in the organization, such as department heads. Success will be measured against clearly stated performance targets set out in the plan.

A business plan is usually combined with detailed budgets to finance the required activities.

The purpose of a business plan

A business plan is drawn up to:

- support the launch of a new organization or business idea
- attract new funds from banks, grant providers, or venture capitalists
- support strategic planning
- identify resource needs
- provide a focus for development
- work as a measure of business success.

Entrepreneurs may have plenty of original ideas, but they often lack business experience. If banks are to lend funds to new businesses, they want to be confident they will be paid back with interest. Since the risk of new business failure is very high – up to 80 per cent over the first two years in some sectors – banks will only want to lend to those businesses with a low risk of failure. To persuade a bank to lend it money, a business needs to prove that it has done its homework, knows where it is going, and how it is going to get there. In other words, it needs a plan.

A good business plan may be of significant use to stakeholders. For potential investors, it will provide a basis for assessment of risk by detailing how the business will use a bank loan or investment. For employees, it will identify specific objectives and goals and provide a focus for action and a source of motivation. For suppliers, analysis of the business plan may identify whether there are likely to be long-term advantages from a commercial relationship with the business.

For the local community and pressure groups, access to the business plan will provide the basis for assessing the organization's role in the community.

Businesses that have become successful will have usually started off with a clear plan. This is often in the style of a document called the "Business plan" which can be presented to potential investors or other interested groups such as the government or the bank manager.

The elements of a business plan

There are six elements of a business plan:

- the business idea, aims and objectives
- business organization
- HR
- finance
- marketing
- operations.

Each element has a specific focus and should address key questions, as set out in Table 1.1.5.

Student workpoint 1.3

Be a communicator

Using the business you discussed in the workpoint on page 12, create a business plan and present it to the rest of the class.

Table 1.1.5. The key questions for a business plan

Element	For this element the focus is on:	Key questions to address are:
Starting the business – the idea	setting out the business idea in the right context	What is the core idea and what are the objectives of the business? How will the product work? Does it have a **unique selling point (USP)**? How will the product be developed? Why should it succeed?
Business organization	how the business will be organized	Where will the business be located? What structure will it have? What type of business will it be? Who will make what decisions? How will the owner or owners share out the profits? Are there any legal requirements necessary to start up the business?
HR	how the business will be staffed	Who will have what responsibilities and what rewards should they expect? What will be the **HR plan**? What type of contract will be used?
Finance	how the business will be financed	Where and how will the entrepreneur source the start-up capital and at what cost? This unit should include projected **budgets, income statements,** and **cash-flow forecasts.**
Marketing	how best to market the product	What market research has been done? Has a **sales forecast** been made? Is the product to be targeted at a particular **segment of the market** or will it be mass marketed? What will the **promotional mix** be? How will the product be distributed?
Operations	how the product will be made	How will production be organized? How many units will the business produce? How long will production take? Is there likely to be a **lead time**? What is the **supply chain** likely to be?

Revision checklist

✓ Businesses combine human, physical and financial resources to produce goods and services.

✓ Human resources are the people needed to carry out the aims of the organization. Physical resources include buildings, machinery and raw materials. Financial resources include the money needed to make the product or service.

✓ There are four main sectors of business activity:

   ✓ the primary sector generally involves the acquisition of raw materials.

   ✓ the secondary sector involves processing raw materials, usually to create a product

   ✓ the tertiary sector is where most service businesses sit

   ✓ the quaternary sector provides services that focus on knowledge

✓ An entrepreneur is an individual who demonstrates enterprise and initiative in order to make a profit.

✓ An intrapreneur is an individual employed by a large organization who demonstrates entrepreneurial thinking in the development of new products or services

✓ Businesses are started for many reasons. Steps involved in starting up a business include: researching the market, planning the new business, establishing legal requirements, raising finance and testing the market.

✓ A new business might face challenges at each stage. These can be both things within its control and external factors beyond its control.

✓ The elements of a business plan are: the idea, business organization, human resources, finance, marketing and operations

Practice question

Starbucks® and Tata Coffee

Starbucks® is a multinational coffee shop chain based in the United States (US). *Starbucks®* is in discussions with *Tata Coffee*, an Indian company, about opening *Starbucks®* coffee shops in the fast-growing Indian market. The Indian government limits the entry of foreign-owned retail chains into India.

Tata Coffee grows and sells its own coffee. It is owned by *Tata Group*, the largest Indian business conglomerate*. *Starbucks®* and *Tata Coffee* are considering forming a strategic alliance or a joint venture. For the past seven years, the two companies have done business with each other. *Starbucks®* has purchased coffee from various suppliers in India (for its coffee shops in Europe and the US), including from *Tata Coffee*.

Forming a strategic alliance or a joint venture with *Tata Coffee* will allow *Starbucks®* to enter the Indian market. Additional advantages for *Starbucks®* include:

- *Starbucks®* could open coffee shops inside hotels of the *Tata Group's* nationwide hotel chain

- *Tata Group* would consider allowing *Starbucks®* to open coffee shops in the numerous retail chains that it owns.

Coffee has long been popular in southern India but not in the north. Over the past decade, however, consumption of coffee in the north has increased significantly, as new coffee shop chains with more choice, appeal to young Indians with disposable income. India (with its population of over 1 billion) is developing fast (with a growth rate of 8% of its GDP this year). *Starbucks®* has carried out research and found that the global brand name "*Starbucks®*" is already well-known in India, although there are no *Starbucks®* coffee shops there yet.

The competition in India is intense. *Café Coffee Day®*, an Indian company, dominates the market. An Italian company owns the other big coffee shop chain, *Barista™*.

[Source: adapted from "Starbucks to broaden dealings in India", *International Herald Tribune*, 14 January 2011]

a) Define the term *multinational company*.   [*2 marks*]

b) Explain the importance of branding for the decision of *Starbucks®* to enter the Indian market.   [*4 marks*]

c) Explain **one** PEST factor that may influence the decision of *Starbucks®* to enter the Indian market.   [*2 marks*]

IB, Nov. 2012

---

* *conglomerate*: a company that is made up of a number of different companies and business that is typically in diversified fields and, often, different sectors of the economy

1.2 Types of business organization

By the end of this chapter, you should be able to:

→ Distinguish between the private and the public sectors

→ Outline the main features of the following types of for-profit (commercial) organizations:
- sole traders
- partnerships
- companies/corporations

→ Outline the main features of the following types of for-profit social enterprises:
- cooperatives
- microfinance providers
- public-private partnerships (PPP)

→ Outline the main features of the following types of non-profit social enterprises:
- non-governmental organizations (NGOs)
- charities

Main features of profit-based (commercial) organizations

Profit-making businesses come in many types of legal organization and existence, but the most common are the following:

- sole traders
- partnerships
- companies or corporations
- for-profit social enterprises
  - cooperatives
  - micro-financers
  - public–private partnerships (PPPs).

The common feature of all of these types of business is that one of their aims is to generate profit. The profits a business receives can be shown by the following formula:

> **Profits = total revenues – total costs**

Total revenues, often called "sales", are all the income received by the business in a specified period of time. Total costs are all the costs incurred by that business in the same period of time. The way that revenue and expenses are measured is actually more complex than this simple formula suggests, but for now the simple form is enough.

The difference between them can be expressed as shown in Figure 1.2.1.

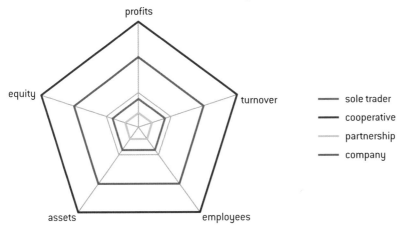

Figure 1.2.1. Revenue, expenses, and profits in different types of organization

Sole trader

Most people starting their own business typically begin with a limited budget and a simple organization. Facing these constraints, they often choose to operate as a sole trader (sometimes called a sole proprietor), which is the simplest form of business to organize. Being a sole trader fulfills many of the reasons people start a business: being their own boss, seeing a gap in the market and wanting to respond quickly, creating their own product, serving the community, or just living their dream.

The main features of a sole trader business include the following:

- **The sole trader owns and runs the business.** Sole traders may employ other people, including those empowered to make some of the decisions, but the sole traders themselves make management decisions and have ultimate responsibility for the business.

- **No legal distinction exists between the business and the sole trader.** The sole trader *is* the business and, thus, is liable for all the debts of the business or other claims (such as the outcome of a lawsuit). In other words, sole traders have "unlimited liability".

- **The finance is usually limited.** Here, finance refers to the money that the business has available for use. It can come from the personal savings of the sole trader or from other sources, such as a loan from family and friends or from a bank. Regardless, sole traders typically have limited finance, either because their personal savings are limited or because family, friends, banks, and other financial institutions may be reluctant to lend the sole trader money because of the high failure rate of start-up businesses.

- **The business is close to the customer.** A sole trader is usually a small business that allows the sole trader to interact with each customer. Sole traders get to know their customers on an individual

Monique owns and runs her own café business - she is a sole trader basis, which allows them to provide a more personalized service than larger businesses.

- **The sole trader has privacy and limited accountability.** Most of the time, sole traders do not have to declare their finances to anyone except the tax authorities, which want to know how much profit the business has made for tax purposes. Sometimes, as well, sole traders borrow money or enter into a financial contract (such as a lease) and lenders or lessors may need to see financial statements. In general, however, sole traders have a high degree of privacy.

- **Registering the business is generally relatively easy and inexpensive – and quick.** Although laws vary from country to country, in general starting and operating as a sole trader is simpler than for other types of legal organizations. Sole traders usually have less legal paperwork to fill out and file. Sole traders make all decisions themselves and therefore do not have to devote time to discussion and to building consensus for decisions.

One of the greatest advantages of being a sole trader is that all profits from the business belong to the sole trader, as no legal distinction separates the owner from the business. Other advantages of operating as a sole trader include:

- complete control over all the important decisions

- flexibility in terms of working hours, products and services, and changes to operations

- privacy, as sole traders generally do not need to divulge information

- minimal legal formalities

- close ties to customers, which can give a competitive advantage.

The success of businesses operating as sole traders depends on the drive, enthusiasm, and health of the sole traders themselves. Any of these can falter. Sole traders also have other disadvantages, which include the following:

- Competing against established businesses all by yourself can be a daunting challenge.

- There may be stress and potential ineffectiveness because the sole trader makes all the decisions, often with limited time to make them and limited opportunity to seek advice from others.

- There will be lack of continuity in the event of a serious accident or the owner's death – the business itself may not continue.

- There may be limited scope for expansion as the owner spends all his or her time running the business.

- Generally, there will be limited capital, which may also create a burden on the business. The focus will be more on having sufficient cash for day-to-day operations than on looking to the future.

- There is unlimited liability of the owner for any faults, debts, or mistakes made.

The majority of sole traders remain small businesses and typically the business comes to an end when the sole trader retires or dies. Sometimes, sole traders want to stay small, which allows them to make a decent living and not have to manage (and worry about) the many complexities of operating on a larger scale. Sole traders often have a **niche** in the market and see no need to expand. When sole traders want to expand, often the challenges are too great. Their profits are not large enough to support growth, or the risks of growth are too great. Just surviving may be the chief goal of a sole trader: many sole traders give up or fail within the first few years of existence.

Partnerships

An alternative type of business is that of a partnership. This type of business is formed by two or more people. Often they are friends, associates or people with similar or related skills. Partnerships are popular with professional people with related qualifications, such as doctors, lawyers, accountants, or even business consultancy firms.

The main features of a partnership business include the following:

- **Decisions are made jointly by the partners**, who own and run the business together. Partners may employ other people but they make all the management decisions. Partners also own the business, each partner with a percentage ownership.

- **The business is owned and managed by more than one person.** Although the number of partners is technically unlimited, getting agreement is more difficult as the number of partners increases. Most partnerships have 2–20 partners.

- **No legal distinction exists between the business and the partners**, who are liable for all of the partnership's debts and other obligations. Partners have unlimited liability and legally can be called upon to **pay for 100 per cent** of the partnership's debts even if a partner owns only a small percentage of the business.

- **Finance is usually more available than for a sole trader business.** All partners contribute some capital to start up the business or to "buy into" the business, which usually means more capital than if provided by only one person. Also, banks and other financial institutions are usually more willing to provide finance to a partnership than to a sole trader, as a partnership is considered more stable than a sole trader.

- **Some partners may be "sleeping partners"**, which means that they provide some finance (their investment in the partnership) and expect a share of the profit. Otherwise, however, a sleeping partner performs no other role in the business.

- **The business operated as a partnership can often offer a more varied service than a sole trader.** Often, different partners bring different expertise, and the product or service offerings of the business can vary. This situation is especially true in the case of partnerships of professionals such as lawyers or doctors. For example, a law firm could have lawyers specializing in criminal law, commercial law, international law, or civil law.

- **Partnerships typically have a greater degree of accountability than a sole trader.** Although in most countries partnerships are not legally required to draw up a deed of partnership, partnerships often do. Having a deed of partnership makes good business sense because it is a legally binding document that sets out the rights and duties of the partners.

  It includes information about:

  - responsibilities
  - financing
  - division of profits
  - liabilities
  - procedures for changing circumstances.

  With a deed of partnership, partners know their rights and responsibilities within the partnership, and the likelihood of some major disagreement between the partners decreases.

- **Partnerships are typically more stable than sole traders and have a higher likelihood of continuity.** Drawing up a deed of partnership will slow down registering the business but will help the organization in the long term.

- **Partners do not necessarily share all the profits equally.** Usually, profits are allocated and paid out according to each partner's percentage ownership of the business. If one partner has provided a substantial amount of finance, then that person may expect a greater proportion of profits than the other partners are allocated. In addition, in partnerships with "sleeping partners", the active partners may get agreed-upon salaries or drawings that are considered expenses for the purpose of determining the partnership's profit. Then, after the profit is determined, the profits are allocated to partners according to their percentage ownership.

Partnerships have certain advantages compared to sole traders:

- As partners often bring different skills and qualities, partnerships often have more efficient production through the specialization and the division of labour.

- In general, partners bring more expertise to a business than one person can.

- As partnerships are perceived to have greater stability and lower risk, they generally have access to more finance.

- Partners can help in emergencies or when others are ill or on holiday.

- Partnerships have more chance of continuity as the business will not necessarily end if one partner dies.

Partnerships also have certain disadvantages:

- Each partner has unlimited liability, which means that each partner is legally responsible for all of the businesses debts or actions of any other partner. The one exception to this liability is when, in the deed of partnership, a partner or certain partners are declared "limited

partners". Although the laws vary according to country, in general, limited partners have limited liability but also limited control (both specified in the deed of partnership).

- Compared to businesses that operate as companies (corporations), partnerships usually have less access to loans from banks and other financial institutions. Limited finance can often prevent a business from expanding or maximizing opportunities for making profits.

- An individual partner does not have complete control over the business and has to rely on the work and goodwill of others.

- Profits have to be shared among the partners.

- Partners may disagree, which in the worst case could break up the partnership.

In summary, partnerships are safer than sole traders but also more complex organizations. As multiple partners can typically raise more finance than sole traders and because of the greater inherent stability, partnerships have more of a chance of surviving changing market conditions and have more of a chance of expanding if the conditions are right.

Companies or corporations

Perhaps the most important type of business is the company (corporation in North America) and you can recognize a company as it may have the following abbreviations after its logo:

This business in the USA has registered itself as a corporation

INC – Incorporated (USA/Canada)

LLC – Limited Liability Company (United States)

PLC – Private or Public Limited Company (UK)

PTE – Private Limited Company (UK)

LTD – Limited Company (various)

SA – Sociedad Anónima (Latin America except Brazil and Mexico);

SA – Sociedades Anônimas (Brazil, Portugal)

SpA – Società per Azioni (Italy)

AB – Aktiebolag (Finland, Sweden)

Bhd – Berhad (Malaysia, Brunei)

GIE – Groupement d'Intérêt Economique (France)

GmbH – Gesellschaft mit beschraenkter Haftung (Austria, Germany, Switzerland)

Other countries have other designations and abbreviations. Whichever is used, this type of designation means the same thing: that the business is a joint stock or limited company. This type of business is the only one that can be called a company (corporation) to distinguish it from the other types of business.

A business can become a company by a simple but very powerful process – the business and the owners of the business are legally separated and the liability of the company is distinct from the liability of those who own it. Another feature of a company is that, typically, it has multiple owners, each owning a fraction of the company in the form of **shares** (shares of stock or equity shares) in the company.

The business – the company – has legal existence in its own right. The company employs executives to manage the business and workers who handle the day-to-day operations. Just like sole traders and partnerships, a company has certain responsibilities in the community: it must obey the laws of the land and pay taxes. Unlike sole traders and partnerships, companies keep the profits from their business activities – unless the owners (also called shareholders) decide to pay all or a portion of profits (past or present) to the shareholders in the form of dividends. Shareholders receive a proportion of the profits as dividends at the discretion of the company, and their proportion of the dividends is determined by their proportion of the shares of stock. For example, if a company makes a profit of €1,000,000 and decides to pay total dividends of €600,000, the total payout (€600,000) will be divided by the number of shares of stock issued and outstanding. If that figure were 100,000, the owner of each share of stock would receive a dividend of €6.00 for each share the person owned. If one person owned 20,000 of the issued and outstanding shares, that person would receive €120,000.

Often, individual shareholders own only a part of the business. When that is the case, individual shareholders in theory do not control the business unless they own a majority of the shares. In practice, sometimes a shareholder who owns a lower percentage can still have a deciding weight in the decisions of the company and can, therefore, control it. In the case of very large companies, it is very rare for one person to own all or a majority of the shares of a company. With smaller companies, it is not uncommon for one person to own 100 per cent of the shares or for a small group of family members or friends to own 100 per cent of the shares.

Regardless, shareholders are rewarded for investing in a company in three ways:

1. The **price** of the share(s) they hold may increase in value if the company is performing well. In theory (though not always true in practice), the value of a company is based upon its profits. As profits increase, so too should the total value of its shares. Therefore, individual shares of stock in the company should increase in value at the same rate.

2. The company issues a portion of the company profits as **dividends**. The amount of money each shareholder receives depends on the number of shares each shareholder owns. With small or new companies, dividends are often not paid or are relatively small. With large, established companies, dividends are often paid regularly – once every three months, or quarter – and individuals invest in the company in part because they want the regular dividend income that comes with share ownership in that particular company.

3. The shareholder has **limited liability**, which is one of the single most important features and benefits of owning stock in a company. Unlike sole proprietors or partners in a partnership, shareholders in a company are not responsible in any way for the company's

debts. If the business fails, then all the shareholders can lose is their investment in the company, but no more. For example, if a company goes into receivership (bankruptcy) owing millions of euros or dollars to individuals, banks, and other companies, the shareholders do not have to pay any of those debts. The shareholders' liability is limited to their investment (however, in the event of liquidation of a company, the shareholders are the last party to receive any monies from the sale of the assets of a business; all debts will be paid first).

The cost to the shareholders of investing in a company is as follows:

1. The **price** of the share(s) they hold may decrease in value if the company is not performing well. As noted in point 1 above, in theory the value of a company is based upon its profits. If profit declines, so too (typically) will the value of individual shares.

2. The company may choose not to issues **dividends** if it does not have to. Businesses need funds for many reasons. Companies that are doing poorly may not have sufficient cash on hand to be able to pay dividends. Businesses that are rapidly growing also need money to support the growth (to pay for more investment in equipment and working capital). As a result, many companies rarely or never pay dividends. The entire measurement of the value of the investment is based upon the rise or fall in the stock value.

3. As "owners" often own only a fraction of the shares of the company, owning shares in a firm may not mean that an individual shareholder has any meaningful say in decisions about the business. At the end of 2012, General Electric Corporation (GE) in the United States had 10,405,625,000 issued and outstanding shares of stock. An individual investor owning 100 shares would, practically speaking, have no say at all in a giant company such as GE. To own even 1 per cent of the company (and thus have a 1 per cent say in who the executives are) would require an investment of approximately $2.5 billion dollars.

Typically, businesses choose initially to become a company because the owners of the business want the business to have a separate legal existence from them personally, thus giving the owners, as shareholders rather than as a sole trader or partners, limited liability. There are also other reasons for becoming a company:

- The enhanced status of being a company is generally recognition that the business has been successful.

- Selling shares is a good source of finance for a business, especially one with growing working capital requirements.

- Being a company increases the stability of the business, as a company has a legal existence apart from its owners. If a shareholder or shareholders die, the business continues. In the case of small businesses, the death of a major shareholder, if that person is also an active executive in the firm, can cause some disruption. Nevertheless, the business does continue.

- Companies typically have improved chances of gaining further finance, especially loans, from financial institutions and governments.

Achieving company status is often a turning point in the evolution of a business. Up until the point that a business becomes a company, some questions exist about the survival of the business and its continuity and growth.

As with any legal organization of a business, the choice to become a company has advantages and disadvantages. To take full advantage of becoming a company, a business will have multiple investors and thus a major infusion of capital. However, when this occurs, the original business owner loses some control over the business and could even lose personal involvement in the company. When a business becomes a company, its new owners (the shareholders) may hire executives to make all major decisions. The original business owner (as sole trader or partner) may now be merely an investor.

When a business reorganizes as a company, it can choose to become either of these types of organization:

- private limited company
- public limited company.

The only real difference between the two forms of company is that the private limited company can only sell shares in the company privately: to people known to the owners such as friends, family, and associates. Although the number of shareholders permitted in a private limited company varies from country to country, generally it is a low, around 20. As a result, becoming a private limited company limits the amount of finance available but allows more control to be maintained.

If the business decides to become a public limited company (and the phrase typically used is "the company is going public") then it has to offer its shares in a public place – a stock exchange – based in one of the major financial centres such as London, New York, Frankfurt, Tokyo, Shanghai or Singapore, or online; for example, the FTSE, Wall Street, the NASDAQ, the NIKKEI. Going public opens up the possibility of securing large sums of capital. In 2012, for example, Facebook acquired $16 billion from its "initial public offering" (IPO), or first sale of shares to the public. When a company goes public, it does lose some privacy. Public limited companies have to allow potential investors to see their accounts, which become open to everyone. Further, the business itself has no control over who buys their shares. For example, Microsoft bought US$150 million worth of shares in Apple in 1997.

The main features of a company include the following:

- **The shareholders own but do not run the business.** Their purchase of shares provides finance, but otherwise the shareholders have little input into the day-to-day running of the business. Instead, professional managers are normally employed to make all the management decisions.

- **The business and the owners are divisible.** The shareholders are not liable for any of the debts of the business. The shareholders' liability is limited to their investment in the company because the company and shareholders are separate legal entities. As the business and the owners (shareholders) are divisible, the owners can change.

A person owning shares in the company can decide to sell these shares for any reason whatsoever.

- **The legal existence and many of the details are legally recorded and matters of public record.** To form a company (and thus achieve this separation from the owners), owners of the business must have two documents drawn up and registered with the appropriate government agency (which varies in name from country to country, as do the names of the documents):

  - Memorandum of association – this document records the key characteristics and the external activities of the company being created. For example, the memorandum will provide basic information on the objectives of the business and record the share capital initially required.

  - Articles of association – this document specifies how the company will be regulated internally. It will, for example, explain the initial organization of the executives of the company with their titles and areas of responsibilities (chief executive officer, chief financial officer, etc.) and the rights and responsibilities of each shareholder.

- **Greater finance is generally available.** The initial offering of shares represents a one-time injection of capital to the business. Once the business sells its shares, it receives the price paid at the IPO. Thereafter, the initial shares and any future gains (or losses) in price are to the benefit (or cost) of the shareholders only, unless the company issues and sells additional shares to raise more capital.

- **A company is held to a high degree of accountability.** The owners and the company are separate entities, so from time to time the company must provide information to the shareholders so that they can understand the condition of their investment and so that the company and its management are being held accountable. Information on a company is generally provided by:

  - published, audited company reports annually and, in some countries, unaudited quarterly reports

  - an annual general meeting (AGM) open to all shareholders

  - an extraordinary general meeting (EGM) if called by the shareholders.

- **Compared to other forms of business organizations, companies have greater stability and a higher chance of continuity.** When a shareholder dies or sells shares, the company continues to operate. The death of a shareholder or the sale of shares has no direct impact on the company. All that happens is that one partial owner of the business is replaced by another partial owner. A company can theoretically last for ever because it is independent of the shareholders. The oldest company in the world is a Japanese construction company, Kongō Gumi, which was founded in 578 CE and began operations by building a Buddhist temple. Another example of an exceptionally old company is Stella Artois, which has been operating in Belgium since 1366.

Advantages of operating a business as a company include the following:

- **Access to finance is easier than for sole traders and partnerships.** Companies are perceived to have greater stability and lower risk than sole traders and partnerships. Individuals and institutions are more likely to invest and banks and financial institutions are more likely to make loans to companies.

- **The investor has limited liability.** Investors can lose only the value of the shares and nothing else. By owning small numbers of shares in many different companies, investors can build up safe investment portfolios. Each individual investment is limited, and thus their risks are spread out among many companies. The companies also benefit. Many companies have a huge number of "small" investors (individuals or institutions that own a very small number of shares). However, the sum of the investment of all those small investors can add up to large sums of finance.

- **There is continuity.** The business will not necessarily end if a shareholder dies or sells his or her shares or indeed if any of the directors leave. Companies can go bankrupt and be liquidated (with all of the assets sold off to pay all the liabilities), thus terminating their operations. However, companies have a greater chance of continuity than a sole trader or partnership.

- **There are possibilities for expansion.** Companies have more opportunity to expand because generally they last longer and have more access to finance. For a business to grow, it often needs to invest money in equipment, marketing efforts, or new activities. With fewwer opportunities for finance, many small business, including sole traders and partnerships, cannot take advantage of business opportunities to expand. More often, companies can.

- **An established organizational structure exists.** Managers and workers do not have to change every time a shareholder sells shares. This stability can help the business develop long-term relationships with customers and suppliers alike. It can also allow the business to hire individuals with expertise for individual positions and thus enhance the performance of the business.

Disadvantages of operating as a company include the following:

- **Setting up a company can take time and cost a great deal of money to fulfil the necessary legal requirements.** Whether reorganizing into a company or starting a business as a company, the owners must retain lawyers, have legally required paperwork filled out, and file papers with the appropriate government agencies.

- **Selling shares, especially if the company "goes public",** does not guarantee that the desired or intended amount of finance will be raised. Sometimes IPOs are unsuccessful, and a business has sold itself for relatively little cash. Thus, reorganizing a business as a company or starting up a company involves risk.

- **Owners risk partial or entire loss of control of the business.** If a business decides to become a company, especially for a public limited company, the owners must give up some control of their

business. Even if, during incorporation, former owners still retain 51 per cent of the shares, they must still answer to the new owners (other shareholders). In the case of public companies, loss of control can be significant. Original owners can have a very small percentage of the shares after the firm has gone public.

- **There is loss of privacy.** A public limited company is required to fulfil a number of legal obligations, including publishing its accounts publicly. Many business people unaccustomed to sharing information with others dislike publishing their accounts. Further, if the company's performance has been weak – sales are down or profits are negative – the future performance can be further jeopardized. Some customers may not want to purchase from or do business with a weak company, a situation that can be especially damaging to those business that offer product warranties or after-sales service on products.

- **A company has no control over the stock market.** Share prices may fall, which can damage the image of the company. Such a loss of share value can sometimes occur not because the business has done anything wrong but simply because of an external factor: an election, negative news about another business in the same industry, a downturn in the economy, or a natural disaster.

- **A company has limited control over who buys its shares.** For example, a competitor may want to take over the business. If the shareholders are willing to sell their shares, the company cannot prevent being taken over. Companies are especially vulnerable to being taken over if their share prices fall, which, as noted above, sometimes occurs through no fault of the business itself.

For-profit social enterprises

Although the term "social enterprise" has a slightly different meaning or legal standing in different countries, in general it refers to a form of business that has a social purpose. Social purpose generally means that the organization aims to improve human, social, or environmental well-being. Although social enterprises should and typically do operate to a professional standard (regarding legal existence, proper accounts, management structure, and reporting procedures, etc.), the social aim nevertheless takes priority over any other aim such as growth, maximizing sales, or making profits, which are typical objectives of for-profit organizations. For-profit social enterprises aim to make a profit. However, they do not want to maximize profits if doing so compromises their social purpose.

The for-profit social enterprise can take the form of any of the three models we have seen already (sole trader, partnership, or company). Social enterprises often have one of several other models of business organization, including the following.

Cooperatives

Cooperatives are a form of a partnership whereby the business is owned and run by all the "members" but, unlike partnerships (which in most countries can have no more than 20 partners), cooperatives may have

TOK discussion

Is the label "social enterprise" appropriate?

Can businesses be separated from a profit motive? Can any business be separated from a social purpose?

more than 20 members. Each member participates actively in the running of the business.

There are many types of cooperative:

- **A financial cooperative** is a financial institution the ethical and social aims of which take precedence over profits. Sometimes, for example in the case of credit unions, the social aims might mean lending money at lower rates of interest or providing non-lending services at lower cost than banks or other financial institutions. At other times, a financial cooperative will provide finance (loans) to its members who otherwise might not be able to borrow money.

- **A housing cooperative** is run to provide housing for its members as opposed to providing rent for private landlords. A common activity of a housing cooperative is owning an apartment building and having each "member" entitled to one housing unit in the building. The members, through the cooperative, own the building, and surpluses are reinvested in the building and its operation, so costs to individual members are lower. In addition, housing cooperatives typically have control over who can become a member, thereby ensuring that all members agree to rules and conditions and thus increase the likelihood of social harmony in the building.

- **A workers' cooperative** is a business that is owned and operated by the workers themselves, which does not pay significantly higher wages or salary to managers, and has providing employment to workers as a priority. Often, a workers' cooperative emerges when a business is about to fail. Workers, fearful of losing their jobs, take over the business, sack the managers (or drastically reduce their pay), and reinvest all profits in the business (rather than pay them out as dividends).

- **A producer cooperative** is where groups of producers collaborate in certain stages of production. Producer cooperatives are particularly common in agriculture, such as grape farmers having a cooperative wine-production facility or olive producers having a cooperatively owned press. With producer cooperatives, often the aim is to maximize the utilization of an expensive piece of equipment that individual members, by themselves, could not afford. At other times, cost efficiencies can only be achieved when a stage of the production process is carried out on a large scale. Thus, many producers pool their resources to obtain the cost efficiencies.

- **A consumer cooperative** provides a service to its consumers who are also part owners of the business. In Europe and the United States, a common type of consumer cooperative involved certain grocery stores. Individual consumers would become a "member", which entitles them to purchase groceries at the cooperative, often at lower prices than for-profit grocery stores.

In each case, the cooperative's priority is not to make profit. Rather, the cooperative sells or offers its products or services typically at as close to cost price as possible, thereby lowering the costs to members. However, if its prices are too low, the cooperative runs the risk of failure by not reinvesting in the business (and thus not updating its products

or services) or not having a significant financial cushion to weather a difficult period or an unexpected expense. Thus, cooperatives generally aim to make some profit, but maximizing profit is not their most important aim.

Micro-financiers

Since the work of the Nobel Prize winner Muhammad Yunis, founder of the Grameen Bank in Bangladesh in the 1980s, a whole industry has developed, particularly in low-income economies. The idea is very simple: to provide small amounts of finance to those who traditionally would not have access to it, for example low-income individuals, families in rural communities, and women. The money is lent with specified conditions of use and scheduled repayments. The micro-financier expects to receive repayment of principal and to make a profit on the loans (interest). The loan amounts are small and the interest rates are low, and micro-financiers do not use the aggressive tactics of other forms of moneylenders. While the model has proved to be very profitable for all parties, the main aim has always been to help those who would previously never have had access to finance to take the first steps towards economic independence. In many low-income economies, individuals with good ideas and a strong work ethic have been able to open their own business through the help of micro-finance.

Public–private partnerships (PPP)

A PPP is a business created between a private sector business and the public sector. Typically, a PPP involves the construction of a facility with a social aim (for example in healthcare or education). It could also be for a specific project such as the development of a site for alternative energy or a nature reserve. The business is expected to make a return on the money invested into it, but the priority is not profits. The public sector usually provides the finance and the private business the expertise. Often, the government offers tax incentives to the private sector to take part in the partnership. A PPP may not be limited to small partnerships such as a drug rehabilitation service but can involve large businesses doing big projects. The multinational Swedish company Skanska was involved in a PPP to help construct the Eurotunnel, the channel tunnel between France and the UK.

The main common features of a PPP (for-profit social enterprise) include the following:

- **Profit is important but not the priority** – social aims take precedence. These aims may vary and for-profit social enterprises need to generate profits to ensure the survival and growth of the business. The aim, however, is not to maximize profits but to earn profits sufficient to sustain the business.

- **There is collaboration between the business and the local community.** For-profit social enterprises usually signify a desire for cooperation between the business community and government because both recognize a need being met by ordinary business activity or by government.

- **There is greater democracy in the business than in other organizations.** In for-profit social enterprises, decision making tends to be more consultative and transparent. This style of governance partially stems from the spirit of social enterprises, which are to do good and not typically to devise aggressive business strategies (such as to take market share from competitors or to maximize profits). This style of governance partially stems from the nature of social enterprises, which often rely on support or aid from others (workers willing to work for lower wages, landlords willing to lease properties at discounted rates, etc.). Consultation and transparency convey the social spirit and generate greater willingness on the part of stakeholders to be supportive.

- **The business operates the same functions as any other business.** For-profit social enterprises are businesses, and must attend to production, marketing, HR, and finance decisions, just as in any other business. In some respects, areas of the business have to be run with greater care than other businesses, which often have greater profits and profitability.

Advantages of for-profit social enterprises compared to traditional sole traders, partnerships, and companies include these:

- **A favourable legal status is achieved.** Anyone can engage in activities that are good for humans, society, or the environment. The legal structure of a for-profit social enterprise allows individuals to engage in those activities without being personally liable or accountable to shareholders with traditional (maximizing profits) business interests.

- **There is a strong communal identity.** For-profit social enterprises often have highly motivated employees and other stakeholders working together with a common sense of purpose. Employees often report a high degree of satisfaction, knowing that they are doing something positive for society.

- **There are benefits to the stakeholder community.** For-profit social enterprises help many stakeholders, including the direct beneficiaries of their products and services. They may help the government more, because for-profit social enterprises typically ameliorate human, social, or environmental problems that a government is not addressing, and so help reduce problems in the community.

Disadvantages of for-profit social enterprises compared to traditional sole traders, partnerships, and companies include these:

- **Decision making is complex and time consuming.** In being consultative and transparent, for-profit social enterprises often take a long time to make decisions. If many parties are involved with the decision, which is often the case, this extended decision-making time can limit the effectiveness of the business.

- **There may be insufficient capital for growth.** The business model for a for-profit social enterprise may not sufficient in the long term. Most business rely on healthy profit margins and profits, much of which are retained, for investment in property, plant, and equipment and to provide working capital as working capital requirements

increase with the size of the business. Without large profits, for-profit social enterprises may struggle to survive and expand.

- **There may be insufficient capital for financial strength.** For-profit social enterprises tend to have lower profit margins and profits than traditional for-profit businesses because they often try to make their products and services as inexpensive as possible. As a result, for-profit social enterprises tend not to have deep financial strength that can permit them to survive a recession or times when finance is less available.

Non-profit social enterprises

The main features of non-profit based (commercial) organizations (NPOs) are as follows:

- Some businesses operating in the private sector do not aim to make profits at all. These businesses are also social enterprises – that is, where the main aim is for a social purpose – but they are different from for-profit social enterprises in that they do not aim to make any profits whatsoever.

- Though these social enterprises are run as businesses, they generate (or aim to generate) surpluses rather than profits. A **surplus (sometimes referred to as surplus revenue)** is, conceptually, very similar to a profit. However, rather than be distributed to the owners of the business, the surplus is used to advance the social purpose for which the business was set up.

A surplus is any extra revenue generated after subtracting an NPO's costs. A surplus is calculated as follows:

Surplus = total revenues – total costs

Many non-profit social enterprises are very large: the United Way, Red Cross and Red Crescent, the Mohammed bin Rashid Al Maktoum Foundation, and the Calouste Gulbenkian Foundation are just a few examples. These organizations, and many other large NPOs, are bigger than many traditional businesses.

Social enterprises can take many possible forms, and the differences between them can be subtle (and confusing). Nevertheless, two broad categories of non-profit social enterprises exist: NGOs and charities.

Non-governmental organizations (NGOs)

NGO was a term first used by the United Nations and it has since become a common way to describe a variety of social enterprises. The aim of these various social enterprises is to support a cause that is considered socially desirable. Some of these NGOs are concerned with a single issue, such as **Save the Whales** or with a broader spectrum such as **Greenpeace**. Others may be apolitical, such as the **Aga Kahn Development Network,** while others have political aims, such as **Amnesty International** and the **National Rifle Association**. Regardless, a common element of these is that they are not organized or run by any government.

Student workpoint 1.4

Be a researcher

Look at the websites for two NGOs – one local and one international. Make notes about when they were established, the work they do and any recent news articles about them. Can you find any information about their funding and organization?

What are the main similarities and differences between the two NGOs?

Charities

Charities are a specific form of NGO whose aim is to provide as much relief as possible for those in need. Charities differ from other NGOs in that their focus is on philanthropy and a desire to help those who cannot help themselves.

Some charities are single-event charities that provide, for example, emergency aid for specific natural disasters or war. Other charities focus on a single issue: Save the Children or Oxfam. As with regular NGOs, charities may be apolitical such as the Red Cross and Red Crescent and Half the Sky. Others can be partisan and or have particular preferences, such as the Catholic Charities USA. Nevertheless, the idea is that the business is not run by any government and that it operates in the private sector of the economy.

In addition to the common features of social enterprises mentioned above, common features of non-profit social enterprises include the following:

The surplus generated from a charity's business activities, such as this second-hand clothes shop, are used to advance the social purpose of the organization.

- **Profits are not generated** – instead, these businesses generate surpluses and surpluses are used to advance the social purpose of the business. Sometimes non-profit social enterprises retain surpluses, in a fashion similar to retaining profits, for the capital requirements of the organization. Typically, the surpluses are used directly to provide the goods and services for which the charity was created.

- **Donations are important** – these businesses cannot rely on government funding or other forms of income, so a large part of their revenues comes from voluntary donations from individuals. In some cases (the Calouste Gulbenkian Foundation, for example), the charity has an endowment and the proceeds from the endowment provide reliable ongoing revenues. Nevertheless, virtually all charities want to do more – provide more goods and services for those in need – and welcome large and small donations from individuals and organizations.

- **There is unclear ownership and control.** Who owns a charity? Who should decide who sits on the board of directors? Who selects new board members? Should individuals who contribute large amounts of money to a charity have a larger say in the operation of the charity than others? How are managers selected? What is appropriate compensation? The issue of compensation is especially thorny when the charity is huge, such as the United Way, and its management requires the skills of executive officers of major, for-profit companies. Should the head of a multinational charity be paid the same amount as the CEO of a multinational company? To attract executives of the necessary calibre and skill-set, are for-profit corporate salaries necessary? These kinds of questions routinely plague charities and can be the source of discontent among stakeholders if not handled effectively.

Finally it is also worth noting that there is one clear distinction between NGOs and charities: charities, because of their charitable status and philanthropy, are exempt from paying taxes. Other NGOs, as with all other businesses, are not exempt.

Non-profit social enterprises have many advantages compared to any of the businesses discussed above. These are some of the advantages:

- **They help people or causes in need.** Individuals, organizations, and governments almost never have sufficient resources to solve all of the needs of local people and/or communities. Non-profit social enterprises cannot address all the needs either. Nevertheless, for the specific groups or causes that are supported, the work of non-profit social enterprises is crucially important and valuable.

- **They can foster a philanthropic spirit in the community.** People may feel good about helping others, which can foster socially constructive views in general. In turn, positive attitudes in a community can make it a better place to live and can improve the general business climate.

- **They can foster informed discussions in the community about allocation of resources.** As noted above, individuals, organizations, and governments almost never have sufficient resources to solve all the needs of local people and/or communities. The actions of non-profit social enterprises and the individuals working for and contributing to them can lead to better information about local and distant problems, issues, and causes. With better information, individuals and organizations, including various government agencies, can carry out more informed decision making.

- **They can innovate.** Employees or members are often "forced" to be creative – to try new ideas and tactics to address problems and find solutions – because non-profit social enterprises are not tied to profits.

Non-profit social enterprises have many disadvantages compared to any of the businesses discussed above. These disadvantages include the following:

- **The lack of control but intense lobbying can lead to socially undesirable goods.** For example, High North Alliance in Norway lobbies for Artic coastal communities and seeks to protect the rights of whalers. In effect, it supports consumption of whale meat.[1] In the United States, the power of two non-profit lobbying groups, the National Rifle Association and Gun Owners of America, effectively lobby state and national legislatures in the United States to prevent meaningful restrictions on gun ownership, including the possession of hand guns and assault weapons. Both gun ownership and gun-related deaths are far higher in the United States than in other industrial countries.[2]

- **Sometimes the employees of non-profit social enterprises have a passion and zeal that ill serve the organization or its cause.** Greenpeace employees, for example, have at times taken direct action, acting as pirates by boarding whaling ships, which is illegal and can lead to loss of support for the organization or business.

- **Funding can be irregular.** Non-profit social enterprises are generally very reliant on donations, which can be a problem in economic recessions.

CULTURE

Many NGOs work across national boundaries, providing assistance and aid all over the world.

What cultural difficulties might they encounter? Do some research to find examples of such difficulties.

1 Business organization and environment

---

[1] http://www.reuters.com/article/2008/03/03/us-climate-whaling-idUSEIC37493020080303. Accessed 5 October 2013

[2] http://abcnews.go.com/blogs/health/2013/09/19/u-s-has-more-guns-and-gun-deaths-than-any-other-country-study-finds/. Accessed 5 October 2013.

Revision checklist

✓ Businesses in the private sector are owned and controlled by individuals or groups of individuals.

✓ Businesses in the public sector are owned and controlled by governmental authorities.

✓ Sole trader businesses are owned and managed by a single person. The individual is liable for any debts the businesses might incur. Registering a business as a sole trader is relatively quick and easy.

✓ A partnership is a business owned and managed by more than one person. Decisions should be made jointly and all partners will be equally liable. Multiple partners can bring different kinds of expertise, and may also bring extra sources of finance.

✓ Companies and corporations have multiple owners – usually shareholders. When a business has registered as a company or corporation, the owners themselves are legally separate from the business, so they are no longer liable for debts.

✓ For-profit social enterprises have a social mission, but still aim to make a profit.

✓ A social mission is the main aim of non-profit social enterprises. Any money made is called surplus. Most charities fall into this category.

Practice question

Ecosoluciones

Ecosoluciones is a non-profit research organization located in Madrid, Spain. One of their objectives is to try to introduce non-polluting sources of electricity in developing countries.

One successful application of their research was the Alumbre Project. This provided electricity created by wind generators to the remote village of Alumbre, Peru, which previously had none.

In Alumbre, wind generators were installed by *Ecosoluciones* to supply, for the first time, electricity to a textile factory, one of the few firms in the area operating in the secondary sector. *Ecosoluciones* also agreed to maintain and repair the generators. There was a complete transformation in the production process. The factory was able to buy new machinery. Productivity increased dramatically. New jobs were created.

Ecosoluciones also promised, in partnership with *Peru Telecom* and the Peruvian government, to help fund the improvements in communication between Alumbre and the rest of Peru. This also allowed regional trade to develop. The entire community experienced significant improvements in their

quality of life. The Peruvian government saw this as a practical solution to develop other depressed areas* of the country.

Unfortunately in 2008 a severe financial crisis hit Europe and the Spanish government suspended part of its funding for research organizations such as *Ecosoluciones*. As a direct result, the management of *Ecosoluciones* felt it may no longer be able to maintain Alumbre's wind generators.

[Source: adapted from http://ecoworldly.com/2008/06/17/ wind-power-blows-into-peru-and-brightens-future/, 17 June 2008]

a) Define the term *secondary sector*. [2 marks]

b) Prepare a PEST analysis for the textile factory in Alumbre. [6 marks]

c) Contrast the objectives of non-profit organizations such as *Ecosoluciones* to those of profit-based organizations. [5 marks]

d) Discuss **two** possible areas of conflict between stakeholders in the Alumbre Project. [7 marks]

IB, May 2010

---

* depressed area: a region or locality where business, employment, and stock-market values have declined severely or are at a very low level of activity

1.3 Organizational objectives

By the end of this chapter, you should be able to:

→ Explain the definitions and roles of vision statement and mission statement

→ Define aims, objectives, strategies and tactics and explain their relationships

→ Explain why organizations change objectives and innovate in response to changes in internal and external environments

→ Describe ethical objectives and corporate social responsibility (CSR)

→ Outline the reasons why organizations set ethical objectives and the impact of implementing them

→ Explain the evolving role and nature of CSR

→ Prepare a SWOT analysis of a given organization

→ Examine the Ansoff matrix for different growth strategies of a given organization

Vision and mission statements

Successful businesses have a clear identity, shared values and a sense of purpose that all stakeholders identify with. To create or reinforce this identity, communicate these values, and maintain focus on the purpose, many businesses produce mission and vision statements. Some businesses will have one of these, others both. When properly done, both types of statement can help a business reach its loftiest aims and stay focused day to day.

Mission and vision statements are sometimes confused. They have, however, different purposes. The vision statement is more forward looking and speaks to the long-term aims and highest aspirations of a business. A mission statement is more grounded in the aim of accomplishing objectives to achieve the mission, an intermediate step on the way to the vision. The two statements should complement each other, with the vision statement being produced first. Less specific than a mission statement, the vision statement serves as a guiding principle or principles.

Table 1.3.1. Comparison of vision and mission statements

	Vision	**Mission**
Concept	**What** do we want?	**Why** are we doing what we are doing?
Purpose	A vision statement points to the **future**. It is what the business would like to see itself as.	A mission statement, based upon where the business is **now**, communicates what needs to be done in order to achieve the vision.
Audiences	To internal stakeholders, the vision statement **inspires** and motivates employees. For external stakeholders, the vision statement **binds** them to the business by giving a sense of shared beliefs.	To internal stakeholders, the mission statement provides a means for **accountability** by defining key performance indicators. For external stakeholders, the mission statement measures how **successful** the business is at achieving its vision.
Change	As an expression of the business core values, the vision should *never* change.	A mission statement may change: in a world of dynamically changing external environments, a mission statement *may* need to be modified to meet new circumstances.

Aims, objectives, strategies, and tactics

Businesses may also distinguish between aims and objectives and between strategies and tactics. All of these concepts are interdependent and all these terms, including vision and mission, are linked in some way or another. Figure 1.3.1 is an attempt to show their relationship with each other.

TOK discussion

"Futurists" or "futurologists" are regularly wrong. In light of the unpredictability of the future, to what degree is planning for the future good use or a misuse of a business's resources?

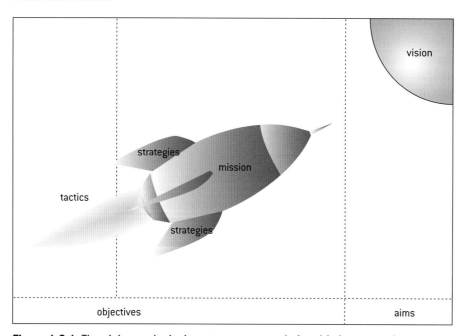

Figure 1.3.1. The vision and mission statements – relationship between aims, objectives, strategies, and tactics

The aims of a business are its long-term goals – what it wants to achieve in the future. An example of an aim might be: "We want to be profitable every year through the production of tasty, high-quality meat products". Another aim might be more focused on the delivery of the service: "We aim to deliver

consistently high-quality plant and garden products through a helpful sales staff". The vision statement is a summary of these aims (sometimes literally the sum of these aims, at other times with modified wording).

Two examples of vision statements of major corporations you probably know (and the products of which you might use) are from Microsoft and Toyota USA.

Examine their vision statements:

- Microsoft: "A personal computer in every home running Microsoft software".
- Toyota USA: "To be the most successful and respected car company in America".

In both cases, the vision statements are brief and express aspirations that are high and long term. They are inspirational. Both statements convey a sense of confidence in purpose. Further, they convey the sense that, if the companies are not at this lofty place yet (Microsoft running software in every home or Toyota USA being the most successful and respected car company in America), they will not give up until they have reached their aspiration.

In contrast to aims, objectives are the medium- to short-term goals that clarify how the business will achieve its aims and reach its vision. A mission summarizes these objectives.

> ### Key term
>
> **Vision statement**
>
> a philosophy, vision or set of principles which steers the direction and behaviour of an organization

Student workpoint 1.5

Be reflective

You might be aiming for a grade 7 in IB Business Management. What might your personal vision statement be?

What might your personal mission statement be?

Does your school have a mission statement? If so, what does it mean for you as a pupil? What does in mean for your teachers? If not, try and design one!

Objectives should have specific characteristics. They also come in three types:

- **Strategic objectives** – sometimes referred to as global objectives – are the medium- to long-term objectives set by senior managers to guide the company in the right direction to achieve the aims.
- **Tactical objectives** are the medium- to short-term objectives set by middle managers to achieve the strategic objectives.
- **Operational objectives** are the day-to-day objectives set by floor managers (and sometimes workers themselves) so that the company can reach its tactical objectives.

Table 1.3.2. Vision and the three types of objective

Vision (summary of aims)	Strategic objectives	Tactical objectives	Operational objectives
Long-term and highest aspiration	Long-term goals	Medium or short-term goals	Day-to-day goals

Businesses use the term **hierarchy of objectives** to describe the relationship between all of these goals. At the top of the hierarchy are the aims, which are few in number and set by the entrepreneur or the chief executive officer (CEO). The aims are (and should be) rather general. How the business achieves these aims is through the next level of managers – the senior managers (directors or executives). These strategic objectives will be greater in number and concrete. Ideally, these objectives will also be SMART (see below for details). With SMART objectives, the entrepreneur or CEO has some fair and measurable way to assess the performance of the executives and their divisions. If SMART objectives are not met, the CEO must ask: Were the objectives properly set, or did the directors or executives not perform properly in meeting the objectives? If the directors or executives vastly exceed the objectives, the CEO may decide to set more ambitious objectives the following year.

Businesses achieve their strategic objectives through the next tier of objectives, those that are tactical. Tactical objectives tend to be greater in number than strategic objectives and are usually set by the next level of managers – the middle managers (heads of department or supervisors). At the lowest level, operational objectives will be set: floor managers will determine specific objectives that, in sum, ensure that the tactical objectives will be met.

Consider the hierarchy of objectives shown in Table 1.3.3.

Table 1.3.3. The hierarchy of objectives

Aim	Strategic objective	Tactical objective	Operational objective
To be the most successful car dealership in the city	To have the highest market share of car dealerships in the city	To hire and retain enough salespeople so that the dealership has sufficient salespeople to serve customers at all times	To have the average amount of time that a customer waits to be greeted by a salesperson to be less than two minutes

In the example in Table 1.3.3 the CEO sets the aim that a particular car dealership should be the most successful in the city. The head of sales determines that the best way to measure success is by having the highest market share of any car dealership in the city. The sales managers realize that to have the highest market share within a specified time frame means having more qualified sales staff to serve customers. Then the salespeople, realizing that their chance of making a sale increases the sooner they greet the customer, agree as a group that no customer will go more than two minutes without being greeted and offered service by a salesperson – even if it means that salespeople will not finish their coffee during their break.

An important difference between aims and objectives is that objectives are concrete and can be translated into something specific and measurable. A vision such as "To be the most successful and respected car company in America" is motivating, but it is also (purposely) vague. This vagueness allows almost everyone to feel connected to it, but vagueness and abstractness are not qualities that employees can act on in unison.

Student workpoint 1.6

Be reflective

Here are the vision statements of two large organizations:

Oxfam: A just world without poverty

Amazon: Our vision is to be earth's most customer centric company; to build a place where people can come to find and discover anything they might want to buy online.

What do the statements reveal about the aims and attitudes of the organization? Look carefully at the words that each statement uses – what affect do they have on you?

Businesses are effective when they take that vision and transform it into specific objectives. The best business objectives are SMART. **SMART objectives** are as follows:

Specific – Is the objective clear and well defined? Objectives should relate to the nature of the business and be unambiguous. Rather than set an objective that the business "should grow", a smart objective would clarify that it wants to "increase its membership" or "increase the number of units sold" or "increase market share".

Measurable – Can the objective be measured to see whether it has been achieved or not? Not only should the objective be specific but it should also be measurable, as each of the above cases were (number of members, number of units sold, size of market share).

Achievable – Can the objective be achieved (is it realistic)? When objectives are achievable, they can be motivational. Objectives that are beyond the reasonable reach of a business or its employees can have the opposite effect, with employees giving up because they think or fear that they cannot reach the objective. Achievable goals also reduce dissonance and distractions (when employees or managers wonder how other aspects of the business are going to support these objectives).

Relevant – Is the objective actually of any use? Businesses can set objectives that are distractions from the main purpose of the company or, more commonly, set objectives for specific employees that are not relevant to the employees' area of responsibility. At a school, telling a member of the custodial staff that the objectives are for students to achieve high IB scores is not particularly relevant. Telling the custodial staff that, to lower expenses, they need to reduce the amount of cleaning supplies by 7 per cent is relevant.

Time-specific – Has a sufficient time frame been set? If objectives do not have a time frame or deadline, they are not meaningful. For a car dealership to tell the sales staff that the number of cars sold per salesperson must increase by 5 per cent is meaningless unless the sales staff is told the date by which the new sales target is to be met.

A **business strategy** is a plan to achieve a strategic objective in order to work towards the aims of the business. This strategy will be medium to long term and will require senior managers to make the decisions approved by the owners and/or the CEO.

Strategies are not unplanned or spur of the moment; they involve careful analysis of:

- where the business is

- development of a plan (strategy) of how to get where the business wants to be (aims)

- careful consideration of how to implement the strategy

- a periodic evaluation process (in well-run organizations) to determine whether the plan is working or, after a specific period of time, has worked.

Specific

Measurable

Achievable

Relevant

Time-specific

STRATEGY

Whatever the business, devising a strategy means asking 'who, when, what, where, why?'

What are the implications of missing one of these questions?

A **business tactic** is a plan to achieve a tactical objective to work towards the strategies of the business, which themselves are the path to reaching the aims of the business. This tactic will be short term and will require middle managers to make the decisions approved by the senior managers. Tactics are easier to change. They are less closely tied to the long-term health of the firm but rather focus on how to achieve measurable targets within the strategy.

A business can have a sound strategy but a poor tactical plan. A strategic objective, for example, might be offering food that is perceived by restaurant customers to be of the highest quality of its type in a market area. One tactic for determining customers' satisfaction might be customer count or observing customers' reactions as they eat the food. A better tactic might be to obtain a more direct form of customer feedback on food quality (but it might not be a better form if the direct feedback does not otherwise fit with the marketing mix of the restaurant).

The need for organizations to change objectives

Businesses often need to change objectives. Sometimes this requires changing strategic objectives. More commonly, it involves changing tactical objectives and, day to day, floor managers and supervisors change operational objectives. Regardless of the level, objectives change because of changes in either of these environments:

- the internal environment, which refers to changes in the conditions within the business

- the external environment, which refers to anything outside the business that nonetheless has a bearing on its operation or performance.

Changes in the internal environment might include the following:

Leadership – change of leadership often can lead to a change in aims and objectives. A famous example is when, in 1996, Steve Jobs returned to Apple. Sometimes new leaders brought into a company will have a different leadership style from their predecessor, which can require significant changes to objectives.

HR – the term "human resources" covers a vast array of elements of a business. Conditions related to HR can change and can alter objectives all down the hierarchy. Industrial action, which refers to actions taken by unions or other forms of organized labour, can often precipitate change in an organization.

Organization – business organizations change. A merger or acquisition, such as when Kraft took over Cadbury, can have a ripple effect through an organization causing the new organization to rethink many of its objectives. In other instances, some internal pressures may cause an organization to modify one aspect of its business. However, given the interconnectedness of all the business functions, changes in one area can require changes in another, including changes to strategic or tactical objectives.

Product – products are sold in a marketplace. Sometimes, the performance of the product in the marketplace may require changes in either the product or sometimes an entire product line. In the 1980s, for example, because of market pressures Lucozade reoriented itself as a sports drink, and sales tripled. With this change in the branded identity of the product, from an illness-curing beverage to an energy-providing sports drink, many different aspects of Lucozade's strategic and tactical objectives had to change (which led to an even greater number of changes in operational objectives).

Finance – All business activity must be financed. When the circumstances of finance change, especially when sources of finance become fewer and the amount of finance decreases, organizations have to modify their strategies or change the emphasis of their business. In 2009, FIFA football introduced the "Financial Fair Play" rule, which modified how much money teams could spend on players, and teams had to respond.

Many other sets of circumstances can change finance. After the world recession began in 2008, for example, many banks raised lending standards and businesses had to make adjustments because they had more limited access to capital to finance activity.

Operations – ideally, most businesses are innovating constantly, not just by offering new products but also by developing better methods for producing or delivering their core service or product – that is, by innovating their operations. Sometimes changes in operations occur for more everyday reasons, such as relocating a factory. Whether because of innovation or the more everyday reason, changes in operations can necessitate other changes in objectives.

If any of the above internal factors are altered, then the business may well have to respond or even pre-empt them by changing its objectives. Changes can also occur in the external environment. Usually, a business has limited or no control over the external environment, and often objectives have to change in response to them. Often, business people and teachers and students use a "STEEPLE" framework to frame issues related to the external environment. Steeple factors are as follows:

Social – this refers to changes in society or culture, such as demographic change (social) or cultural change (such as an increased preference for expensive coffees, like those supplied by Starbucks or Coffee Aroma). Social changes such as these may force the business to reappraise its objectives. One example is the business of education. More women are attending university and obtaining degrees than they did a few decades ago and, as a result, universities are modifying many of their objectives, from course offerings to residential practices, to suit the greater number of women.

Technological – today is an era of rapid technological change, which can change the environment for business in any number of ways. A product a business offers can be rendered obsolete or uncompetitive because of technological innovation (think how quickly Blackberry went from being a "hot" product to one that struggles to compete with new smartphones). Technological innovation can force changes in production techniques if a competitor develops new methods for producing products more cheaply than other businesses. Technological changes can also force a business to change for "softer" reasons. All businesses need to be more aware of their environment and their actions in it because information technologies allow communication in ways previously unknown. Today, for example, Nike would have a harder time manufacturing shoes in low-income economies and using child labour compared to several decades ago, when companies could often follow those tactics without being discovered.

Economic – changes in the market conditions, such as the presence of new competitors, or simply changes in the economy, such as the global financial crisis that began several years ago, can have a profound influence on businesses and force them to change strategic and tactical objectives. For example, because of changing economic conditions interest rates on loans can increase, raising the cost of capital for businesses and preventing capital investment. If a company sells a product the demand for which is income elastic (see more on this in Unit 4.x), sales may fall in an economic downturn. For many reasons, changing economic conditions can force a business to change.

Ethical – sometimes quickly, sometimes slowly, the values of a society can change. Changes in ethical values in a society encourage or even force a business to change its practices. Fifty years ago, relatively few businesses were deeply concerned about sustainable business practices – Paul Hawken's concept of "natural capitalism" was unheard of. Today, even if the owners or executives of a business were not genuinely concerned about sustainable practices, external stakeholders will almost certainly expect their business not to harm the environment, or at least to minimize that harm. In a host of other ways – ethics in lending, diversity in hiring, attentiveness to sexual harassment, product safety – changes in society's values have led to changes in many businesses' objectives.

Political – change to the political system very often forces business to change its approach. Multinational businesses plan for this possibility and often will have a "country risk assessment" before investing in a particular country. A country risk assessment attempts to determine the likelihood that drastic political change in a country could put at risk the investment or operations of a business there. Political risk, however, can occur at home. If the outcome of a political election determines that the legislature of a country changes from centre-left to centre-right, the business environment can change. Sometimes, though, political change can occur unexpectedly and not from the results of an election. Legislatures can decide to take action because of a scandal, a crime, or even an accident, that in turn affects the business environment.

Legal – when responsibility for legislation changes from one party to the other, or one coalition to another, changes in the legal environment often occur. Regulation, taxes, and a host of other factors can be changed merely by statute, and businesses have to respond. In the 1980s in the United States, for example, many individuals across the country grew tired of the number of fatal or traumatic injuries occurring to young people due to excessive alcohol consumption. One by one, most state legislatures raised the minimum drinking age in the

United States from 18 to 21 years. Many taverns, bars, and clubs that targeted customers in the 18–20-year-old range had to modify their business strategies.

Ecological – growing environmental awareness and the "green" revolution have had a significant effect on many businesses, for example with the emergence of hybrid cars. Ecological factors can affect businesses in ways other than the now-dominant focus on sustainability. Ecological depletion, such as from fisheries off the coast of Canada, or through some types of mining, can force a business to change strategies. Large oil companies, sometimes notorious for their ecological disasters such as huge oil spills, are nonetheless highly innovative as they search for new sources of energy, especially clean energy, in anticipation of rising demand and declining traditional sources or energy, such as oil.

Why organizations set ethical objectives

Ever more commonly today, business are establishing for themselves ethical objectives. Objectives such as these are goals based on established codes of behaviour that, when met, allow the business to provide some social or environmental benefit or, at the least, not to hurt society or the environment in the process of making a profit. For example, a business might aim to expect all its employees to be treated without discrimination, harassment, or even favouritism. Another ethical objective might be always to treat customers with respect and honesty. Ethical objectives can cover a whole range of activities and today many businesses are setting them.

Businesses may set themselves ethical objectives for some very good commercial reasons, including these:

This poster from the clothing company Matalan clearly states the business's ethical policy

- **Building up customer loyalty** – repeat customers are vital to most businesses. Customers are more likely to return to a business they trust and respect, and ethical objectives and ethical action foster this.

- **Creating a positive image** – both existing and potential customers are likely to shop at businesses with good reputations. The opposite is certainly true: customers will avoid businesses with reputations for untrustworthiness.

- **Developing a positive work environment** – businesses that have well-motivated staff who enjoy working for the business have a competitive advantage. Businesses with strong ethical objectives can be attractive to many potential employees and serve to improve morale and motivation.

- **Reducing the risk of legal redress** – being unethical can cost a company money, not only from dissatisfied customers not returning or from the bad word-of-mouth reports generated by unethical behaviour. Sometimes unethical behaviour can lead to legal redress by the government, by other businesses or by the customers themselves. Even if a business "wins" in court, the process can be expensive and cause significant damage to the firm's reputation.

- **Satisfying customers' ever-higher expectations for ethical behaviour** – with improved ICT and the worldwide web, business decisions and actions are more visible than ever before. Today, consumers are aware of what is considered ethical and unethical behaviour and often "punish" unethical behaviours by not patronizing certain businesses. Few businesses can disregard public opinion.

- **Increasing profits** – opportunities for businesses to behave ethically are growing. Banks will often not lend to dubious businesses, clothes manufacturers will not use "sweatshop" workers, and coffee houses use "fair trade" coffee. Many people today seek out and purchase from businesses that behave ethically, which can lead to higher profits.

The impact of implementing ethical objectives

When a business implements ethical objectives, many areas of the business environment will be affected. The effects may be on the following:

- **The business itself** – although in the long run the business may experience benefits from implementing ethical objectives, in the short term costs are likely to rise, and employees, accustomed to certain norms and practices, may **resist change**.

- **Competitors** – competitors may have to respond to maintain their **market position**.

- **Suppliers** – if the business implementing ethical objectives includes the policy of buying only from other ethical businesses, suppliers may have to respond in order to protect their orders.

- **Customers** – customers are likely to trust the business more and develop a strong **brand loyalty**.

- **The local community** – businesses that have and follow ethical objectives generally see an improvement in their relationship with the local community, which can benefit them in terms of employment and goodwill.

- **Government** – feeling pressure from voters and other stakeholders, increasingly local, regional, and national levels of government are recognizing businesses with ethical objectives, overall creating a government–business environment fostering ethical objectives.

The difference between ethical objectives and corporate social responsibility

Ethical objectives are specific goals that a business may set for itself based on established codes of behaviour. Ethical objectives differ, but are closely related to corporate social responsibility (CSR). CSR is the concept that a business has an obligation to operate in a way that will have a positive impact on society. As part of its CSR policy, a business would want to assess its actions. As a result of such an assessment,

the business may wish to implement a particular ethical objective. For example, a business might open a crèche facility (an early childhood day-care centre) for its employees.

The importance of corporate social responsibility

CSR is broader and less specific than ethical objectives. A company committed to CSR is intending to act as a good "**corporate citizen**": in all matters acting responsibly and in a manner that benefits society as a whole. A business committed to CSR not only obeys laws but also interacts responsibly and honestly with customers and reduces its impact on the environment. By recognizing its CSR, a business is more than likely to have a **sustainable business model**. By building strong links with society and the environment, the business is more likely to be a valued part of the society.

Many businesses, and increasingly big businesses, see themselves and want to position themselves as role models – as leading citizens – setting the standard for everyone for responsible behaviour. In an international context this might be more difficult because of different opinions of ethical values, but with globalization and the greater integration of the world's economies through the actions of multinational companies this can still be possible. Although many businesses do not reach their highest aspirations for CSR, since around 1980 the movement towards CSR has been significant and led to dramatic changes in the attitudes and practices of businesses.

SWOT analysis

SMART objectives are part of a coherent strategic plan. In the 1960s, a business tool – the SWOT analysis – was developed to help business set these objectives. Although use of this tool has not been without criticism, in general many businesses rely on SWOT analyses for planning purposes.

SWOT analysis is meant to be the first stage in the planning process. It helps managers to brainstorm the perceived **strengths**, **weaknesses**, **opportunities**, and **threats** facing the business. These elements are combined in a matrix as shown in Table 1.3.4.

Table 1.3.4. The SWOT matrix

	Positive factors	Negative factors
Internal to the business	Strengths	Weaknesses
External to the business	Opportunities	Threats

The SWOT matrix is based on perceptions. The wider the sources and the more reliable the data, the stronger will be the analysis of the SWOT factors. The opposite is also true. If a SWOT analysis is done in a poor, sloppy, or uninformed fashion, it can actually mislead a business. Like any business tool, it is useful only when thoughtfully and properly applied.

A SWOT analysis for a given organization

Table 1.3.5 shows an example of a SWOT matrix for Apple Inc. (as of January 2013).

Table 1.3.5. SWOT matrix for Apple Inc.

Strengths	Weaknesses
● Well recognized among most consumers ● Fourth largest player in the global mobile phone market ● 18.5% market share of global smartphone market ● Strong brand image provides an edge over competitors ● Very profitable – $100 billion cash reserves ● Focused research and development creating stylish products ● Provides integrated operating systems, hardware, application software and service to its customers	● Patent infringement lawsuit may affect financial condition and operating results 　■ January 2010 　■ Nokia 2012 Samsung dispute ● Product recalls may harm Apple's reputation 　■ 2010, antennae problems in iPhone 4 ● Product defects harm Apple's reputation and add significant warranty and other expenses 　■ 2012 embarrassing discard of Google maps and the failure of Apple's own maps for the iPhone 5. ● Poor design and limited innovation in the latest products ● Death of the inspirational leader Steve Jobs in 2012 ● Loss of share value (25% in three months Sep–Dec 2012) ● Proprietary systems that do not allow individuality ● Price – other products are more affordable and of similar quality ● Foxcom – has been a PR disaster for Apple
Opportunities	**Threats**
● Strong growth in smartphone ● Strong growth in tablet markets ● Mobile advertising market is forecast to reach approximately $25 billion by 2015 ● Increased scope in the educational market ● Streaming and television markets have great potential	● Rising popularity of Google Android may affect its market share 　■ 350,000 Android smartphones are activated daily; 150,000 iPhones are activated daily 　■ More firms like HTC and Motorola are using Android ● Intense competition may affect revenues and profitability ● Increasing popularity of Kindle Fire ● The business sector is not dominated by Apple – the field is more open

Source: Adapted from Datamonitor's Apple Inc. Company Profile SWOT Analysis
http://paigebalash.wordpress.com/2012/02/28/where-is-apple-going-now-swot-analysis-of-apple-inc-2/

Note that the purpose of a SWOT analysis is not to brainstorm the strengths and weaknesses of a business strategy itself; it is the first part of developing the strategy by identifying the different strengths and weaknesses of the business. Once these are known, the SWOT matrix can be analysed and so a strategy can be formulated.

SWOT analysis and market position

Use of the SWOT matrix can be strengthened by "pairing" key factors from each quadrant and then adopting a relevant strategy, as shown in Table 1.3.6.

Table 1.3.6. Pairing key factors to determine the relevant strategy

	Strengths	**Weaknesses**
Opportunities	S–O **Growth** strategies	W–O **Re-orientation** strategies
Threats	S–T **Defusing** strategies	W–T **Defensive** strategies

Source: Adapted from: http://www.quickmba.com/strategy/swot/

Growth strategies are best achieved by combining the strengths of a business with the market opportunities, which produces the most positive short-term strategy available from the matrix. The business should pursue growth strategies when it is confident that it has no big issues in any other area.

Defensive strategies are adopted when a business is at its most vulnerable. When threats and weakness exist in combination, the business needs to act defensively and quickly. Defensive strategies are the most "negative" short-term strategies, but they may be necessary to help the business survive.

Re-orientation strategies are adopted when a business focuses on addressing its weaknesses in order to use them for the opportunities available in the market. Re-orientation strategies are positive and long term. Their adoption assumes that the business will first address its weaknesses, then can re-orientate itself in a new direction.

Defusing strategies are designed to eliminate threats in the market by focusing on the strengths of a business. Defusing strategies assume that the business does not need to look for new market opportunities but can simply defuse the threats through a focus on core strengths. This is a neutral and medium- to short-term strategy. For instance, if Apple had considered its SWOT matrix (Table 1.3.5) then it may have focused on re-orientating strategies – see Table 1.3.7.

Table 1.3.7. Apple SWOT analysis – re-orientating strategies

Strengths	Weaknesses
	• Product defects harm Apple's reputation and add significant warranty and other expenses
	■ 2012 embarrassing discard of Google maps and the failure of Apple's own maps for the iPhone 5.
	• Poor design and limited innovation in the latest products
	• Death of the inspirational leader Steve Jobs in 2012
Opportunities	**Threats**
• Mobile advertising market is forecast to reach approximately $25 billion by 2015	
• Increased scope in the educational market	
• Streaming and television markets have great potential	

Apple may conclude that it needs to signal to the market that the business lives on after Steve Jobs. To do so, it must create new products (in the growing streaming and television markets) to rescue its reputation as an innovative producer. Such a move would also signal a move away from the intensely competitive tablet and smartphone markets – just as the company did in the past when it moved away from the home computer market and into digital music.

The Ansoff matrix

Another business tool to help businesses plan and set objectives is the Ansoff matrix, which was designed by Igor Ansoff in 1957. Many businesses use the Ansoff matrix to help plan their growth strategies.

The matrix looks at the growth potential in terms of the market and product, and considers both the existing markets and products, and new markets and products (see Figure 1.3.2).

Product

		Existing	New
M a r k e t	Existing	Market penetration	Product development
	New	Market development	Diversification

Figure 1.3.2. The Ansoff matrix

There are four possible growth strategies, explored below.

Market penetration occurs when a business grows by increasing its market share, selling more of its existing products in the same market. Market penetration is considered the safest option but opportunities for increasing market share may be limited by the competitors in the market. Market penetration relies heavily on promoting brand loyalty in order to encourage repeat customers and on promotion in general to lure customers away from the competition. Television soap operas, telenovelas, or even Hollywood blockbusters with sequels that tell more or less the same story, such as "Toy Story", "Shrek" or "Iron Man", would fall into this category.

Key factors to increase the chance of success are:

- the growth potential of the market
- the strength of customer loyalty
- the power and ability of competitors.

Market development expands the market by looking for new markets or for new **market segments** in the existing market. Market development is a riskier strategy than market penetration, as the business may not understand the new markets. For example, Starbucks was unsuccessful when it opened coffee stores in Australia. Wal-Mart also was unsuccessful when it expanded into Germany. Wal-Mart had underestimated the loyalty of the German public to existing (German) superstores. Successful market development requires different approaches from market penetration.

Key factors to reduce the risk of market development are:

- effective market research
- having local knowledge on the ground
- having an effective distribution channel.

Product development is the development of new products for the existing market. Sometimes it may be a genuinely and wholly new product. Often, however, so-called "new" products are upgrades of existing products such as the iPad, iPad 2, iPad 3, iPad mini and all the different variations. At other times, a "new product" is a variation on an existing product. For example, this was the case when Singapore Airlines introduced their budget airline "Scoot" to fight off competition from Australian budget airlines.

Product development is riskier than market penetration, with much depending on how loyal the customers are to the original products. Key factors to reduce the risk of product development are:

- effective market research
- having a strong research and development system
- having first mover advantage.

Diversification is the riskiest growth strategy a business can pursue. When diversifying – introducing a new product into a new market – a business combines two elements of risk:

- lack of familiarity and experience in the new market
- the untestedness of any new product.

> **TOK discussion**
>
> Long before business tools such as SWOT analysis and the Ansoff matrix existed, businesses operated successfully. Do these tools add value? To what degree, if any, do they obscure rather than clarify?

1 Business organization and environment

When Apple moved away from home computing and entered the digital music market and then the handphone market, it successfully diversified. Many attempts at diversification, however, have failed. For example, a British cement producer 'Blue Circle' decided to produce lawnmowers. Its rationale was that people using their cement to build garden patios would want a lawnmower to cut the grass. Blue Circle's failed attempt at diversification was a factor contributing to the takeover of the business in 2001.

Key factors to reduce the risk of diversification are:

- effective market research
- due diligence testing to determine:
  - the attractiveness of the market
  - the cost of entering the market
- recognition of the existing business
- possible tie-ups with other businesses with the necessary experience.

Apple's iPod is an example of successful diversification

Revision checklist

✓ A vision statement should encapsulate what the business hopes to be in the future. It should remain constant.

✓ A mission statement describes what the business is doing now. It might need to be modifies as time passes.

✓ Aims are long-term goals.

✓ Objectives are short-medium-term goals which allow a business to meet its aims. Objectives should be SMART (specific, measurable, achievable, relevant and time-specific).

✓ A business strategy is an over-arching plan of objectives which will enable aims to be met.

✓ Business tactics are the actions and objectives which allow a business to implement strategy.

✓ Ethical objectives are goals that a business sets for itself based on established codes of behaviour.

✓ Corporate social responsibility (CSR) is the concept that all businesses have an obligation to operate in a way that will have a positive impact on society.

✓ A SWOT analysis is a tool used in business planning. It involves analysing strengths, weaknesses, opportunities and threats, both inside a business and externally.

✓ The Ansoff matrix is used to plan business growth. It considers new and existing products and new and existing markets to identify opportunities. It allows a business to identify areas of market penetration, market development, product development and diversification.

Practice question

Predicting the future

Traditional secondary research to identify trends, to forecast and to provide data about seasonal and cyclical variation is increasingly outdated, particularly as many products are sold through e- commerce.

Today online forecasting is becoming popular. *Google™'s* chief economist has found a correlation between sales of products (such as cars and holidays) and levels of online *Google™* searches for information about those products.

To make market predictions, market researchers are increasingly using social media* to collect online messages in order to understand consumers' moods. They use web-based data to build a "real time" measure of consumer emotions and preferences and then use the results for predicting consumers' behaviour. Some companies such as *Coca Cola®*, *Starbucks®* and *Disney* already use social media for online market research.

Dr Bollen of Indiana University, United States, found that:

Twitter users' collective mood changes coincide with national events.

A correlation exists between trends in national mood (expressed in millions of *Twitter* messages) and changes in share prices. Three days after an increase in anxiety levels, share prices tend to fall (although it is unclear why this happens).

Investors use social media to guide their decisions.

Users of social media share information online about feelings and purchasing intentions. They are unconcerned by market researchers using software such as "Wise Window" to follow them constantly in order to forecast demand.

Technologically advanced software can recognize sarcasm, double meanings and cultural references. However, interpreting slang expressions remains a challenge.

Mr Watts, an Internet researcher at *Yahoo!®*, said that to be useful, a forecasting technique must add something new to what is already known. The use of social media will only add value to forecasting if other sources of information are limited. He warned that sophisticated methods based on the analysis of *Twitter* messages, blog postings or *Facebook®* pages have limitations.

[Source: adapted from "Can Twitter predict the future?" *The Economist Technology Quarterly*, 4 June 2011 and John Plunkett, *Media Guardian*, 25 July 2011]

---

* social media: refers to various forms of relatively new electronic technologies that allow individuals, groups and organizations to communicate with one another. The communication is "virtual" (across the world wide web and through electronic transmission) and is typically interactive. One frequent feature is the ability of a participant to pass on a communication it has received to other persons, groups, or organizations.

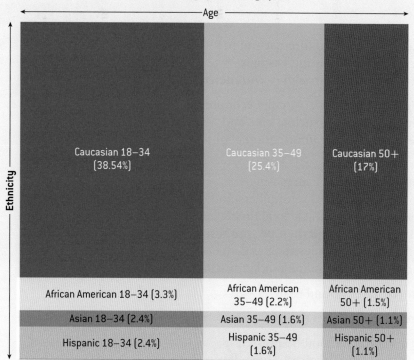

Twitter Demographics (Infographic)

a) Describe **one** advantage and **one** disadvantage to an organization of using e-commerce. [4 marks]

b) (i) Explain **one** benefit of sales forecasting for an organization. [4 marks]

    (ii) Distinguish between seasonal **and** cyclical variations to predict sales trends. [4 marks]

c) Examine the usefulness of traditional secondary research to identify market trends and for forecasting. [6 marks]

d) Evaluate the use of "social media to collect online message in order to understand consumers' moods" for making market predictions. [9 marks]

IB, Nov. 2013

1.4 Stakeholders

By the end of this chapter, you should be able to:

→ Outline the interests of internal stakeholders

→ Outline the interests of external stakeholders

→ Discuss possible areas of mutual benefit and conflict between stakeholders' interests

Stakeholders are any individual or groups of individuals who have a direct interest in a business because the actions of the business will affect them directly. They are called stakeholders because they have a stake or interest in the business. Sometimes the stake is directly financial (they are shareholders, lenders, suppliers, or employees) and at other times it is less direct, such as the community in which a business operates. Nevertheless, all stakeholders have an interest in the business.

Internal and external stakeholders

In general, we usually talk about two types of stakeholder:

- **Internal stakeholders** are individuals or groups that work within the business.

- **External stakeholders** are individuals or groups that are outside the business.

In practice, grey areas exist between internal and external stakeholders:

- Employees of a business live in the community where the business is located. As employees, they are internal stakeholders; as residents of the community, they are external stakeholders.

- In democratic societies, employees (internal stakeholders) are voting citizens and thus in some way are external stakeholders, as voting citizens have some claim on the government.

- Consultants to a business, such as financial planners, are external to the business. They are people brought in largely because of their expertise in a particular area. However, once hired, in some fashion they have an internal position.

- Small shareholders in large publicly traded companies, like all shareholders, are considered internal stakeholders, even if they own a tiny fraction of a large publicly traded company, for example Apple or General Electric (GE). However, someone who owns a small stake, such as 100 shares, of a large publicly traded company has virtually no ability to influence the business and in most respects is external to the business.

In addition, in other instances individuals have multiple stakeholder interests: employees who own shares and managers, who are part of the management team, have multiple stakeholder interests.

The interests of internal stakeholders

- **Shareholders** focus on returns on their investments.

- **The CEO or managing director** focuses on coordinating the business strategy and delivering profits and returns that satisfy the shareholders.

- **Senior managers** focus on the strategic objectives for their functional areas.

- **Middle managers** focus on the tactical objectives for their functional areas.

- **Foremen and supervisors** focus on organizing tactical objectives and formulating operational objectives.

- **Employees and their unions** focus on protecting their rights and working conditions.

The interests of external stakeholders

- **Government (at all levels)** focuses on how the business operates in the business environment.

- **Suppliers** focus on maintaining a stable relationship.

- **Customers and consumers** focus on the best product that meets their needs.

- **People in the local community focus** on the impact of the business in the local area.

- **Financiers** focus on returns on their investments.

- **Pressure groups** focus on how the business has impact on their area of concern.

- **The media** focuses on the impact of the business in terms of news stories.

Note that **competitors** are *not* considered to be stakeholders. Although a business may have an indirect impact on competitors through its actions in the marketplace, the competition does not have anything directly at stake with the business itself. In fact, the competitor usually wants the business to fail.

Possible areas of mutual benefit and conflict between stakeholders' interests

Groups of people with a common interest, such as a business, may also have differences of opinion. This situation makes sense: although all stakeholders have a "stake" in the business, their focuses are different.

Consider the example of a pay rise for employees. Shareholders may object to the idea, as it could decrease profits and, therefore, their return on investment. At the other end of the spectrum are the employees

> ### Key terms
>
> **Stakeholder**
>
> an individual or group who has an interest, often financial, in the activities and success of an organization
>
> **Shareholder**
>
> an individual who owns a share or shares in a company
>
> **Competitor**
>
> another business or organization offering very similar goods or services

themselves, who would favour pay rises, which would give them a higher standard of living.

In between these two positions, various stakeholders would be of mixed mind.

- The CEO and senior managers would in principle probably support paying higher wages, as this would make the employees happier. However, the CEO and senior managers, with responsibility for meeting profit targets and return on investment ratios, would also be worried that pay rises would lower profits.

- Managers may also be concerned that, by reinforcing the use of extrinsic motivating factors, a pay rise might undermine their efforts to foster a culture of intrinsic motivation.

- Those in the local community would in principle favour higher wages for employees, as it would mean that employees would have more money to spend in the local community – at restaurants and shops, etc. However, if the pay rises in any way threatened the existence of the business, the community would not favour the idea.

Thus, any decision of importance, such as a general pay rise at the business, will elicit different reactions from different stakeholders. In this situation, there may be friction and alliances may be formed as each stakeholder group jockeys for position.

One feature of successful businesses is that the interests of stakeholders are sufficiently satisfied most of the time. In some instances, managing stakeholders' interests is not particularly complicated. An individual running a small shop as a sole trader typically has relatively few internal stakeholders: the sole trader and perhaps an employee or two. While in theory the business would have several external stakeholders, such as the community, the government, financiers and suppliers, these external stakeholders typically (though not always) have such a small stake in the business that the decisions of the shop are relatively inconsequential. Thus, for this type of business, satisfying the interests of stakeholders is not complicated. What is required mostly is being profitable enough to pay for expenses and provide the sole trader with an income, and to be in compliance with laws and government regulations and with community standards.

For other types of business, especially large ones, coordinating the interests of stakeholders is a much more formidable challenge. When a large business operates a factory in a small city or in a town, the factory may be the most important employer in the area. In this instance, the various stakeholders have a major stake in the success of the business. For example, in the case of a factory that is the main employer in a town, a 20-per-cent reduction in the workforce might lead to reduced expenses for the business. It might also mean greater productivity out of the workforce that was not retrenched, if the workers retained were pressured into working harder to make up for the smaller workforce. Shareholders might be happy with this outcome, as might the CEO and senior managers (who might receive greater year-end bonuses). The workers, however, would be dissatisfied. Those losing their jobs would be unhappy. Even those keeping their jobs would not like seeing their co-workers go. Even if the business were not pressuring the remaining workers to work harder to make up for the lost work of those retrenched, a general sense of fear – of more job cuts – would affect the workers.

Many other stakeholders would be affected as well. Just a few of the implications for the local community and the local government would be as follows:

- Many employees would struggle to find new jobs, and government expenses (support for the unemployed persons) would increase.

- Probably many people would move away from the town, selling houses or moving out of rental flats, thus depressing the real estate market.

- When families move away, the number of children in the school may fall, thus leading to lay-offs of teachers in the school.

- Local businesses would suffer, as fewer employees of the factory would mean fewer people with the resources to purchase at local shops and restaurants.

Large businesses or those businesses that have complicated stakeholder interests often perform a **stakeholder analysis**. The first step is to prioritize or rank the interests of various stakeholders. One conceptual approach to this step is to determine how "close" each stakeholder is to decision making in the business. This is shown in Figure 1.4.1.

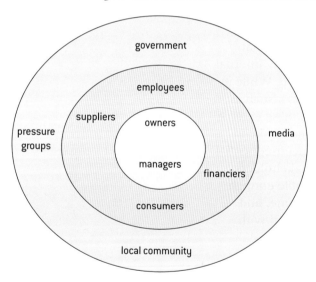

Figure 1.4.1. The comparative closeness of stakeholders to decision making

Under this approach, owners and managers are central to decision making, while suppliers, employees, financiers, and consumers are further removed. Most distant are government, pressure groups, the media and the local community. Decision makers try to satisfy those stakeholders closest to the centre.

Another conceptual approach involves a tool called **stakeholder mapping**. Numerous models for mapping stakeholders exist. One particularly valued model was formulated by Johnson and Scholes and called the power–interest model.

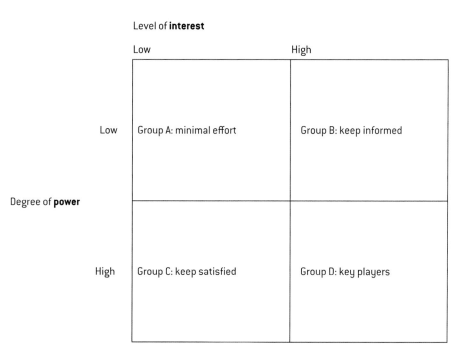

Figure 1.4.2. The power–interest model (Johnson and Scholes)

Source: Johnson, G and Scholes, K (1999) *Exploring Corporate Strategy*, 5th edition, Prentice Hall Europe

By placing each stakeholder group in the matrix, a business can decide on likely strategies.

Stakeholders in group A. These stakeholders, who have minimal interest in the business and have limited power over it, are rarely a problem for the business. Owners and managers fairly safely ignore these stakeholders, or at least devote limited energy and attention to satisfying their interests.

Stakeholders in group B. For owners and managers, making this group feel included is important. Newsletters, events, and other ways of conveying a sense of belonging are important.

Stakeholders in group C. This pivotal group of stakeholders must be kept satisfied. They have the power to influence other groups. The business must find ways to flatter the self-esteem of members of this group to make them feel important.

Stakeholders in group D. These stakeholders are the most important. The business must not merely communicate with them but also consult with them before any major decisions are made. The business should focus on their needs in preference to the others. Failure to involve and satisfy these stakeholders can have very negative consequences for the business.

Group A	**Group B**	**Group C**	**Group D**
Least important to the business			Most important to the business

Revision checklist

✓ Stakeholders are individuals or groups who have a direct interest in the business.

✓ Internal stakeholders are individuals or groups that work within the business, such as employees and managers.

✓ External stakeholders are individuals or groups outside the business, such as customers and suppliers.

✓ The interests of the various stakeholders will differ. Interests might include return on investment, the impact on the local area, working conditions and the quality of the product produced.

Practice question

Anigam

Anigam is one of the biggest multinational companies operating in the animal drugs industry. In many countries, *Anigam* is well known for its promotional campaigns. It uses both above the line and below the line promotion.

Anigam has a portfolio of animal drugs at different stages of their product life cycle:

- Anitox is the first animal drug that *Anigam* developed and sold. It is a business-to-business (B2B) product used in veterinary clinics worldwide. Anitox has a high 25% share of the global market. That figure has been stable for the last 10 years. Anitox is a well-established product in a market that is saturated and growing very slowly.

- A range of animal drugs was launched four years ago. One of them, Anisan, helps prevent heart attacks in aging animals; it already has a high 15% share of a rapidly growing market. Some other animal drugs, however, are not performing as well: for example, Aniplus, which is designed to strengthen animals' immune systems against the flu and other contagious diseases. The market for products such as Aniplus is growing rapidly, but it is very competitive.

- Last year, *Anigam* launched a new drug called Anislim which helps to reduce obesity in domestic animals. Thanks to significant introductory marketing efforts and an appropriate promotional mix, the first sales results were good. It is, however, too early to forecast whether present sales for Anislim will be maintained.

a) Analyse *Anigam's* portfolio of animal drugs by applying the Boston consulting group (BCG) matrix. [*5 marks*]

b) With reference to *Anigam* **and one** other company of your choice, discuss reasons for the increase in the number of multinational companies. [*7 marks*]

IB, Nov. 2013

1.5 The external environment

By the end of this chapter, you should be able to:

→ Prepare a STEEPLE analysis of an organization

→ Exaplain the consequences of a change in any of the STEEPLE factors for a business's objectives and strategy

The impact of the external environment on a business

All businesses, no matter how small or big, operate in an environment. In business, "environment" does not have the narrower meaning of "ecology", as the word usually means or implies. Rather, in business, environment refers to various conditions (including ecological) external to the business. Even when a business manages to control its internal environment – that challenge alone can be difficult – elements external to a business will still have an impact on it.

Businesses have only limited means to influence the elements of the external environment. They can, however, plan and make contingency plans for changes in the elements of the external environment. One common tool for this type of planning process begins with a **STEEPLE** analysis, which highlights and focuses on these external elements. Earlier versions of STEEPLE analysis included a **PEST** or a **PESTLE** analysis. All elements of those analyses were incorporated in the STEEPLE framework, shown in Figure 1.5.1.

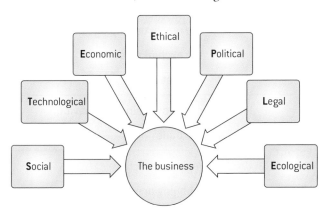

Figure 1.5.1. The STEEPLE framework

What is the difference between PEST, PESTLE and STEEPLE analyses?

- **PEST –** Political, Economic, Social and Technological

- **PESTLE –** Political, Economic, Social, Technological, **Legal and Ecological**

- **STEEPLE –** Social, Technological, Economic, Ecological, Political, Legal **and Ethical**.

The addition of the extra elements (first legal and ecological and then ethical) reflect an evolution in business practices and thinking over the last 50 years as businesses have grown larger. Many have become multinational and even global, so they have had to consider the different legal frameworks in which they operate. A similar transformation has occurred with the addition of ecological and ethical. Whereas 50 years ago many businesses focused only on making profits, today most businesses have broader concerns, including striving towards sustainable practices and treating all stakeholders ethically.

The impact of changes in any of the STEEPLE factors

If any of the STEEPLE factors change, this will have an impact on the objectives and strategy of a business. In a STEEPLE analysis, a business first considers particular influences of each element on the business. Then the business conducts an analysis to determine the most important influences. Once the most important influences are isolated, the business can develop a strategy to take them into account. Common influences are listed in Table 1.5.1.

Table 1.5.1. Common influences in a STEEPLE analysis

Social influences include:	• lifestyles • social mobility • demographics	• education • fashions or tastes.
Technological influences include:	• technological improvements • new technology transfer • infrastructure	• ICT • research and development costs.
Economic influences include:	• the economic or business cycle • the rate of economic growth • the rate of inflation	• the rate of unemployment • the exchange rate • interest rates.
Ethical influences include:	• corruption • transparency	• codes of business behaviour • fair trade.
Political influences include:	• political stability • trade policies	• regional policies • lobbying or electioneering.
Legal influences include:	• regulations • employment laws	• health and safety legislation • competition laws.
Ecological influences include:	• depletion of renewable resources • global warming	• organic farming • carbon footprints.

Not all businesses react to the influences or changes shown in Table 1.5.1 with the same degree of energy or purpose. Often, a business might not need to be concerned with changes in particular laws (if they are not

relevant to the business) or to changes in fashion or tastes (if its product or service is not determined by fashion or tastes). How the business will react to (or try to pre-empt) these influences will be a function of their relevance to its current strategy and objectives.

Businesses that are flexible and can adapt to change will be more successful than businesses that are inflexible and do not adapt. Being an **early adaptor** and having **first mover advantage** can be very useful for businesses that move fast enough. Planning based on STEEPLE elements often allows a business to determine changes to environmental factors, which may give it the opportunity to respond and perhaps even to have a first mover advantage.

ToK discussion

To what degree are businesses limited in how much they can "know" about the external environment?

Case study

Cat's Store, Japan

Cat's Store was the first 'cat café' to open in Tokyo, Japan. Customers pay a fee to visit the café, where they can sit with the cats who live there. There are now around 40 cat cafés in Tokyo, with many more throughout Japan and, increasingly, across the world.

A STEEPLE analysis for Cat's Store might consider the following factors:

Social – is the interest in cats a fad or a trend? Is there a risk that a new animal could become more 'fashionable'? Is the population ageing? Is the café visiting by more young people than elderly people?

Technological – How can the café best market itself in an online world? Social media such as Instagram and Twitter could be used to generate buzz. Is the café utilizing the most efficient technology?

Economic – visiting a cat café is a luxury that people may not be able to afford if the economy slows down. Can the café owners afford to pay for vet bills?

Ethical – is it ethical to keep the cats in the café? Are the standards of cleanliness and hygeine adequate?

Political – is there a risk that animal rights campaigners could call for laws to be changed? Could a new goverment change the rules?

Legal – the café is subject to strict health and safety and animal rights regulations. Could these change? What if a customer was injured by a cat? Do customers need to sign a disclaimer?

Ecological – each cat will require food, shelter and warmth. What is the ecological effect of this?

Student workpoint 1.8

Be a thinker

Work in a pair or group to create a STEEPLE analysis for one of the following businesses:

- local restaurant
- international hotel chain
- high-street bookshop
- local car mechanic
- global electronics manufacturer
- online clothing retailer

You might base your analysis on a real company. Present your findings to the rest of the class and discuss the differences in your findings.

Revision checklist

✓ A STEEPLE analysis is a way of evaluating all the external factors which might influence the success of a business.

✓ The factors are: social, technological, economic, ethical, political, legal and ecological.

✓ If any of the factors change, a business may need to adapt its strategy.

Practice question

China

China, with a population of some 1.3 billion people, is hungry for economic growth. Between 1979 and 2000, its GDP grew at 9.7% per year on average. Young Chinese drink coffee at *Starbucks*, talk on mobile phones and use the Internet for their news and fashions. By night the neon signs illustrate the extent of foreign investment. They display *Nestlé*, *Samsung*, *Canon*, *Pepsi* and *Standard Chartered*. Shanghai, Beijing and the coastal cities are as dynamic now as Hong Kong was a few years ago.

With world demand for ICT products and services falling, companies in expensive markets, such as the US and Japan in particular, have turned from innovation towards cutting costs. In China more than two million university graduates qualify each year. Wages are about 50 cents per hour. American manufacturers, pay more than $6. US companies such as *Dell* and *Siemens* as well as *Acer* of Taiwan and Japan's *Sony* and *Hitachi* have moved production to China. Foreign motor manufacturers are now among the highest Chinese taxpayers. Boom towns such as Shenzen create an image of China as a country full of technology fanatics. It has 40 million Internet users and 178 million mobile-phone owners which is more than in America.

However, the wealth gap between rich and poor is widening. China is bureaucratic with a centrally planned economy. There are political risks associated with the new government, but after a year as a member of the World Trade Organization (WTO), China can claim to have achieved about 70% of the tariff cuts agreed to on entry. Overall tariffs have come down from 15% to 12%. However, some agricultural tariffs have risen and new rules, such as health and safety requirements, discriminate against foreign firms who also complain about illegally copied books, music and software.

[Source : *IT puts fire in the belly of dragon economy* – The Times, 12 Dec 2002 and *China: Welcome the Final Frontier* – Sunday Times 3 Nov 2002]

a) Evaluate the extent to which globalization is encouraged by the development of new ICT (information and communication technology). [*7 marks*]

b) Using a STEEPLE framework analyse the potential advantages and disadvantages to foreign firms of locating in China. [*6 marks*}

IB, May 2004

1.6 Growth and evolution

By the end of this chapter, you should be able to:

→ Define the terms economies and diseconomies of scale

→ Discuss the merits of small versus large organizations

→ Outline the difference between internal and external growth

→ Explain the following external growth methods:

  • mergers and acquisitions (M & As) and takeovers

  • joint ventures

  • strategic alliances

  • franchising

→ Explain the role and impact of globalization on the growth and evolution of businesses

→ Outline reasons for the growth of multinational companies (MNCs)

→ Evaluate the impact of MNCs on the host countries

Economies and diseconomies of scale

Businesses that expand or increase their scale of operations can often use the larger scale to become more efficient. Scale of operations refers to the size or volume of output. When a business increases its scale of operations, it produces more or in greater volume. When a business increases its scale of operations and in the process becomes more efficient, the business has achieved **economies of scale**. The term "economies of scale" refers to the reduction in average unit cost as a business increases in size. However, sometimes a business experiences inefficiencies as it becomes larger. When this situation occurs, the business has achieved **diseconomies of scale**, which refers to an increase in average unit cost as the business increases in size.

Efficiency is measured in terms of costs of production per unit. For a more complete explanation of the different types of cost of production, refer to Unit 5. For now, think of costs of production with the following formula:

Total costs = fixed cost + variable cost

Using the abbreviations TC for total cost, FC for fixed cost and VC for variable costs, the formula is:

TC = FC + VC

Fixed costs are costs that do not change as production changes. For example, if a business operates in a rented (leased) factory, the monthly rent payments are the same regardless of the quantity of production of the business. **Variable costs** are costs that vary as production changes.

For example, if a furniture manufacturer expands production, then it will require more raw materials (wood, metal springs, cloth, leather, etc.).

Further costs are known as **average costs** or **unit costs** or **average unit costs**. All three refer to total cost per unit, which can be calculated with the following formula:

$$\text{Average cost} = \frac{\text{total cost}}{\text{quantity produced}}$$

And if AC is average cost (Unit costs or average Unit costs) and Q is quantity produced, the formula becomes:

$$AC = \frac{TC}{Q}$$

As we saw above, TC refers to total cost, derived from adding FC and VC. Thus, average cost can also be calculated with the following formula:

$$AC = \frac{FC + VC}{Q}$$

Expressing the formula in this way helps to explain the concepts of economies and diseconomies of scale. First, as the business expands by producing a greater quantity, variable costs increase. However, the fixed costs are spread over a greater quantity of units produced. As a result, the average costs go down. Thus, the business becomes more efficient. It has achieved economies of scale.

Sometimes when a business expands, it starts to experience inefficiencies that increase average unit costs. This situation refers to diseconomies of scale. For example, imagine that a business expands production year on year. As it does, it initially achieves economies of scale. One reason for this is that the fixed cost of rent is being spread out over a larger number of units produced. However, at some point in time (if growth continues), the business will be at its maximum production level for the size of its factory. It will be at 100 per cent capacity utilization (See Unit 5). The business will have to acquire different or additional space to expand production.

In this scenario, remember, the business is expanding year on year. When acquiring different or additional space – another factory or a larger factory, for example – the business should probably not acquire just enough space for the next year or even for the next two years. It should probably acquire a significantly greater amount of space. That way, the business can grow for years to come without having the cost and disruption of changing locations frequently.

When a business doubles its factory size, its capacity utilization will go down (initially) and its rent will increase. In our example, in the old factory or old space, the business had 100 per cent capacity utilization. When the space is doubled but production remains the same (initially), capacity utilization will decrease from 100 per cent to 50 per cent. The business's rent expense will increase significantly (it will probably double). The higher rent will now be spread over the same (or a slightly higher) number of units produced. With the higher rent, initially, the business will have higher average unit cost. Thus, it will have achieved diseconomies of scale.

Figure 1.6.1 shows this progression.

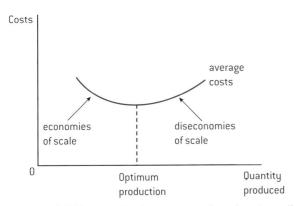

Figure 1.6.1. Progression from economies of scale to diseconomies of scale

As the business grows, it produces more output and initially the average costs go down. The business becomes more efficient. After the point of lowest average costs, the business is at "optimum production". In our example using rent as the chief fixed cost, optimum production would also be the point where the business is at 100 per cent capacity utilization. As the business continues to expand, it starts to become more inefficient. Average costs start to rise. The minimum point of the average cost curve is the optimum level of production. At that point, average costs are at the lowest and profits are at their maximum.

Efficiency is not related to production alone. A business can become more efficient if it can lower average unit costs, regardless of the area of the business in which the savings per unit occur.

Table 1.6.1. Internal economies of scale (efficiencies that the business itself can make)

Type	Explanation	Example
Technical	Bigger units of production can reduce costs because of the **law of variable proportions** – the increase in variable costs spread against a set of fixed costs.	Operating a container ship with one crew, fuel bill and berthing fee is cheaper than running two or more smaller vessels. Similarly, the A380 passenger airline will be cheaper to operate than two traditional long-haul aircraft; an articulated lorry will be cheaper to operate than two or three smaller vehicles.
Managerial	A bigger business can afford to have managers **specializing** in one job as opposed to trying to do everything.	Managers specializing by function, such as production, marketing, finance, and HR, as opposed to having a "general" manager, can typically work with greater efficiency.
Financial	Bigger businesses are less **risky** than smaller businesses.	Banks and other financial institutions charge lower rates of interest on loans or overdrafts to businesses they consider safe.
Marketing	Bigger businesses can **direct** more effective marketing campaigns.	Only large business can afford sponsorship of major sporting events such as the Olympic Games, the Super Bowl or the Football World Cup, which are especially higher yielding promotions per dollar, pound or euro.

| Purchasing | Big businesses can gain discounts by **bulk buying** – buying in large quantities. | Supermarkets such as Wal-Mart or Tesco buy large quantities of food at very low prices from farmers. |
| Risk bearing | Big businesses can afford to produce a bigger product range and in doing so spread the risk of one product failing – **hedging their bets**. | Pepsi Co owns a number of different brands such as Pepsi, Gatorade, Tropicana, Lipton's Teas, Quaker Oats, and Lays. |

Table 1.6.2. External economies of scale (efficiencies that the business achieves because someone else has expanded)

Type	Explanation	Example
Consumers	A shopping mall increases the number of potential of customers as more people go to the mall compared to an independent shop because of the ease of one-stop shopping. So, a whole range of other businesses benefits from someone else building the infrastructure.	A shopping mall, an international airport, and a business park or zone all require servicing and maintenance as well as their core business.
Employees	Labour concentrations – some cities or geographic areas concentrate on certain industries or sectors. Individual businesses located in those areas and operating in the industry that has the concentration can often benefit from lower recruiting and training costs.	Hollywood is famous for having many actors and others skilled in various aspects of film and television production. London is a major banking centre, where numerous professionals in financial services live and work.

As we have noted, however, if a business expands too much, then it can achieve diseconomies of scale in the same area.

Table 1.6.3. Internal diseconomies of scale (inefficiencies that the business itself can make)

Type	Example
Technical	A container ship can be too big to berth in a harbour, an airplane too big to land at smaller airports, or a lorry too large to drive on minor roads.
Managerial	Businesses may have "over-specialized" managers who cannot (or will not) work outside their area of expertise or for everyone's benefit, which often occurs in the investment and commercial banking sectors.
Financial	Sometimes big businesses with large amounts of "surplus" cash make poor investments. Poor decisions occur because the businesses do not think through the consequences of investment choices – Singapore Airlines bought a 49% stake in Virgin Atlantic for US$ 965 million in 1999 but in 2012 sold its stake to Delta Airlines for US$ 360 million.
Marketing	Sometimes big businesses can make big marketing mistakes. In the 1990s, Hoover offered free flights to anyone who spent more than US$150 on a vacuum cleaner. Hoover did not realize that, for many people, an expensive vacuum cleaner was worth buying if it included a free flight anywhere in the world! When Hoover refused to honour the deal, the courts ordered the company to pay US$ 50 million in compensation to customers. Weakened by this expense, Hoover was acquired by a competitor, Candy.
Purchasing	Large businesses often buy too much stock, which can be costly if the capital funds used to purchase the stock are greater than the cost savings from buying in large quantities. Stock can also become spoilt, obsolete or unfashionable. The first stock market crash was as a result of too many tulips being bought by Dutch traders in the 17th century.
Risk bearing	In 2005 eBay bought Skype in the hope of broadening its range but in 2011 sold it to Microsoft.

Table 1.6.4. External diseconomies of scale (inefficiencies that the business achieves because someone else has expanded)

Type	Example
Employees	If one geographic region becomes too concentrated on one economic activity, typically a shortage of skilled workers in the industry will occur. For an individual business this relative shortage of skilled workers means that the business will have to pay higher wages than before to attract and retain skilled workers.

The merits of small versus large organizations

Not all businesses want to expand. Many businesses simply prefer to remain small. Some business owners do not want the headache of growing their business or managing a large business.

Many businesses offering **high-end products** (high-quality, specialized products) and service businesses prefer to stay **close to their markets** and their clients. For example, among the many tent manufacturers, only a few make "portaledges", which are portable hanging tents used by big-wall climbers. Serving this niche market means that the manufacturers stay close to their small pool of customers and remain entrenched in the culture of big-wall climbing.

Many professional firms also prefer to stay small. In the legal sector, some law firms are large multinational companies, but around the world many small practices exist, their lawyers preferring to serve a small group of familiar clients. In accountancy, four major firms serve clients around the world – the so-called Big Four. However, countless small accounting firms serve the needs of small businesses everywhere in the world.

This 'portaledge' tent is an example of a niche market product

Advantages of being a big business

These are some of the advantages of being a big business:

- **Survival** – large firms have a greater chance of surviving. They are less likely to fail and less likely to be taken over by another firm.

- **Economies of scale** – large firms typically enjoy economies of scale, which translate into greater profits, higher returns, and a healthier balance sheet.

- **Higher status** – large firms have greater status than smaller ones. However fashionable some clothing brands may be, working for a larger firm such as Abercrombie & Fitch or Benetton can provide status to employees and can motivate managers and other employees.

- **Market leader status** – McDonald's is the market leader in fast-food restaurants in most of the industrial world. All by itself, McDonald's can shape market habits, giving it a competitive advantage.

- **Increased market share** – large companies that have a large market share can control the market by determining prices and deciding which services will be the industry standard.

Advantages of being a small business

- **Greater focus** – because customers do not expect small business to "be all things to all people", small businesses can focus investments where they want and where they believe the greatest profitability lies. They may have lower profits than larger businesses but often they have greater profitability and higher returns on investment.

- **Greater cachet** – small businesses sometimes have more cachet, a greater sense of exclusiveness, than larger businesses. As a result, some small businesses are able to charge more for their goods and services, leading to higher profit margins.

- **Greater motivation** – having more prestige can motivate managers and other employees. Sometimes, as well, employees are motivated by the idea that they matter to the business. Very large businesses sometimes have a hard time conveying the sense that all employees matter.

- **Competitive advantage** – being small, providing a more personalized service, and being flexible can give a competitive advantage.

- **Less competition** – sometimes a market is so small (a true niche market) that big businesses do not even want to consider getting involved. This situation often means a market with limited competition.

The difference between internal and external growth

Businesses with growth as a strategy have two broad options to choose from:

- internal (organic) growth
- external (fast-track) growth.

Internal growth is often known as organic growth because it occurs slowly and steadily and occurs out of the existing operations of the business. Although it may take a long time, a business can grow this way without taking many risks. The business expands by simply selling more products or by developing its product range. Although most businesses that are growing internally still have to borrow money from banks for major capital outlays, such as to update or expand property, plant, and equipment, most of the expansion from internal growth is self-financed using retained profits.

External growth is a quick and riskier method of growth than internal growth. Instead of selling more of its own products itself, the business expands by entering into some type of arrangement to work with another business, such as:

- a merger and acquisition or takeover (M & A)
- a joint venture
- a strategic alliance
- a franchise.

External growth usually requires significant external financing. Although the risks are greater, the potential rewards are that the business can increase market share and decrease competition very quickly.

External growth methods

There are many ways of expanding externally but some of the most common are as follows:

M & As

This type of expansion occurs when two business become **integrated**, either by joining together and forming a bigger combined business – a merger – or by one business taking over the other – an acquisition. When the acquisition is unwanted by the company being acquired, the term typically used is "takeover" or "hostile takeover".

One result of a merger, acquisition, or takeover is the same: one bigger business. However, the underlying business reason for the integration can vary. In general, integration occurs for one of the following four reasons, although the process is very different.

Integration can happen in four ways:

- **Horizontal integration** occurs when the two businesses integrated are not merely in the same industry broadly but actually in the same line of business and in the same chain of production (as outlined in Unit 1.1). The Italian car maker Fiat's acquisition of Chrysler Motors was an example of horizontal integration.

- **Backward vertical integration** occurs when one business integrates with another business further back (at an earlier stage) in the chain of production. Backward vertical integration usually occurs when a business wants to protect its supply chain. In 2008, for example, Starbucks bought a coffee manufacturer, The Clover Brewing System, to make sure Starbucks had control over processing the coffee beans.

- **Forward vertical integration** occurs when one business integrates further forward (to a later stage) in the chain of production. Forward vertical integration usually occurs when a business wants to ensure a secure outlet for its products. For example, in 2002 the Walt Disney Corporation (Disney) merged with the major US television broadcasting and multimedia company, American Broadcasting Corporation (ABC). The combined firm, Disney–ABC Television Group, ensures that Disney has a secure television and multimedia outlet for its products (and provides ABC with an additional supplier of high-quality programming).

- **Conglomeration** occurs when two businesses in unrelated lines of business integrate. This type of integration is also known as diversification and occurs for many reasons but mainly to reduce overall corporate risk. For example, the Indian company Tata Group has among its many businesses Tata Chemicals, Tata Steel, Tata Television, Tata Motors and Taj Hotels. If any one of the businesses – the chemical business or the steel business – were to fail, Tata Group would still have successful businesses in other industries.

INNOVATION

When two businesses are integrated, they find themselves sharing ideas, people and resources.

How might this encourage innovation?

Another reason that a business may diversify is to have complementary seasonal activity. If a business that does most of its sales in the summer months purchased a business that had most of its sales in winter months, the new, combined enterprise would not have long periods of inactivity.

Integration has many advantages for businesses, including economies of scale, complementary activities, and control up or down the chain of production. However, M & As can be costly and typically include, in addition to the cost of the business being acquired, high legal and consulting fees. Sometimes when one company acquires or combines with another company, especially if the takeover is hostile, a culture clash occurs. Employees from the two companies do not work well together.

Joint ventures

Joint ventures occur when two businesses agree to combine resources for a specific goal and over a finite period of time. As a result, a separate business is created with funding by the two "parent" businesses. After the defined time period is over, the new business is either dissolved or incorporated into one of the parent businesses, or the two parent firms decide to extend the time frame. Although a joint venture may be temporary in nature by opening up new areas of business, considerable transfer of specialist skills can occur. This transfer of skills, knowledge, and expertise could benefit either party in the future. Sometimes in a joint venture one of the partners begins to play a dominant role and then buys out the other.

The Channel Tunnel, which links the UK and France, was built as part of a joint venture

Examples of joint ventures include Sony–Ericsson (2001–2012), Channel Tunnel Group–France-Manche (1985–1994), New Zealand Post–DHL 2004–2012), and BMW – Brilliance (formed in 2003 and ongoing). Joint ventures have the advantage that the two firms typically enjoy greater sales, but neither loses its legal existence or its identity. Joint ventures also have the advantage that the two businesses forming the joint venture can bring different areas of expertise, in combination with what the other business brings, to create a powerful combination. However, sometimes joint ventures do not produce the desired outcome or a company realizes that it could have accomplished what the joint venture is doing without having to share the profits with the other company. At least conceptually (though not always legally), a joint venture is a partnership. All partnerships run the risk that a disagreement between partners will occur. Sometimes a disagreement may be so severe that the effectiveness of the partnership is compromised or the partnership (or joint venture) breaks apart.

Strategic alliances

Strategic alliances are similar to joint ventures because they involve businesses collaborating for a specified goal. However, strategic alliances differ from joint ventures in several fundamental ways:

- **More than two businesses may be part of the alliance**. Strategic alliances often, though not always, involve more than two businesses. In the airline industry, the Star Alliance has 27 airlines, including Singapore Airlines, Lufthansa, South African Airways and United, in the alliance.

- **No new business is created**. No new legal entity comes into existence but rather a strategic alliance is typically an agreement to work together for mutual benefit.

- **Individual businesses in the alliance remain independent**. The existing businesses may agree to share resources but they remain independent and often otherwise compete against each other.

- **Strategic alliances are more fluid than joint ventures**. In a strategic alliance, membership can change without destroying the alliance.

All of these strengths are also weaknesses. The more businesses that are involved in a strategic alliance, the more challenging coordination and agreement becomes. Without legal existence, the alliance has less force than a legally extant enterprise. Individual businesses may gain benefit from the alliance (presumably they think they will, otherwise why would they join the alliance?). However, remaining independent means that the individual businesses do not get the capital strength of legal merger with other enterprises, nor do they enjoy economies of scale that other forms of external growth provide. Lastly, greater fluidity of members also means that the alliance lacks stability.

Franchises

Franchising, another form of external growth, is becoming increasingly popular for businesses that want to expand globally. Franchising involves the following:

- An original business, known as the **franchisor**, that developed the business concept and product, then sells to other businesses the right to offer the concept and sell the product.

- Businesses, known as the **franchisees**, buy the right to offer the concept and sell the product. In other words, the franchisee sells the products developed originally by the franchisor. The franchisee usually also has to be consistent with, and in some instances identical to, the original business concept developed by the franchisor.

A business that starts to franchise is the franchisor. Franchising is often a rapid form of growth because the franchisor does not actually have to produce anything new. Instead, the business (the franchisor) sells that right to other businesses (the franchisees). Franchisees can be individuals, partnerships, or companies. Franchising is proving particularly attractive as a means to grow globally. The franchisor has a host or home country. The franchisor can then sell to other businesses in the other places where it wants to expand – as long as it finds buyers of the concept of the enterprise. The franchisees typically have knowledge of local markets, local conditions, and local cultures. Franchisees also know local languages, which is especially helpful if the franchisor wants to grow in many countries of the world.

There are many examples of franchises in many different areas of business, including:

- McDonalds – fast food

- Budget – car hire

- Hilton – hotels
- Kumon – education
- Blockbuster – entertainment
- Wokinabox – fast food
- Spar – food stores
- Benetton – clothes
- Body Shop – cosmetics
- Edo – fast food.

An outlet of Spar in Berlin, Germany

The cost of the franchise comes in two parts. First, the franchisee must pay for the franchise itself – essentially a right to operate a business offering the franchisor's concept and product. Then the franchisee must typically pay royalties – a percentage of sales or a flat fee – which goes to the franchisor. Both the franchisor and the franchisee have specific responsibilities in their relationship. These responsibilities vary somewhat according to individual business concepts and industries. For example, McDonald's franchisee agreements would not be exactly the same as those of Yum! Brands (KFC, Taco Bell, and other restaurants), nor exactly the same as the franchise agreement for Enterprise Rental Cars. However, in general, the division of responsibilities between franchisor and franchisee are as follows.

The **franchisor** will provide:

- the stock
- the fittings
- the uniforms
- staff training
- legal and financial help
- global advertising
- global promotions

The **franchisee** will:

- employ staff
- set prices
- set wages
- pay an agreed royalty on sales
- create local promotions
- sell only the products of the franchisor
- advertise locally.

Which party provides the outlet and which party provides the start-up costs can vary considerably according to the strength of the brand. Some brands, such as McDonald's, are especially strong. Only very rarely does a McDonald's restaurant close. A new McDonald's restaurant is almost certain immediately to have strong name recognition and high sales, so the franchisor is in a strong position to dictate the terms of owning a McDonald's franchise. Other brands have less market power. In those circumstances, the franchisor may have less bargaining strength when setting the rights and responsibilities of the franchisor and franchisee.

For businesses (regardless of legal organization), acquiring a franchise has many advantages and disadvantages compared to developing their own business model. For the franchisee, advantages and disadvantages are as follows.

Advantages	**Disadvantages**
The product exists and is usually well known.	The franchisee:
The format for selling the product is established.	• has unlimited liability for the franchise
The set-up costs are reduced.	• has to pay royalties to the franchisor
The franchisee has a secure supply of stock.	• has no control over what to sell
The franchisor can provide legal, financial, managerial, and technical help.	• has no control over supplies
	• makes all the global decisions.

Franchisors also have advantages and disadvantages.

Advantages	**Disadvantages**
The franchisor:	The franchisor:
• gains quick access to wider markets	• loses some control in the day-to-day running of the business
• makes use of local knowledge and expertise	• can see its image suffer if a franchise fails or does not perform properly.
• does not assume the risks and liability of running the franchise	
• gains more profits and the sign-up fees.	

Do some franchisees eventually become tired of the control of the parent company? Perhaps, but by then, the operators of the franchise may have enough expertise to start their own independent business. On the other hand, many franchisees, even if tired of the control of the franchisor, enjoy the great profitability that can come with a successful franchise. Regardless, for the franchisor, selling franchises is an easy and fast way to break into new markets with a minimum of difficulty and risk and is a way to gain an advantage over its competitors.

The impact of globalization

Globalization has had significant impact on businesses' growth and evolution. Globalization is the process by which the world's regional economies are becoming one integrated global unit. The process is not wholly new. The Roman Empire, the Silk Road, the Age of Exploration, the British Empire and other historical examples and periods saw some degree of economic global interdependence. Nevertheless, since the Second World War, the phenomenon known as "globalization" is different from earlier forms of interdependence.

First, just in terms of intensity, scale, speed, and economic value of goods and services being exchanged, global interdependence today is on a completely different order of magnitude from that seen in earlier periods or circumstances.

Second, current globalization is being characterized by a relatively small number of extremely large "post-national" businesses. Post-national means that, although these companies have a home of record (the "home" office is legally registered in one country), the businesses are otherwise transnational; apart from the legal home of record, these businesses consider no place their home or every place their home. They will do business wherever they can make a profit. Loyalties are to the company itself, and to its profits, and not to any country.

Globalization can have a significant impact on the growth of domestic businesses for the following reasons:

- **Increased competition** – large foreign businesses can force domestic producers to become more efficient as the domestic consumer has more choice. "Greater efficiency" can mean lower-cost goods and services for consumers. However, one way that businesses become more efficient is by slowing the growth in wages of its workers and extracting greater productivity out of them.

- **Greater brand awareness** – domestic producers have to compete with big brand names and so need to create their own **unique selling point** (**USP**). Sometimes they do this by emphasizing the local or national origins of their products compared to the "foreign" products sold by multinationals and global firms. Regardless, creating a USP, even if forced to do so, can make many businesses more competitive and efficient.

- **Skills transfer** – foreign businesses, no matter how big, must use some local knowledge: at least some of their workforce must be local, which will lead to a two-way transfer of knowledge and skills. The multinational or global firm will learn from the workers hired in particular countries, while those workers can learn new approaches and develop new skills.

- **Closer collaboration** – whether through joint ventures, franchises, or strategic alliances, domestic producers can create new business opportunities.

Reasons for the growth of multinational companies

A multinational company is a business that operates in more than one country or is legally registered in more than one country. The connotation of the word "multinational" may be global or operating in many countries, but multinational has a narrower meaning. A small company operating in the small countries of Luxembourg and Belgium is a multinational, whereas a large company registered in and operating only in the United States is not.

Multinational companies are the biggest type of business and in fact they often generate more revenues than the country they operate in.

For example, Table 1.6.5 shows a comparison of the world's leading countries and businesses in terms of GDP and sales revenues.

Table 1.6.5. The world's leading countries and businesses – GDP and sales revenues

Rank	Economy	US$ millions	Rank	Economy	US$ millions
1	United States	14,991,300	18	Turkey	774,983
2	China	7,318,499	19	Switzerland	659,308
3	Japan	5,867,154	20	Saudi Arabia	576,824
4	Germany	3,600,833	21	Sweden	539,682
5	France	2,773,032	22	Poland	514,496
6	Brazil	2,476,652	23	Belgium	513,661
7	United Kingdom	2,445,408	24	Norway	485,803
8	Italy	2,193,971	25	Royal Dutch Shell	484,489
9	Russian Federation	1,857,770	26	Exxon Mobil	452,926
10	India	1,847,977	27	Wal-Mart Stores	446,950
11	Canada	1,736,051	28	Austria	417,656
12	Spain	1,476,882	29	South Africa	408,237
13	Australia	1,379,382	30	BP	386,463
14	Mexico	1,153,343	31	Sinopec Group	375,214
15	Korea, Rep.	1,116,247	32	United Arab Emirates	360,245
16	Indonesia	846,832	33	Thailand	345,672
17	Netherlands	836,074	34	Denmark	333,616

Source: Adapted from World Bank & Fortune Global 500, 2011

Four factors have allowed multinational companies to grow so rapidly and with such a reach:

- **Improved communications** – not only ICT but also transport and distribution networks

- **Dismantling of trade barriers** – allowing for easier movement of raw materials, components and finished products

- **Deregulation of the world's financial markets** – allowing for easier transfer of funds and also tax avoidance

- **Increasing economic and political power of the multinational companies** – which can be of enormous benefit especially in middle- and low-income countries.

The impact of multinational companies on the host countries

Multinational companies can have both positive and negative impacts on the host (domestic) countries in which they operate.

Advantages for the host country include:	Disadvantages for the host country include:
• **economic growth** – multinational companies can boost the domestic economy by providing employment, developing a local network of suppliers, and paying taxes and providing capital injections.	• **profits being repatriated** – the multinational companies may pay into the local tax system but the bulk of their profits will be rerouted away from the host country.
• **new ideas** – multinational companies may introduce new ways of doing business and new ways of interacting socially.	• **loss of cultural identity** – the appeal of domestic products, ways of doing business, and even cultural norms may suffer. This is especially important for the younger generations who are more likely to buy global brands.
• **skills transfer** – multinational companies may help develop the skills of local employees. Domestic businesses can benefit from starting their own business with the skills learned.	• **brain drain** – many highly skilled employees may look to work for the multinational company in another country.
• **more choice of products** – the domestic market will benefit as the variety of products will increase.	• **loss of market share** – as multinational companies take over more of the domestic market, domestic producers may suffer.
• **short-term infrastructure projects** – multinational companies often help to build infrastructure (for example roads to the factory, schools for workers' children).	• **short-term plans** – multinational companies may not plan on staying for a long time – if lower-cost producers can be found elsewhere, they may move out at short notice.

Revision checklist

✓ An economy of scale occurs when the costs of a business go down as the business grows. For example, if a publisher prints 7000 books they might be able to negotiate a cheaper price for paper than if they only printed 500.

✓ The reverse of this is a diseconomy of scale – where the cost goes up as the business gets larger i.e. the business becomes less efficient.

✓ Small organizations might benefit from greater focus, greater cachet and motivation, competitive advantage and less competition.

✓ Large organizations might benefit from economies of scale, market-leader status, and high market share.

✓ Internal (or organic) growth is the gradual expansion of a business from within.

✓ External growth can be quicker and riskier. A business might experience this sort of growth through a merger with another company or an acquisition, through a joint venture of through franchising.

✓ Multinational companies (MNCs) operate in more than one country.

✓ Due to improved communication and less restricting regulations, the number and size of MNCs has grown rapidly in recent years.

✓ MNCs have both positive and negative effects on the countries in which they operate.

Practice question

Bauli's panettone

The large Italian company *Bauli* produces a variety of baked products such as croissants and biscuits, but it is most famous for its *panettone*[1], a specialty at Christmas. The original producers of *panettoni* were small luxury bakeries, which could bake a few expensive *panettoni* relatively easily. Michele Bauli claims that the quality of his product is what explains the company's success: "High investment in research and technology allows us to guarantee a uniform quality that small luxury bakeries find hard to achieve". It could be argued, however, that *Bauli's* success is mainly based on its low price. A *panettone* produced by a luxury bakery typically costs €30. A *Bauli panettone* costs €8.

Bauli produces on an industrial scale. Baking 12 million *panettoni* per year for sales across Italy and in European and American markets is a major challenge of workforce planning. *Bauli* meets the seasonal demand[2] for *panettoni* by hiring 1200 temporary workers for four months each year (from August to November). The company has also made significant technological innovations.

According to Michele, "Attention to ingredients and the use of new technologies in production give the *panettone* a shelf-life of five months". *Bauli* has also developed a broader product mix, including the Colombo cake, which is popular at a different time of the year. The broader product mix reduces the need for temporary workers.

Bauli has not relied only on internal growth. In 2009, the company purchased two subsidiaries of the multinational food group *Nestlé*. As both subsidiaries produce *panettoni*, these acquisitions have increased *Bauli's* market share. They will also help *Bauli* meet the growing demand for *panettoni* in American markets.

[Source: adapted from http://www.economist.com/, 10 December 2009]

With reference to Bauli, evaluate the benefits of small versus large organizations. [*7 marks*]

IB, Nov. 2011

---

[1] *panettone*: in Italian *panettone* is singular, *panettoni* is plural
[2] seasonal demand: demand that varies at different times of the year

1.7 Organizational planning tools (HL only)

By the end of this chapter, you should be able to:

→ Describe the planning tools that organizations can use:

- fishbone diagram
- decision tree
- force field analysis
- Gantt chart

→ Evaluate the value to an organization of these planning tools

To help businesses to achieve their objectives, managers may wish to use organizational planning tools, including:

- fishbone diagrams
- decision trees
- force field analysis
- Gantt charts.

Each of these tools has strengths and weaknesses. As long as users are aware of their limitations, these tools can help managers to plan.

The fishbone diagram

While working for Kawasaki in the 1960s, Kaoru Ishikawa developed the fishbone diagram as a tool to help identify quality problems. The diagram attempts to show the **cause and effects** of quality problems. The tool is usually used with small groups of managers, or **quality circles**.

Ishikawa designed the fishbone diagram for the "4 Ms" of manufacturing: method, manpower, machine, and materials. Since then, the tool has been applied to the "4 Ps" for service businesses (places, procedures, people and politics) and the "4 Ss" for administration (surroundings, suppliers, systems, and skills). Managers may use all these terms in various combinations according to individual circumstances. The general idea is to provide a tool to help **brainstorm** the causes and the effects of a quality problem.

The fishbone diagram is closely linked to Sakichi Toyoda's concept of "**5 whys**", a questioning technique he developed to provide better quality and service at the Toyota Corporation. The "5 whys" technique is intended to get people to probe more deeply into the nature of quality problems or customer dissatisfaction. In its simplest form, the "5 whys" presumes that what someone reports as a problem may just be merely a symptom of some other underlying problem. When the "5 whys" technique is followed, the goal is to determine and fix the underlying problem. In doing so, not only is the underlying problem resolved but so is the original symptom (and possibly many other symptoms showing up in various areas of the business).

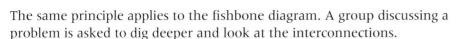

The same principle applies to the fishbone diagram. A group discussing a problem is asked to dig deeper and look at the interconnections.

1. The idea is that the **effect** of the problem is placed in the head of the fish. For example, Figure 1.7.1 shows the fishbone diagram prepared by an airline losing **market share** and wishing to address the issue.

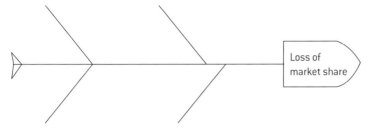

Figure 1.7.1. Fishbone diagram – the effect of the problem

2. Then each fishbone is allocated to a particular factor that may have **caused** the problem. Typical factors are set out below, but it is also possible to create other factors relevant to a particular problem.

Table 1.7.1. The "4 Ms", "4 Ps" and "4 Ss" in relation to different types of business

Manufacturing	Services	Administration
Manpower	Places	Surroundings
Methods	Procedures	Suppliers
Materials	People	Systems
Machines	Politics	Skills

In this case the airline may decide to use the "4 Ps" to brainstorm, as shown in Figure 1.7.2.

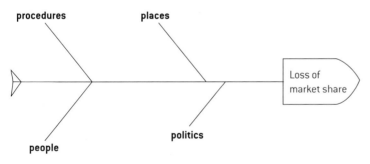

Figure 1.7.2. Fishbone diagram using the "4 Ps"

3. After discussion by the group, each factor is broken down into a subfactor and is drawn as a smaller fishbone coming out of the original one.

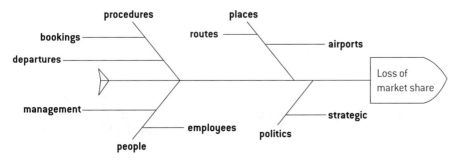

Figure 1.7.3. Fishbone diagram showing subfactors

4. Finally, after brainstorming and discussion, the group discards those issues ("fishbones", large or small) that are not the root cause of the problem, thus identifying which fishbone is the problem. In this example, involving an airline losing market share, the fishbone analysis determined that the airline had insufficient Asian routes in that expanding market.

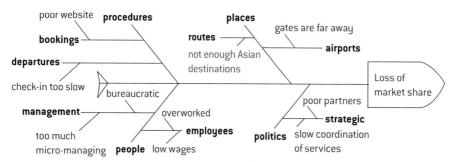

Figure 1.7.4. Fishbone diagram showing the root cause of the problem

The fishbone diagram has many benefits and limitations.

Benefits	**Limitations**
The fishbone diagram:	The fishbone diagram:
• is motivating as it brings people together to discuss problems	• may show causes of a problem but not show specific solutions
• is flexible – applicable to virtually any situation	• can be divisive and lead to arguments
• is simple and visually attractive	• requires knowledge and honesty to justify assertions
• can highlight many factors before singling out the most significant.	• begins the process of fixing a problem and requires a follow-up process.

Decision trees

A decision tree is a planning tool designed to help simplify complex decisions. It is similar to a probability tree used in mathematics. By providing a clear visual structure, a decision tree can help managers make sensible strategic decisions.

To construct a decision tree, certain conventions should be followed.

1. Where a choice has to be made, the decision is represented by a square 'node' and the possible choices as lines stemming from the node with the choice written above the line.

   For example, a business has to decide whether to build a new factory from a choice of three new sites (A, B or C). These nodes are numbered in order to identify them correctly, as shown in Figure 1.7.5.

2. If any given decision has multiple possible outcomes, these outcomes are represented by a circle node. Possible outcomes are represented by lines stemming from the circle with the outcome written above the line. Again, the nodes are numbered to help identify them (see Figure 1.7.6).

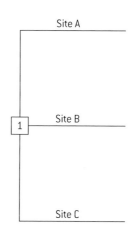

Figure 1.7.5. Decision tree – initial stage of analysing three new sites

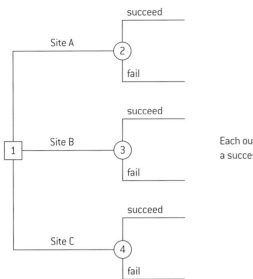

Each outcome has a possibility of being a success or a failure.

Figure 1.7.6. Decision tree – sites analysed for success or failure

3. Then, using whatever data is available, the manager estimates the probability that the outcome actually happens. As with the mathematics probability trees, the sum of all probabilities stemming from one outcome node must always be 1 (or 100 per cent).

These possibilities are put below the line for that particular outcome, as shown in Figure 1.7.7.

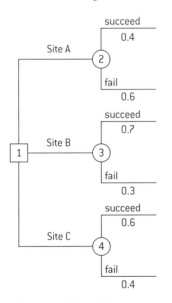

Choice	Outcome and probability
A	• succeed 40% • fail 60%
B	• succeed 70% • fail 30%
C	• succeed 60% • fail 40%

Figure 1.7.7. Decision tree – probability of outcomes

4. Using the best data available, the manager must then make an estimate of the values of that outcome actually happening. These values are written at the end of the line represented by that outcome, as shown in Figure 1.7.8.

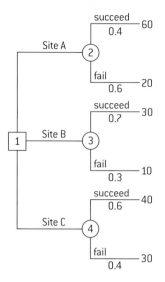

Figure 1.7.8. Decision tree – probability of outcomes

Choice	Outcome	Probability	Returns (US$ m)
A	succeed	40%	60
A	fail	60%	20
B	succeed	70%	30
B	fail	30%	10
C	succeed	60%	40
C	fail	40%	30

5. Then, again using the best data available, the manager estimates the costs of the choices being considered (see Figure 1.7.9). If no costs are incurred in the choice, a figure "0" need not be shown. The costs are written under the respective choice lines.

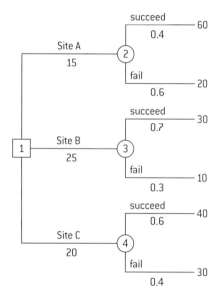

Choice	Cost US$ m
A	15
B	25
C	20

Figure 1.7.9. Decision tree – cost of outcomes

6. The manager can now calculate the results, known as the **expected values** (EV). Each outcome node will have an EV based upon the following formula:

$$\text{Expected value node}_x = (\text{probability}_{x1} \times \text{return}_{x1}) + (\text{probability}_{x2} \times \text{return}_{x2})$$

So in this case the calculations are as follows:

$EV_2 = (0.4 \times 60) + (0.6 \times 20) = 36$

$EV_3 = (0.7 \times 30) + (0.3 \times 10) = 24$

$EV_4 = (0.6 \times 40) + (0.4 \times 30) = 36$

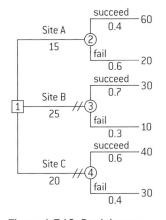

7. The decision would normally be the outcome that gives the highest EV. However, in this case, the manager must include the costs incurred by building the factories. The cost is subtracted from the EV for each choice. This process then indicates the best choice: the EV with the highest value:

$$EV_2 - cost_A = 36 - 15 = US\$21 \text{ million}$$

$$EV_3 - cost_B = 24 - 25 = (US\$1 \text{ million})$$

$$EV_4 - cost_C = 36 - 20 = US\$16 \text{ million}$$

8. The decision taken is to build the factory at **site A**.

   As shown in Figure 1.7.10, this is indicated on the decision tree by crossing out the choices not taken with the symbol //

   Using a decision tree has benefits and limitations.

Figure 1.7.10. Decision tree – selection of site A

Benefits	**Limitations**
A decision tree:	A decision tree:
• gives a clear answer to a complex decision	• is based on estimates of both outcomes and probabilities of outcomes
• is flexible and can be applied to many situations	• is based on quantitative data and so ignores qualitative issues
• is simple and visually attractive.	• can be difficult to draw for highly complex decisions with multiple outcomes and interrelated choices.

Force field analysis

Force field analysis was originally designed by Kurt Lewin as a model for use in psychological experiments. It has since been adopted as a planning tool for businesses. Lewin's force field analysis uses the **management of change** concept to focus on the factors working for and against a planned change in an organization.

1. First, the **change factor** being considered is highlighted. For example, a business may be thinking of changing its logo.

Change
the logo

2. Then the decision makers brainstorm factors acting positively for that change, which are **driving forces,** and factors working negatively against that change, so-called **restraining forces**.

Driving forces		**Restraining forces**
Market research reveals that consumers are tired of the current logo		The founder of the business created the logo and her family do not want to change it
The logo has not been changed for 20 years		The logo is familiar to the loyal customers
Market research reveals that 60% of potential customers do not recognize the logo	Change the logo	The logo is recognized as a symbol of good-quality products
New brands entering the market are gaining recognition for innovative and modern products		The logo is patented and creating a new one would be costly to design and protect

3. The manager then gives each factor a **weight** corresponding to that factor's importance. Although managers can use any scale they want, typically with a force field analysis the scale is from 1 to 5, with 5 being the strongest weighting. Sometimes, the forces are drawn with arrows that reflect their weighting to give a simple visual picture:

Driving forces				**Restraining forces**
Market research reveals that consumers are tired of the current logo	5		1	The founder of the business created the logo and her family do not want to change it
The logo has not been changed for 20 years	2		3	The logo is familiar to the loyal customers
Market research reveals that 60% of potential customers do not recognize the logo	3	Change the logo	1	The logo is recognized as a symbol of good-quality products
New brands entering the market are gaining recognition for innovative and modern products	4		2	The logo is patented and creating a new one would be costly to design and protect

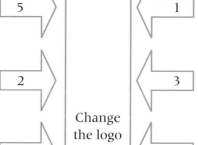
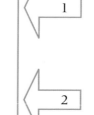

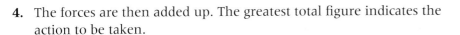

4. The forces are then added up. The greatest total figure indicates the action to be taken.

    Restraining forces = 7

    Driving forces = 14

    In this case, the decision would be to change the logo.

Using force field analysis has many benefits and limitations.

Benefits	**Limitations**

Force field analysis:

- gives a clear answer to a difficult decision

- is flexible and can be applied to many situations

- is simple and visually attractive.

Force field analysis:

- involves interpretations in determining which factors to include

- is based on estimates of the value of each individual factor

- is based on mainly qualitative data, not quantitative issues.

Gantt charts

The Gantt chart was developed by Henry Gantt as a tool to help plan work schedules. It is commonly used for production projects that have multiple tasks. It is a means of organizing production in order to determine the most efficient use of resources, whether raw materials, labour, or capital. It also gives the project managers a clear overview of the whole project. Progress of the whole project can be measured against key deadlines (milestones).

The charts on the following pages take the example of a music producer who wants to plan the production of a new CD.

1. First the producer must create the framework by creating a matrix, shown in Table 1.7.2. The horizontal axis is measured in time (days, weeks or months) and the vertical axis is split up into the individual tasks that need to be completed before the CD is finally produced.

Table 1.7.2. Gantt chart matrix

	Tasks	Jan	Feb	Mar	Apr	May	June	July	Aug	Sept	Oct	Nov	Dec
1	Band writes the music for 10 songs												
2	Band writes the lyrics for 10 songs												
3	Initial recording by the band												
4	Full production by the band and other musicians												
5	Creation and design of the cover artwork												
6	Production of the completed CDs												
7	Production of the online version												
8	Promotion of individual songs on radio shows												
9	Promotion by interviews and press releases												
10	Promotion of the music through concerts												

2. The tasks are then scheduled. Some must follow sequentially but others need not be. The order, time, and sequence of tasks is denoted by shading in parts of the matrix, as shown in Table 1.7.3.

Table 1.7.3. Gantt chart matrix showing timing of tasks

	Tasks	Jan	Feb	Mar	Apr	May	Jun	July	Aug	Sep	Oct	Nov	Dec
1	Band writes the music for 10 songs												
2	Band writes the lyrics for 10 songs												
3	Initial recording by the band												
4	Full production by the band and other musicians												
5	Creation and design of the cover artwork												
6	Production of the completed CDs												
7	Production of the online version												
8	Promotion of individual songs on radio shows												
9	Promotion by interviews and press releases												
10	Promotion of the music through concerts												

3. Once the schedule has been created, then the management team can always check for progress as the project is running. Managers do this check by marking off the tasks as time elapses. Typically, the manager colours in the chart as each task has been completed.

Consider the example in Table 1.7.4.

Table 1.7.4. Gantt chart matrix showing progress checks

	Tasks	Jan	Feb	Mar	Apr	May	Jun	July	Aug	Sept	Oct	Nov	Dec
1	Band writes the music for 10 songs												
2	Band writes the lyrics for 10 songs												
3	Initial recording by the band												
4	Full production by the band and other musicians												
5	Creation and design of the cover artwork												
6	Production of the completed CDs												
7	Production of the online version												
8	Promotion of individual songs on radio shows												
9	Promotion by interviews and press releases												
10	Promotion of the music through concerts												

If in April the project looks like Table 1.7.4, the business knows that the artists are running slightly behind schedule. The business needs to readjust its plans accordingly.

Using a Gantt chart has many benefits and limitations:

Benefits	Limitations

A Gantt chart:

- gives a clear picture of current progress of the various tasks
- gives a clear picture of the overall project
- is flexible and can be applied to many situations
- is simple and visually attractive
- allows managers to plan the use of resources to complete the project in the most efficient manner.

A Gantt chart:

- is based on estimates of the timings of each task
- is difficult to follow when applied to very complex projects
- is based on mainly qualitative data, not quantitative data (such as costs)
- cannot separate out interdependent tasks
- places a premium on meeting deadlines (milestones), which may lead to erosion of the quality of the work.

> **TOK discussion**
>
> If business is a human enterprise, is it possible to quantify (express in numerate form) various business scenarios? What role should "human" methods, such as intuition, emotion, and "hunches" play in business decision making?

The value of these planning tools

Each of these organizational planning tools can be useful for a business. However, they have different uses and are not applied at the same time and for the same reasons. All of the tools have limitations, which should be borne in mind by potential users.

Also, each tool is just one available to managers and should be used together with other tools, data, or techniques. The value of each tool depends on the circumstances and the way it has been applied. Table 1.7.5 indicates factors that should be taken into account before using the tools.

Table 1.7.5. Factors relating to different business analysis tools

Tool	Fishbone diagram	Decision tree	Force field analysis	Gantt chart
What is its major area of focus?	It is used to help a business react to issues that require quality improvements and may involve the whole business.	Senior managers use it to indicate the most effective direction from a variety of options.	It is used to facilitate management of change.	It is used for day-to-day project management by middle managers but is open to all to view.
What time frame is involved?	It is a short-term response to an identified problem.	It is used for medium- to long-term planning of future directions.	It is used for medium- to long- term planning of future directions.	It is used for short- to medium- term projects.
At what level of planning is it used?	Tactical planning	Strategic planning	Strategic planning	Tactical planning
Which part of the decision making process is it used for?	Initial – brainstorming	Final – based on as much information as possible	Initial – brainstorming	Ongoing
What should it be used with?	Quantitative data	Qualitative data	Quantitative data	Quantitative data
Which departments should use it?	Mainly production (but it can be used by all departments)	Mainly production and marketing	All departments	Production

Revision checklist

✓ A fishbone diagram allows businesses to look closely at problems and identify underlying causes.

✓ A decision tree provides a clear visual structure to help mangers simplify complex decisions and identify the most appropriate outcome.

✓ A force field analysis is used to help businesses manage change. It focusses on the factors which might influence the planned change.

✓ Gantt charts are used to plan complex projects and schedules. They enable businesses to allocate resources appropriately and give a clear overview of the entire workflow.

Practice question

Primature Inc

Following a 13% increase in orders over the last six months, *Primature Inc* is considering the expansion of its production facilities. It is presently producing at 98% of its production capacity. The production manager is examining two expansion options:

Option 1 – The construction of an extra production line in the present factory building at a cost of $1.5m. This will increase capacity by 16%.

Option 2 – The construction of an additional factory unit at a cost of $3.5m. The new building could be designed to allow for cell production and just in time (JIT) management. This would cut costs and provide additional future production flexibility and human resource advantages. Capacity could be increased by a maximum of 40%.

The recent increase in orders is as a result of improved economic conditions. However, the finance director is not convinced it is wise to invest in either option before it is clear that the increase in economic growth will be maintained. He believes unit price and revenues can be increased at current output, provided economic growth remains constant or improves. Economists differ on their forecasts for the next five years. 40% of those asked believe that the economy will strengthen over the next five years. 30% believe that average growth over that period will remain constant, whilst 30% believe there will be a decline in economic growth. The production manager estimates the following profit/loss outcomes for each of these predictions:

	Option 1 (new line) $m	Option 2 (new factory) $m	Option 3 (no expansion, increase unit price) $m
Economy strengthens	6	9	4
Constant economic growth	3	4	3
Declining economic growth	1	2	−1

a) (i) Construct a fully labelled decision tree showing *Primature Inc's* options with the financial costs and outcomes for each option.

[*3 marks*]

    (ii) Using your decision tree, decide which option *Primature Inc* should select on purely financial grounds. Show full working to support your choice. [*4 marks*]

b) Describe **three** benefits of using decision trees. [*3 marks*]

c) Evaluate the extent to which additional non-financial and financial factors may support, or not support, the choice of option selected for *Primature Inc* in your answer to question (a)(ii). [*10 marks*]

IB, May 2008

2 HUMAN RESOURCE MANAGEMENT

2.1 The functions and evolution of human resource management

By the end of this chapter, you should be able to:

→ Define human resource planning (workforce planning)

→ Explain the concept of labour turnover

→ Identify internal and external factors that influence human resource planning (such as demographic change, change in labour mobility, new communication technologies)

→ Outline common steps in the process of recruitment

→ Define the following types of training:
- on the job (including induction and mentoring)
- off the job
- cognitive
- behavioural

→ Define the following types of appraisal:
- formative
- summative
- 360-degree feedback
- self-appraisal

→ Outline common steps in the processes of dismissal and redundancy

→ Describe how work patterns, practices and preferences change and how they affect the employer and employees (such as teleworking, flexitime, migration for work)

→ Explain outsourcing, offshoring and re-shoring as human resource strategies

→ Evaluate how innovation, ethical considerations and cultural differences may influence human resource practices and strategies in an organization

HR (or workforce) planning

Human resources are critical for any business. The issue of human resources (HR) is especially important for businesses operating in the tertiary and quaternary sectors. Nevertheless, all businesses must ensure

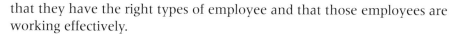

that they have the right types of employee and that those employees are working effectively.

Successful businesses are likely to have a clear framework for how to get the best from their human resources. HR planning is a continuous process. Businesses strive to make sure that their employees are in jobs for which they are properly trained and properly suited. At the same time, as part of HR planning, a business estimates its future HR needs (the correct type and number of employees), so that as rarely as possible the business has too many employees (which increases costs) or too few employees (which can hurt productivity). This framework for how to get the most from their human resources is referred to as the HR plan or workforce plan. With large businesses, this plan will almost always be a written document that can be referred to. With smaller businesses, the plan may not be written but decided upon by and remain "in the head" of the director of HR or the owner of the small business.

Labour turnover

Labour turnover refers to the movement of employees into and out of a business in a given time period (usually a year) and is an indicator of how stable a business is.

Labour turnover is usually measured by the following formula:

$$\text{Labour turnover} = \frac{\text{number of staff leaving over a year}}{\text{average number of staff employed in a year}} \times 100$$

A high labour turnover rate suggests that the business has labour problems. For some reason or reasons, employees do not stay for a long period of time. By itself, high labour turnover suggests that workers are dissatisfied by some aspect of their employment situation. This source of dissatisfaction may also affect workers who remain at the business and may lead to lower productivity. When a business has high labour turnover, the business must frequently hire new labour, which can cause problems for the business. Recruitment and training can be expensive. New workers are often less productive than those who are established in the business. High turnover can affect employees' motivation, as it leads to some interruption in work practices and routines. In addition, high turnover communicates to employees that the business has a problem with some aspect of employment there. Even if workers are otherwise satisfied in their jobs, high labour turnover may lead them to believe that they should be dissatisfied.

Business can anticipate certain circumstances when labour turnover will be higher than others. In a booming economy, employees tend to look for new opportunities since jobs are plentiful. In addition, younger employees tend to swap jobs more often than middle-aged employees.

Finally, some labour turnover can be good for a business. A low turnover rate may indicate a stable business, but stability can lead to complacency and lack of progress. New employees tend to bring energy and new ideas, especially if they have just left college or have been retrained and/

or reskilled. Sometimes, a business has employees of lesser productivity or who make minimal contributions to the business but otherwise provide no basis for separation (being fired or sacked). When a worker such as this leaves a business, managers may actually be happy.

The HR plan should be designed to make sure that the labour turnover rate is kept at an acceptable level, which will vary according to the industry and the skill and experience requirements for the position. A grocery store chain might expect (even if it did not want) fairly high labour turnover among its cashiers, but a law firm would not want to see high turnover among its experienced lawyers. Managers would pay close attention to any significant changes in the labour turnover rate. Labour turnover can quickly get higher as a result of a significant change in circumstances either in or outside the business. By tracking the labour turnover rate, the business can try to correct internal factors or mitigate against external factors.

TOK discussion

To what degree should businesses resist workforce planning and instead base human resources on the strengths and weaknesses of its current and available workforce?

The internal and external factors that influence HR planning

Many factors can influence an organization's HR plan. Even before a business employs someone, some **external factors** can have an effect on the pool of labour available for potential employment. Also the business itself may change and **internal factors** influence the HR plan that is already in place. This is shown in Figure 2.1.1.

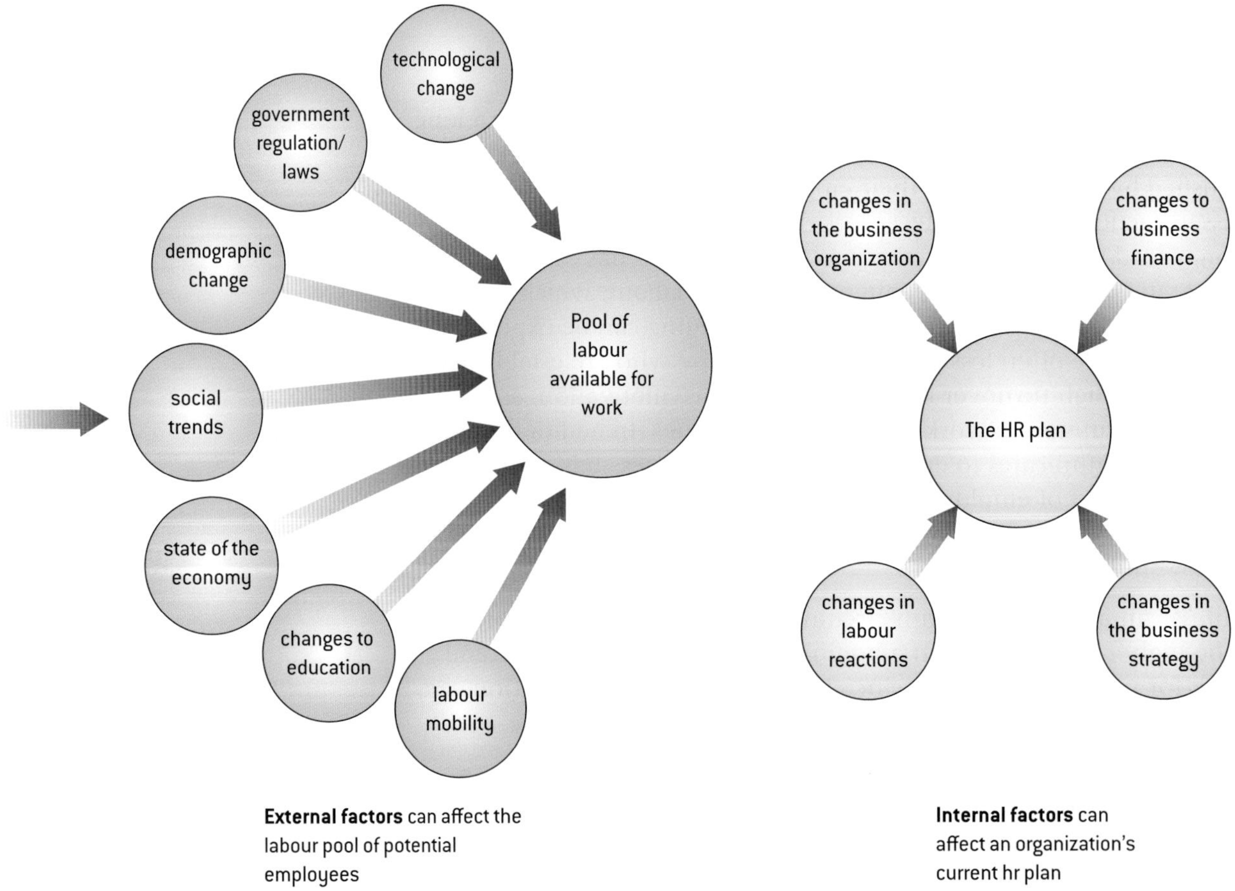

External factors can affect the labour pool of potential employees

Internal factors can affect an organization's current hr plan

Figure 2.1.1. External and internal factors affecting the HR plan

The **external factors** have an impact on the size and availability of the pool of potential employees for the business and include the following:

- **Technological change** – improvements in ICT can lead to more **teleworking** and working from home. Infrastructural improvements, such as new roads or other transport links, can make employing someone from further away easier than before.

- **Government regulations** – changes in laws or government regulations regarding health and safety issues can influence a potential workforce. Laws or government regulations can affect maximum weekly working hours or contractual issues, such as equality in the workplace irrespective of age, gender, ethnicity, or disability. Laws generally determine obligations such as pension provisions or age of retirement.

- **Demographic change** – an ageing population, reduced fertility rates, or changes in internal and external migration patterns are just some of the demographic changes that can have an impact on the potential employees available and their specific requirements to work.

- **Social trends** – changes in society, such as the role of women in society, a rise in the number of single parent families, or the importance of leisure in the "work–life balance" can all have significant impacts on the labour pool.

- **The state of the economy** – an economic boom will lead to a strain on the pool of labour available and consequently lead to increased wages; a recession will have the opposite effect as more unemployed workers are available and so may accept lower wages.

- **Changes in education** – some would consider changes in levels of education a factor of demography. Regardless, rising or falling education levels can have a direct impact on the suitability of labour for employment. Also relevant is the range and type of courses available to students.

- **Labour mobility** – many factors can influence labour mobility, which can refer either to occupational mobility (changing occupations) or geographical mobility (changing locations). In either case, the mobility of the workforce significantly affects the labour pool.

The **internal factors** stem from within the business itself and will have an impact on the current HR plan, which may have to change as a result of the following:

- **Changes in business organization** – businesses change the way they are organized to better meet their strategic objectives. Any reorganization can affect the current HR plan. Organizational

Recent technological change has meant that more people in certain sectors can work from home

2 Human resource management

changes affecting the HR plan can also occur when a business acquires another business or is acquired.

- **Changes in labour relations** – labour relations can have a significant impact on workforce planning. If the labour force chooses to unionize, for example, the business will now have to contend with the work requirements of the union. If the power of a union decreases, on the other hand, the business may have more flexibility with workers. Either way, the long-term labour circumstances will change.

- **Changes in business strategy** – whether in response to changes in circumstances in the market or to the business re-orientating itself, changes in business strategy may well lead to amendments to the plan.

- **Changes in business finance** – the financial situation of a business will have a bearing on the HR plan. A business that has limited resources may not be able to pay the highest wages and salaries, which can affect recruitment and retention. Other financial factors can have an impact as well. Unfunded pension liabilities can influence available resources for the current workforce, or a significant increase in profitability may allow for a greater number of staff.

The HR (or workforce) plan

There are four parts to the HR plan, which follow an individual's career path as the employee progresses in the business:

- **recruitment** – how the business recruits the right person for the right job

- **training** – how the business ensures that employees receive proper professional development, whether initial training or ongoing professional development

- **appraisal** – how the employee's job performance is evaluated

- **termination or dismissal** – how the business manages the situation when the employee leaves, whether voluntarily (the employee leaves of his or her own free will) or involuntarily (the employee is fired for cause or is retrenched).

The processes of recruitment

The first stage of the HR plan can be split into three parts:

- identification

- application

- selection.

The identification process

Identification	The business realizes that it needs a new employee because of a change in its internal factors.
Job description	This gives details about the job, such as: • the job title • what the employee will have to do • the employee's responsibilities.
Person specification	This gives details about the type of person required to do the job, such as: • the skills required to do the job • the qualifications necessary • what experience is necessary.
Internal or external recruitment	The business has to weigh up the advantages of recruiting internally by promotion (or redeployment), such as it being: • cheaper • quicker • more efficient as the person would know how the business works. It then has to weigh up the advantages against the disadvantages. For example, recruiting internally: • limits the pool of potential candidates • may cause resentment • causes the "domino" effect as the person promoted would leave a vacancy to be filled, and so on down the hierarchy. Searching externally would be the reverse of all of the above.

The application process

Application	The business has to decide how to find the best applicants for the job.
Job advert	The business will need to consider: • where to place the advert so it is seen by the right people • what should be included in the advert so the applicants have sufficient information • the legal requirements that have to be met.
Application form or résumé (CV)	What is the most appropriate tool to process the applications? Every tool should include the same elements (personal details, skills and qualifications, work experience, interests and hobbies, and references) but application forms are: • standardized (so they are useful for jobs with lots of possible applicants) • designed specifically to match the job requirements • focused on the issues that the business wants • legally binding. However, a résumé (CV): • is better for jobs with limited applicants (such as senior posts) • is more personal and can reveal more about the applicant • can be more flexible • is quicker as it can be prepared beforehand.

Internal or external agency	The business has to weigh up the advantages of finding the best applicants internally by using its HR department, such as it being:
	<ul><li>cheaper</li><li>quicker</li><li>more efficient as the HR department will know precisely what the business requires.</li></ul> It then has to weigh up the advantages against the disadvantages. For example, using its HR department: <ul><li>limits the pool of potential candidates; agencies may have plenty more applicants in their databases</li><li>may cause a lack of focus in other areas</li><li>may not cater for specialist skills, in contrast with an agency, for example that specializes in administrative vacancies.</li></ul>

The selection process

Selection	The final part of the process of recruitment is the selection of the best applicant for the job.
Shortlisting	The business will have to discard many applicants on the basis of: <ul><li>their overall quality</li><li>how many are required for interview</li><li>any legal requirements that have to be taken into account.</li></ul>
Testing	Many businesses like to subject the shortlisted applicants to some form of test, to be used as a complement to the final interview. These tests can be: <ul><li>aptitude (task-oriented activities, designed to test understanding and application of theories or concepts)</li><li>psychometric (personality questionnaires, designed to test reasoning skills and personality traits)</li><li>team based (exercises designed to focus on the qualities necessary for working in project teams).</li></ul>
Interviews	The interview is the final part of the recruitment process and there is no one best style of interview. It will depend on circumstances but may include the following: <ul><li>face to face (one to one)</li><li>panel (with more than one person)</li><li>video conference (or telephone)</li><li>multi-stage (one interview leads to another)</li><li>multi-day (conducted over a number of days).</li></ul>

Training

The second stage of the HR plan, training, can help an employee's professional development. Training can keep the employee up to date with the latest ideas and technologies. It may lead to the employee finding a new career path by being reskilled. Training might even prevent the employee from losing a skill that they had learned previously – deskilling.

However, training is also important for a business. It can:

- improve the quality of the work

- lead to greater productivity

- motivate the employee

- reduce labour turnover.

In some countries a full-time worker has the right to be allowed to take time off to train.

Training can take many forms, including the following:

- **Induction** – training that focuses on making a new employee familiar with the way the business functions and with lines of authority (who to report to, for example). A good induction programme helps to ensure that new employees settle in quickly so that they can begin work straight away.

- **On-the-job** – when employees are trained while they are doing their normal job. Often on-the-job training occurs through mentoring, which is when an experienced employee guides the employee being trained. Another common type of on-the-job training is shadowing, when one employee follows, or "shadows", another to learn a new skill.

- **Off-the-job** – when the employee is given time off from work to attend training away from the job. That training may be a workshop, conference, or course run by consultants, agencies, or educational institutions. Today, many managers choose to earn an MBA with the support of their employer. In light of the importance of education in contemporary post-industrial economies, many employers pay for courses at local universities, even if the coursework is not otherwise required of the employees – businesses just want to see their employees gain a better education.

Another way to think about training is not how and where it occurs, but rather what the aim of the training is. Most often, training is about learning discrete skills or knowledge to enhance job performance. Other forms of training enhance employees in other ways. These other forms of training include the following:

- **Cognitive training** – which is training not focused on a particular aspect of the business. Rather, it helps employees develop their thinking and processing skills. The assumption is that with enhanced thinking and processing skills (that is, cognitive skills), they can make quicker and more effective decisions.

- **Behavioural training** – like cognitive training, behavioural training does not focus on a particular aspect of the business. Instead it helps employees develop their interpersonal skills (how they work with others) and intrapersonal skills (how to manage emotions). Behavioural training is useful for employees working in project teams and positions of leadership by concentrating on, for example, emotional intelligence or stress management.

On-the-job training is often led by an experienced employee

Student workpoint 2.1

Be a thinker

A new restaurant is opening in your local town. It will sell expensive food cooked by a highly-trained and well-known chef. The restaurant is advertising for waiters and waitresses. Draw up a job description for this role, including a detailed person specification.

Once you have finished, think about how you'd change the job description to suit a busy fast food restaurant.

Appraisal

The third stage of the HR plan is appraisal, which occurs when the performance of the employee is reviewed.

Appraisal is different from a more traditional form of employee review know as inspection. Under a system of inspection, managers review employees' performances and make judgments based on their observations. Communication tends to be one-way (the employee is not given the opportunity to respond) and top–down (from manager to employee). Often, in a system of inspection, the process focuses on the negative indicators of performance – what the employee has failed to do, or the frequency with which the employee did not meet targets.

Under a system of appraisal, employees may respond to, or even initiate, discussion. Communication is two-way, and managers include constructive feedback in order to foster a positive and inclusive working environment. Appraisal is supposed to be a non-threatening, non-judgmental and supportive process.

Benefits of appraisal

For an employee, appraisal can:

- be motivating

- be instructive – employees can learn from past mistakes

- help employees progress along their career path

- lead to a change in career direction.

For the business, appraisal can:

- act as a check on performance

- help to review new initiatives

- be useful to record and document performance

- be motivating as it formally recognizes good performance.

Appraisal systems can be costly and time consuming, especially when done well. Good appraisal systems tend to have certain characteristics:

- **They are not directly linked to pay or promotion.** Linking appraisal to pay or promotion can lead to mercenary behaviour, "back stabbing" (when people try to sabotage others' positions or performances in order to look better themselves), and a poisonous atmosphere.

- **Appraisal systems are separate from disciplinary systems.** Sometimes employees have to be punished for some failure to perform. Appraisal, on the other hand, is supposed to be positive. Linking appraisal to punishment destroys the whole essence of appraisal.

- **Good appraisal systems require minimal paperwork.** Having employees fill out numerous forms or having line managers excessively documenting their performance is time consuming. In addition, it puts the focus of the process on discrete accomplishments, many of which may be accomplishments in name only, rather than on more substantive issues.

- **Appraisals provide an honest exchange of views.** Appraisal has to be transparent. Everyone involved should know their role and the role of those around them. Though appraisal should be positive overall, conversations should be honest, with appropriate conversations about areas of strength and areas needing improvement.

Appraisal systems may include these methods of appraisal:

- **Formative** – because appraisal is intended to be a learning process, often it is a continuous approach to evaluate performance during an employee's time at work. Appraisal is typically run on a one-to-three-year cycle. The focus is on giving employees feedback when appraisees have done well and also in areas in which they have had difficulties. The idea is to help employees improve. This type of appraisal presumably "forms" the employee.

- **Summative** – this measures an employee's performance according to set standards. A summative assessment has an element of making a judgment of whether the employee passed or failed. Summative assessment tests employees' knowledge and skills against clear and explicit markers and then sums up (thus, summative) how an employee has performed against the standards. Summative appraisal is usually conducted at the end of a project, a contract, or a specific goal. Failure should not necessarily lead to termination.

- **360 degree** – this method provides each employee with the opportunity to receive performance appraisal not only from their line manager but also from between four to eight co-workers, subordinates and even customers or clients. This method involves an element of **upward appraisal** and is the most complex, having multiple perspectives. The 360-degree appraisal is often used with CEOs and other executives who serve and interact directly with several groups of stakeholders (see Figure 2.1.2).

- **Self-appraisal** – this is an important part of the performance appraisal processes outlined above or it can be used by itself. With this method of appraisal, individual employees reflect on their own performance. Usually this reflection is done with the help of a self-appraisal form on which employees rate themselves on various performance indicators. Typically, employees can also suggest their training needs, and discuss their accomplishments, strengths, weaknesses, and any potential problems faced during the relevant time period.

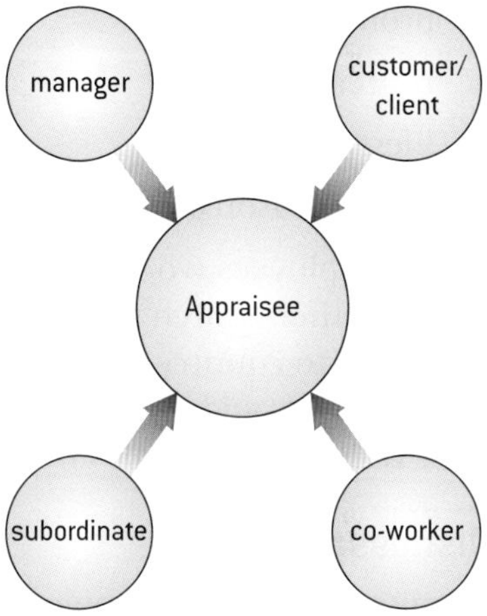

Figure 2.1.2. 360-degree appraisal

Termination, dismissal, and redundancy

The final stage in the HR plan is when an employee leaves the business. This situation might happen because:

- the employee chooses to leave the business

- the business decides that the employee should no longer work there

- both the employer and the employee agree that separation is in the best interests of both parties.

Good businesses will have a set of procedures ready to deal with this part of the HR plan to minimize the impact of losing employees and acquiring new ones.

For several reasons, termination of a business relationship does not happen too often:

- As employees develop more skills and experience, the cost of replacing them increases considerably and so businesses are very reluctant to go through the whole HR process again.

- Many businesses prefer such policies as redeployment, or, in times of recession, reducing the working hours rather than having to "let workers go" only to have to re-employ them (or other people) when business picks up again.

- Finally, employees have rights. If a business breaks employment contracts unnecessarily, it could face legal action initiated by the ex-employee on the basis of "unfair dismissal". Court cases are expensive and can result, additionally, in damages paid by the business to unfairly dismissed employees.

Nevertheless, from time to time, an employee has to leave a business, which can occur in one of three ways.

Termination

Employees can "terminate" or leave the business at the end of their contract for a variety of reasons, including:

- change of career

- professional development

- promotion

- retirement

- lifestyle choice

- family reasons.

These employees would expect to receive a reference from the employer to use in their search for their new job. Though the practice varies according to country, industry, and the level of the employee, in general employees should give some advance notice to their employer of when their resignation will be effective.

Dismissal

Dismissal is when an employee has broken one (or more) of the terms of their contract. The reasons may include:

- continually missing work

- poor discipline

- drug or alcohol abuse

- theft or dishonesty.

Employees may sometimes be dismissed for reasons other than non-performance under their employment contract. Generally, these circumstances occur when an employee has done something that might harm the image of the business, which may be:

- a conviction for an offence or imprisonment

- an unresolvable personality clash with a co-worker

- refusal to accept a company reorganization that changes the terms of employment.

If employees are dismissed, they would not expect to receive a reference. However, employees should receive a "period of notice" – a specified length of time when they may continue to work (for example a "two-week notice"). In some instances, employees do something so bad that they face a "summary dismissal", which takes effect immediately. Summary dismissals can also happen when the employer fears that the employee facing dismissal will damage the property of the business (either actual physical damage or, more commonly today, damage to computer files or systems) or steal from the business (for example, take computer files that are the property of the business).

Redundancy

Redundancy may happen when a business no longer has any work for an employee, causes for which may include:

- a drop in demand for the business's products

- changing market circumstances

- a recession

- restructuring of the industry

- the business becoming insolvent or bankrupt

- the job someone has been doing being replaced by mechanization when the employer introducies new technology (i.e. the job can be done by a machine)

- relocation of the business

- restructure or reorganization of the business

- a merger or takeover.

In these cases, because employees have lost their job through no fault of their own (that is, their employment is not ended for "cause"), they would normally expect to receive a redundancy payment and a letter of reference. The amount of the redundancy payment can vary from country to country and by industry. Typically, the longer an employee has been with the business, the greater the redundancy payment will be (one month's pay for every year of employment, or some other formula).

When a large number of positions are made redundant, deciding which employees to retain can be difficult for managers. They would normally have two options to offer:

- **Voluntary** redundancy – typically, this is the preferred option as it reduces the stress and animosity that the decision can generate. With the voluntary approach, some employees may choose to be made redundant. They may have wanted to look for a new job anyway. They receive the redundancy payment and a letter of reference, which will help them in their efforts to get a new job. The problem with the voluntary approach is that the business may lose employees it would prefer to retain or retain employees it would prefer to lose.

- **Involuntary** redundancy – this approach is typically less desirable than the voluntary option. Involuntary redundancy may be based on age, years of service, or some other criterion or criteria. If not constrained by a some type of agreement with the unions or some other form of labour agreement, the benefit of the involuntary approach is that the business can have more influence over which employees will leave based upon the criteria it selects.

Changes in work patterns, practices, and preferences

Over the past 50 years, many changes that affect employers and employees have occurred in work patterns, practices, and preferences. Some of these changes have stemmed from external factors affecting the pool of labour. For example, social trends have led many employees to want a better work–life balance and many businesses are trying to respond to the desires of their employees. Other social trends have stemmed from internal factors affecting businesses, which can benefit from some of the new work practices.

Some of the factors changing the working environment include:

- privatization and the move away from public-sector to private-sector employment

- increased migration of potential employees in a country or region and across the globe

- increasing participation of females in the workforce

- changing educational opportunities

- increasing urbanization and the consequent rise in stress levels

- an ageing population and increasing average age of the workforce.

Changes in work patterns

One change has been in the patterns of work – the types of jobs required by businesses as well as the types of jobs people want. Table 2.1.1 shows the results of some opinion polls analyzing the most sought-after jobs in selected countries.

Table 2.1.1. The ten most sought-after jobs in selected countries in 2013

	USA	India	Singapore	South Africa	El Salvador
1	Actuary	IT personnel	Financial adviser	Engineer	Skilled labour
2	Bio-medical engineer	Retail staff	Electronics specialist	Driver	Sales agent
3	Software engineer	Healthcare worker	Engineer	Skilled tradesperson	Technician
4	Audiologist	Hospitality staff	IT personnel	Labourer	Engineer
5	Financial planner	Engineer	Media personnel	Manager/ executive	Bilingual administration staff

	USA	India	Singapore	South Africa	El Salvador
6	Dentist	HR personnel	Accountant	Teacher	Manager
7	Occupational therapist	Aviation personnel	Actuary	Legal staff	Driver
8	Optometrist	Psychologist	Retail worker	Secretary/PA	Mechanic
9	Physical therapist	Financial adviser	Property agent	Technician	Logistics personnel
10	Computer systems analyst	Teacher	Brand manager	Accountant	Accountant

Table 2.1.2 shows the ten least sought-after jobs in 2013 in the United States, based on a recent opinion poll.

One significant change that has happened, especially with the improvements in ICT, has been an increase in occupational and geographical mobility. Today it is much easier for individuals to determine "growing" occupations – occupations for which the number of positions will be expanding – and which occupations are contracting. Traditional mail services, for example, are decreasing the need for letter carriers because of email, electronic banking and online bill payment services. For letter carriers, or other individuals in contracting professions, it is relatively easily to learn which occupations are growing and then seek to acquire the necessary skills for those positions. Thus, occupational mobility is more common than in earlier eras.

Similarly, ICT also provides opportunities to match people seeking positions with countries or regions with shortages of people with certain skills. The United Kingdom and Belgium, for example, have shortages of both nurses and chefs. Many countries have shortages of pharmacists and ICT professionals. Before the ICT revolution, matching skilled people to places where they were needed was vastly more challenging than it is today. ICT allows for faster processing of data (who has what skills and what skills are needed in particular geographic regions). Then, ICT allows for easier dissemination of that information. Recently, BBC News ran an article that contained an interactive schematic showing what types of skilled employees different countries needed.[1] A result of this improved information is that many people are migrating because of work.

Changes in work practices

Not only have the types of jobs changed. The nature of work routines has changed as businesses have responded to greater demands for more flexible working practices.

Work practices in decline

Full-time work
↓
Permanent contracts

When employees work the maximum hours per week accepted by law (for example, working 35 hours a week in Europe).

An employee who has been hired for a position without a predetermined time limit.

Table 2.1.2. The ten least sought-after jobs in 2013 in the United States

USA 2013	
1	News reporter
2	Lumberjack
3	Military personnel
4	Actor
5	Oil rig worker
6	Dairy farmer
7	Meter reader
8	Mail carrier
9	Roofer
10	Flight attendant

Source: http://www.careercast.com/jobs-rated/worst-jobs-2013

Student workpoint 2.2

Be reflective

Look at the jobs listed in tables 2.1.1 and 2.1.2. Do any results surprise you? What factors are likely to influence people's opinions? Do you think money is the only consideration?

---

[1] http://www.bbc.co.uk/news/business-21938085

Work practices on the increase

Part-time work	When employees work less than the full-time weekly maximum hours.
Temporary	Work that is on a fixed-term contract usually of a temporary nature (for example, to cover maternity leave). The employee would normally sign up to an agency who finds work for the employee.
Freelance	When someone who is self-employed works for several different employers at the same time.
Teleworking	Work taking place from home or a telecommunication centre. Usually the employee would have a core number of hours he or she has to work at the office, the remainder from home.
Homeworking	When an employee works from home. Usually the employee would have a core number of hours he or she has to work at the office, the remainder from home.
Flexitime	Work involving a set number of hours of an employee's own choosing. Usually the employee would have a core number of hours he or she has to work at the office; the rest is up to the employee.
Casual Fridays	When an employee is allowed to wear less formal dress on a Friday so that it is easier to go away at the weekends.
Three-day weekend	Instead of working, say, five days of eight hours, the employee works four days of ten hours and so has a three-day weekend.

Student workpoint 2.3

Be an inquirer

Talk to people you know – teachers, parents and friends about their work. What can you find out about the ways in which they work – does everyone work a similar number of hours per work? Are these hours fixed? Where do they work from?

Case study

Work-life balance in France

In 2000, the French government reduced the statutory working week from 39 hours to 35 hours. Now, under a new deal, French employers' federations and unions have signed a legally binding labour agreement that requires employers to make sure staff "disconnect" outside of working hours.

The deal, which affects around 250,000 employees in the technology and consultancy sectors (including the French sectors of Google, Facebook, Deloitte and PwC), means that employees will have to resist the temptation to look at work-related material on their computers or phone—during their free time. Companies must ensure that their employees come under no pressure to do so.

Exam-style questions

Explain the impact on a) employers and b) employees of this new change. [6 marks]

Discuss the impact this change might have on the culture of businesses in France. [8 marks]

Changes in work preferences

Instead of working continuously for 20 to 30 years for the same business, many employees are now adapting their work routines to suit changing lifestyles. These are some of the most common methods:

- **Career breaks** – an employee decides to stop working for a time, usually a year or more, before returning to work in the same career. Sometimes the employer formalizes this and agrees to take the employee back after the break – this is known as a "sabbatical".

- **Job share** – two or more employees decide to share a job in order to free up more time for other activities.

- **Downshifting** – an employee gives up a senior position or highly paid employment in order to change career into another lower-paid field or area of interest.

- **Study leave** – an employee is granted time off work to acquire a new qualification such as an MBA.

Outsourcing and offshoring as HR strategies

HR costs can be significant for many businesses, particularly for service-based businesses operating in the tertiary or quaternary sectors. Many businesses have therefore adapted their HR plans to match the changes in work patterns, practices, and preferences. In doing so, they cut costs and gain a competitive advantage.

One method has been **outsourcing** (also known as subcontracting or contracting out work). Outsourcing occurs when a business cuts back on its operations to focus on its core activities. This way, it does not need to employ as many workers.

Imagine a smartphone company with current annual salary costs for design, manufacturing, and distribution of US$42 million per year, as shown in Figure 2.1.3.

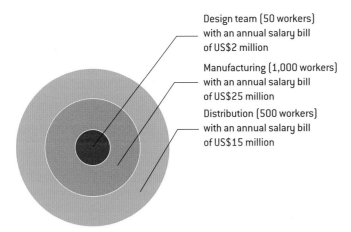

Design team (50 workers) with an annual salary bill of US$2 million

Manufacturing (1,000 workers) with an annual salary bill of US$25 million

Distribution (500 workers) with an annual salary bill of US$15 million

Figure 2.1.3. Smartphone manufacturer before using outsourcing

Design team (50 workers) with an annual salary bill of US$2 million

Figure 2.1.4. Smartphone manufacturer after using outsourcing

However, if the business were to outsource manufacturing and distribution, it would have US$40 million available, as shown in Figure 2.1.4.

Although the business would have to pay subcontractors to complete the work, it could cut costs by doing this. The subcontractors are likely to be specialists in either manufacturing or distribution. They probably have fewer inefficiencies and greater productivity in these areas of expertise and so would most likely charge less than the cost of the smartphone business doing the work itself.

In addition to the lower production costs (which can be calculated by the cost to buy/cost to make formulas in Unit 3), the smartphone business not only saves on its wage bill. It will also save on all the other costs of employing people. Medical, maternity, and holiday pay, pensions, and other benefits that businesses provide to full-time employees are extremely expensive. In the United States, as a "rule of thumb", these benefits are typically equal to 50 per cent of an employee's salary. Thus, the cost saving is likely to be even greater than the US$40 million wage bill. By outsourcing, the business saves significant amounts of money. The benefit to the business is not just the cost savings. Now, it can focus on its core activity – designing innovative products.

An extension of outsourcing is **offshoring**: when a business outsources outside its home country. With improved global communication, offshoring has been a growth area in the modern business environment. Businesses take advantage of the huge wage differences between workers doing the same job but in different areas of the world. Many customer service call centres, for example, have been offshored from the United Kingdom and the United States, where wages are high, to India, where many people speak English fluently and wages are far lower.

> ### Why offshoring?
>
> Simple mathematics is often the answer:
>
> - In the USA, an architect might be paid $3,000 a month. An architect in the Philippines would get around £250 a month.
>
> - A Java programmer earns $60,000 a year in the United States and makes $5,000 annually in India.
>
> Through outsourcing, businesses can cut their operational costs by 20–40 percent.
>
> British Airways calculates that it saves US$23 million a year for every 1,000 jobs it relocates to India.
>
> Adapted from http://www.economist.com/media/globalexecutive/outsourcing_revolution_e_02.pdf

Examples of typical business functions that can be outsourced include:

- in **marketing**, using an advertising agency

- in **operations management**, licensing a producer to make your product

- in **HR**, employing an agency to "headhunt" potential staff

- in **finance**, hiring accountants to run an external audit.

ETHICS

It is easy to say that, because production costs are cheaper elsewhere, then production should be moved offshore. But there are many ethical implications for businesses to consider. Think about the people in the original location, and the people in the 'offshore' location – what effect will off-shoring have on them? Hold a debate arguing for and against offshoring for a business of your choice.

Key terms

Outsourcing

when a business subcontracts a process, such a manufacturing or packaging, to another business or organization

Offshoring

outsourcing a process or service to another country in order to reduce costs

The impact of innovation, ethical considerations, and cultural differences

Innovation, ethical considerations, and cross-cultural differences can also have an impact on the HR plan and the business's ability to implement it successfully.

Innovation

Innovation or its opposite – inertia – can have a major impact on the HR plan. A business committed to being innovative must have a greater strategic focus on HR than any other business function. Innovations come from people. The business will not be successfully innovative unless it recruits and retains the right people. Developing a supportive and stimulating business environment – a vital part of HR planning – will help the creative process.

A business such as Google prides itself on being innovative and employing creative individuals. The Google office shown in Figure 2.1.5 reflects this approach.

Figure 2.1.5. One of Google's offices

Ethical considerations

A strong connection has always existed between HR planning and ethical behaviour. HR plans are based on relationships, which are reflected in the way that the business treats its employees. Not only should businesses treat their employees ethically, today it must do so. With the Internet, people have greater ability to send and receive information. Social network sites, in particular, can be places where employees treated badly can tell other how they have been treated. As a result, businesses have to be careful to act in an ethical manner – or at the least to create that appearance.

Ethical issues that might be addressed through the HR plan can be seen in Figure 2.1.6.

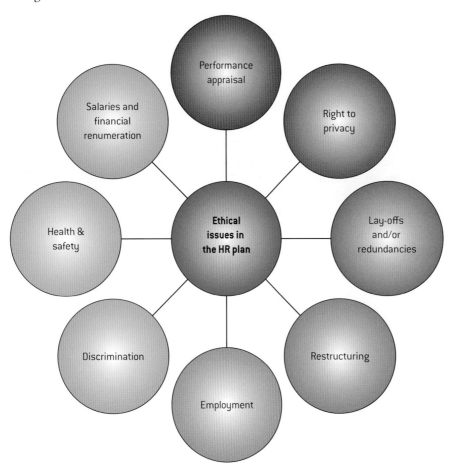

Figure 2.1.6. Ethical issues in the HR plan

One example of how improved information in the contemporary era has intersected with ethical considerations involved executive compensation in the banking sector. Through the news and other forms of ICT, a perception emerged that some executives were awarding themselves excessive salaries and other forms of financial rewards not matched by their performance. Many stakeholders in the banking sector got very angry about this situation. As a result, many changes occurred in financial packages to executives of many banks.

Cultural differences

Cultural differences can also have a significant effect on the HR plan for any business that employs a multicultural workforce. Such businesses would naturally include multinational businesses operating in different countries. Many domestic businesses also employ migrant workers. Lastly, the citizenry of many countries is increasingly diverse, as children of migrant workers grow up as citizens in their parents' adopted country. Businesses that adapt their HR plan to suit a more varied cultural workforce are more likely to be successful with a diverse workforce, especially if their markets are as diverse as their workforce.

In the HR context, Figure 2.1.7 highlights some of the factors that might affect the cultural expectations of a business's employees.

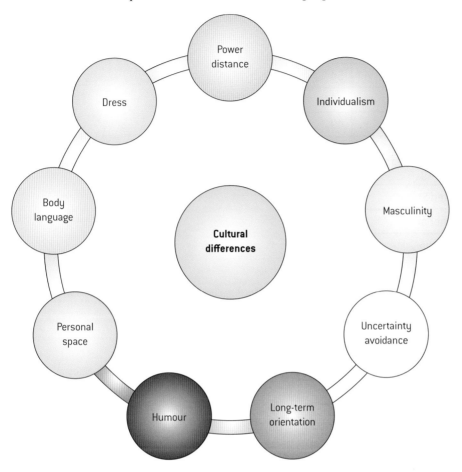

Figure 2.1.7. Cultural differences in the HR plan

The concept of power distance was developed by Geert Hofstede to indicate the acceptance by society of inequality.

According to Hofstede, employees from a society with a high level of power distance would not expect to be consulted and included in decision making. They are more accepting of authority. Employees from countries with a low score would expect the opposite. Some example scores from Hofstede's power distance index (PDI) are shown in Table 2.1.3.

As this one axis of difference shows, people from different parts of the world and from different cultures have different expectations. Training people to work in diverse workforces can reduce potential misunderstanding and friction that can emerge from cultural differences. It can also help businesses to take advantage of one of the most important benefits of a diverse workforce: increased innovation and creativity. Innovation occurs when people see a problem and solve it. When people from different backgrounds are gathered together to solve problems, the diversity of perspectives increases the likelihood that a successful and novel solution will be found.

Table 2.1.3. PDI scores for selected countries

Country	PDI	Country	PDI
Malaysia	104	Spain	57
Panama	95	Pakistan	55
Philippines	94	Japan	54
Mexico	81	Italy	50
China	80	Argentina	49
Egypt	80	South Africa	49
Saudi Arabia	80	Hungary	46
Ecuador	78	United States	40
Indonesia	78	Netherlands	38
India	77	Australia	36
Singapore	74	Costa Rica	35
Brazil	69	Germany	35
France	68	United Kingdom	35
Hong Kong	68	Switzerland	34
Thailand	64	Finland	33
Zambia	64	Norway	31
Chile	63	Sweden	31
Portugal	63	Ireland	28
Uruguay	61	New Zealand	22
Greece	60	Denmark	18
South Korea	60	Israel	13
Iran	58	Austria	11
Taiwan	58		

Source: http://www.clearlycultural.com/geert-hofstede-cultural-dimensions/power-distance-index/

Revision checklist

✓ Human resource planning is a strategy to ensure that employees are selected, used and developed in the most effective way.

✓ Labour turnover is the movement of employees in and out of a business over a given period of time.

✓ Human resource planning can be influences by both internal and external factors.

✓ The most common steps in the process of recruitment are identification, application and selection.

✓ On-the-job training takes place as part of day-to-day work. It is usually led by an experienced employee who can act as a mentor to the trainee.

✓ Off-the-job training allows employees time off work to attend external training.

✓ Cognitive training is not focussed on a particular aspect of the business but helps employees to develop their thinking skills.

✓ Behavioural training helps employees develop interpersonal skills.

✓ Appraisals allow employees and their employers to review performance during a given timeframe. The main methods are: formative, summative, 360 degree and self-appraisal.

✓ Employees may leave a business due to termination, dismissal or redundancy.

✓ As working practices and patterns have changed, businesses have had to adapt their HR strategies.

✓ Outsourcing occurs when organizations contract other organizations to carry out certain functions, allowing them to concentrate on core activities.

✓ Offshoring is when functions are outsourced to another country, perhaps because labour is cheaper or production is quicker.

Practice question

Dome Hospital in Ghana

Today, 13 000 nurses who were trained in sub-Saharan African countries such as Ghana work in Australia, the United Kingdom (UK), Canada and the United States (US). Recently, the UK has saved millions of US$ in the cost of training UK nurses by recruiting Ghanaian ones. The government of Ghana, however, had spent a similar amount in training the same nurses who now work in the UK.

The migration of nurses is driven by workforce shortages in countries such as the US and the UK. Given these demographic changes, *Dome Hospital* in Ghana is experiencing severe difficulty in recruiting locally trained nurses.

Recruitment agencies in Ghana have tried a number of different methods to encourage Ghanaian nurses to come back home. They have used recruitment events and have set up a web site to attract nurses to fill vacancies. They also offer improved pay and working conditions, a free flight home and payment of moving expenses. *Dome Hospital* is considering the introduction of job enrichment schemes to increase non-financial motivation.

Dome Hospital has conducted primary research with Ghanaian nurses working in the UK and has discovered that they have encountered a lack of opportunities for experience and promotion.

Dome Hospital has been approached by *Afua*, a non-governmental organization (NGO), which is concerned about Ghanaian hospitals' ability to retain nurses. *Afua* is determined to help and is calling for changes in international law to reduce the mobility of nurses from developing to developed countries. *Afua* will probably offer *Dome Hospital* advice and guidance on recruitment and retention, but not direct funding. *Afua*, however, has considerable knowledge of other NGOs with financial resources.

[Source: adapted from http://www.medicalnewstoday.com/articles/98545.php, 21 September 2009]

a) Define the term *primary research*.   [*2 marks*]

b) Explain **two** non-financial rewards that *Dome Hospital* could use to encourage Ghanaian nurses to stay in Ghana.   [*6 marks*]

c) Analyse the likely benefits for *Dome Hospital* of *Afua's* support.   [*5 marks*]

d) Discuss the advantages **and** disadvantages of *Dome Hospital's* recruitment strategy.   [*7 marks*]

IB, May 2011

By the end of this chapter, you should be able to:

→ Define the following terminology to facilitate understanding of different types of organizational structures:

- delegation
- span of control
- levels of hierarchy
- chain of command
- bureaucracy
- centralization
- decentralization
- de-layering

→ Describe the following types of organization charts:

- flat/horizontal
- tall/vertical
- hierarchical
- by product
- by function
- by region

→ Explain changes in organizational structures (such as project-based organization, Handy's "Shamrock Organization")

→ Describe how cultural differences and innovation in communication technologies may impact on communication in an organization

Even the most chaotic of start-ups with more than one owner must have some sense of organization, roles, and responsibilities, at least if the business is to survive. When a business succeeds and grows, then it must develop a formal plan clearly outlining the structure of the organization. An organizational structure formally represents the roles and responsibilities of a business, as well as the reporting lines between individuals in the business.

Organizational charts

The most common form of presenting the structure of an organization is through an **organizational chart** – a diagram that outlines the formal roles, responsibilities, and reporting lines. An example is given in Figure 2.2.1.

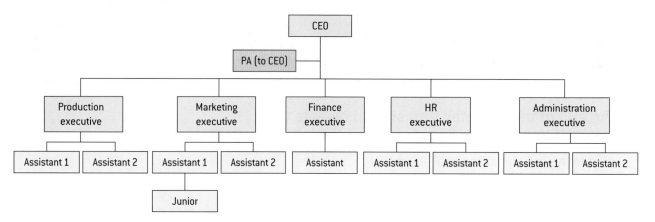

Figure 2.2.1. An organizational chart for a business

Terminology

Figure 2.2.1 shows a typical organizational chart for a business.
A few terms help describe the organizational structure in an
organizational chart:

- **Levels of hierarchy** – this term refers to how many levels of
  responsibility are in a business. Each level indicates a level of
  seniority in the business. In this case, four levels range from most
  senior, the chief executive officer (CEO), to the most junior, the
  "junior" working in the marketing department.

Each level of hierarchy indicates **line managers** – people who have
the authority to make decisions and who bear responsibility for the
outcomes of those decisions.

Note that the personal assistant (PA) to the CEO is not included in
the levels of hierarchy. This employee is known as a **staff manager** –
someone with the authority to communicate a decision made by the
CEO without the responsibility for that decision. Other types of staff
managers could be secretarial and administrative staff.

- **Chain of command** – this is the formal route by which a decision
  must travel through the organization. Traditionally, decisions travel
  from the top of the organization downwards and are therefore
  often referred to as commands. In this case, if the CEO wants to
  communicate with the junior in the marketing department, then
  the message would pass through the chain: from the CEO to the
  marketing executive then to marketing assistant 1, and finally to
  the junior.

Note that the PA is outside the chain of command but of course would
be the one typically to communicate the message.

- **Span of control** – Span of control refers to how many
  subordinates are directly under the authority of a manager and
  whom managers are responsible for. In this case, the span of control
  of the CEO is five. Note the various assistants and the junior are not
  included in the span of control and nor would be any staff manager
  such as the PA.

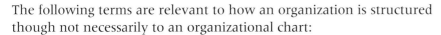

The following terms are relevant to how an organization is structured though not necessarily to an organizational chart:

- **Delegation** – this occurs when a manager gives authority for a particular decision but not the responsibility for the outcome of that decision. That remains with the manager. Delegation is more likely when the span of control is wide. A manager who has a narrow span of control usually keeps a tighter control on all decisions.

- **Centralization** – a high degree of centralization indicates that all major decision making is maintained within a small group of managers operating close to the head of the business. This type of organizational structure is usually associated with businesses that have many levels of hierarchy and narrow spans of control – so that key managers can keep more effective control of their subordinates. Delegation rarely happens in such an organization and leadership is more likely to be autocratic.

- **Decentralization** – this is the opposite of centralization. In a decentralized organization senior managers may maintain core strategic decisions, but other decision-making authority is delegated to middle managers. This type of organizational structure is usually associated with businesses that have fewer levels of hierarchy and wider spans of control – so that key managers allow greater freedoms to their subordinates. Delegation is more likely to happen in such an organization and leadership is more likely to be **democratic**.

- **Bureaucracy** – originally a term referring to non-elected officials serving in government, today this term means any administrative system. In business the term indicates the relative importance of rules and procedures. An organization that is "bureaucratic" has many rules and procedures and set ways of doing things. Personal initiative, flexible thinking and delegation are not expected. This type of organizational structure is usually associated with businesses that are well established and have been operating for many years. As such they are more likely to have many levels of hierarchy. Typically, such organizations require paperwork to get tasks accomplished and have "red tape" to show that procedures have been correctly followed. Delegation is not likely.

- **De-layering** – this occurs when a business reduces the levels of hierarchy by removing layers of management. This business strategy is usually associated with businesses that are well established and have been operating for many years. As such they are more likely to have built up many levels of hierarchy. The concept of de-layering is intended to reduce bureaucracy and increase the decision-making capability of middle managers. De-layering typically reduces costs as the business does not have to employ so many levels of managers.

Types of organizational chart

There are many different types of organizational structure. The most common are described below.

Tall organizational structure

A tall organizational structure is the traditional organizational form of a business and is common in well-established businesses. It has the following features:

- many levels of hierarchy
- narrow spans of control
- centralized decision making
- long chains of command
- autocratic leadership
- limited delegation.

Flat organizational structure

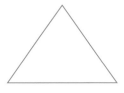

A flat organizational structure is a modification of the more traditional structure and has become popular with businesses set up since the 1960s or with those attempting to reinvent themselves. Flat organizations have the following features:

- few levels of hierarchy
- wider spans of control
- decentralized decision making
- shorter (though more diffuse) chains of command
- democratic leadership
- increased delegation.

Organizational structure by hierarchy

Another way to show an organizational structure is by showing hierarchy. Individuals at the top have more authority than those below them. This is the traditional way of presenting an organizational structure and is shown in Figure 2.2.2.

Organizational structure by function

An organizational structure can be presented by function – indicating what employees do. Employees are grouped by department (see Figure 2.2.3). They will then be organized by seniority.

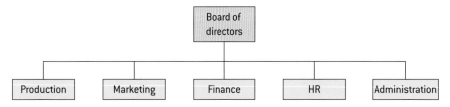

Figure 2.2.3. Organizational structure by function

TOK discussion

Why can organizational charts be misleading?

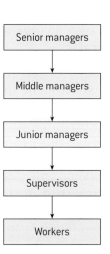

Figure 2.2.2. Organizational structure by hierarchy

Organizational structure by product

Another typical way of presenting an organizational structure is by what the business produces. For example, Figure 2.2.4 shows a publisher organized by what types of books it produces.

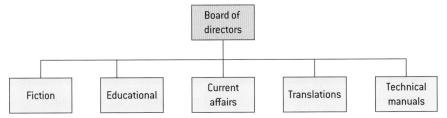

Figure 2.2.4. Organizational structure by product

Organizational structure by region

A further typical way of presenting an organizational structure is according to where the business operations are. Figure 2.2.5 shows an example structure for a multinational corporation.

Figure 2.2.5. Organizational structure by region

Changes in organizational structures

As well as these standard types of organizational structure, some businesses have attempted to adapt their structure to take account of changes in the business environment. Two examples of this are:

- project-based organization
- shamrock organization.

Project-based organization

This structure is designed to be more flexible and responsive to market demands. In a project-based organizational structure, a business's human resources are organized around many projects. Project-based organizations have project managers who run teams of employees focusing on individual projects. After the project is completed, the team is split up and reassembled to begin another project. Typically, many teams operate at once, but they have no need to interact with each other because each team is focused on completing its own project. Each team "borrows" members of different departments to complete the project such as accountants, operations managers and marketing specialists.

This type of business structure is common in construction or IT, where businesses are often under contract to run a number of different projects at the same time. It is also known as a matrix structure as often the organizational teams are shown as a matrix (see Table 2.2.1).

Table 2.2.1. Matrix of organizational teams

	Operations management	Finance	Marketing	HR	Administration
Project 1 manager	4 employees	2 employees	1 employee	1 employee	1 employee
Project 2 manager	3 employees	2 employees	2 employees	2 employees	1 employee
Project 3 manager	3 employees	2 employees	1 employee	1 employee	1 employee
Project 4 manager	3 employees	2 employees	2 employees	2 employees	1 employee
Project 5 manager	3 employees	2 employees	1 employee	1 employee	1 employee

Shamrock organizations

This type of organization is based on a model suggested by the Irish management theorist Charles Handy[1].

He argued that businesses can be more flexible by taking advantage of the changes in the external environment and its impact on workforce planning. His idea uses the national symbol of Ireland – the shamrock – which is a type of clover and has three leaflets on each stem.

The model suggests that businesses can reduce costs, gain competitive advantage and increase response time by trimming their workforce to retain only a **multiskilled core**, which is concerned with the creation or delivery of a product or service. All other supporting, non-central functions are outsourced wherever possible to the **periphery**:

- The first leaf of the shamrock represents the **core managers, technicians and employees** essential to the business.

- The second leaf Handy calls the **contractual fringe**, because non-core activities are subcontracted out to specialist businesses.

- The third leaf consists of a **flexible workforce** made up of part-time, temporary, and seasonal workers.

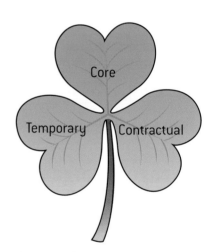

Figure 2.2.6. The shamrock model

Communication

An important element of the organizational structure is how a business communicates with its stakeholders. Communication is integral to how a business functions. Successful businesses communicate effectively with both their internal and their external stakeholders.

---

[1] Handy, C, 1989, *The Age of Unreason*, Harvard Business School, Boston MA, USA

Communication can take two routes: formal communication, which is channelled through the organizational structure, and informal communication outside the "proper" channels. The communication loop in Figure 2.2.7 shows the process by which a message is communicated.

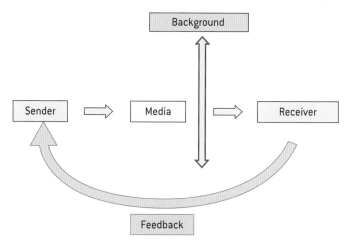

Figure 2.2.7. The process of communicating a message

The sender of the message is said to encode the message by deciding what form the message should take, then the sender chooses what he or she considers the appropriate media through which to deliver the message. The receiver is the person who gets the message and decodes it.

If the message has been delivered successfully, then the sender should receive some form of feedback to show that the message has been understood and acted upon successfully. However, the message may not get through clearly – because of so-called background noise. Background noise can be anything from the wrong choice of media to something outside the control of either party. Background noise can even be due to deliberate interference.

Communication can take several forms using a variety of different media, which increases the likelihood that the message will get across. Sometimes, different methods of communication are combined. The most common forms of communication include the following.

Verbal

This communication relies on the spoken word. Formal verbal communication occurs in:

- interviews
- meetings
- lectures
- presentations
- telephone conversations (recorded).

Informal verbal communication might include:

- face-to-face conversations
- gossiping
- telephone conversations (unrecorded).

Open plan offices like this are becoming more common. What effect could this have on formal and informal communication?

2 Human resource management

Verbal communication can be quick, direct and effective, especially if combined with other forms of communication. It also allows for immediate feedback. However, the message can be misunderstood if the sender uses the wrong language, does not speak clearly, or does not allow for feedback.

Visual

This form of communication relies on sight. Formal visual communication can take place through:

- presentations
- videos
- notice boards
- signs
- sign language
- symbols
- maps.

Informal visual communication might include:

- body language
- gestures.

Visual communication can be effective as it can be permanent, recognizable, and immediate. However, this type of communication can be difficult, especially for those who have limited sight or if the communication is not positioned appropriately. It can also be less effective if the image or picture requires interpretation, as some cultures may respond differently to the same image.

Written

Written communication relies on the written word. Formal written communication is found in:

- reports
- letters
- notices
- bulletins
- forms
- press releases.

Informal written communication might include:

- memos*
- emails*
- texts
- blogs.

Written communication can be effective. Records of the message may be kept, and written communication can be amended or revised. However, written communication can be considered impersonal and often the "tone" of the message may be lost. In addition, feedback is not immediate.

Student workpoint 2.4

Be reflective

What would be the most appropriate method of communication in these situations:

- your manager needs to tell all staff that the office will be closed tomorrow for emergency maintenance

- you want to persuade your managers that your new product idea is a good one. You have done lots of research and have figures and data to back up your arguments

- a new product is launching globally in two months' time. It will be the first of its kind and you want it to sell well

You might choose more than one method for each scenario. Think about what influences your choices so that you can justify your decision.

---

* In some organizations, memos and emails would be considered formal communication.

Revision checklist

✓ Delegation occurs when a manager gives authority for a particular decision to someone else. The manager still holds responsibility for the outcome of that decision.

✓ The span of control is how many employees are directly under the authority of a particular manager.

✓ A level of hierarchy is a level of responsibility within a business.

✓ The chain of command is the formal route though which a decision must travel. Usually, decisions are made at the highest level and are communicated down.

✓ Bureaucarcy refers to rules and procedures within an organization.

✓ Centralization occurs when the majority of decisions are made by a small group of individuals in a senior position within the business.

✓ Decentralization is found where decisions are made by middle managers. Senior management is likely to retain control of key strategic decisions.

✓ De-layering occurs when a business reduces the levels of hierarchy by removing layers of management.

✓ A flat organizational structure has few levels of hierarchy and tends to have a wide span of control. Decision making is decentralized.

✓ A tall structure has many levels of hierarchy and narrow spans of control Leadership tends to be autocratic and decision making in centralized.

✓ Organizational structures can be organized by hierarchy, by function, by product or by region.

Practice question

Casas Carreras

Paolo Carreras, founder of *Casas Carreras* in 1950, had a vision to become the largest retailer in Brazil. He ran his business in a very autocratic fashion. *Casas Carreras* always had a tall organizational structure. Managers were always expected to consult Paolo on major decisions.

Consequently, decision-making was slow and salespeople complained that their ideas were rarely communicated to senior management.

By 2001, *Casas Carreras* had become the largest retail chain store in Brazil. As many of the items *Casas Carreras* sells are large household items (such as stoves, refrigerators and washing machines) a key driver of this growth was credit cards being made available to most Brazilians. However, sales growth at *Casas Carreras* has slowed in recent years.

Paolo died in 2006 and ownership of the business was passed to his daughter Suzanna.

Suzanna believes that the business is too bureaucratic: she is planning to make it more flexible and more responsive to market needs. She believes the managers do not have sufficient incentives and is proposing to offer them greater freedom by creating a flatter organizational structure. They will have greater independence as long as they meet revenue and profit targets. Suzanna proposes that a store manager would have the right to cut prices by as much as 10%, and a regional manager by up to 25%, without consulting executive management.

At present, salespeople are paid a monthly salary of $350. Suzanna wants to reduce the monthly salary to $200 (the minimum wage as required by law) but salespeople will be able to improve their income by earning 5% commission on sales. As a result, the average salesperson could earn $500 per month.

a) Analyse **one** advantage and **one** disadvantage of changing the organization of *Casas Carreras* from a tall to a flatter structure.

[*5 marks*]

b) Evaluate the impact of the proposed payment scheme for salespeople on their job satisfaction, motivation and productivity.

[*7 marks*]

IB, Nov. 2009

2.3 Leadership and management

By the end of this chapter, you should be able to:

→ Outline the key functions of management

→ Describe management versus leadership

→ Discuss the following leadership styles:

- autocratic

- paternalistic

- democratic

- laissez-faire

- situational

→ Explain how ethical considerations and cultural differences may influence leadership and management styles in an organization

Management is made up of the people in organizations charged with making sure tasks, whether large or small, are accomplished. They are not the people who do the work of the organizations. Rather, they are the people with a special set of responsibilities who ensure that the work of the company is performed. For example, in a television manufacturing company, those in management roles are not actually making the televisions on the shop floor. Rather, they have some supervisory role making sure televisions are made, and made according to company standards. Management covers a range. Top management includes the CEO and the various people in charge of each of the major business functions (HR, accounting and finance, marketing, and operations management). Other levels of management exist, all the way down to the floor supervisors. To some degree, even they are part of management.

The key functions of management

In *Administration Industrielle et Générale* (1916), Henri Fayol[1] outlined five major functions of management based upon his experiences as a manager at a large French coal mine:

Planning – managers must plan. They must set strategic objectives, tactical objectives, even operational objectives, all of which have implications throughout the organization.

Organizing – managers must then make sure that the business has sufficient resources to achieve its objectives. This process requires careful organization, as too many resources tie up too much capital; too few mean that the organization's objectives cannot be met.

---

[1] Fayol, Henri, 1916, *Administration Industrielle et Générale*

Commanding – managers must then make sure that all individuals know which duties they are to perform. If necessary, managers must also make sure that employees receive instruction in how they are to perform their tasks.

Coordinating – managers must bring together the various resources to achieve objectives. In many types of business, various different activities are going on, with each activity contributing to the output of the businesses. Managers must coordinate these activities, making sure that each activity is done when and where it is supposed to be.

Controlling – managers control. They have power over a given situation to achieve objectives. They have power to test, or "control for", quality so that processes can be changed if necessary. They also have power to expand or reduce the scale of operations as conditions require.

Fayol argued that these functions were universal and could therefore be applied to any organization.

Management versus leadership

A manager is responsible for planning and overseeing the work of a group, monitoring the group's progress, and ensuring that the plan is put into effect. A manager therefore deals with complexity. Many would argue that a manager is task-oriented; that is, a manager is focused on getting tasks accomplished in a timely manner rather than on leading people. To get tasks accomplished, managers:

- instruct and coordinate people

- help subordinates to resolve problems

- generally have technical expertise and bring that technical expertise to bear (by setting strict schedules, precise instructions)

- have authority by virtue of their position in the organization

- generally like to make the organization function (and therefore tend not to challenge the organization).

In contrast, a leader's role is more emotional since a great leader will have the ability to inspire people to follow him or her voluntarily. A leader spends a great deal of time and energy building relationships and, thus, a leader is relationship-oriented. Leaders:

- motivate and inspire with their personal qualities

- often rely on instincts even in the face of evidence that they are choosing the less safe option

- have vision – and others follow them because of that vision

- often have the vision that the organization should be doing things in a totally different way and inspire the confidence that can lead to systemic change and innovation.

TOK discussion

To what degree is it misleading to claim that a manager and a leader are different? How helpful is this terminology?

Leadership styles

Leadership styles can be categorized as follows.

Autocratic

Autocratic leaders hold on to as much power and decision-making authority as they possibly can. They tend not to consult (or only minimally consult) employees when making a decision. Their orders should be obeyed and employees should welcome the structured environment and the rewards they receive.

This style of leadership is most likely to be used when subordinates are unskilled, not trusted, and their ideas are not valued. It is also more likely in an organization that focuses on results and has to make urgent decisions that depend highly on the manager. Many in the military rely on an autocratic style, which is often accompanied by very detailed instructions and close supervision. In some situations subordinates may expect – and like – to be told what to do since they cannot second-guess.

Autocratic leadership will probably be unsuccessful when employees have the opposite characteristics to those just described. Highly skilled individuals who have experienced democratic systems and who like to do things their own way are unlikely to tolerate an autocratic manager – and may well leave the organization.

A benefit of autocratic leadership is that lines of authority are clear and decisions can be made quickly. What the leader communicates is what is to be followed. Employees come to depend on the guidance but also to execute instructions precisely. The major negative aspect of an autocratic leadership style is that employees tend not to develop the ability to manage on their own or to make decisions. And rarely, in any business, can the leader make all the decisions.

Paternalistic

Paternalistic leadership shares some features with autocratic leadership in that the leader has considerable authority over employees. Unlike autocratic leaders, however, a paternalistic leader views the employees as "family" – a figurative family, certainly, but a family all the same. "Paternalistic" derives from the Latin word for "father", which gets at the heart of the paternalistic style. Paternalistic leaders have great concern for the employees of the business.

Paternalistic leaders are like parents. They provide employees with a sense of safety. The employees come to believe that, no matter what, the business will stand by them. As a result, paternalistic leaders often get total loyalty, even blind trust, from employees. If employees like this style of leadership, they will probably remain at the business for a long time and become totally committed to it, the leader, and the leader's aims.

A positive aspect of paternalistic leadership is that employees take great pride in the organization and do whatever is necessary to make it successful. They take some (figurative) "ownership" of the business, in part because they do not want to let the leader down. However, paternalistic leaders place great importance on loyalty, which may mean that they do not have a fully objective, critical eye when evaluating employees' performance. Thus, paternalistic leaders may come across as "playing favourites" (and they may actually play favourites). Further, employees, knowing they are part of a "family", may at times take advantage of the leader and his or her loyalty to them.

Democratic

The democratic manager involves employees in decision making and informs them about issues that affect them. Democratic leadership can occur across a spectrum. At one end is the truly democratic leader. This type of leader facilitates the democratic process and honours it as much as possible and practical. Truly democratic leadership is rare in business or any organization, as ultimately one role of a leader is to make decisions. Thus, a more common type of democratic leader is one who consults employees regularly. However, as a practical matter and because the leader is ultimately responsible for the decisions of the team, the leader will have the final say.

Democratic leadership is probably the most popular style among employees, possibly because for most people the word "democracy" has positive emotional connotations. They also like being involved in the decision-making process, especially when the decisions have a major impact on them. The democratic leader can produce results in terms of quantity, since many employees like the trust, cooperation, and sense of belonging that go with it. Employees feel as though they have a voice.

The democratic leadership style may not always work out. It is likely to be most effective when used with skilled, free-thinking, and experienced subordinates who enjoy the relationships and chaos that can result from belonging to a highly effective team. Nevertheless, the democratic process may slow down decision making and may prove too costly. The style also requires a positive "chemistry" in the team. If this characteristic is absent, no amount of democracy can make the style work.

Laissez-faire

Laissez-faire means "to leave alone". In this leadership style the manager gives employees considerable freedom in how they do their work. Employees can set their own goals, make their own decisions, and resolve problems as they see fit.

This management style may be appropriate when employees can be trusted to do their job because they are motivated, skilled, and educated. Universities tend to be "laissez-faire", as university lecturers, researchers and professors, who are generally world experts in their field, resist being told what to do. In other professions, as well, individual practitioners demand considerable freedom. It may be appropriate when working with a culture based around the individual and where people can work successfully on their own.

The benefit of a laissez-faire style is that many employees enjoy the freedom it provides and it can foster creativity and innovations. However, the individual interests of the employees may diverge too far from the focus of the organization, and the organization can veer away from its vision and aims. From an employee's perspective, a laissez-faire leadership style may be unnerving, as this type of leader does not give much guidance and may not provide much feedback. Precise instructions and a watchful eye can give comfort to employees, whereas a laissez-faire style requires confident and disciplined employees. In instances where a leader adopts a laissez-faire style and the employees are not disposed to be successful under it, the results can be disastrous.

Situational

Situational leadership rests on the notion that different situations require different styles of leadership. Thus, no one style of leadership would ever be deemed "the best". Sometimes, the nature of the employees (unskilled workers versus highly trained professionals) will determine which leadership style fits the situation. At other times, the nature of the circumstances will determine the most appropriate style. In emergency situations, even highly democratic leaders will often become autocratic: to lead the employees and the organization quickly and efficiently through the emergency. Sometimes, in situations where the outcome of the decision is not altogether consequential for the organization as a whole but may influence employee morale, even autocratic leaders may allow democracy: let the employees decide.

The benefit of situational leadership is that leaders match their style to the circumstances at hand. On the other hand, a leader may too frequently change styles or may change styles when the circumstances of the situation determining the switch are not clear to employees. In either of these scenarios, the leader may come across as unpredictable or arbitrary, which may demotivate employees.

In summary, the style of leadership is likely to be influenced by:

- the subordinates (subordinates' skills, age, education, expectations, and motivation)

- the decision (whether urgent, important, or consequential)

- the leader (the leader's character, values, experience, and expectations)

- the environment (whether creative, standardized, repressive, democratic, or compliant).

Ethical considerations and cultural differences

Now let's look at how ethical considerations and cultural differences may influence leadership and management styles in an organization.

Ethical considerations

Ethical considerations can influence both leadership styles and management styles, though in somewhat different ways. Leaders, as opposed to managers, focus on "doing the right thing" with respect to their people, whereas managers tend to do the right thing with respect to their organizations.

Student workpoint 2.5

Be reflective

Draw a table showing the advantages and disadvantages of the five leadership styles discussed here.

2 Human resource management

Leaders are focused on people. As a result, they focus on building relationships and on inspiring employees. To accomplish these objectives, leaders have to do more than merely say that they care about "their people". They must actually demonstrate that care when circumstances require.

Leaders guide organizations toward ethical ends. In the military, for example, leaders are those who risk their own lives to protect the lives of their subordinates. In business, leaders are willing, if necessary, to take the blame for bad outcomes to the organization if it means serving their employees by protecting them from excessive or unwarranted criticism. A leader might, for example, intervene when a manager wants to sack a young employee who made an error of judgment on the grounds that the employee was inexperienced. The leader might argue that the right thing to do is to give the employee a second chance. In this instance, the leader is taking a personal risk – responsibility not only for the employee's error of judgment but, arguably, for any future errors of judgment the employee might make. Another example of ethical considerations is when a leader adopts ethical objectives for the organization, even when some stakeholders object – typically because ethical objectives have a financial cost. So central is ethical behaviour to leadership that many would argue that an unethical leader is not a leader at all.

On the issue of ethical considerations, managers are often criticized. They are criticized as being bureaucratic and "rule followers" and for putting their own positions and rewards ahead of their employees'. Most of the time, this criticism of managers is somewhat unfair. Managers, in contrast to leaders, see their ethical obligations more to the organization or business than to the employees. The manager supervising a young employee who has made a major error in judgment sees the employee as a liability to the business. From this perspective, the manager believes that the right thing to do is to sack the employee to prevent further errors in judgment, which could cost the business money. However, if a manager is too hasty in sacking an employee or is not giving the individual due process and fair consideration, the manager deserves the type of criticism mentioned above. If, to protect themselves from criticism, managers are too hasty in sacking an employee, they are not focusing on the interests of their organization but rather on their own career.

In summary, most leaders and managers are influenced by ethical considerations. With leaders, ethical considerations are centred on people, whereas with managers ethical considerations are centred on the organization. When people in these roles behave unethically, whether they are leaders or managers, they really are not leading people or managing an organization. They are, unethically, putting their own interests ahead of others'.

INNOVATION

'If a manager is innovative, the business will be innovative'

How true do you think this statement is? Does an innovative management style necessarily mean that the business will produce innovative goods and services?

Student workpoint 2.6

Be a thinker

Define the following leadership styles:

- Autocratic
- Paternalistic
- Democratic
- Laissez-faire
- Situational

Cultural differences

Cultural differences, too, can influence leadership and management. The most famous treatment of this concept is the work of Geert Hofstede (see also Unit 2.1), who over his business and academic career developed and refined his cultural dimensions theory. According to Hofstede, cultural influences relevant to business have five dimensions:

- power distance
- individualism
- uncertainty avoidance
- masculinity
- long-term orientation.

Different cultures value individualism (Anglo-American cultures), for example, whereas others (such as the Japanese culture) value group cohesion. The style of leadership or management that an individual adopts will be influenced by the culture from which they originate and should also be influenced by the cultures of the people they lead or manage. Employees from cultures with great power distance prefer (and arguably function better, at least initially) in organizations with autocratic leaders. On the other hand, employees from countries or cultures with low power distance might resent an autocratic leader and would probably perform better under democratic leadership.

Revision checklist

✓ The key functions of management are to plan, to organize, to command, to coordinate and to control.

✓ A manager's role is to plan and oversee the work of a group. In contrast, a leader's role is to motivate and inspire.

✓ Autocratic leaders hold onto as much power as they can. They make all decisions and their instructions should be obeyed.

✓ Paternalistic leaders also have a lot of decision-making power. They have concern for their employees and instil trust and loyalty.

✓ A laissez-fiare leadership style allows employees much freedom. Employees can set their own goals and manage problems as they see fit.

✓ A democratic leader will involve employees in decision making and inform them of issues which will affect them.

Practice question

Rox and Inclusive Music (IM)

Rox was a music band managed by Michel Mbappe. The band enjoyed considerable commercial success thanks to Michel's autocratic leadership style. He personally made all decisions. Rox had given generously to local schools and other non-profit organizations. The band received many awards for their acts of corporate social responsibility. Their last CD "Action Not Words" had brought them considerable fame.

In June 2010, Michel was asked to help finance the start-up of a new non-profit music school called "Inclusive Music" (*IM*). *IM's* aim was to support young musicians from low income families. At first, Michel was very enthusiastic and prepared a business plan. Unfortunately, he realized that Rox could not afford to finance *IM* fully. External sources of finance other than contributions from Rox would be needed for *IM* to grow. Until then *IM* would only have a limited budget for marketing and market research.

In June 2011, *IM* opened with the mission statement "Action not words". To support its mission, it offered free lessons and allowed students to borrow musical instruments. Michel asked a popular former singer, Louis Marsaud, to be the school's director. Louis adopted a laissez-faire leadership style, hoping it would allow creativity among students. Initial student attendance was lower than expected and quickly worsened. Within three months, many instruments had gone missing and many students were no longer attending music lessons.

IM's finances were deteriorating, and Louis could not attract external sources of finance.

Michel took action and organized a concert by Rox to promote *IM*. He also examined *IM's* accounts and discovered a significant liquidity problem. Without consulting anyone, he dismissed Louis. In the music media, Michel received much criticism for dismissing Louis. Journalists argued that the two main problems were *IM's* vague mission statement and poor marketing. However, Michel aimed to ensure that *IM* became sustainable in the long term.

a) Define the term *corporate social responsibility*. [*2 marks*]

b) Identify **two** possible causes of a liquidity problem. [*2 marks*]

c) Explain how the following may have contributed to *IM's* financial problems:

   (i) its mission statement. [*3 marks*]

   (ii) its limited marketing budget. [*3 marks*]

d) Analyse the appropriateness of Michel's autocratic leadership style, for the running of an organization such as *IM*. [*6 marks*]

e) Discuss **two** possible medium- to long-term external sources of finance that *IM* could use to help solve its financial problems.

  [*9 marks*]

IB, Nov. 2012

2.4 Motivation

By the end of this chapter, you should be able to:

→ Describe the following motivation theories:

- Taylor
- Maslow
- Herzberg (motivation –hygiene theory)
- Adams (equity theory)
- Pink

→ Explain the following types of financial rewards:

- salary
- wages (time and piece rates)
- commission
- profit-related pay
- performance-related pay (PRP)
- employee share ownership schemes
- fringe payments (perks)

→ Define the following types of non-financial rewards:

- job enrichment
- job rotation
- job enlargement
- empowerment
- purpose/the opportunity to make a difference
- teamwork

→ Discuss how financial and non-financial rewards may affect job satisfaction, motivation and productivity in different cultures

Intrinsic and extrinsic motivation

In this unit we will be studying the factors that influence a person to work. If managers can motivate employees, it is more likely that those managers will achieve their goals. All the writers and researchers you will be reading about in this unit will be referring to intrinsic and extrinsic motivators.

Intrinsic motivation occurs when someone gets satisfaction from an activity itself without threats or rewards from outside. Employees are more likely to be intrinsically motivated if they are in the following work situations:

- They can see that their success is a result of something they have done; if they put in more work they will achieve more positive outcomes.

- They have some control over their results – they are given a degree of freedom.
- They are interested in the work they are doing.

Rewards are extrinsic motivators – motivators that come from outside the individual. In the workplace, pay is an obvious example. Extrinsic motivators provide satisfaction that the job itself may not provide and may compensate workers for the "pain" or dissatisfaction that they experience at work.

Frederick Winslow Taylor

Taylor was a mechanical engineer who observed the phenomenal contribution science had made to agriculture and the Industrial Revolution and he wanted to apply scientific methods to management to achieve similar results. He published research between 1894 and 1912 and is often referred to as the founder of scientific management, since his ideas on management attempted to apply scientific methods of measurement under controlled circumstances to maximize output.

Taylor believed that standardization of work methods and enforced adoption of the best ways of working were the ways to ensure that output would be maximized in the shortest possible time. It is worth recalling that Taylor's ideas were adopted when many poorly educated Americans were leaving agriculture and starting to work in factories. In this situation it is perhaps understandable that managers may have decided to take a more hands-on style in decision making. The introduction of Taylor's ideas and methods was often resented by workers and provoked numerous strikes.

Taylor is perhaps most famous for his time-and-motion study. This involved breaking a job down into its component parts and measuring how long it took to perform each task. One of his most famous studies involved shovels, but we'll take a different example. If you watch how a hamburger is prepared in a large and busy fast-food restaurant, then you will get some idea of the huge benefits that can arise if each "bit" of the system is managed precisely. The burger is cooked at a given temperature, for a precise amount of time on each side. The fries are also cooked at a given temperature for a precise amount of time. Each worker will have a specific role and will not move far from his or her position to minimize time wasted in movement. The result of all this is consistent fast food, cooked quickly and efficiently at low cost. Skill has been largely removed from the system, so employees can be employed at low cost and with little training.

Abraham Maslow

Maslow is most famous for proposing a hierarchy of human needs to explain motivation. He argued that people have a number of needs and arranged these in terms of their importance.

Key terms

Intrinsic motivation

motivation which comes from the satisfaction of carrying out a particular activity

Extrinsic motivation

motivation derived from external factors, such a money

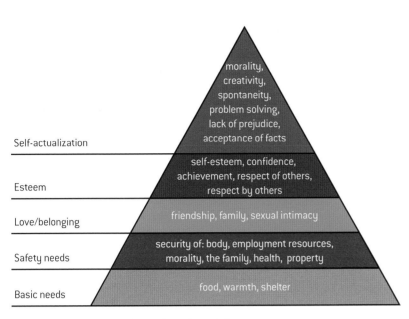

Figure 2.4.1. Maslow's hierarchy of needs[1]

The basic needs at the bottom of the diagram are most important and an individual will suffer anxiety if they are not met. The first four levels are considered basic needs. Once these needs are met, they go away or no longer cause anxiety.

The remaining needs are growth needs. Once these needs are initially fulfilled, they do not go away. In fact, the individual will strive to find new ways to satisfy these needs. These needs involve people fulfilling their potential; being the best they can be in as many areas as possible.

One of the key issues for managers is that, once a need is satisfied, providing more of the same will not motivate a worker. So in Taylor's factories, workers will have initially been motivated by the need for food, warmth, and shelter, but the failure of his factories to satisfy higher-level needs may explain why his methods often resulted in labour unrest.

Frederick Herzberg

Herzberg developed a two-factor theory of motivation based on hygiene needs and motivational needs.[2] Hygiene needs are those factors that provide dissatisfaction at work if they are not attended to. At school you will probably be demotivated if the classrooms are not clean, or if the heating is not working properly. If these things are satisfactory, however, it is unlikely to lead to motivation. Hygiene factors are the things that are necessary for you to get started, but they don't drive you to succeed.

Motivators are the things that get you working because you get some intrinsic reward from them. For example, if you play in a football team

[1] "Hierarchy of needs", developed 1943–54 and published in Maslow, Abraham, 1954, *Motivation and Personality*, Harper & Row, New York

[2] Herzberg, Frederick I, 1959, *The Motivation to Work*, Wiley and Sons, New York

you will probably be motivated by the successes you have notched up and the recognition you get for playing as part of the team.

Herzberg's "hygiene" needs are:

- company policy and administration
- relationship with supervisor
- work conditions
- salary
- company car
- status
- security
- relationship with subordinates
- personal life.

Herzberg's research identified that true motivators were other completely different factors:

- achievement
- recognition
- the work itself
- responsibility
- advancement.

He argued that people have a number of needs and arranged these in order of their importance.

John Adams

Another theorist, John Adams developed a theory called the equity theory based upon the concepts of "inputs", "outputs", and "equity".[3] His theory is that employees will be motivated when they perceive that a balance, or equity, exists between their inputs into the business and their outputs from it.

Inputs are those affective and cognitive qualities that an employee brings to a business or organization. Inputs include:

- ability
- adaptability
- attitude
- dedication
- determination
- effort
- flexibility
- hard work
- knowledge
- loyalty
- personal sacrifice
- skill
- support from co-workers and colleagues
- time
- tolerance
- trust in superiors.

Outputs are what an employee receives from working at the organization. Outputs can be negative and thus in some sense subtract from the positive

---

3 Adams, John S, 1965, "Inequity in social change", *Advanced Experimental Social Psychology*, 62: pp. 335–43

outcomes (though Adams did not believe that inputs and outputs could be quantified). Typically, outputs are positive and include:

- fringe benefits
- job security
- praise
- recognition
- reputation
- responsibility
- reward
- salary
- sense of achievement
- stimuli
- thanks.

When employees believe that their outputs are greater than their inputs, they will be motivated. If, however, employees are giving more (inputs) to an organization than they receive (outputs), they will be demotivated. Employees want some degree of equity between what they give to the organization and what they receive. Motivation, according to this theory, is based upon a perception of fairness.

The sense of fairness is not restricted solely by the employee's relationship to the organization. Employees also compare their "ratio" of inputs to outputs and compare it to other employees. If employee A perceives that employee B has a more favorable input-to-output ratio, employee A will suffer a loss of motivation.

Daniel Pink

Pink argued that older motivational models developed in the early 1900s and largely stemming from the premises of Taylor's scientific management are flawed.[4]

These older motivational theories assumed that work was mostly a series of simple, uninteresting tasks. From this perspective, the best way to get people to work was to give them rewards and carefully monitor their performance. These types of theories assume that humans largely respond to rewards and punishments. A manager can increase productivity either by offering more rewards (pay, benefits, etc.) or increasing punishments for failure to perform.

According to Pink, work today has changed. Rewards and punishments may have motivated employees in the industrial era of the early 20th century, when tasks were routine, unchallenging, and highly controlled. Today, however, employees' tasks are more complex and challenging, and require creativity and problem-solving skills. In this context, the old reward and control system is not merely ineffective; it may actually have negative results, for both the employees and for the business. Here is why: promises of rewards or the threats of punishment actually narrow the focus and intellectual range of employees (employees focus on the reward rather than solving the problem), which diminishes their capacity to innovate or be creative. Thus, older systems of motivation stemming from the ideas of Taylor actually are ineffective for the business. Workers have less capacity to accomplish the complex tasks they face. These systems are also bad for employees. With less capacity to accomplish tasks and do their jobs, workers lose motivation and get less satisfaction from their work.

[4] Pink, Daniel H, 2009, *Drive: The Surprising Truth About What Motivates Us*, Riverhead Books (Penguin USA), New York

Pink argues that businesses have to tap into employees' intrinsic motivation, which psychologist Harry F. Harlow called the "third drive". The first drive of humans is biological: their requirement to satisfy hunger, thirst, sex, and other biological needs. The second drive is the response to rewards and punishments. The third drive is intrinsic motivation, which occurs when someone gets satisfaction from an activity itself without threats or rewards from outside. Pink proposes that businesses should adopt a revised approach to motivation that fits more closely with post-industrial jobs and businesses: self-determination theory (SDT). According to SDT, human beings want to be autonomous, to achieve self-determination, and to be "connected" to other people and the world at large. When people are liberated to pursue these ends, they can accomplish more and have more rewarding lives. Businesses should create settings that allow for the following:

- **Autonomy** – an environment that permits employees to shape their own lives. As much as possible, businesses should give employees freedom in when they work (time), how they do their jobs (technique), who they work with (team), and what they do (task).

- **Mastery** – opportunities that allow employees to learn, innovate, and create new things. Employees will achieve mastery when they are given tasks that matter to them and are neither too easy nor too difficult. Easy tasks bore employees; tasks beyond employees' capabilities cause excessive anxiety. Tasks fostering mastery are those that allow employees to "stretch" themselves and develop their skill set further.

- **Purpose** – a sense that their work betters their own lives and the world. Employees must know and understand the organization's purposes (other than profit) and how each person contributes to these purposes. To Pink, businesses should emphasize "purpose" goals as much as profit goals as reaching profit goals has no positive impact on a person's well-being (it may actually have a negative impact).

TOK discussion

Business and psychological studies of motivation assume that a "science" to understanding human motivation is possible. To what degree, at both an individual and group level, is the science of motivation misleading?

Case study

Happiness at work

A happy working environment is a win-win situation. Research shows that happy people are healthier, more productive, have more ideas, are more likely to go beyond the responsibilities of their job, and are less likely to leave or be off sick. Happiness is contagious so, if your team is happy – you and others around them are more likely to be happy too.

As a manager or leader you can influence the happiness of those in your team. This doesn't mean that work can't be serious, or that you need to be telling jokes constantly. There is a lot more to happiness at work than that.

Recent research is suggesting more and more ways that we can increase happiness at work.

Changing an organization's culture or incentive system can be complicated and take a long time, and may not always be possible if you are not near the top of the hierarchy, but here are some ideas for things that will make a difference:

- make an effort to understand what makes your employees happy

- focus on people's strengths

- give feedback which encourages growth and improvement

- acknowledge and celebrate successes in meetings – don't just focus on problems

- give your employees the opportunity to shape their own jobs

adapted from www.actionforhappiness.org

Exam-style questions

Define the terms 'motivation' and 'hierarchy' [4 marks]

Outline the benefits of using non-financial rewards to motivate employees. [4 marks]

Motivation in practice

Many organizations devise complex payment systems in an effort
to reward and motivate their employees. Unfortunately, no perfect
payment systems exists. Table 2.4.1 identifies some of the major issues of
financial rewards that need to be considered.

Table 2.4.1. Financial rewards – main issues

Type of financial reward	How it is paid	Motivation factors	Disadvantages
Salary	Employees are paid a sum of money per month.	The main motivator is likely to be the security of receiving a regular income.	The employer is typically relying on the professionalism of the staff to provide the quality and quantity expected.
Wages (time rates)	Employees are paid an hourly rate, or for a number of hours per week. It is possible that overtime rates of pay are used too.	The main motivator is likely to be the security of receiving a regular income and the opportunity to receive overtime pay.	It is possible that employees will work slowly since their pay is not based on output. If overtime rates apply then employees could benefit financially from ensuring that the work is extended to cover time over the usual hours of the working day.
Wages (piece rates)	Employees are paid for each unit (or batch) produced.	The main motivator is likely to be the fact that increased output will bring a measurable benefit.	This might involve tedious and repetitive work and employees may not have control of their results if they rely on others, for example to supply materials. Employees may work quickly to get as much money as possible. It may be that a system of checks will have to be put in place to ensure that quality standards have been met. There may be an emphasis on quantity rather than quality.
Commission	Employees are paid by results, for example, a flat fee or a percentage for each item sold.	The main motivator is likely to be the fact that employees will be rewarded by results.	Employees may not have control over results (and this income). For example, during a recession sales commission will fall in many industries. Employees may be tempted to sell products that are not in the best interests of the customer or business and this could create problems for the organization. For example, a bank employee who sells a mortgage to a customer will receive the commission, but the bank may suffer financially if the customer subsequently defaults on the loan.
Profit-related pay	The amount an employee receives is linked to the amount of profit the business makes.	Sharing the financial rewards of a business may encourage a sense of belonging and a desire to contribute to its success.	Productivity may be a consequence of the profitability of the business rather than the cause. If profits fall then employees could experience a demoralizing loss through no fault of their own.

Type of financial reward	How it is paid	Motivation factors	Disadvantages
Performance-related pay (PRP)	PRP is usually a bonus paid in addition to the employee's ordinary compensation.	PRP is ordinarily used with those employees whose productivity or output cannot be measured precisely. However, the pay is based upon pre-established performance targets. Ordinarily, in a PRP system, employees receive a salary and are expected to reach certain targets. Employees exceeding the targets are then paid an additional amount. The assumption is that employees will be motivated by the opportunity to make extra money by performing better than the targets.	As long as the tasks are repetitive tasks that involve physical skills, PRP can enhance performance. However, when cognitive tasks are involved, PRP may actually reduce productivity. In addition, PRP can cause divisions in a business if the evaluation of employees' performance is based upon subjective factors.
Employee share-ownership schemes	These come in two forms. The first is as some type of bonus; however, the payment is shares in the business rather than cash. The second is some type of employee savings plan whereby employees are allowed to purchase shares through a payroll deduction (typically a fixed amount per pay period) without having to pay brokerage fees. Some employers will also offer a "match" programme (for example, for every $1 the employee invests in shares the company will give (or "match") the employee's contribution with $0.50.)	Employee share schemes, when offered as a bonus, can motivate in the same ways that other types of bonuses do. Even when an employee share-ownership scheme is simply a savings plan, a benefit is that employees become partial owners of the business, which is thought to provide an incentive for employees to work harder (as they now have a "stake" in the business.)	When offered as a bonus, the basis for awarding the bonus must be clear and, ideally, measurable to avoid accusations of "favouritism" in granting them. If employees have all their savings in a company match plan, both their salaries and their savings are tied to the viability of the business.

Type of financial reward	How it is paid	Motivation factors	Disadvantages
Fringe payments (perks)	Fringe payments, or perks, are the many types of extras that businesses offer their employees. They can include medical insurance, a car, and private pension plans, among other forms of payment. They often include perks related to the nature of the business (a hotel chain may offer discounted rates at its hotels to employees).	Employees like fringe benefits, as often they have substantial value. While employees may have to claim some fringe benefits for tax purposes, many do not have to be claimed. This provides the employee with an additional benefit: for the business to pay for fringe benefits on a pre-tax basis is much cheaper than for employees to pay for these items with after-tax salary. Thus, the business is able to give more value to employees than if it paid them the equivalent amount in additional salary.	If fringe benefits are not given equally to all employees or on a clear, fair basis, division among the staff can result. In addition, employees can come to expect certain fringe benefits and may become angry if some perks are taken away.

Table 2.4.2 gives examples of types of non-financial reward.

Table 2.4.2. Non-financial rewards – main issues

Type of non-financial reward	Main features	Motivation factors	Disadvantages
Job enrichment	Job enrichment makes an employee's job "richer", or more meaningful and rewarding, by allowing employees to use the full range of their abilities. Typically, job enrichment involves supervising employees less and making the responsibilities of the position more challenging. Often enrichment will mean that an employee does the entirety of a production process to have a greater sense of ownership and responsibility in what they produce.	Employees typically prefer to have responsibilities that are challenging. Employees who are more satisfied are typically more motivated to work hard.	Job enrichment cannot be applied in all work situations, either because of the type of work involved or because of the calibre of the workers.
Job rotation	Job rotation involves having an individual employee rotated through different divisions in a business over a period of time. It is often used with young employees as a form of training but can be used at many different stages of a career.	Job rotation benefits companies as it gives them employees who have a better sense of the "big picture" of the business. For employees, rotation provides additional training and the acquisition of new skills and knowledge, which can lead to new opportunities with the business (or with other organizations).	Job rotation means employees go through periodic productivity dips as they begin in a new division and must go through a training phase before they understand fully the new position.

Type of non-financial reward	Main features	Motivation factors	Disadvantages
Job enlargement	Job enlargement may include job rotation or job enrichment. It may involve giving employees more tasks to do, sometimes because of a shortage of staff.	In general, employees prefer some variation in the tasks they must do.	If job enlargement is nothing more than giving employees additional duties, it may increase employee dissatisfaction.
Empowerment	Empowerment involves giving individuals access to resources and information to do their jobs and the power to make decisions. In an employment context, empowerment means giving employees considerable control over how their jobs should be done.	Empowered employees generally believe that they can be instrumental in changing things and learning new skills so that they can be part of the change process. Employees find this rewarding.	Businesses run some risk that the empowered employees will not be able to manage the responsibility they have been given. Employees may make decisions that are not fully productive or cost the business unnecessarily.
Purpose or opportunity to make a difference	Purpose or opportunity to make a difference in the world refers to the ability of businesses or other organizations to connect employees to the aims of the organization other than profit. Non-profit organizations have this advantage, as they typically exist to meet some social or environmental need. Many for-profit businesses today, however, have adopted the other-than-profit aims to their objectives.	Many individuals want to do more than merely make money. They want to know that they are making a difference in the world and are connected to purposes larger than themselves or their organization. People tend to find these purposes intrinsically motivating.	If for-profit organizations overemphasize social or environmental aims, employees may lose focus on the profit-making objectives.
Teamwork	Teamwork involves working cooperatively with a group of people to achieve a goal.	The success of teams can be crucial to organizations' performance, so an organization will strive to have high-performance teams. Individuals tend to be energized by working in teams, which creates a sense of group cohesion and common purpose.	When successful, teamwork can have great yields for organizations. However, team failures can amplify dissatisfaction and, thus, weaken employees' productivity.

All of the above financial and non-financial rewards have differing degrees of effectiveness in different countries and cultures. In general, in developing countries, many people are unaccustomed to making significant incomes. Work is a contemporary version of traditional industrial production: a series of simple, uninteresting tasks. Further, many traditional forms of social cohesion (family, village, labour association, etc.) remain strong. In these contexts, financial rewards tend to be important. Wages based upon piece rates can be especially motivating.

In developed countries, circumstances have changed significantly in the last 50 years. Individuals are accustomed (and in many developed countries virtually guaranteed) high standards of living. Economies have largely shifted to the tertiary and quaternary sectors, where work tasks tend to be more complex and require cognitive processes. Finally, traditional forms of social cohesion have weakened. In these contexts, people are increasingly interested in non-financial rewards. Personally satisfying work, teamwork and making a difference in the world are of considerable importance to workers.

Generalizations such as the above can be misleading. In all economies, some people are mostly interested in making money, while others are mostly interested in non-financial objectives.

Revision checklist

✓ Frederick Winslow Taylor believed that the standardization of working practices and enforced adoption of the most effecient ways of working were the key to ensuring maximum output in the shortest time.

✓ Abraham Maslow argued that human needs can be categorized in levels of importance. The more needs an employer can satisfy, the more motivated a worker will be.

✓ Frederick Herzberg distinguished between 'hygeine needs' and 'motivational needs'. Motivational needs are the ones which truly motivate workers.

✓ John Adams' equity theory suggests that employees will be most motivated when they can see a balance between what the but into a business and what they get out of it.

✓ Daniel Pink suggests that the workplace has changed dramatically since earlier observers developed their theories. Pink argues that businesses must nurture their employee's in-built motivation.

✓ Financial rewards include salary, time and piece rate wages, commission, profit-related pay, performance related pay, share ownership schemes and fringe payments.

✓ Non-financial rewards include job enrichment, job rotation, job enlargement, empowerment, purpose, and teamwork.

Practice question

Fish Packaging in Reykjavik

The firm *Fish Packaging Ltd* owns a fish packaging plant in Reykjavik, Iceland, and sells frozen fish to the domestic market. Workers in the plant are paid $10 per hour to pack fish into boxes.

They are expected to pack approximately 13 kg per hour. When local fishing boats do not go out fishing, there is nothing to pack. When this happens the workers stay at home and are still paid $4 per hour.

The workers are concerned about a number of issues including:

- poor weather has led to local fishing boats fishing less, so workers are staying home more often

- an autocratic leadership style

- a lack of involvement in day-to-day decision making

- a shortage of protective clothing

- insufficient rest breaks during the working day

Management complains that workers seldom exceed the target of 13 kg per hour and are also concerned about the possible imposition of fishing quotas by governments. Furthermore, the fish packaging industry has been badly hit by the competition of Russian factory ships. Management feels it has to make some changes and is considering the introduction of a piece rate payment system.

a) (i) Describe the difference between time rate and piece rate payment systems. [*2 marks*]

    (ii) Explain **two** disadvantages and **one** advantage of introducing a piece rate payment system at *Fish Packaging Ltd*. [*6 marks*]

b) Explain **two** external factors that could influence *Fish Packaging Ltd*. [*4 marks*]

c) Using appropriate motivation theory, evaluate possible changes the management of *Fish Packaging Ltd* could introduce to improve the motivation of the work force. [*8 marks*]

IB, May 2008

2.5 Organizational and corporate cultures (HL only)

By the end of this chapter, you should be able to:

→ Define the meaning of organizational culture

→ Outline elements of organizational culture

→ Outline types of organizational culture

→ Discuss the reasons for, and consequences of, cultural clashes within organizations when they grow, merge and when leadership styles change

→ Explain how individuals influence organizational culture and how organizational culture influences individuals

The term organizational culture, or corporate culture, refers to the attitudes, experiences, beliefs, and values of an organization. These are generally considered the elements of corporate culture. The ways that individuals in an organization dress, or treat each other and those outside the organization often reflect the culture of the organization. If an individual joins an organization and does not share its values and beliefs, it is highly likely that person will not stay there long. This situation is described as a culture clash.

Managers may try to influence the culture of an organization. Doing so, however, is difficult, especially at established and old institutions with low staff turnover (institutions with a strong corporate culture). Nonetheless, setting the values and the way things get done is a role of managers. New managers will spell out their beliefs and values to staff and expect staff to behave in a manner that reflects the beliefs managers have set. In an organization, different cultural norms exist in different departments. The factors that will influence these will be the head of department, the members of the team, the senior managers, the culture of the country in which the organization is operating and the culture of the nationality of the department members.

Types of organizational culture

Charles Handy

Handy introduced a highly memorable way of viewing organizational culture when he described four distinct organizational cultures – power culture, role culture, task culture and person culture.

Power culture

A power culture exists when a few individuals retain the essential power. Control comes from these individuals and spreads out across the organization. Power cultures have few rules and procedures. People are usually judged by their results rather than how those results are achieved, since ends are more important than means. Swift decision making can result, but the decisions may not be in the long-term interests of the organization. The collapses of the US energy-trading giant Enron and the family-owned merchant bank Barings Bank are attributed to dominant power cultures. Family businesses and merchant banks often have power cultures.

Handy represented a power culture as a spider's web. The power comes from the spider; a web with no spider has no strength. The spider can reward or punish. In a power culture, individuals who do not fit in are unlikely to work there for long.

Role culture

In a role culture, employees have clearly defined roles and operate in a highly controlled and precise organizational structure. These organizations are usually tall hierarchical bureaucracies with a long chain of command. Power stems from a person's position. Position and a "rule book" (corporate procedures) play dominant roles in decision making, which is often slow and detailed. In role cultures, people avoid taking risks. Civil services, military organizations, and nationalized industries often have role cultures.

Handy uses the symbol of a temple or building to describe a role culture. Temples or buildings are old and exist in stable environments. The oldest buildings in a town often house organizations with role cultures – government offices and the main post office are often the oldest buildings in town.

Task culture

The task culture describes a situation when short-term teams address specific problems. Power within a task culture shifts from person to person, since different people with different skills can lead the team at different times. Many people like the idea of a task culture because they like to work in a rapidly changing environment. A strong team spirit with a great deal of emotional energy can emerge. However, divisive decisions can seriously damage the team. This passion for a team can be highly constructive, but the reverse can also be true. The task culture often features the crossing lines of a matrix structure.

Handy used the image of a net to describe the task culture. The strength of a net is its different strands. The task culture is often found in management consultancies, where a team enters an organization to work on projects. Once a project is completed, the team will break up and a new team (or net) will form for another project. In schools, drama departments may resemble a task culture. Different teams produce a major theatrical production and then a new team emerges for the next one.

Person culture

A person culture exists where individuals believe themselves to be superior to the organization and just want to do their own thing. These organizations are where employees simply go to work and they see themselves as separate from it – as free spirits. Some professional partnerships, such as architecture firms and some university departments, can be predominantly person cultures. There, each specialist brings a particular expertise to the organization.

Handy represents person culture as a constellation of stars. Each star (or person) is unique and different, and individuals operate on their own. Person cultures are difficult to manage. Individuals preferring this culture will often find working in organizations difficult because the constraints they impose on these individuals seem unbearable.

Edgar Schein

Schein described three levels of organizational culture.[1]

Organizational attributes

You sense organizational attributes when you walk into an organization. When entering a government building in a communist country, stern signs or warnings are everywhere. Often visible is a picture or statue of a dominant leader. People may speak in hushed tones and dress in a conformist fashion. Outsiders are viewed with suspicion. What is seen, heard, and felt reflects the culture.

Professed culture

Some organization "profess" their culture with slogans, statements, or images that project a certain image. These slogans, statements, or images give clues to how the organization operates. Websites of most large organizations give clear statements of what the businesses profess to believe or value. These sites contain statements about commitment to employees, customers, charities, and other stakeholders. These are what Schein classified as elements of professed culture.

Organizational assumptions

People who have been with an organization for a long time will often talk about "how things really get done" as opposed to the "official" channels. These people are referring to the organizational assumptions. This aspect of the organization is the most ephemeral.

People are often afraid to talk about organizational assumptions or will not really be able to articulate them. The people who understand organizational assumptions best are those who have been there the longest. They know how things really get done—even if the "official" organizational structure and literature state otherwise.

This insight helps Schein to explain the difficulty that people new to an organization often have. The best way to understand organizational assumptions is to work closely with someone who has been with the organization for some time. Even if that person knows how things "really work", the truth may be unmentionable. The existence of organizational assumptions also helps explain why some managers new to an organization may find it difficult to initiate change.

[1] Schein, Edgar H., 1965, *Organizational Psychology*, Englewood Cliffs, Prentice-Hall, NJ, USA

> **Student workpoint 2.7**
>
> ### Be a thinker
>
> Suggest one type of business organization which would suit:
>
> - power culture
> - role culture
> - task culture
> - person culture
>
> Are there advantages and disadvantages in every case?

Culture clashes

Reasons for culture clashes

When individuals enter an organization or when two or more organizations merge together, "culture clashes" can occur. Reasons for these clashes include the following:

- **Different comfort levels with diversity** – some organizations are used to diversity; others are ethnocentric.

- **Different degrees of formality** – some organizations are highly formal whereas others are informal.

- **Different languages** – organizations typically have a language that is the norm. Individuals who do not speak the language well often experience difficulties. Misunderstanding can also occur if differences exist in mode of non-verbal communication.

- **Different leadership styles** – when two organizations merge, individuals can experience changes in leadership styles. For example, if an organization with an authoritarian leadership style acquires a company accustomed to democratic leadership, both leaders and employees will find the situation difficult.

- **Different orientations to tasks and to people** – some organizations are task-oriented and others are relationship-oriented.

- **Different practices** – all organizations, even those from the same country, have some difference in practices compared to other organizations. These differences can be greater when organizations are from different countries or cultures.

- **Different senses of time** – in some cultures, time is fixed: exact appointment times and schedules are taken very seriously. Other cultures have a more fluid sense of time.

Consequences of culture clashes

Businesses combine for different reasons. In a merger, owners and management of the two firms anticipate achieving benefits, such as economies of scale or increased market share, from combining the resources of the organizations. In an acquisition or takeover, the acquiring organization has similar goals. However, sometimes when businesses combine, culture clashes occur for the reasons noted above. The overarching consequence of a culture clash when two or more companies combine is that the new organization does not achieve the expected benefits.

The consequences of a culture clash can be significant. Leaders of the business should develop a strategic plan for managing the merger, including harmonization of the two cultures. Similarly, when a change in leadership occurs at an organization, managers need to anticipate that employees may struggle with the new leadership style. The most severe consequences of a failure to harmonize cultures or prepare for new leadership can include the actual failure of the business. However, the signs of such a serious consequence may take several years to reveal themselves – typically when final accounts are prepared after the first several years of the new, larger organization. Evidence of problems as significant as potential failure may take a long time to appear, so managers must be keenly sensitive about recognizing early indicators of a culture clash. Early indicators include:

- **Lack of focus** – employees may not understand the values and aims of the new organization or the new leader and, thus, are not focused on organizational aims.

- **Preoccupation with the merger** – employees focus their attention and energy on the fact of the merger or the fact of a new leader, rather than on their own jobs. Productivity and job performance suffer.

- **Sense of division** – employees focus on the differences between the employees from the merging companies rather than on their common purpose and their many similarities. Or, in the case of a new leader and new leadership styles, some employees may think that they have fallen out of favour.

- **Sense of isolation** – while managers focuses on the strategy of the new organization, employees feel isolated and ignorant of what is happening.

- **Unresponsive management** – employees feel that managers are not concerned for their well-being.

If these early indicators go unaddressed, the organization can then experience more serious problems, including the following:

- **Lower productivity** – workers in the new organization do not produce expected efficiencies but actually find working in the new organization more difficult because of unfamiliarity with norms and procedures.

- **Higher labour turnover** – dissatisfied with the new organization and fearful that they may not have a place in it, many employees may seek new jobs. Increased labour turnover is especially troublesome when a primary purpose of the merger was to form greater human capital.

- **Various types of conflict in the workplace** – when differences between cultures occur, conflict is likelihood to increase. The stress of a merger can "bring out the worst" in people,

- **Decreased profitability** – if workers are less productive, if labour turnover increases, and conflict in the workplace increases, the business will have to devote important resources to these problems, which is likely to lower profits.

- **Bankruptcy or failure** – if the problems from a merger are severe enough and profitability falls too much, the organization can actually run the risk of bankruptcy or failure.

Organizational culture and individuals

Now let's look at how individuals influence organizational culture and how organizational culture influences individuals.

Culture is a very tricky issue to address in organizations, as it is simultaneously everything and, paradoxically, nothing. Culture is everything because it is the sum of values, attitudes, beliefs, practices, and norms of an organization. It is the sum total of the organization and thus can influence everything that happens in a business. Even though businesses with high-performing cultures typically attract high-performing individuals, such businesses usually also transform people into high-performing individuals. New employees can "feel" the energy of the organization and intuitively sense the hierarchy of values in the business. Employees will then strive to fit in by shaping their values, attitudes, beliefs, practices, and norms to the organization. Today, knowing the power of organizational culture over individuals, virtually all serious leaders of businesses treat the issue of culture as a high priority and with great purpose.

On the other hand, though individuals often remark that they can "feel" the culture of an organization, in a literal sense they cannot. Culture cannot be seen, heard, tasted, smelled, or touched. Culture is an abstraction from values, attitudes, beliefs, practices, and norms of individual employees and groups of employees. When someone asserts "We need to change the culture of our organization", they actually mean that values, attitudes, beliefs, practices, and norms must change. In other words, what changes is not "culture", but rather what individuals think, value, and do. From this perspective, individuals can influence organizational culture significantly. For example, imagine that an individual joins an organization where the practices of employees include long, unauthorized breaks and too much time sending personal emails. If the new employee decides not to follow these practices and only takes authorized breaks and sends only the occasional personal email, that person is starting to influence the culture of the organization.

What happens in this scenario? Possibly fellow employees, grumbling "She will make us all look bad", will be hostile to the new employee for violating unofficial company practice. Possibly fellow employees will think her odd and not care; they are not going to change their behaviours regardless of what any new employee does. Possibly, however, she will inspire others – other employees, for example, feeling guilty about long breaks and many emails but lacking the courage to break with the culture of the organization.

TOK discussion

Culture cannot be heard, seen, smelled, tasted, or touched, only behaviour can.

Is it correct to speak of "culture" at all?

Revision checklist

✓ Organizational culture is the attitudes, beliefs and values of an organization.

✓ Power culture exists when a few individuals retain most of the power.

✓ In role culture, each employee has a clearly defined role and operates within a highly-controlled structure.

✓ In task culture, teams address specific problems within a defined time-frame.

✓ Person culture exists where individuals believe that they are superior to the organization and just do their own thing.

✓ Reasons for culture clashes include: different degrees of formality, different leadership styles, different languages, different senses of time and urgency.

Practice question

Recruiting a new CEO

A company can spend a large amount of money to recruit a well-known and successful Chief Executive Officer (CEO) from outside the organization. However, recently published research suggests that recruiting externally is not only costly, but it is also risky, disruptive and demotivating.

Two long-term studies of 36 large public limited American companies found the following:

- The companies that promoted CEOs internally performed better than those that recruited externally.

- "Outsider" CEOs (recruited externally) have a significantly higher failure rate than "insider" CEOs (recruited internally). 40% of "outsider" CEOs stayed for two years or less.

- The average financial reward package for "outsider" CEOs, including salary, bonuses and profit-related incentives, was 65% higher than for those appointed internally.

- "Outsider" CEOs feel empowered to impose rapid change and to assert their authority on the company, even before they really understand the organizational culture. The arrival of an "outsider" CEO is often quickly followed by the departure of senior managers.

- "Outsider" CEOs are very good at rapid cost-cutting and eliminating unprofitable products/activities, a skill that is very valuable when a competitive advantage needs to be gained or restored in a competitive environment.

Apple, *Dell*™, *Microsoft*®, *Intel*®, *McDonalds*® and *Nike*® are successful American companies that appointed CEOs internally between 1998 and 2007.

A comparison of average performance indicators between 1998 and 2007 is shown below:

	Companies led by an "insider" CEO	Companies led by an "outsider" CEO
Return on capital employed (ROCE)	20.3%	15.8%
Revenue growth	11.9%	4.4%
Earnings per share	13.9%	4.6%
Net profit margin	7.9%	6.0%

Some critics of the two American studies argue that companies promoting CEOs internally usually have a strong corporate culture and are already efficient and profitable. These critics also argue that the performance indicators in the table do not measure the exact contribution of individual CEOs.

[Source: adapted from Alexandra Frean, "The value of hiring chief executives on the inside track", *The Times*, 4 April 2011]

a) Describe **two** possible influences on organizational culture. [*4 marks*]

b) (i) Explain the importance of earnings per share to a shareholder. [*2 marks*]

(ii) Distinguish between **two** external methods of recruitment that an organization could use to recruit a new CEO. [*4 marks*]

c) Examine the usefulness to an organization of rapid change management imposed by a new "outsider" CEO. [*6 marks*]

d) Discuss whether organizations that promote CEOs internally are more likely to be successful. [*9 marks*]

IB, Nov. 2013

2.6 Employer and employee relations (HL only)

By the end of this chapter, you should be able to:

→ Discuss the role and responsibility of employee and employer representatives

→ Define the following industrial/employee relations methods used by:

- employees: collective bargaining, slowdowns/go-slows, work-to-rule, overtime bans and strike action

- employers: collective bargaining, threats of redundancies, changes of contract, closure and lock-outs

→ Outline sources of conflict in the workplace

→ Explain the following approaches to conflict resolution:

- conciliation and arbitration

- employee participation and industrial democracy

- no-strike agreement

- single-union agreement

→ Outline reasons for resistance to change in the workplace (such as self-interest, low tolerance, misinformation and interpretation of circumstances)

→ Evaluate human resource strategies for reducing the impact of change and resistance to change (such as getting agreement/ownership, planning and timing the change and communicating the change)

→ Describe how innovation, ethical considerations and cultural differences may influence employer-employee relations in an organization

This unit discusses employer and employee relations. As with any aspect of business that is governed or influenced by the laws of a country, situations can differ from country to country. Nevertheless, what follows is generally applicable in many countries.

Collective bargaining

The situation when the management team and workers have representatives who negotiate on the terms and conditions of employment is called collective bargaining. Large organizations do not have the time to negotiate with individual employees. For both workers and managers, having employer and employee representatives to negotiate makes better sense.

Sometimes the collective bargaining system may not work and an industrial dispute may arise. A common way in which workers take action is when they go on strike. A strike is when employees stop working to force an employer to meet their demands. However, employees have other means of resolving labour disputes. Employee representatives may try to keep negotiating. Workers may start a "go slow", which means they deliberately work below their potential. Alternatively they may "work to rule", which involves working strictly by the company rule book – and following every rule in the organization would probably bring it to a standstill. An overtime ban occurs when employees refuse to work overtime. In this case, the organization may find it very difficult to operate. Finally, strike action occurs; that is, workers withdraw their labour.

At the same time, an employer can use a public relations (PR) campaign to try to put forward its case. The employer might also threaten workers with redundancy or make changes to their contract of employment. It might also lock employees out.

Sources of conflict

The primary causes of conflict between workers and the management team in the workplace include the following:

- **Change** – this can be driven by either internal or external factors. Either way, change can cause stress. Not all employees will respond well to new technology, for example. Having employees adapting poorly to change increases the likelihood of conflict in the workplace.

- **Different interests** – workers, who in certain respects have a lesser stake in business than managers or the shareholders, focus on their individual goals, which may include more flexibility in the workplace or higher wages. Managers sometimes believe that workers do not sufficiently consider the goals of the business.

- **Different values** – individuals see the world differently. Lack of acceptance and understanding of these differences can cause conflict. Often, workers have a culture that differs from that of the management team.

- **External factors** – any number of external factors can disrupt the workplace: changes in the economic environment can affect the resources available to the business, migration of labour can bring in new workers unaccustomed to an organization's traditional culture, and political changes can lead to new laws and regulations that workers or managers do not like.

- **Insufficient resources** – no organization has unlimited resources. Managers must decide how resources are allocated. Frequently, employees think that they have to compete for available resources just to do their jobs. Having insufficient resources also touches employees' pay. Conflict often arises when workers or managers demand more pay.

- **Poor communication** – sometimes managers and workers clash because lack of communication has created misunderstanding. Even when managers or workers have tried to communicate, misunderstandings can occur.

- **Poor performance** – sometimes people do not do their jobs properly, a situation that can happen at all levels of an organization.

TOK discussion

When looking out at the world, capitalists tended to see the world as composed of individuals. Peoples of left-wing political persuasions generally see the world in groups – groups of capitalists, groups of workers, etc. Which perspective is closer to the truth?

People not doing their jobs properly, whether managers or workers, has an impact on others and can lead to conflict. If the problem is addressed (the non-performing employee is reprimanded, demoted, or even sacked), that too can cause conflict.

Approaches to conflict resolution

Conciliation and arbitration

Sometimes the employer and employee representatives will seek help from a third party to resolve a dispute. This process is often referred to as conciliation and arbitration. The aim of conciliation is to bring together the groups in dispute and help them to find a resolution. An independent third party is usually called in to conciliate on the dispute. In this situation, both parties outline their positions by providing appropriate evidence. This evidence is then assessed and a judgment is made.

Employee participation and industrial democracy

In industrial democracies, often partial or complete participation by the workforce in the running of an organization occurs. At one extreme, industrial democracy implies workers' control over industry, perhaps linked with workers' ownership of the means of production, as with producer cooperatives. Another approach is the appointment of worker or trade union representatives to company boards or governing bodies. For others, industrial democracy takes the form of "worker participation", such as collective bargaining in which trade unions negotiate with managers. A fourth approach places less stress on power sharing and more on consultation and communication: managers are seen as retaining all responsibility for decisions but make arrangements to consult employee representatives before changes are introduced.

No-strike agreement

A no-strike agreement occurs when a trade union has agreed not to undertake industrial action unless procedural steps have first been undertaken. It can also mean that a union has agreed to rule out any possibility of taking industrial action. Unions usually agree not to strike when the management team has agreed to certain conditions. For example, the management team may have agreed to inflation-proof pay rises, or agreed to refer all disputes to arbitration should no agreement be made between managers and unions.

Single-union agreement

Where one union is recognized as the only representative of employees, it is called a single-union agreement. This situation saves managers the difficulties of negotiating with several unions and reduces competition between the unions to get a higher pay increase than rival unions. It also helps to avoid the disruption to the organization if only one of several unions is in dispute with managers. When multiple unions are involved, one union can disrupt the production process for the whole organization.

Reasons for resistance to change

For many reasons, employees may resist change in the workplace. Change is typically "forced" on them by managers because of changes in the internal or external environments. Whereas managers typically view change as desirable (or necessary) for the health of the organization and for profitability, workers are often threatened by change. There are specific reasons that workers and employees often resist change:

- **Discomfort** – employees are often happy with the current situation and want to maintain the status quo.

- **Fear** – changes often makes employees afraid simply because they do not know what will happen.

- **Insufficient reward** – employees often perceive that implementing the change requires them to do more work for no increase in compensation.

- **Lack of job skills** – employees may not have the skills necessary to perform in the changed work environment.

- **Loss of control** – when managers insist on change, employees feel that they do not have control over their lives.

- **Mistrust** – employees sometimes do not trust managers.

- **Poor communication** – employees do not know why the business needs to change.

- **Poor timing** – change is brought about for the needs of the organization but might occur at a time that, for either professional or personal reasons, may fit poorly with the needs of employees.

- **Prior experience** – an employee may have had a bad experience with change in an another organization or at an earlier time with his or her current employer.

- **Social support** – an employee who works with a group of people who resist change may choose to resist for the sake of maintaining social relationships.

HR strategies to reduce the impact of change

Good organizations do not blindly move forward with change but rather lead and manage employees through a change process. When effectively done, a change process helps to reduce the resistance and transition the organization to its new and desired set of circumstances.

Organizations and managers can reduce the impact of change through various steps. The first is simply assessing the potential impact of the change, assessing employees' potential reaction to it, and determining the degree to which managers can control the change process. Thereafter, the management team should take the following steps:

1. Develop a vision for the change process and the desired outcomes. If necessary, the business may have to realign its largest aims and vision for the organization.

2. Forecast and allocate the necessary resources to implement the change.

Student workpoint 2.8

Be a researcher

Use the internet to research an industrial dispute that has occured in your country.

Describe:

- What casued the dispute? Was it one or a combination of many factors?

- What strategies were adopted by a) the employees and b) the employers

- What was the outcome of the dispute? Was there a clear 'winner'?

3. Involve employees in the change process from the outset so that employees are not surprised and so that they do not feel powerless.

4. Regularly communicate to all appropriate stakeholders how the change process is unfolding. Managers should not be afraid to report problems or implementation dips. Pretending that problems in the process are not occurring when they clearly are will weaken employees' confidence. On the other hand, managers should report successes in the change process to inspire confidence.

5. Train employees in advance of those changes that affect them directly, which should allow them to see the benefits of change immediately. If employees are not properly trained, the fears of lack of competence will be heightened.

6. Routinely communicate the benefits of the changes.

7. Be aware of the stress that change can cause and support employees as much as possible, before, during, and after change.

Revision checklist

✓ Employee and employer representatives act on behalf of employees and employers in negotiations.

✓ Collective bargaining is a negotiation between employees (usually through a trade union) and their employers to agree wages and working conditions.

✓ Slowdowns occur when workers deliberately work less efficiently than they can.

✓ When employees work-to-rule they follow every rule and regulation exactly, which often means slowing down production.

✓ An overtime ban is when employees refuse to work any more than their contracted hours.

✓ When workers strike, they refuse to work and may also protest outside their workplace.

✓ Employers may negotiate by making threats of redundancies or changing the terms of employees contracts. This would put pressure on workers and might persuade them to agree to a settlement.

✓ A lock-out involves closing the business for a short time, preventing employees from working and being paid.

✓ Potential sources of conflict involve change, differing interests or values, external factors such as the economy, poor communication and poor performance.

✓ Conflicts can be resolved through conciliation and arbitration, industrial democracy, no-strike agreements, and single-union agreements.

✓ Successful organizations use their HR strategy to manage employees through the process of change.

2 Human resource management

INNOVATION, ETHICS AND CULTURE

Innovation, ethical considerations, and cultural differences may influence employer–employee relations in an organization.

Innovation is a two-edged sword. On the one hand, innovation makes an organization dynamic and often enhances the reputation and increases the profitability of a business. However, if an organization is "too dynamic" (that is, constantly changing), employees may find the situation too stressful. They may grow weary.

Ethical considerations can also influence employer–employee relations. When going through the change process, for example, if managers fail to consider fully the human element, employees may draw the conclusion that changes being undertaken benefit only the organization's managers and owners, especially if retrenchment of employees is involved. Conversely, managers can build trust if they treat employees ethically: whenever possible, retraining employees for new jobs, giving them adequate time to learn, and providing support throughout. In general, whether it is a static situation or a changing environment, employers should treat employees well, with ethical considerations in mind. Treating employees well can be costly, but in the long run doing so generally pays off.

Finally, cultural differences, both within an organization and relating to the broader culture of where the business is located, play a role in employer–employee relations. Some cultures have traditions of workplace democracy, others of paternalism, still others of authoritarian management. Regardless, these internal and external cultures influence managers' and workers' expectations and, thus, employer–employee relationships.

Practice question

Get Going

Get Going is a charity that was created fifteen years ago to provide wheelchairs to disabled people. After a successful start, the business has been experiencing financial problems. This has led to low motivation among employees and some are considering leaving the charity.

Recent changes in the organization from a tall to a flat structure have led to communication problems and the chief executive is keen to solve the issues. Rumours have started about job losses and this has led to employees becoming more unhappy and fearing change.

a) Explain how the aims and objectives of a charity may be different from those of a profit making organization. [*4 marks*]

b) Examine the effects on *Get Going* of moving from a tall to a flat organizational structure. [*6 marks*]

c) Identify **two** examples of formal and **two** examples of informal communications that might be used in *Get Going*. [*4 marks*]

d) Evaluate **two** solutions to the problems of poor communications in *Get Going*. [*6 marks*]

IB, May 2005

3 FINANCE AND ACCOUNTS

3.1 Sources of finance

> **By the end of this chapter, you should be able to:**
> → explain the role of finance for businesses in terms of **capital expenditure** and **revenue expenditure**
> → comment on the following internal sources of finance: **personal funds, retained profit** and **sale of assets**
> → comment on the following external sources of finance: **share capital, loan capital, overdrafts, trade credit, grants, subsidies, debt factoring, leasing, venture capital** and **business angels**
> → define **short-, medium-** and **long-term finance**
> → discuss the appropriateness, advantages, and disadvantages of sources of finance for a given situation.

Introduction

All forms of business organization need funding for the various activities they undertake. The money could be needed for a variety of reasons, including starting a business, for its day-to-day operations, or for its future growth and expansion. As a result, businesses need to ascertain or be clear on the exact purpose of their finance. This purpose can be classified as either **capital expenditure** or **revenue expenditure**.

Capital expenditure

This is money spent to acquire items in a business that will last for more than a year and may be used over and over again. Such items are known as **fixed assets** and include machinery, land, buildings, vehicles, and equipment. These fixed assets are needed for the purpose of generating income for the business over the longer term. Due to their high initial cost, most fixed assets can be used as **collateral** (financial security pledged for repayment of a particular source of finance such as bank loans). Capital expenditures are therefore long-term investments intended to assist businesses to succeed and grow. For example, purchasing a van by a business is termed capital expenditure because the benefits accrued to the business from this will be spread over the long term.

Revenue expenditure

This is money spent on the day-to-day running of a business. These payments or expenses include rent, wages, raw materials, insurance, and fuel. They do not involve the purchase of longer-term, fixed assets. Revenue expenditure needs to be covered immediately to keep the business operational and should therefore provide immediate benefits, unlike capital expenditure which has a long-term focus. Businesses need to be cautious not to have consistently high revenue expenditure as this will make it difficult for them to build sufficient capital in order to make long-term investments. In addition, it may make it extremely difficult for them to get out of a sudden crisis situation. For example, if a school is spending most of its money paying salaries and bonuses to teachers or paying food suppliers, and these costs are not checked, it may be unable to build new classrooms to accommodate any increases in student demand. In a business, a high level of expenses may also erode the profits.

The sources of finance for a business can be obtained from either internal sources or external sources.

Internal sources of finance

Internal finance is money obtained from within the business and is usually from already established businesses. Some of these sources include the following.

Personal funds

This is a key source of finance for sole traders and it comes mostly from their own personal savings. By investing with their personal savings, sole traders maximize their control over the business. In addition, this investment shows commitment to the business and is a good signal to other investors or financial institutions that the business might need to approach for additional sources of finance. It is a preferred source of finance because it is cheap and easily available, and no interest will need to be paid. However, it poses a great risk to the owners or sole traders because they could be investing their life's savings. In addition, if these savings are not large it may prove difficult to start or maintain a business, especially if this is the only source of funding.

Retained profit

This is the profit that remains after a business has paid tax to the government (corporation tax) and dividends to shareholders. It is also known as **ploughed-back profit** and may be reinvested into the business, becoming an important source of finance for the organization. Importantly, retained profits do not necessarily represent surplus cash available to a business. Rather, they represent how the business has managed its profits. For example, whether it has distributed them as dividends or reinvested them in the business. If reinvested, they are reflected as increases to assets which could include cash. The advantages of retained profit include the following.

Key terms

Capital expenditure

money spent to acquire fixed assets in a business

Revenue expenditure

money used in the day-to-day running of a business

Key terms

Personal funds

a source of finance for sole traders that comes mostly from their own personal savings

Retained profit

profit that remains after a business has paid corporation tax to the government and dividends to shareholders

- It is cheap because it does not incur interest charges.

- It is a permanent source of finance as it does not have to be repaid.

- It is flexible as it can be used in a way the business deems fit.

- The owners have control over their retained profits without interference from other financial institutions such as banks.

However, there are some disadvantages:

- Start-up businesses will not have any retained profit as they are new ventures.

- If retained profit is too low, it may not be sufficient for expansion.

- In some cases owners may overuse the retained profit and leave no buffer for emergencies or for future growth opportunities.

- A high retained profit may mean that either very little or nothing was paid out to shareholders as dividends.

Sale of assets

This is when a business sells off its unwanted or unused assets to raise funds. These assets that are no longer required by the business include obsolete machinery or redundant buildings. To raise cash, businesses could also sell off any excess land or equipment they may not be using. The advantage of selling assets is that it is a good way of raising cash from capital that may be tied up in assets that are not being used. No interest or borrowing costs are incurred. The drawback is that it may only be an option available to established businesses and not new ones that may lack any excess assets to sell. In addition, it may be time-consuming to find a buyer to sell the assets to, especially in the case of obsolete machinery. In some cases businesses may adopt a **sale and lease back** option, which involves selling an asset that the business still needs to use. In this case the business will sell the asset to a specialist firm that then leases the asset back to the business.

> **Key term**
>
> **Sale of assets**
>
> when a business sells off its unwanted or unused assets to raise funds

3 Finance and Accounts

> **Student workpoint 3.2**
>
> ***Be a researcher***
>
> Using an Internet search engine such as Google, find at least five organizations that rely to a large extent on internal sources of finance to operate. What are the main internal sources they use, and why?

External sources of finance

External finance is money obtained from sources outside the business. These could be from institutions or individuals willing to provide the funds. Some of these external sources of finance include the following.

> **Key term**
>
> **Share capital**
>
> money raised from the sale of shares of a limited company

Share capital

This is money raised from the sale of shares of a limited company and is also known as **equity capital**. Buyers of these shares are known as **shareholders** and may be entitled to dividends when profits are made. The term **authorized share capital** suggests the maximum amount the shareholders of a company intend to raise. Unlike private limited company shares that are not sold to the public, the shares of public limited companies are sold in a special share market known as the **stock exchange**. This is a regulated and organized market where securities (for example shares and bonds) are purchased by and sold to willing investors. The oldest stock exchange in the world is the London stock exchange. Other global exchanges include Bombay, Tokyo, Nairobi, Johannesburg, and New York stock exchanges. The advantage of share capital as a source of finance is that it is a permanent source of capital as it will not need to be redeemed (repaid by the business). Another is that there are no interest payments and this relieves the business from additional expenses. On the other hand, shareholders will expect to be paid dividends when the business makes a profit. In addition, for public limited companies the ownership of the company may be diluted or change hands from the original shareholders to new investors or shareholders via the stock exchange.

Loan capital

Also known as **debt capital**, this is money sourced from financial institutions such as banks. Interest is charged on the loan to be repaid; however, these repayments (installments) are usually spread evenly until the full loan amount (principal plus interest) is paid. The interest rates may be either fixed or variable. A **fixed interest rate** is one that does not fluctuate and remains fixed for the entire term of the loan repayment. A **variable interest rate**, on the other hand, changes periodically based on the prevailing market conditions. The advantage of this source of finance is that it is accessible and can be arranged quickly for a firm's specific purpose. Its repayment is spread out over a predetermined period of time, reducing the burden to the business of having to pay it in a lump sum. Large organizations can negotiate for lower interest charges depending on the amount they wish to borrow. The owners still have full control of the business if no shares are issued to dilute their ownership.

However, there are drawbacks. The capital will have to be redeemed even though the business is making losses and in some cases collateral (security) will be required before any funds are lent out. Failure to pay the loan may lead to the seizure of a firm's assets. If variable interest rates increase, a firm that took this option may be faced with a high debt repayment burden.

Overdrafts

This is when a lending institution allows a firm to withdraw more money than it currently has in its account, which is called overdrawing from the account. In most cases the overdrawn amount is an agreed amount that has a limit placed on it. Interest is charged only on the amount overdrawn. However, exceeding the limit set may attract higher

The trading floors of the New York (top) and Tokyo (bottom) stock exchanges

Key terms

Loan capital

money sourced from financial institutions such as banks, with interest charged on the loan to be repaid

Overdrafts

when a lending institution allows a firm to withdraw more money than it currently has in its account

additional costs. The advantage of a bank overdraft is that it provides an opportunity for firms to spend more than they have in their account (even in situations where there is no money in the account), which greatly helps in settling short-term debts such as paying suppliers or the wages of staff. It is a flexible form of finance as its demand will depend on the needs of the business at a particular point in time. Charging interest only on the amount overdrawn may make it even cheaper than loan capital. With an overdraft facility, banks can cover a firm's cheques to prevent them from bouncing. The major drawback is that banks can ask for the overdraft to be paid back at very short notice. In addition, due to the variable nature of an overdraft, the bank may at times charge high interest rates.

Trade credit

This is an agreement between businesses that allows the buyer of goods or services to pay the seller at a later date. In essence, no immediate cash transaction is done at the time of trading. The credit period offered by most creditors (trade credit providers) usually lasts from 30 to 90 days; jewellery businesses are known to extend it to at least 180 days. A major advantage of trade credit is that by delaying payments to suppliers, businesses are left in a better cash-flow position than if they paid cash immediately. It is also an interest-free means of raising funds for the length of the credit period. A disadvantage is that debtors (trade credit receivers) lose out on the possibility of getting discounts had they purchased by paying cash. In addition, delaying payment to creditors after the agreed period may lead to the development of poor relations and suppliers may even refuse to engage in future transactions with the debtors.

Grants

These are funds usually provided by a government, foundation, trust, or other agency to businesses. In order to receive a grant, businesses will be expected to write a proposal showing how they plan to use the money. In most cases **grant makers** (providers of the grant) are very selective on who receives the grant. Governments, for example, would prefer to offer grants to businesses that agree to set up in areas of high unemployment so as to improve the welfare of people living in that area. Foundations such as the Bill and Melinda Gates Foundation offer most of its grants to US-based organizations including other tax-exempt organizations, with a focus on promoting social responsibility. A key advantage of a grant is that it does not have to be paid back by the recipient. The downside is that it mostly comes with "strings attached" depending on the objective of the grant maker.

Subsidies

A subsidy is financial assistance granted by a government, a non-governmental organization (NGO) or an individual to support business enterprises that are in the public interest. Farm subsidies are common subsidies given to domestic farming industries. In most cases the cash subsidies are given to help these industries survive in a very competitive

Key terms

Trade credit

an agreement between businesses that allows the buyer of goods or services to pay the seller at a later date

Grants

funds usually provided by a government, foundation, trust, or other agency to businesses that do not need to be repaid

Subsidies

financial assistance granted by a government, a non-governmental organization (NGO), or an individual to support business enterprises that are in the public interest

3 Finance and Accounts

environment by being able to sell their produce at low market prices, while still being able to reap financial gain. In situations where the market price goes below the cost of production, this is known as **subvention**. A major advantage of granting subsidies is that it helps businesses to increase their demand for goods by charging lower prices for their products. Like grants, subsidies do not need to be repaid. A drawback, especially with government subsidies, is that they are often marred by political interference in the subsidization process.

Debt factoring

This is where a business sells its invoice to a third party known as a debt factor. It is a financial arrangement where the factor takes on the responsibility for collecting the debt owed to the business. The debt factor may immediately pay the business between 80–90 per cent of the money owed on the invoices and then proceed to collect the full amount from these debtors. The remaining 10–20 per cent of sales revenue counts as part of the debt factor's profit. The higher the debt owed the more willing the debt factors will be to pay upfront, due to the possibility of getting a higher percentage profit. An advantage of debt factoring is that a business gets immediate cash that it can use to fund other activities or projects. In addition, the risk or responsibility of collecting the debt is passed on to the factor. The disadvantages are that a business loses a percentage of its profits because it does not receive the full debt repayment and debt factors are known to charge high administrative and service fees to do their job. In addition, a business may risk losing a loyal customer if the debt factors use harsh means of collecting debt such as threatening to take the customer to court for failing to pay the debt.

Leasing

This is where a business (lessee) enters into a contract with a leasing company (lessor) to acquire or use particular assets such as machinery, equipment, or property. This allows a firm to use an asset without having to purchase it with cash. Periodic or monthly leasing payments are made by agreement between the lessor and lessee. In some cases businesses may get into a **finance lease** agreement where, at the end of the leasing period, which usually lasts for more than three years, it is given the option of purchasing the asset. Large organizations such as airlines and electronic and car companies are known to lease their assets. A major advantage of leasing is that a firm does not need to have a high initial capital outlay to purchase the asset. Second, the lessor takes on the responsibility of repair and maintenance of the asset. In addition, leasing is useful when particular assets are required only for short periods of time or occasionally. In the long haul, though, leasing can turn out to be more expensive than the outright purchase of an asset due to the accumulated total costs of the leasing charges. Moreover, a leased asset cannot act as collateral for a business seeking a loan as an additional source of finance.

Venture capital

This is financial capital provided by investors to high-risk, high-potential start-up firms or small businesses. Venture capitalists usually fund

Key terms

Debt factoring

a financial arrangement where the debt factor takes on the responsibility for collecting the debt owed to the business and provides the business with a percentage of the owed debt in cash

Leasing

a source of finance that allows a firm to use an asset without having to purchase it by cash

Venture capital

financial capital provided by investors to high-risk, high-potential start-up firms or small businesses

start-ups that find it difficult to access money from other financial institutions or capital markets. Venture capitalists include specialist organizations and investment banks. They own a stake in the businesses they invest in with the expectation of benefiting from future profits. However, due to the high risks involved, they expect the firms needing the funds to produce a thoroughly researched business plan to help mitigate the risk of investment. The key advantage of venture capitalists is that they provide funding to businesses that other institutions might regard as too high a risk. In addition, in an effort to protect their investment they are involved in the firm's decision making by providing the required guidance where it is needed. The disadvantage is that venture capitalists may set very high profit targets for the start up businesses they invest in and if these are not attained they usually increase their equity stake in these firms, often by a large percentage.

Business angels

Also known as **angel investors**, these are very affluent individuals who provide financial capital to small start-ups or entrepreneurs in return for ownership equity in their businesses. They invest in high-risk businesses that show good potential for high returns or future growth. They may provide a one-time initial capital injection or continually support the businesses through their lifetime. A major advantage of business angels is that they give more favourable financial terms than other institutions or lenders of small or start-up businesses. This is because they are known to invest in the person rather than how viable a business venture is. In addition, they focus on helping a business succeed by using their extensive business experience coupled with good financial capital. The key disadvantage is that angel investors may assume a good degree of control or ownership in the businesses they invest in, therefore diluting the ownership of the entrepreneur.

> ### Key terms
>
> **Business angels**
>
> highly affluent individuals who provide financial capital to small start-ups or entrepreneurs in return for ownership equity in their businesses

Case study

Vodafone and Safaricom Kenya: Extending the Range and Reliability of Financial Services to the Poor in Rural Kenya

In Kenya there are less than two million bank accounts serving the country's population of 32 million people. The reasons for this disparity include the high cost of banking and the fact that the majority of the people have low incomes with a large percentage of them living on an average of one dollar a day. Such people do not feel comfortable interacting with commercial banks that typically target middle and upper income customers. Micro-Finance Institutions (MFIs) such as Faulu Kenya do successfully provide financial services for the poor, but they are hampered by poor infrastructure and low levels of technology.

In order to address this problem Safaricom Kenya, one of the two mobile service providers currently operating in Kenya, developed an appropriate technology. The result was MPESA, an electronic money transfer product aimed at making financial transactions faster, cheaper and more secure. MPESA allows transfer of money between individuals, transfer of money between individuals and businesses, cash withdrawal and deposit at registered retail outlets as payment for goods and services through the mobile phone short message service (SMS). MPESA account holders can deposit or withdraw money into or from their virtual accounts at Safaricom vendor shops or at an increasing number of outlets such as supermarkets and petrol stations. Once the money is in their accounts, they can use it to pay bills, transfer to other people or purchase goods and services.

In October 2005, MPESA trials were successfully launched in Kenya, featuring eight Safaricom dealer shops and 450 Faulu Kenya clients and concluded in May 2006. Vodafone Group Plc provided 990,000 Sterling pounds and DFID 910,000 pounds sterling to finance the pilot project. Consult Hyperion a British ICT firm developed the technology that was utilized by mobile service provider Safaricom Kenya through dealers, retailers and MFIs among others. The product has been successfully launched by Safaricom and plans are underway to recruit more financial institutions and retail outlets. Trials on new training methods for potential MPESA users are also under way. Vodafone also plans to introduce the system in other developing countries.

Exam-style questions

1. Describe two challenges encountered by Micro-Finance Institutions such as Faulu Kenya.   [4 marks]

2. Explain two advantages and one disadvantage of Micro-Finance Institutions for Kenyan people.   [6 marks]

3. Compare and contrast the financial services provided by Safaricom's MPESA with those of commercial banks in Kenya.   [10 marks]

Student workpoint 3.3

Be a researcher

Find out how the various sources of finance for private sector organizations compare with the sources for public sector organizations.

Short-, medium- and long-term finance

In determining whether to classify a source of finance as short, medium or long term, it is important to consider the investor's personal preference or the type of asset under consideration. The type of finance should therefore be matched to the type of asset being financed. Thus, a long-term asset should be financed with long-term finance, a medium-term asset should be financed with medium-term finance and a short-term asset with short-term finance. There is no uniformly agreed way of determining the exact duration of a source of finance, but most financial literature uses the following definitions.

Short-term finance

This is money needed for the day-to-day running of a business and therefore provides its needed working capital. This is finance that lasts for one year or less. External short-term sources of finance are usually expected to be paid with 12 months of a trading or financial year. Examples of short-term finance include bank overdrafts, trade credit and debt factoring.

Medium-term finance

This is money mostly used to purchase assets such as equipment or vehicles that have useful lifespans for a specific period of time. This source of finance has a duration period of between one year and about five years. Examples of medium-term sources include leasing, medium-term bank loans and grants.

TOK discussion

What role does intuition play in financial decision making?

Is there a moral obligation for financial institutions to lend to every start-up business?

Long-term finance

This is funding obtained for the purpose of purchasing long-term fixed assets or other expansion requirements of a business. The duration of the finance may be anywhere from more than five to around 30 years. Long-term finance sources include long-term bank loans and share capital.

Student workpoint 3.4

Be knowledgeable

Prepare and complete a table that classifies the following sources of finance into short, medium or long term:

- debt factoring
- retained profit
- trade credit
- leasing
- sale of assets
- venture capital
- share capital
- overdrafts
- loan capital
- subsidies.

Factors influencing the choice of a source of finance

In determining the appropriateness of using a particular source of finance for a given situation, firms need to consider a number of factors which can influence their decision. Some of these factors are explored below.

Purpose or use of funds

Businesses will need to match the source of finance carefully to their specific requirements. What exactly will the finance be used for? Will it be used for the purchase of long-term fixed assets or for the short-term day-to-day running of the business? Long-term loan capital may be appropriate when purchasing a fixed asset, while trade credit may be suitable if raw materials are needed urgently in the business.

Cost

Businesses will need to consider thoroughly all the costs associated with obtaining a source of finance. Such costs include interest payments, administration costs, and costs associated with a share issue. In addition, the **opportunity cost** (the next best alternative that is forgone after choosing one source over the other) is also an important consideration when deciding on the most appropriate source of finance.

Status and size

Public limited companies can obtain finance from various sources, whereas sole traders will not be able to. This is because sole traders are less well known and smaller in size than public limited companies. For example, the issue of shares is a source of finance that is only possible for public limited companies and not sole traders. In addition, large organizations have added collateral that they can use to negotiate for lower interest rates from financial institutions.

Amount required

For small amounts, firms may consider mostly short-term sources of finance such as bank overdrafts while, for larger amounts, long-term bank loans or the issue of shares are available options. Therefore varying sources will be used depending on the amount required.

Flexibility

This looks into the ease with which a business can switch from one source to another. In some cases businesses will need additional sources at particular points during their trading period which could be influenced by, for example, seasonal changes in demand that may require short-term sources of funding. The availability of such sources of funding in such a short period also determines how flexible it is.

State of the external environment

This involves factors that the business has no control of. For example, increases in interest rates or inflation (persistent increases in average prices in an economy) will greatly affect the purchasing decisions of both consumers and producers. Consequently, this will affect the choices businesses make in sourcing their finance. Taking up a bank loan with rising interest rates may not be the best choice for a firm because of the increased cost involved.

Gearing

This refers to the relationship between share capital and loan capital. If a company has a large proportion of loan capital to share capital it is said to be **high geared**, while a company that is **low geared** has a smaller proportion of loan capital to share capital. For example, assume there are two companies, company A and company B, each with a total capital of $60 million. Company A may have a loan capital of US$10 million and share capital of US$50 million, while company B may have a loan capital of US$40 million and share capital of US$20 million. Company A is therefore low geared compared to company B which is high geared. High-geared businesses are viewed as risky by financial institutions and they will be reluctant to lend money to such firms. These businesses will therefore need to seek alternative sources of finance. One way of measuring gearing is by calculating the gearing ratio (see section 3.6).

INNOVATION

Read the summary from the *Finance for Innovation* (http://www.awt.nl/upload/documents/publicaties/tekst/as36.pdf)

What in your opinion would you consider to be the best source of finance for innovation? What factors may influence your decision on this source of finance? Carry out research on how various global businesses are funding their innovations.

MTN Uganda achieves one of the most remarkable mobile money growth rates working with Fundamo

MTN Uganda's MobileMoney service achieved one of the most remarkable and rapid growth rates ever witnessed in the mobile financial services industry. In a year after launching, the service had registered more than one million users, 16% of its subscriber base. Today, it remains one of the world's most successful MFS deployments.

The success of the service, however, has gone far further than simply connecting the previously unbanked. The introduction of mobile payments has led to a fundamental shift in the rural and peri-urban economies.

About MTN Uganda

In October 21 1998, MTN Uganda launched commercial services in Uganda. MTN has since grown to be the leading mobile operator in the country.

MTN adopted a wireless approach to providing telecommunications services to the Ugandan market, which proved to be a convenient and fast method of rolling out services. Despite insufficient infrastructure (power, roads etc.) MTN now covers the majority of both the urban and rural population

Uganda's financial position – the opportunity for MTN

There are over 30 banks in Uganda, but a banking penetration rate of no more than 10%.

The traditional banking model involves taking branches to various locations, an option that is not compatible with poor countries such as Uganda that cannot afford to make the investment required for such a complex infrastructure.

Furthermore, some traditional banking branches were unable to support the number of customers they can generate in an area. The advent of mobile money provided everyone with the opportunity to access financial inclusion.

This presented an opportunity for MTN Uganda to provide banking services using mobile.

The power of the MTN Fundamo partnership

MTN MobileMoney was launched as a way to allow the consumers to send and receive money, top up airtime and perform many other services using a mobile phone. MTN Uganda saw the pressing need to offer services to a population desperate for financial inclusion, and it turned to Fundamo to help roll out the ambitious national project.

MTN MobileMoney makes use of the basic Fundamo platform with an additional layer of services designed specifically for the Ugandan environment and to meet regulatory requirements.

MTN and Fundamo spent over a year in Africa before the launch of Mobile Money, interviewing potential users of the service from all age-groups and business sectors. This market research allowed Fundamo to refine aspects of the service to make sure that it would be well received and met the needs and aspirations of the Ugandan communities.

MTN MobileMoney is an electronic wallet service that enables you to send and receive money anywhere in Uganda using your phone. MTN MobileMoney users are able to:

- Send money to any MTN mobile phone user; registered or not.
- Send money to mobile phone users on other local networks using the MTN agent network.
- Withdraw cash at any authorised MTN MobileMoney agent.
- Pay bills such as DStv, anywhere conveniently with immediate results.
- Buy airtime for themselves and others on the MTN network directly and conveniently.
- Manage their MTN MobileMoney accounts.

The go-to-market strategy was designed to ensure rapid uptake of the services. However, even the highest hopes of the partners were exceeded by the response. It was testament to the robust Fudamo platform that MTN was able to continue to sign up new customers onto the system, relying on the integrity of the Fundamo solution.

The system was designed at the outset to handle complex transactions as the long-term view was to migrate the users onto newer services like international remittances and mobile insurance.

MTN Uganda's success has been referenced in a number of articles looking at mobile money implementations in the developing world. The reason for the success has been the non-traditional, below the line methods used by MTN. The distribution model of "by the people, for the people" has relied on empowering the local population through education and solid entrepreneurial opportunity.

Over 2500 MobileMoney 'foot soldiers' were trained on the system. Equipped with basic infrastructure such as photocopiers, marquees, relevant marketing material and transport, the foot soldiers canvassed new users across the country.

Fundamo invested an enormous amount of time ensuring that the sign-up process was both simple and logical, while complying with all regulatory requirements. The service menu was also designed to work with even the most rudimentary handsets to ensure the service is as inclusive as possible.

Service agents are incentivised using a commission-based system which rewards them immediately upon the sign-up of new user, and on transactions levels. This was a significant boost to local communities and was warmly welcomed by governments who are looking for SMME job creation. More importantly, it has meant that agents are driven to ensure customer satisfaction and are always on the lookout for ways to make the user-experience more rewarding.

Results

In just over a year MTN Uganda registered 1 million MobileMoney service users - 16% of its subscriber base.

MTN Uganda continues to be one of the most successful Mobile Money deployments globally to date. It continues to innovate introducing new, useful services on a regular basis such as paying government pensions through the system.

Due to the success of the project, Western Union announced that it had chosen Uganda as the first country to roll out its international remittance service in partnership with MTN.

Once the new international remittance service was activated, MTN subscribers registered for MobileMoney were able to receive Western Union Money Transfer transactions in their mobile accounts. In addition, MobileMoney users in certain countries are now able to send Western Union Money Transfer transactions directly from their mobile phones for pay-out at one of Western Union's agent locations in territories around the world.

Adapted from : http://www.fundamo.com/PDF/Case%20 study/MTN%20Uganda%20Case%20Study.pdf

Exam-style questions

1. Outline the main activities of MTN Uganda in the financial services sector. [4 marks]

2. Explain how three different stakeholders have been affected by the introduction of MTN Mobile money. [6 marks]

3. To what extent have MTN and Fundamo reached their strategic objectives in Uganda? [10 marks]

Revision checklist

✓ Capital expenditure is money spent to acquire fixed assets in a business, which include machinery, land, buildings, vehicles and equipment, while revenue expenditure is money spent on the day to day running of a business with expenses that include rent, wages, raw materials, insurance and fuel.

✓ Internal sources of finance, which are obtained within the business, include personal loans, retained profits and sale of assets.

✓ External sources of finance that are obtained outside the business include share capital, loan capital, overdrafts, trade credit, grants, subsidies, debt factoring, leasing, venture capitalists and business angels.

✓ Short-term finance which lasts for one year or less provides a business with its needed working capital. Medium-term finance that lasts from more than one year to about five years is mostly used to purchase assets such as equipment or vehicles. Long-term finance with a duration of more than five years to thirty years, is funding obtained for the purpose of purchasing long term fixed assets or other expansion requirements of a business.

✓ In deciding on the appropriate source of finance to use businesses need to consider; the purpose of the funds, cost, flexibility, their status and size, amount required, gearing and the state of the external environment.

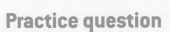

Practice question

Three Hills Driving School

Three Hills Driving School provides driving instructions to people interested in obtaining a licence to drive a car. They target people aged 18 to 25 who are mostly students who have finished high school and/ or university students.

It is owned by Maria who set it up two years ago using her savings. Her capital expenditure was about $90,000 in the first year while her revenue expenditure was half that amount in the same year. She plans to sell her business after five years as a going concern. Due to increased demand she plans on buying more cars and employing more instructors. Therefore, she will need to seek alternative sources of finance to fund this. She is debating between taking up a long term loan or a bank overdraft.

a) Differentiate between capital expenditure and revenue expenditure   *[4 marks]*

b) Comment on two benefits and two drawbacks of raising money using ones savings   *[6 marks]*

c) Explain two medium term sources of finance available to Maria to help her expand her business   *[6 marks]*

d) Evaluate the view that taking up a long term loan would be a preferable option than a bank overdraft for Maria's business expansion plans.   *[9 marks]*

3.2 Costs and revenues

Introduction

Costs and revenues are very important factors that determine the success of any business. Businesses therefore need accurate and reliable information about them for effective decision making.

Cost refers to the total expenditure incurred by a business in order to run its operations.

Revenue is a measure of the money generated from the sale of goods and services.

Profit is calculated by finding out the difference between revenues and costs. A high positive difference is a good indicator of business success.

Types of costs

Fixed costs

These are costs that do not change or vary with the amount of goods or services produced. They are expenses that have to be paid regardless of any business activity the firm engages in. They are mostly time related and are usually paid per month, per quarter, bi-annually, or per year. They remain fixed in the short run. The short run is defined as a period of time when at least one factor of production (resource needed to produce goods or services) does not change. Examples of fixed costs include rent, insurance, salaries, and interest payments. For instance, if a firm usually pays a rent of $5,000 per month and decides to take a week's holiday, this rent will still need to be paid despite the holiday. It is therefore important to note that fixed costs do not change due to a change in output in the short run.

Variable costs

These are costs that vary or change with the number of goods or services produced. They are expenses that change in proportion to business activity. Variable costs are volume related as they are paid per quantity produced. These are costs that can be incurred both in the short run or in the long run (a period of time when all factors of production are variable). They are also pegged to sales, in that an increase in sales or output sold leads to an increase in variable costs. If no units are produced then no variable costs are incurred. Examples of variable costs include raw material costs, sales commissions, packaging, and energy usage costs.

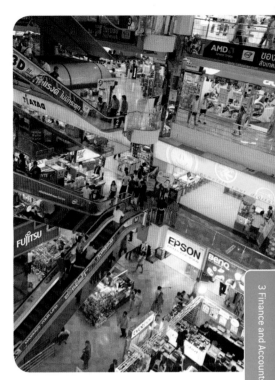

All fixed costs (total fixed costs) added to all variable costs (total variable costs) gives us the total costs. Hence, total costs (TC) = total fixed costs (TFC) + total variable costs (TVC).

Semi-variable costs

These are costs comprising both fixed and variable components. Semi-variable costs remain fixed for a given level of production or consumption, after which they become variable when the set level is exceeded. Such costs are also known as **semi-fixed costs** or **mixed costs**. The greater the production levels the higher will be the total costs; however, when no units are produced the firm still incurs fixed costs. Labour costs are an example of semi-variable costs. The fixed cost would be the salary paid per month to the worker for regular hours worked, while the variable cost is any payment such as overtime made for working extra hours. Another example would be a monthly rental for a phone line (standing charge) which constitutes a firm's fixed cost, while the call charges (number of calls made) make up its variable cost.

Direct costs

These are costs that can be identified with or clearly attributed to the production of specific goods or services. They are expenses that can directly be traced to a particular product, department, or process (known as cost centres). Some examples of direct costs include the cost of flour used in making bread in a bakery, the cost of labour used in car production in a manufacturing firm, and the cost of chicken in a fast-food restaurant selling only chicken products. Generally, direct costs include raw materials, direct labour, and packaging costs.

Indirect costs

These are costs that are not clearly identified with the production of specific goods or services. They are expenses that are not directly traceable to a given cost centre such as product, activity, or department. As a result, they are difficult to assign to particular cost centres. They are also known as **overheads** or **overhead costs**. Examples include rent, office staff salaries, audit fees, legal expenses, insurance, advertising expenditure, security, interest on loans, and warehouse costs.

Rent on business premises is an indirect cost

Raw materials are a direct cost

Key terms

Fixed costs

costs that do not change with the amount of goods or services produced

Variable costs

costs that change with the number of goods or services produced

Semi-variable costs

costs comprising both fixed and variable components

Direct cost

costs that can be identified with the production of specific goods or services

Indirect cost

costs that are not clearly identified with the production of specific goods or services

3 Finance and Accounts

Student workpoint 3.5

Be a researcher

Research the following organizations and identify the various costs they incur:

- An airline

- A mobile phone company

- A high school

- A hospital

- A bank

Classify the costs into either fixed, variable or semi-variable. Which of these costs can also be categorized as direct or indirect?

Total revenue

This is the total amount of money a firm receives from its sales. It is calculated by multiplying the price per unit by the number of units sold:

Total revenue = price per unit × quantity sold

Abbreviated as TR = P × Q

where TR is total revenue, P is price per unit and Q is the quantity sold.

For example, if a toy-producing firm charges US\$8 per toy and sells 200,000 toys a month, then its total revenue for the month will be (US\$8 × 200,000) = US\$1,600,000 or US\$1.6 million.

Total revenue, also known as sales revenue or turnover, should not be confused with earnings or profits, which take costs or expenses into account. In addition, total revenue includes all income received, whether the goods or services were sold on credit or cash. However, a firm's revenue is obtained not only from its trading activities. Other revenue streams include the following:

- Rental income – a business could receive income from rent it collects from property it has invested in. A seasonal business could also hire out its office or factory space during times when demand for its products is low.

- Sale of fixed assets – this could be from the sale of unused or underutilized assets in a business.

- Dividends – a business could be a shareholder in other businesses and is entitled to a share of the profits, also known as dividends.

- Interest on deposits – holding substantial amounts of cash in the bank can lead to a business earning good levels of accumulated interest on the money if the interest rates are favourable.

- Donations – these could be a cash gift made by an individual or organization targeting mostly charitable organizations.

- Grants and subsidies – see section 3.1.

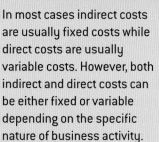

Key terms

Revenue

a measure of the money generated from the sale of goods and services

Total revenue

the total amount of money a firm receives from the sale of goods or services, found by multiplying the price per unit by the number of units sold

TOK discussion

To what extent is mathematics a vital input in knowing the costs and revenues of a business?

Revision checklist

✓ Fixed costs are costs that do not change with the amount of goods or services produced and are paid regardless of any business activity the firm engages in. Variable costs are costs that vary with the number of goods or services produced or that change in proportion to business activity.

✓ Total cost is the summation of all fixed and variable costs

✓ Semi-variable costs are costs that have both fixed and variable components and are also known as *semi-fixed costs* or *mixed costs*.

✓ Direct costs are expenses that can be directly traced to a particular product, department or cost centres while indirect costs are not clearly identified with the production of specific goods or services.

✓ Total revenue is the income gained from the sale of goods and services. It is also known as *sales revenue* or *sales turnover*.

✓ Available revenue streams to businesses include rental income, sale of fixed assets, dividends, interests on deposits, donations, grants and subsidies.

Practice question

TAK

TAK is a sole proprietorship business set up by Tom that focuses on providing tour and travel services to tourists. The set up costs included a good amount of fixed costs and variable costs grew as he ran his business. As he operated his business Tom became aware of semi-variable costs that also had an impact on his costing. In his first year he did not make any profit because his revenue was quite insignificant especially following the downturn in the economy. He has therefore resorted to cut down on his costs and seek for more revenue streams so as to guarantee a profit by the close of next year. He has approached a financial consultant to help him improve the performance of his business.

a) Define the following terms

    (i)   fixed costs   *[2 marks]*

    (ii) revenue   *[2 marks]*

    (iii) profit   *[2 marks]*

b) Using examples explain the term "semi-variable costs"   *[5 marks]*

c) Explain three ways the financial consultant may advise Tom on how to improve his revenue streams   *[9 marks]*

3.3 Break-even analysis

Contribution

Contribution is an important concept when determining the overall profitability brought about by given products in a business. However, it is vital to note that it is not the same as profit. Contribution can be used in calculating how many products need to be sold in order to cover a firm's costs. It determines how much a product contributes to its fixed costs and profit after deducting the variable costs.

Contribution per unit refers to the difference between the selling price per unit and variable cost per unit:

Contribution per unit = price per unit – variable cost per unit

For example, if a business sells tables for $150 each and its variable cost per table is $60, then the business makes a contribution of $90 per table towards paying its fixed costs.

Total contribution is calculated when more than one unit is sold. It is found by subtracting the total variable costs from the total sales revenue:

Total contribution = total revenue – total variable cost

Following from the above example, if the business sells 100 tables at the same price of $150 and a variable cost of $60 per table, then:

$$\text{Total contribution} = (\$150 \times 100) - (\$60 \times 100)$$
$$= \$9,000$$

This $9,000 will contribute towards the firm's total fixed costs and profit.

Alternatively, the total contribution can be calculated by multiplying the contribution per unit by the number of units sold:

Total contribution = contribution per unit × number of units sold

Still using the above examples:

$$\text{Total contribution} = \$90 \times 100$$
$$= \$9,000$$

Contribution and profit

After establishing what the contribution is, **profit** can be calculated. Here we will also need to know the total fixed costs incurred by the business. Using this, the formula for profit is therefore:

> **Profit = total contribution − total fixed costs**

If the business described above incurs a total fixed cost of $5,000 then its profit will be:

Profit = $9,000 − $5,000

= $4,000

Clearly we can see that contribution is not the same as profit, as contribution only removes the variable costs from sales revenue, while in calculating profit firms must also subtract the fixed costs.

Student workpoint 3.6

Be knowledgeable

A mobile phone company sells two phone models. Model A phones each sell for $250 while Model B phones sell for $180 each. In the month of January 2012, 1,000 Model A phones were sold while 1,500 Model B phones were sold. Model A's variable cost per unit was $90 and Model B's was $70 per unit. If the total fixed costs incurred by the mobile phone company that month amounted to $10,000, calculate:

a) the contribution per unit for each model

b) the total contribution for each model

c) the profit for the mobile phone company that month.

Breaking even

After gathering information about pricing and fixed and variable costs, a firm will need to calculate how many units or what level of output it needs to sell to cover all its costs. This level of output occurs where the total costs equal the total revenue, which is also known as the **break-even point**. At this point a business will neither make a profit nor a loss. Breaking even is especially important for start-up businesses or businesses engaging in new ventures so as to establish the minimum number of products they need to sell to cover all their costs.

Break-even chart

This is a graphical method that measures the value of a firm's costs and revenues against a given level of output. The break-even point can be identified by plotting the total cost and total revenue figures on a graph. The horizontal axis measures the output or units of production while the vertical axis measures the costs and revenues.

When drawing a break-even chart, the following points need to be carefully considered. (See Figure 3.3.1.)

- Fixed costs (FC) need to be paid no matter what level of output and, because they are constant at these levels, they are represented by a horizontal continuous line.

- With no units of output there will be no variable costs (VC). Therefore the VC line starts from zero (origin). The higher the number of units produced the higher the variable costs will be. The total variable costs are found by multiplying the number of units produced by the variable cost per unit. In most cases the VC line may not be included in the break-even chart.

- Since fixed costs still have to be paid with no output produced, the total cost (TC) line begins where the fixed cost (FC) line starts. Importantly, it follows the same trend as the VC line.

- With no output sold there will be no revenue. Therefore the total revenue (TR) line begins from the origin (zero). The greater the number of units sold the greater the total revenue will be.

- The break-even point is the point where the TC line intersects with the TR line. At this point the break-even revenue/costs as well as the break-even level of output can be read from the graph.

- The left of the break-even point shows the loss made by a firm, whereas the right of this point shows the profit obtained.

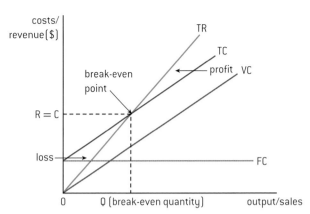

Figure 3.3.1. A break-even chart

Margin of safety

Businesses may need to know how much output they need to produce beyond the break-even point as well as how much output or sales could fall before a loss is noted. A measure of the difference between the break-even level of output and the actual (current) level of output is known as the **margin of safety** or **safety margin**. It is the range of output over which profit is made. The greater the difference between the break-even quantity and the sales levels, the greater the safety net or the safer a firm will be in its profit earnings. (See Figure 3.3.2.)

Margin of safety = current output − break-even output

For example, if the break-even quantity is 2,500 units and actual or current output is 4,000 units then the margin of safety is 1,500 units or 60 per cent above the break-even quantity. As a positive value this is a favourable position for a firm.

However, a firm producing below the break-even point or making a loss will be experiencing a negative margin of safety position. For example, if the break-even quantity is 2,500 units and the current output is 1,800 units the margin of safety will be −700 units, with the negative sign denoting that current output level is below the break-even level of output.

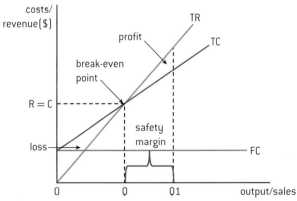

Figure 3.3.2. A break-even chart with margin of safety

Note: Q denotes break-even output and Q1 denotes current output.

Student workpoint 3.7

Be knowledgeable

The following information was provided by David, a candle producer, based on his monthly production and sales.

Table 3.3.1

Quantity of candle boxes sold	Price per candle box (US$)	Revenue from candle box sold (US$)	Fixed costs (US$) [Total]	Variable costs (US$) [Total]	Total costs (US$)	Profit/ (Loss) (US$)
0	$10	0	2,000	0	2,000	(2,000)
200	$10	2,000	2,000	1,200	3,200	
400	$10	4,000	2,000	2,400	4,400	
600	$10	6,000	2,000	3,600	5,600	
800	$10	8,000	2,000	4,800	6,800	1200
1,000	$10	10 000	2,000	6,000	8,000	
1,200	$10	12 000	2,000	7,200	9,200	

Referrring to Table 3.3.1, answer the questions below.

1. Complete the profit/(loss) column.

2. Calculate the variable cost per candle box.

3. Draw a break-even graph using the information in the table and show the break-even quantity on your graph.

4. Show on the graph the margin of safety at 1,200 candle boxes sold.

Calculating break-even quantity

1. Using contribution per unit

Break-even quantity can be calculated using the following formula:

$$\text{Break-even quantity} = \frac{\text{fixed costs}}{\text{contribution per unit}}$$

For example, a shirt retailer incurs fixed costs amounting to $3,000 a month. The variable cost per shirt is $12 and the selling price for each shirt is $22. Using the above formula:

$$\text{Break-even quantity} = \frac{\$3,000}{\$22 - \$12} = 300 \text{ shirts}$$

2. Using the total costs = total revenue method

We saw in section 3.2 that total revenue (TR) = P × Q and

total costs (TC) = total fixed costs (TFC) + total variable costs (TVC)

where TVC is variable cost per unit (VC) × Q.

Using the above example of the shirt retailer, the break-even quantity can be calculated as shown below:

Total revenue (TR) = total costs (TC)

P × Q = TFC + TVC

22 × Q = 3,000 + (12 × Q)

10 × Q = 3,000

Q = 300 shirts

Both methods shown above give a break-even quantity of 300 shirts that the retailer needs to sell in order to break even.

Profit or loss

The break-even chart showed that any sales that exceed the break-even quantity generate **profit** for a business, while sales that are less than the break-even quantity lead to **losses**.

Profit can be calculated using contribution as seen earlier above. Moreover, profit or loss can also be calculated using the following formula:

Profit = total revenue (TR) − total costs (TC)

Assuming the shirt retailer sold 1,000 shirts a month, the profit per month would be calculated as follows:

Profit = TR − TC

Profit = [P × Q] − [TFC + TVC]

= [22 × 1,000] − [3,000 + (12 × 1,000)]

= $22,000 − $15,000

= $7,000

The shirt retailer would therefore be making a profit of $7,000 on selling 1,000 shirts a month.

What would be the profit or loss if in another month only 200 shirts were sold, assuming the price and other costs remain constant?

Target profit

Target profit output

The break-even chart can be used to determine the level of output that is needed to earn a given level of profit. Output found this way is known as target profit output and the expected profit is known as target profit. As shown in Figure 3.3.3, to attain a target profit of $1,500 ($9,600 − $8,100) the bicycle producer will need to sell 80 bicycles.

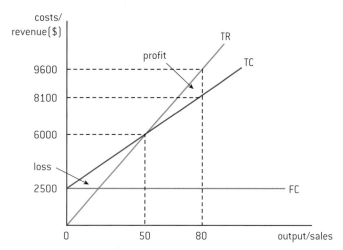

Figure 3.3.3. The break-even chart of a bicycle producer

The producer needs to sell 80 bicycles to reach the target profit

An alternative method of getting target profit output is by using the following formula, which is a modification of the break-even formula:

$$\textbf{Target profit output} = \frac{\textbf{fixed costs} + \textbf{target profit}}{\textbf{contribution per unit}}$$

Using the information for the bicycle producer, where fixed costs amount to $2,500, variable cost per unit is $70, price per bicycle is $120, and the target profit is $1,500, the target profit output can be calculated as follows:

$$\text{Target profit output} = \frac{2,500 + 1,500}{120 - 70} = \frac{4,000}{50} = 80 \text{ bicycles}$$

The result obtained using the calculation method confirms what was obtained using the break-even chart method.

The above formula can also be used in calculating target profit and target price.

Calculating target profit

Assuming that the bicycle producer's fixed costs remain at $2,500, contribution per unit is $50 and the target profit output is now 100 bicycles, what is the target profit?

This is found as follows by incorporating the target profit output formula:

$$\frac{\$2,500 + \text{target profit}}{\$50} = 100$$

$$\$2,500 + \text{target profit} = 100 \times \$50$$

$$\text{Target profit} = \$5,000 - \$2,500$$

$$\text{Target profit} = \$2,500$$

Calculating target price

Target price can also be calculated using the formula above. If the fixed costs are $2,500, the variable cost per bicycle is $50, the target profit is $6,500 and the target profit output is 200 bicycles, the target price can be calculated as follows:

$$200 = \frac{\$2,500 + \$6,500}{\text{target price} - \$50}$$

$$200 \,(\text{target price} - \$50) = \$9,000$$

$$200 \,(\text{target price}) - \$10,000 = \$9,000$$

$$\text{Target price} = \frac{\$19,000}{200} = \$95 \text{ per bicycle}$$

Therefore to target a profit of $6,500 at a target profit output of 200 bicycles, the bicycle producer will need to sell each bicycle for $95.

Break-even revenue

The break-even revenue can be determined using a break-even chart, as seen in Figure 3.3.3, which establishes it to be $6,000 at an output level of 50 bicycles. It is clear that the break-even revenue is obtained at the point where the total revenue equals the total costs, i.e. it is the revenue required to cover both the fixed and variable costs in order for a firm to break even. At this point the break-even revenue is equal to the break-even costs.

It can also be calculated using the following formula:

$$\boxed{\textbf{Break-even revenue} = \frac{\textbf{fixed costs}}{\textbf{contribution per unit}} \times \textbf{price per unit}}$$

Using the previous example of a bicycle producer, if price per bicycle is $120, variable costs are $70 and fixed costs are $2,500, then applying the above formula we get:

$$\text{Break-even revenue} = \frac{\$2,500}{50} \times \$120 = \$6,000$$

This calculation shows that the break-even revenue is $6,000 – the same as that shown in Figure 3.3.3.

Key terms

Break-even chart

a graphical method that measures the value of a firm's costs and revenues against a given level of output

Break-even quantity

a measure of output where total revenue equals total costs

Profit

the positive difference between total revenue and total costs

Margin of safety

the output amount that exceeds the break-even quantity

Target profit output

the level of output that is needed to earn a specified amount of profit

3 Finance and Accounts

Student workpoint 3.8

Be a thinker

XYZ Ltd has the capacity to produce 180,000 units of its key product per month. The fixed costs amount to $600,000 per month, while the variable costs are $15 per unit. The selling price for each product is $20.

1. Calculate the:

    a) monthly profits at maximum capacity

    b) break-even quantity

    c) break-even revenue.

2. The company has a profit target of $250,000 per month. Calculate the:

    a) output level needed to reach the target profit

    b) price it will need to charge to achieve the profit target at a capacity of 150,000 units.

Effects of changes in price or costs

The break-even chart can be used as a helpful decision-making tool as it can show the impact on break-even quantity, profit, and margin of safety as a result of any changes in price or cost. The new position after the changes can then be compared with the previous position to provide future direction in the business.

1. Changes in price

Figure 3.3.4 shows the effect of an increase in price. This leads to a shift of the total revenue line from TR_1 to TR_2. This indicates that the sales revenue has increased at all levels of output. The firm will also break even at a lower level of output and there will be higher profits at every output level. This can also lead to an increase in a firm's margin of safety.

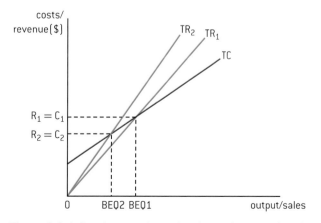

Figure 3.3.4. Break-even chart showing an increase in price

2. Changes in costs

a) Increase in fixed costs

Figure 3.3.5 shows the effect of an increase in fixed costs (FC_1 to FC_2), leading to an upward parallel shift of the total cost line from TC_1 to TC_2. An increase in fixed costs leads to an increase in total costs by the same amount at every level of output. Break-even quantity also increases and profits decrease at all levels of output. This also decreases the margin of safety.

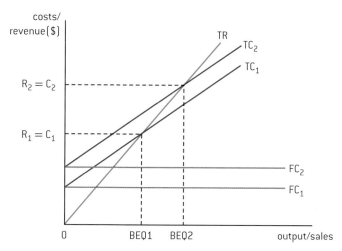

Figure 3.3.5. Break-even chart showing an increase in fixed costs

b) Increase in variable costs

Figure 3.3.6 shows the effect of an increase in variable costs. Increases in variable costs increase the gradient of the total cost line. This is shown by the shift of the total cost line from TC_1 to TC_2. This leads to a rise in the break-even quantity and reduces the margin of safety.

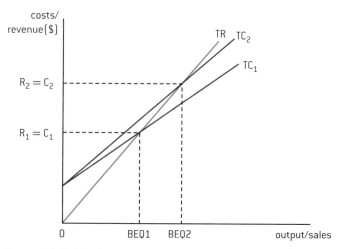

Figure 3.3.6. Break-even chart showing an increase in variable costs

Student workpoint 3.9

Be a thinker

A chocolate business is considering which of the following three prices to charge its customers per chocolate:

A $1.50   **B** $2.00   **C** $2.50

The following information is useful in its decision making:

- fixed costs: $100 000
- variable cost per chocolate: $1
- current output: 300 000 chocolates.

1. For each price, calculate:

    a) the break-even quantity

    b) the margin of safety

    c) the profit or loss

    d) break-even quantity as a percentage of the current output.

2. If the variable costs per chocolate increase to $1.20, recalculate parts (a) to (d) above.

3. Comment on your observations from questions 1 and 2.

Benefits of break-even analysis

- Break-even charts provide an easy and visual means of analysing a firm's financial position at various levels of output.
- At a glance, by using the charts, the management of a business is able to determine the profit or loss, margin of safety, break-even quantity, and break-even revenue or cost.
- Formulae can also be used to give more accurate results when calculating the above.
- Changes in prices and costs and their impact on profit or loss, break-even point, and margin of safety can be compared by using the charts or by calculation.
- Break-even analysis can be used as a strategic decision-making tool such as deciding on key investment projects or whether a business should relocate or merge with another firm.

Limitations of break-even analysis

- Break-even analysis assumes that all the output produced by firms is sold with no possibility of stocks being built up or held. In reality, many businesses may hold stocks to cater for any sudden changes in demand. Stocks may also build up because goods cannot be sold.
- It assumes that all revenue and cost lines are linear, i.e. represented by straight lines. This is not always the case. Offering price reductions

Student workpoint 3.10

Be knowledgeable

1. JTS Ltd produces clocks and sells them to a number of countries globally. The following monthly information is provided.

    Maximum capacity: 200,000 clocks

    Current output and sales: 160,000 clocks

    Selling price: $12
    Fixed costs: $900,000

    Variable cost: $ 4 per clock

    The management propose that a possible reduction in price per unit to $10 would lead to an increase in sales and help them reach their maximum capacity.

    a) Construct a break-even chart using the original price and current output level

    b) Use the chart to determine:

        (i) Break-even quantity

        (ii) The margin of safety

        (iii) Profit at current output

    Use the calculation method to check your answers.

    c) Construct a second break-even chart to show the situation after the price reduction. Repeat the tasks in part (b) above using the new chart.

    d) Recommend which of the proposals JTS Ltd should pursue.

or discounts will influence the slope of the revenue line. The slope of the variable cost line will also change if a firm pays overtime wages in an effort to increase output. This change will then influence the slope of the total cost line.

- Apart from showing fixed and variable costs, semi-variable costs are not represented on the break-even chart. If these are included it makes the process more complex.

- A break-even chart may not be very useful in changing or dynamic business environments. For example, the break-even chart may not cope with sudden changes in prices, costs, or technology.

- The accuracy and quality of the cost and revenue data used determine the effectiveness of break-even analysis. Unreliable or inaccurate data may influence the conclusions reached in the overall analysis.

- Fixed costs may change at different levels of activity. It would be preferable to represent these fixed costs as a "stepped" line. For example, in order to increase output a firm may need to double its capacity. This may lead to sharp rises in fixed costs, thereby complicating break-even analysis.

Revision checklist

✓ Contribution per unit is the difference between the selling price per unit and variable cost per unit while total contribution is the difference between the total revenue and the total variable cost.

✓ Profit can be obtained by getting the difference between the total contribution and the total fixed cost or by subtracting the total costs from the total revenue to obtain a positive value.

✓ A break even chart is a graphical method that measures the value of a firm's costs and revenues against a given level of output and helps in identifying the break-even point.

✓ Margin of safety measures the difference between the break-even level of output and the actual (current) level of output in a business.

✓ Break-even quantity can be calculated by dividing the total fixed costs by the contribution per unit.

✓ Target profit output formula is $\dfrac{\text{Fixed costs} + \text{target profit}}{\text{Contribution per unit}}$

✓ Break-even revenue formula is $\dfrac{\text{Fixed costs}}{\text{Contribution per unit}} \times \text{Price per unit}$

Exam tip

Most IB examination questions require the use of models with straight revenue and cost lines.

TOK discussion

"What you measure is what you get." What, if anything, does this tell you about the role of measurable objectives in business decision making?

Do results obtained from quantitative methods always outweigh qualitative ones?

3 Finance and Accounts

Practice question

Dan Electro

Dan Bowen is a sole trader who sells digital cameras directly to consumers. He owns an online business and all sales are processed electronically under the business name *Dan Electro*. The office, storage place and call centre are located together in an expensive and desirable city centre location.

Dan started the business three years ago by borrowing a considerable amount of money from a bank. He used his residential property as collateral* for the loan.

The cameras are bought and shipped from a reputable and reliable overseas supplier who charges a high price for good quality cameras and prompt transportation. Dan has to pay in advance for the cameras. *Dan Electro's* customers are very loyal and see their purchase as good value for money. Repeat purchases comprise a large percentage of *Dan Electro's* sales. Some customers have even indicated that they would pay a higher price for the cameras because of their quality and the good service he provides.

Dan is now worried about the forecasted rise in interest rates, inflation and an increase in online competition. *Dan Electro* may face some cash flow difficulties in the coming years. He is considering various strategies in order to prevent such possible cash flow difficulties.

Financial information for 2010 (all figures in US$)			
Fixed costs per year			
Rent	Marketing	Administration	Interest payments
20 000	4000	5000	1000
Variable costs per camera			
Camera	Transportation	Direct labour	**Price per camera**
135	45	20	250

Dan is expected to sell 700 cameras in 2010.

a) (i) Define the term *variable costs*. [2 marks]

   (ii) Identify **two** advantages for Dan of operating as a sole trader. [2 marks]

b) (i) Construct a fully labelled break-even chart for *Dan Electro* for 2010. Calculate and indicate the break-even point, the margin of safety and the projected profit at 700 cameras (*show all your working*). [7 marks]

   (ii) Calculate the number of cameras *Dan Electro* must sell in order to double the projected profit (*show all your working*). [2 marks]

   (iii) Calculate the price per camera that needs to be charged (at expected sales of 700 cameras) in order to double the projected profit (*show all your working*). [2 marks]

   (iv) Explain **two** possible limitations of the break-even model as a decision tool for *Dan Electro*. [4 marks]

c) Examine **two** possible strategies for *Dan Electro* to prevent cash flow difficulties. [6 marks]

IB, Nov 2010

---

* collateral: the borrower's property is offered to the lender as security if the loan is not paid back

3.4 Final accounts

3 Finance and Accounts

By the end of this chapter, you should be able to:

→ discuss the **purpose of accounts to different stakeholders**

→ examine the principles and **ethics** of accounting practice

→ prepare and interpret final accounts, namely the **profit and loss account** and the **balance sheet**

→ describe the different types of **intangible assets**

→ calculate and distinguish between the **straight-line** and **reducing-balance** depreciation methods (HL only)

→ explain the strengths and weaknesses of the **straight-line** and **reducing-balance** methods **(HL only)**.

Purpose of accounts to different stakeholders

Final accounts are financial statements compiled by businesses at the end of a particular accounting period such as at the end of a fiscal or trading year. These records of accounts including transactions, revenues, and expenses help to inform internal and external stakeholders about the financial position and performance of an organization. Internal stakeholders include shareholders, managers, and employees, while examples of external stakeholders are customers, suppliers, the government, competitors, financiers, and the local community. The purpose of accounts to each of these stakeholders is explored below.

Shareholders

Shareholders will be interested in knowing how valuable the business is becoming throughout its financial year. They will be keen to establish how profitable the business is in order to assess the safety of their investment. They check on the efficiency of the business in investing capital in order to make a worthwhile return on their investment. The performance of the directors is also of interest to them: they want to see whether they need to be motivated further or replaced.

Managers

Final accounts are used by managers to set targets, which they can use to judge and compare their performance within a particular financial year or number of years. These will help them in setting budgets, which will then help in monitoring and controlling expenditure patterns in various departments. Knowing the financial records will therefore greatly assist managers in strategic planning for more effective decision making in the businesses.

Employees

A profitable business could signal to employees that their jobs will be secure. This may also indicate that they could get pay rises. The potential for business growth could also help to strengthen these two aspects of job security and salary increases. However, an increase in profitability does not necessarily lead to pay increases for employees, leading them to involve trade unions to negotiate further on their behalf.

Customers

Customers will be interested in knowing whether there will be a constant supply of a firm's products in the future. This will determine how dependent they should be on the business and how secure it is. If a firm lacks security, perhaps due to low profitability, customers will go elsewhere where supply is reliable and guaranteed.

Suppliers

Suppliers can use final accounts to negotiate better cash or credit terms with firms. They can either extend the trade credit period or demand immediate cash payments. The security of the business and thus its ability to pay off its debts will be a key concern for suppliers.

The government

The government and tax authorities will check on whether the business is abiding by the law regarding accounting regulations. They will be interested in the profitability of the business to see how much tax it pays. A loss-making business will be of grave concern to the government because it could mean an increase in unemployment, which could be detrimental to a country's economy.

Competitors

Businesses will want to compare their financial statements with those of other firms to see how well they are performing financially. They will look for the answers to key questions:

- Are their competitors' profitability levels higher than theirs or are the competitors struggling financially?
- How do the competitors' sales revenues compare with theirs?

Financiers

These include banks that will check on the creditworthiness of the business to establish how much money they can lend it. This will also depend on the gearing of the business because a high-geared business will have problems soliciting funding from financial institutions (see section 3.1). Banks will thoroughly assess the accounts of a business in order to be confident that it will be able to pay back its loan with interest.

The local community

Residents living around a particular business will want to know its profitability and expansion potential. This is because it may create job

opportunities for them and lead to growth in the community. However, the residents will also be concerned about whether the businesses will be environmentally friendly and whether their accounts consider costs such as air or noise pollution.

Principles and ethics of accounting practice

Professional accountants have a responsibility to act in the public interest. They not only have to satisfy the needs of their employer or client but should observe and comply with a particular code of ethics and conduct. Ethics in accounting is the study of moral values and judgments as applied in the accounting process. A code of ethics is therefore a set of principles, usually based on the firm's core values, that guide accountants on the standards that need to be upheld. A code spells out the "rules" for behaviour with respective pre-emptive warnings. For a deeper understanding of how principles and ethics are applied in accounting practice, read the following case study about the Association of Chartered Certified Accountants (ACCA).

Case study

ACCA code of ethics and conduct

The Association of Chartered Certified Accountants (ACCA) is a global body for professional accountants that offers business-relevant qualifications to people seeking careers in accountancy, finance and management.

The Code of Ethics and Conduct (the Code) is binding on all members of ACCA, and any partner (or director) in an ACCA practice. However, it is also binding on the staff of such a practice, regardless of whether or not they are members of ACCA or any other professional body. The Code is divided into three parts. Part A sets out the fundamental principles of professional ethics for professional accountants and provides a conceptual framework for applying those principles. Parts B and C illustrate how the conceptual framework is to be applied in specific situations. These parts provide examples of safeguards that may be appropriate to address threats to compliance with the fundamental principles and also provide examples of situations where safeguards are not available to address those threats.

Some of the most important areas of the Code, from the point of view of a practitioner, are discussed below and in other available fact sheets.

The fundamental principles

Within the Code, as noted above, the fundamental principles are set out in Part A. As a member body of the International Federation of Accountants (IFAC), ACCA is required to apply ethical standards that are at least as stringent as those stated in the International Ethics Standards Board for Accountants

Code of Ethics for Professional Accountants (the IESBA Code). Whenever the IESBA Code is revised, the *ACCA Rulebook* is reviewed, and updated as necessary, to ensure that it remains aligned with the IESBA Code.

The fundamental principles set out the obligations placed on all members, whether or not they are in practice. The five principles are set out below.

- **Integrity** – members shall be "straightforward and honest in all professional and business relationships". The *ACCA Rulebook* (and the IESBA Code) goes on to state that integrity implies not merely honesty, but fair dealing and truthfulness.

- **Objectivity** – members shall not allow bias, conflicts of interest or the undue influence of others to compromise their professional or business judgment.

- **Professional competence and due care** – members have a continuing duty "to maintain professional knowledge and skill at a level required to ensure that clients or employers receive competent professional service". Members shall "act diligently in accordance with applicable technical and professional standards when providing professional services".

- **Confidentiality** – members shall respect the confidentiality of information "acquired as a result of professional and business relationships", and shall not disclose any such information to third parties "without proper and specific authority or unless there is a legal or professional right or duty to disclose". Similarly, confidential information acquired as a result of professional and business relationships shall not be used to the personal advantage of members or third parties.

- **Professional behaviour** – members shall comply with relevant laws and regulations and shall avoid any action that may discredit the profession. The *ACCA Rulebook* goes further, and states that members shall "behave with courtesy and consideration" towards all with whom they come into contact in a professional capacity.

Source: http://www.accaglobal.com/content/dam/acca/global/PDF-members/2012/2012c/CofEC.pdf

Exam-style questions

1. Outline the objectives of the ACCA Code of Ethics and Conduct. [4 marks]

2. Apply three principles of the ACCA Code of Ethics and Conduct to an organisation of your choice. [6 marks]

3. Discuss the benefits and the limitations of a Code of Ethics and Conduct such as the one produced by the ACCA. [10 marks]

The main final accounts

The profit and loss account

This is also known as the **income statement** and shows the records of income and expenditure flows of a business over a given time period. It therefore establishes whether a business has made a profit or loss and how this was distributed at the end of that period. It is divided into three parts: the **trading account**, the **profit and loss account**, and the **appropriation account**.

(a) The trading account

The trading account shows the difference between the sales revenue and the cost to the business of those sales. It is shown as the top part of the income statement that establishes the **gross profit** of the business (see Table 3.4.1). In calculating gross profit the following formula is used:

> **Gross profit = sales revenue − cost of sales**

Sales revenue is the income earned from selling goods or services over a given period. Cost of sales or cost of goods sold (COGS) is the direct cost of producing or purchasing the goods that were sold during that period. The formula for cost of sales is as follows:

> **Cost of sales = opening stock + purchases − closing stock**

For example, a firm at the beginning of a trading period had $500 worth of stock. It then bought more stock during this period valued at $800. It then closed this period with stock valued at $200. What is its COGS during the period?

COGS = $500 + $800 − $200

COGS = $1,100

What would its gross profit be if it sold 400 units of a product at $10 each?

Sales revenue = $10 × 400 = $4,000

Gross profit = $4,000 − $1,100

    = $2,900

TOK discussion

Many businesses are introducing statements about their environmental, social or ethical performance together with other financial information. How can we effectively measure these social variables?

(b) The profit and loss account

This is the second part of the income statement that shows the net profit before interest and tax, net profit before tax, and net profit after interest and tax (see Table 3.4.1).

To find out net profit before interest and tax, expenses are subtracted from the gross profit shown in the trading account. These expenses comprise indirect costs or overheads which are not directly linked to the units sold. Examples include advertising costs, administration charges, rent, and insurance costs. Therefore:

> **Net profit before interest and tax = gross profit − expenses**

Net profit before tax is calculated by subtracting interest payable on loans from the net profit before interest and tax:

> **Net profit before tax = net profit before interest and tax − interest**

Then, the net profit after interest and tax is found by deducting corporation tax (tax on company profits) from net profit before tax:

> **Net profit after interest and tax = net profit before tax − corporation tax**

(c) The appropriation account

This is the final part of the profit and loss account that shows how the company's net profit after interest and tax is distributed (see Table 3.4.1). This distribution is in two forms, either as dividends to shareholders or as retained profit (ploughed-back profit). Retained profit is calculated using the following formula:

> **Retained profit = net profit after interest and tax − dividends**

Table 3.4.1 Profit and loss account for XYZ Ltd

XYZ Ltd		
Profit and loss account for the year ended 30 June 2012		
	US$ million	
Sales revenue	800	**Trading account**
Cost of goods sold	250	
Gross profit	550	
Expenses	300	
Net profit before interest and tax	250	**Profit and loss**
Interest	20	**account**
Net profit before tax	230	
Tax	40	
Net profit after interest and tax	190	
Dividends	50	**Appropriation**
Retained profit	140	**account**

3 Finance and Accounts

Student workpoint 3.11

Be a thinker

Profit and loss account for BTW Ltd for the year ended 31 December 2012	
	$000
Sales revenue	950
Cost of goods sold	?
Gross profit	650
Expenses	?
Net profit before interest and tax	350
Interest	10
Net profit before tax	?
Tax	40
Net profit after interest and tax	?
Dividends	50
Retained profit	?

a) Complete the above profit and loss account by filling in the missing numbers (indicated by question marks).

b) Identify *four* stakeholders who would be interested in the profit and loss account for BTW Ltd.

c) Explain how the above stakeholders would use the information in this account.

The balance sheet

Also known as the statement of financial position, this outlines the assets, liabilities, and equity of a firm at a specific point in time. It is a snapshot of the financial position of a firm and is used to calculate a firm's net worth. It gives the firm an idea of what it owns and owes, including how much shareholders have invested in it. The basic requirement of a balance sheet is that what a business owns (total assets) must equal what it owes (total liabilities) plus how the assets are financed (equity). This is what makes the balance sheet balance. The three main components of assets, liabilities, and equity are explored below.

Assets

These are resources of value a business owns or are owed to it. They include fixed assets and current assets.

Fixed assets are long-term assets that last in a business for more than 12 months. Tangible examples that are physical in nature include buildings, equipment, vehicles, and machinery. Some of these assets,

> ## ETHICS
>
> In 2002, the Sarbanes-Oxley Act was passed to deter unethical accounting. The Act was passed in response to high-profile scandals including Enron and WorldCom. (http://www.sox-online.com/act. html)
>
> Are there any other global examples of unethical behaviour in accounting that come to mind? How did the firms concerned handle the situation?

such as machinery, usually depreciate (lose value) over time. In this case depreciation is deducted from fixed assets to get net fixed assets. Intangible assets that are non-physical in nature tend to be difficult to value. (These will be looked at later in the unit.)

Current assets are short-term assets that last in a business for up to 12 months. They include cash, debtors, and stock. Cash is money received from the sale of goods and services which could be held either at the bank or by the business. Debtors are individuals or other firms that have bought goods on credit and owe the business money. Stock, also known as inventory, includes raw materials, semi-finished goods, and finished goods.

Liabilities

These are a firm's legal debts or what it owes to other firms, institutions, or individuals. They arise during the course of business operation and are usually a source of funding for the firm. They are classified into long-term liabilities and current liabilities.

Long-term liabilities are long-term debts or borrowings payable after 12 months by the business. They include long-term bank loans and mortgages.

Current liabilities are short-term debts that are payable by the business within 12 months. These include creditors (unpaid suppliers who sold goods on credit to the firm), a bank overdraft (see section 3.1), and tax (money owed to the government such as corporation tax).

When we know what the liabilities of a business are, we can calculate its **working capital** and establish its **net assets**. The amount of working capital a business has is important because it indicates whether the business can pay off its day-to-day bills or running costs. Working capital is also known as net current assets and is calculated as shown below. It is a measure of the short-term financial health and efficiency of a business.

> **Working capital = total current assets − total current liabilities**

To get total assets less current liabilities, we first add all the assets and deduct current liabilities:

> **Total assets less current liabilities = (fixed assets + current assets) − current liabilities**

or

> **Total assets less current liabilities = fixed assets + working capital**

Then to get **net assets**, we subtract long-term liabilities from the above, as shown:

> **Net assets = (total assets less current liabilities) − long-term liabilities**

Having calculated the net assets of the business, we then need to find out how they were financed.

Equity

Also known as shareholder's equity or shareholder's funds, equity includes two aspects, namely share capital and retained profits.

Share capital

This refers to the original capital invested into the business through shares bought by shareholders. It is a permanent source of capital and does not include the daily buying and selling of shares in a stock exchange market or the current market value of shares.

Retained profit

As noted in section 3.1, this is the profit ploughed back into the business obtained from the profit and loss account. It is also known as reserves as it includes profit that the business has made in previous years. This is money owed to the owners but which has been reinvested so as to purchase necessary assets in the business.

From the above, we then note that:

> **Equity = share capital + retained profit**

This equity helps to finance the net assets of the business and enables the balance sheet to balance:

> **Net assets = equity**

Table 3.4.2 is an example of a balance sheet that incorporates what has been discussed above and uses the required IB format.

Table 3.4.2 A statement of financial position

XYZ Ltd Balance sheet as at 30 June 2012	$m	$m
Fixed assets		
Fixed assets	600	
Accumulated depreciation	30	
Net fixed assets		570
Current assets		
Cash	20	
Debtors	15	
Stock	55	
Total current assets	90	
Current liabilities		
Overdraft	10	
Creditors	20	
Short-term loans	15	
Total current liabilities	45	
Net current assets (working capital)		45
Total assets less current liabilities		615
Long-term liabilities (debt)	250	
Net assets		365
Financed by:		
share capital	220	
retained profit	145	
equity		365

Key terms

Balance sheet

a financial statement that outlines the assets, liabilities and equity of a firm at a specific point in time

Assets

resources of value that a business owns or that are owed to it

Liabilities

a firm's legal debts or what it owes to other firms, institutions or individuals

Working capital

also known as net current assets, helps establish whether a firm can pay its day-to-day running costs

Net assets

found by subtracting long-term liabilities from total assets less current liabilities

Equity

also known as shareholders' equity, shows how the net assets are financed using shareholders' capital and retained profit

Student workpoint 3.12

Be a thinker

1. Using Table 3.4.2, prepare another balance sheet for the year ended 30 June 2013 after the following adjustments occurred:

   - Cash increased by US$10 million.
   - Creditors rose by US$15 million.
   - Stock decreased by US$5 million.
   - A long-term loan increased by 10%.
   - Debtors rose by US$5 million.
   - Retained profit fell by US$26 million.
   - The bank overdraft reduced by US$4 million.
   - Net fixed assets, share capital and short-term loans remained the same.

2. Explain **two** uses and **two** limitations of the balance sheet.

TOK discussion

Do financial statements reflect the "truth" about a business?

What role does interpretation play in accounting? For example, how can we compare businesses just by looking at their financial statements?

Intangible assets

These are fixed assets that lack physical substance or are non-physical in nature. However, even though they do not have a physical value they can prove to be very valuable to a firm's long-term success or failure. Some of them are explained below.

Patents

These provide inventors with the exclusive rights to manufacture, use, sell, or control their invention of a product. The inventors are provided with legal protection that prevents others from copying their ideas. Anyone wishing to use the patent holder's ideas must apply and pay a fee to be granted permission to use it. The legal life for most patents is about 20 years; however, this period also depends on the useful life of the patent. Interesting patents include a pen with a scanner, steel kidneys and rubber shoes for horses' health. More details on these and others can be found at: http://www.prv.se/en/Patents/Why-apply-for-a-patent/Examples-of-patents/.

Goodwill

This refers to the value of positive or favourable attributes that relate to a business. It includes a good customer base and relations, strong brand name, highly skilled employees, desirable location and the good reputation a firm enjoys with its clients. Goodwill usually arises when one firm is purchased by another. During an acquisition, goodwill is valued as the amount paid by the purchasing firm over and above the book value of the firm being bought.

Copyright laws

These are laws that provide a creator with the exclusive right to protect the production and sale of their artistic or literary work. Creators include musicians, authors, and film producers. Copyright laws will only apply if the original ideas are put to use such as in the creation of a published novel, a music album or developed computer software. Most copyright lasts for between 50 to 100 years after the death of the creator. As with patents, anyone wishing to use a copyright holder's works must seek permission from them to do so.

'You're fired!' American businessman Donald Trump has attempted to trademark his famous catchphrase

Trademarks

These are a recognizable symbol, word, phrase or design that is officially registered and that identifies a product or business. Trademarks also help to distinguish one firm's products from another's. Anyone who infringes the trademarks of others can be sued by the trademark owners. Trademarks can be sold for a fee and most last for a 15-year renewable period, depending on their use. Examples of popular trademarks include Coca-Cola, KFC, the Nike "swoosh", the McDonald's golden arch symbol, and Donald Trump's catchphrase "You're fired".

Intangible assets are difficult to value, due to their subjective nature and in many cases they will not be shown in the balance sheet. Their value can fluctuate over time and simple changes in the reputation of

an organization can either inflate or deflate a firm's value. As a result, intangible assets can be used to "window dress" or artificially increase the value of a firm just before a purchase. The setting of specific parameters to be used to quantify an intangible asset just serves to increase the complexity and inaccuracy of including it in the balance sheet.

Depreciation (HL only)

This is the decrease in the value of a fixed asset over time. It is a non-cash expense that is recorded in the profit and loss account in order to determine the net profit before interest and tax. Two reasons why assets depreciate include the following:

- Wear and tear – the repeated use of fixed assets such as cars or machinery causes them to fall in value and more money is needed to maintain them.

- Obsolescence – existing fixed assets fall in value when new or improved versions are introduced in the market. With time these "old" assets become obsolete or out of date and are eventually withdrawn.

The IB expects you to know two methods for calculating depreciation, the **straight-line method** and the **reducing-balance method**, as described below.

Straight-line method

This is a commonly used method that spreads out the cost of an asset equally over its lifetime by deducting a given constant amount of depreciation of the asset's value per annum. It requires the following elements in its calculation:

- the expected useful life of the asset, i.e. the length of time it intends to be used before replacement

- the original cost of the asset, i.e. its purchase or historical cost

- the residual or scrap value of the asset, i.e. an estimation of its worth or value over its useful life.

Incorporating the above, the annual depreciation can be calculated as:

$$\text{Annual depreciation} = \frac{\text{original cost} - \text{residual value}}{\text{expected useful life of asset}}$$

Example 1: On 1 January 2012 ABC Company purchased a vehicle costing $30,000. It is expected to have a value of $6,000 at the end of four years. Calculate the depreciation expense on the vehicle for the year ended 31 December 2012.

First, it is important to identify the key elements: the original cost is $30,000, the residual value is $6,000 and the expected useful life is four years.

Then apply the annual depreciation formula:

$$\text{Annual depreciation} = \frac{\$30,000 - \$6,000}{4 \text{ years}} = \$6,000$$

Key terms

Intangible assets

fixed assets that lack physical substance or are non-physical in nature

Patents

provide inventors with the exclusive rights to manufacture, use, sell or control their invention of a product

Goodwill

the value of positive or favourable attributes that relate to a business

Copyright laws

laws that provide creators with the exclusive right to protect the production and sale of their artistic or literary work

Trademark

a recognizable symbol, word, phrase or design that is officially registered and that identifies a product or business

3 Finance and Accounts

The above information can be shown in a table to show the net book value over four years.

Table 3.4.3 Straight-line depreciation at $6,000 per annum

Year	Annual depreciation expense ($)	Net book value on vehicle ($)
0 (present)	0	30,000
1	6,000	24,000
2	6,000	18,000
3	6,000	12,000
4	6,000	6,000

Example 2: Calculate the depreciation expense of the above vehicle if it was purchased on 1 July 2012 with the year ending on 31 December 2012.

In such a case we will be required to charge depreciation for half the year as follows:

$$\text{Depreciation expense} = \left(\frac{6 \text{ months}}{12 \text{ months}} \right) \times \left[\frac{(\$30,000 - \$6,000)}{4} \right] = \$3,000$$

Advantages of straight-line depreciation

- It is simple to calculate as it is a predictable expense that is spread over a number of years.

- It is mostly suitable for less expensive items, such as furniture, that can be written off within the asset's estimated useful life.

Disadvantages of straight-line depreciation

- It is not suitable for expensive assets such as plant and machinery as it does not cater for the loss in efficiency or increase in repair expenses over the useful life of the asset.

- It is known to inflate the value of some assets which may have lost the greatest amount of value in their first or second years, such as motor vehicles.

- It does not take into account the fast-changing technological environment that may render certain fixed assets obsolete very quickly.

Reducing-balance method

This method applies a percentage depreciation rate over the useful life of the asset. It adopts an accelerated depreciation technique whereby the depreciation amount charged to an asset declines over time, i.e. higher depreciation is charged at the beginning of an asset's lifetime and less is charged at the end. Under the reducing-balance method net book value in Year 1 may be calculated as:

Net book value in Year 1 = Cost of original asset − (cost of original asset × rate of depreciation [%])

This is where:

- net book value is an asset's net value and is calculated by deducting the depreciation from the cost of the asset

- rate of depreciation is the percentage fall in the value of an asset over its useful life.

Example 3: Using example 1 above, the vehicle was depreciating at an annual rate of 33%* (see below).

Table 3.4.4 Reducing-balance depreciation

Year	Depreciation ($)	Net book value ($)
0	0	30,000
1	9,900 (30,000 × 33%)	20,100
2	6,633 (20,100 × 33%)	13,467
3	444,411 (13,467 × 33%)	9,022.89
4	2,977.55 (9,022.89 × 33%)	6,045.34

The net book value at the end of four years using this method is about $6,045.

*33% is an approximation obtained using the calculation formula for the depreciation rate. The exact rate is about 33.126%. The formula is as shown below:

$$\text{Depreciation rate} = 1 - \sqrt[N]{\frac{\text{residual value}}{\text{cost of fixed asset}}}$$

Where N represents the expected useful life of the asset.

Residual value is the estimated scrap or salvage value of an asset at the end of its useful life.

Advantages of reducing-balance depreciation

- It more realistically matches the cost and revenue of the business. This is because the higher amount of depreciation provided in the early years is matched against the larger amount of revenue generated by the increased production brought about by the use of the new asset.

- It provides a more accurate measure of depreciation compared to the straight-line method, especially in the valuation of assets over the years.

- it increases non-cash expenses immediately, which lowers the income tax expense in the early years, thereby improving cash flow.

Disadvantages of reducing-balance depreciation

- It is a more complex method of calculating depreciation compared to the straight-line method.

- It charges high amounts of depreciation in the early years, which may not be realistic for some less expensive assets.

- The formula used to obtain the rate of depreciation may be subjective because without residual value it cannot be used.

- It that lowers profits, which some stakeholders, especially if the company is publicly traded on a stock exchange, might object to.

- It defers tax payments for later years. This is not a problem if the company keeps growing and increasing in profits. However, if a company experiences difficulty, growth and profits slow or go down and the company has to delay future capital expenditures, the income tax burden will increase just as the company is facing cash flow pressures from slowed or declining sales and operating profits.

Student workpoint 3.13

Be knowledgeable

Suppose a business has an asset with $2,000 original cost, $200 scrap value, and five years of useful life.

1. Use the straight-line method to determine its annual depreciation charge.

2. Using the formula, calculate its rate of depreciation in the reducing-balance method.

3. In questions 1 and 2 draw and complete the table to show the net book values over the years.

Revision checklist

✓ Final accounts are financial statements compiled by businesses at the end of an accounting period that inform internal and external stakeholders about the financial position and performance of an organisation. Internal stakeholders include shareholders, managers and employees while examples of external stakeholders are customers, suppliers, government, competitors, financiers and local community.

✓ Ethics in accounting is the study of moral values and judgements as applied in the accounting process. A code of ethics is a set of principles usually based on the firm's core values that guide accountants on the standards that need to be upheld.

✓ A profit and loss account shows the records of income and expenditure flows of a business over a given time period and is also known as an *income statement*.

✓ A balance sheet is a snapshot of the financial position of a firm and is used to calculate a firm's net worth. It gives the firm an idea of what it owns (assets) and owes (liabilities) including how much shareholders have invested in it (equity).

✓ Current assets last to up to a year while fixed assets last for more than a year.

Key terms

Depreciation

the decrease in the value of a fixed asset over time

Straight-line depreciation

a method that spreads out the cost of an asset equally over its lifetime by deducting a given constant amount of depreciation of the asset's value per annum

Residual value

an estimation of an asset's worth or value over its useful life, also known as scrap or salvage value

Net book value

an asset's net value at the beginning of an accounting period, calculated by deducting the accumulated (total) depreciation from the cost of the fixed asset

Reducing-balance depreciation

a method where a predetermined percentage depreciation rate is used and subtracted from the net book value of the previous year

✓ Long term liabilities are payable after a year while short term liabilities are payable within a year.

✓ For a balance sheet to balance a firm's net assets should equal its equity.

✓ Intangible assets are fixed assets that lack physical substance or are non- physical in nature and can be very valuable to a firm's long term success. These include patents, copyrights, trademarks and goodwill.

✓ Straight line depreciation method spreads out the cost of an asset equally over its lifetime by deducting a given constant amount of depreciation of the asset's value per annum. Reducing balance depreciation method on the other hand adopts an accelerated depreciation technique whereby the depreciation amount charged to an asset declines over time based on the useful life of the asset. **(HL only)**

Practice question

BBT

BBT is a well-established small private limited company specializing in online education, based in the United States. The owner and founder, Mark Davis, currently owns 100% of the shares and enjoys complete freedom in the running of the company. The business employs three full-time staff who have been with the business for over six years.

BBT has enjoyed many years of expansion in the provision of online education. Mark owns the copyright for his patented software, which provides him with a unique selling point (USP). However, the copyright will expire in the near future. Moreover, several rival companies have recently established a presence in the online education market.

Mark has to raise finance to develop new educational software to maintain or improve his market position. His bank manager has refused to lend funds for the research and development (R&D) of the new software. He said "software has a short product life cycle, and your balance sheet has deteriorated".

Mark's accountant has just presented the following financial information for *BBT* as of 31 October 2010, which raised some working capital and liquidity issues.

a) (i) Define the term *copyright* [2 marks]

(ii) Identify **two** disadvantages for *BBT* of operating as a private limited company. [2 marks]

b) (i) Calculate the missing figures X, Y, Z **and** with those figures and from the financial information provided, construct a complete balance sheet for *BBT* for 2010. [7 marks]

(ii) BBT's net profit before interest and tax as at 31 October 2010 was US$27 695. If interest payments were 10% of this value and corporation tax was 30% Calculate the value of interest paid **and** total corporation tax. [2 marks]

(iii) Using financial and non-financial factors, explain why the bank manager refused to finance the R&D of the new educational software. [6 marks]

c) Examine **two** possible alternative sources of finance that Mark might use to fund the R&D of the new educational software. [6 marks]

IB, Nov 2010

Extract from the balance sheet for BBT for the year ended 31 October 2010

	US$
Capital employed	X
Cash	2000
Creditors	Y
Debtors	28 000
Depreciation	1500
Fixed assets	30 000
Loan capital	0
Net assets	Z
Retained profit	8500
Share capital	2000
Short-term borrowing	0
Stock	0
Total (current assets)	30 000
Total (current liabilities)	48 000

3.5 Profitability and liquidity ratio analysis

3 Finance and Accounts

By the end of this chapter, you should be able to:

→ calculate and interpret the profitability and efficiency ratios: **gross profit margin (GPM), net profit margin (NPM)**, and **return on capital employed (ROCE)**

→ examine possible strategies to **improve the above profitability and efficiency ratios**

→ calculate and interpret the liquidity ratios: **current ratio** and **acid test ratio**

→ discuss possible strategies to **improve the above liquidity ratios**.

Ratio analysis

This is a financial analysis tool used in the interpretation and assessment of a firm's financial statements. It helps in evaluating a firm's financial performance by determining certain trends and exposing its various strengths and weaknesses. It aids in decision making by making meaningful historical and inter-firm comparisons through analysing past ratios and ratios of other businesses in the same or different industries.

The following types of ratio will be explored below: **profitability ratios**, **efficiency ratios**, and **liquidity ratios**.

Profitability ratios

These ratios assess the performance of a firm in terms of its profit-generating ability. Other variables are used in interpreting this profitability. Two types of profitability ratio are **gross profit margin (GPM)** and **net profit margin (NPM)**.

Gross profit margin (GPM)

This is found by dividing the gross profit by the sales revenue, expressed as a percentage. As shown below:

$$\text{GPM} = \frac{\text{gross profit}}{\text{sales revenue}} \times 100$$

Example: A business has sales revenue of US$100 million and gross profit of US$70 million. Calculate its GPM, using the above formula:

$$\text{GPM} = \frac{\text{US\$70 million}}{\text{US\$100 million}} \times 100 = 70\%$$

The business generates a GPM of 70%. This is interpreted to mean that for every $100 of sales the business makes $70 as its gross profit, i.e. every $1 of sales revenue brings in 70 cents as gross profit. Businesses will aim for higher gross profits to help them pay their expenses.

Possible strategies to improve GPM

- A firm might increase prices for products in less competitive markets or markets where consumers are less sensitive to price changes. Raising prices here may increase sales revenue because the quantity purchased may not change significantly with changes in prices. In this case the market may have very few or even lack substitutes. The drawback is that this could damage the image of the business with loyal consumers if they perceive this as a way of "ripping them off" just for higher profits.

- A business might source cheaper suppliers of materials so as to cut down on these purchase costs. This will help in reducing the cost of sales and help increase the GPM. The business will need to be careful, though, not to compromise on the quality of the materials bought, which could lead to customer resentment.

- A firm might adopt more aggressive promotional strategies that will persuade the customers to buy its products (see section 4.5). Businesses need to ensure that they do not use expensive campaigns that will lead to increased costs.

- A business might aim to reduce direct labour costs by ensuring that its staff are more productive or are able to sell more units of the goods produced. Unproductive staff may need to be shed. Care should, however, be taken not to demotivate or decrease the morale of the remaining staff.

Net profit margin (NPM)

This is a measure of the profit that remains after deducting all costs from the sales revenue. It is calculated by dividing the profit before interest and tax by the sales revenue, expressed as a percentage:

$$\text{NPM} = \frac{\text{net profit before interest and tax}}{\text{sales revenue}} \times 100$$

Example: A firm has sales revenue of US\$150 million and a net profit before interest and tax of US\$75 million. Calculate its NPM. This is shown here:

$$\text{NPM} = \frac{\text{US\$75 million}}{\text{US\$150 million}} \times 100 = 50\%$$

The firm therefore makes an NPM of 50%. This means that for every \$100 of sales revenue made, the business generates an NPM of \$50, i.e. every \$1 of sales leads to 50 cents in NPM. A high NPM could mean that a firm is meeting its expenses very well; on the other hand, a low NPM could indicate difficulties in controlling its overall costs. Businesses should therefore look for ways to improve their NPM for better financial performance. In addition to the strategies used to increase GPM, the following can help to boost NPM.

Additional strategies to improve NPM

- A firm can carefully check on the indirect costs to see where unnecessary expenses may be avoided, for example reduce expenditure on expensive holiday packages for senior managers. This could, however, demoralize the managers who have been used to expensive holidays.

- A firm could negotiate with key stakeholders with the aim to cut costs, for example with landlords for cheaper rent or with suppliers for product discounts. However, negotiating for cheaper rent could lead to a firm moving to another location which may not be ideal, with a poorer customer image.

It is important to note that measures to increase revenues and cut costs should be used collectively in an effort to raise both GPM and NPM.

Efficiency ratios

These ratios assess how well a firm internally utilizes its assets and liabilities. They also help to analyse the performance of a firm. One example of such ratios is the **return on capital employed (ROCE).**

Return on capital employed (ROCE)

This ratio measures both the efficiency and profitability of a firm's invested capital. It assesses the returns a firm is making from its capital employed. Capital employed is found by adding a firm's long-term liabilities (loan capital) to its share capital and also to its retained profit, as noted below:

> **Capital employed = long-term liabilities + share capital + retained profit**

This is then used in calculating the return on capital employed as shown below:

$$\text{ROCE} = \frac{\text{net profit before interest and tax}}{\text{capital employed}} \times 100$$

Example: Suppose a business has share capital of US$1 million, retained profit of US$0.5 million and loan capital of US$2 million. It generated a net profit before interest and tax of US$700,000. Calculate its ROCE.

First, the capital employed will need to be calculated as follows:

Capital employed = US$1 million + US$0.5 million + US$2 million
= US$3.5 million

Then, ROCE is calculated as follows:

$$\text{ROCE} = \frac{\text{US\$0.7 million}}{\text{US\$3.5 million}} \times 100 = 20\%$$

The business is making an ROCE of 20%. This means that for every $100 of capital invested, the firm generates $20 as its net profit before interest and tax. Generally, the higher the ROCE the greater the returns businesses get from their capital employed. This acts as an incentive for business owners to inject more money into their businesses for higher returns. It is an important ratio because it analyses and judges how well a firm is able to generate profit from its key sources of finance. Comparisons should also be made on the ROCE of past years, together with those of other firms, to get a better assessment on the performance of a firm.

Additional possible strategies to improve ROCE

In addition to the above strategies on improving GPM and NPM, the following could be used to improve ROCE:

- A firm should try to reduce the amount of loan capital while still ensuring that net profit remains unchanged or does not fall. The problem with this is that the loan capital may be needed to purchase essential fixed assets such as machinery, which will aid in the further production of goods that could be sold to generate more profit.

- A firm might declare and pay additional dividends to shareholders. This will have the effect of reducing the retained profit, and hence raising the ROCE, assuming net profit remains unchanged or does not decrease. The drawback is that reducing retained profit leads to less ploughed-back profit for future investment.

Liquidity ratios

These ratios measure the ability of a firm to pay off its short-term debt obligations. Businesses need sufficient levels of liquid assets to help in meeting their day-to-day bills. Liquidity is a measure of how quickly an asset can be converted into cash. Liquid assets include cash and others such as stock and debtors that can be quickly turned into cash. Two important liquidity ratios are the **current ratio** and the **acid test ratio**.

Current ratio

This ratio makes a comparison of a firm's current assets to its current liabilities. It is calculated using the following formula:

$$\textbf{Current ratio} = \frac{\textbf{current assets}}{\textbf{current liabilities}}$$

Example: A business has current assets totalling $500 000 while its current liabilities amount to $250 000. What is its current ratio?

$$\text{Current ratio} = \frac{\$500\ 000}{\$250\ 000} = 2$$

> ## Key terms
>
> **Gross profit margin (GPM)**
>
> calculated by dividing the gross profit by the sales revenue, expressed as a percentage
>
> **Net profit margin (NPM)**
>
> calculated by dividing the net profit before interest and tax by the sales revenue, expressed as a percentage
>
> **Return on capital employed (ROCE)**
>
> assesses the returns a firm is making from its capital employed

The above firm's current ratio is 2 which can also be expressed as 2:1. This is interpreted to mean that for every $1 of current liabilities the firm has $2 of current assets. A number of accountants differ on the acceptable range of current ratio but many recommend a range of 1.5:2. This range will allow for the availability of sufficient working capital to pay off the short-term debts of the business. A current ratio of below 1:1 means that the current assets are less than the current liabilities, which could put the firm in financial difficulties when it comes to paying its creditors. This depends on the industry the firm operates in. Moreover, a high current ratio should also be avoided. A high current ratio could mean any of the following:

- There is too much cash being held and not being invested, for example by converting to non-current assets.

- There are many debtors, increasing the possibility of bad debts.

- Too much stock is being held, leading to high warehouse storage costs.

Possible strategies to improve current ratio

- A firm might reduce bank overdrafts and choose instead to seek long-term loans. This helps to reduce the current liabilities and hence improve the current ratio. However, increasing long-term loans could increase the interest payable and the gearing ratio of the business (see section 3.6), thereby affecting its efficiency and future liquidity position.

- Another strategy would be to sell existing long-term assets for cash. This increases the available working capital for the business. The disadvantage is that if the long-term assets are needed back the business will face the cost of leasing them.

Acid test (quick) ratio

This is a more stringent indicator of how well a firm is able to meet its short-term obligations. This is because it removes stock as part of the current assets. It is calculated using the following formula:

$$\text{Acid test ratio} = \frac{\text{current assets} - \text{stock}}{\text{current liabilities}}$$

Example: Suppose in the example above the business has stock worth US$ 150 000. What is its acid test ratio?

$$\text{Acid test ratio} = \frac{\text{US\$500 000} - \text{US\$150 000}}{\text{US\$250 000}} = 1.4$$

In the above case, for every $1 of current liabilities the business has $1.4 of current assets less stock. By removing stock the business gets rid of the least liquid of current assets to focus on the most liquid of them. In some cases there is no guarantee that stock can be sold, eventually leading to obsolete items. This ratio indicates to creditors how much of a firm's short-term debts can be met by selling its liquid assets at short notice. As with the current ratio, an acid test ratio of less than 1:1 could mean that the business is not in sound financial health; it may be facing a liquidity crisis (the inability to pay its short-term debts) and should therefore be scrutinized with extreme caution by financial institutions.

However, as with the current ratio, the variation of acid test ratios in different industries needs to be considered. A high acid test ratio has the same implications as a high current ratio except that there is no stock to be considered.

Additional possible strategies to improve acid test ratio

In addition to the strategies to improve the current ratio, the following can help with the acid test ratio:

- A firm could sell off stock at a discount for cash. This will help improve the liquidity position of the business and avail more working capital to pay off its short-term debts. However, selling stock at a discount may reduce the revenue generated from the sold stock, thereby reducing the firm's profits.

- A firm might increase the credit period for debtors to purchase more stock on credit. The problem here is that it may lead to increased bad debts in the business.

Student workpoint 3.14

Be a thinker

1. Referring to Tables 3.4.1 and 3.4.2, calculate and interpret:

    a) **two** profitability ratios.

    b) ROCE

    c) **two** liquidity ratios.

2. Which of the ratios from (a) to (c) are in need of further improvement? Evaluate possible strategies to improve each of those ratios.

Key terms

Current ratio

a ratio that compares a firm's current assets to its current liabilities

Acid test ratio

a stringent ratio that subtracts stock from the current assets and compares this to the firm's current liabilities

---

TOK discussion

Often financial information is presented to the wider audience in statistical, graphical or another form of quantitative summary. Do such simplifying presentations limit our knowledge of accounts?

Case study

Coca-Cola içecek (CCI) – Turkey

Coca-Cola içecek (CCI) has a vision to be one of the leading bottlers of alcohol-free beverages in Southern Eurasia and the Middle East. They currently distribute in

Turkey, Kazakhstan, Azerbaijan, Jordan and Kyrgyzstan. CCI also has over a 33%

interest in Turkmenistan Coca-Cola Bottlers Ltd., the Coca-Cola bottler in Turkmenistan.

In addition, CCI is a party to joint venture agreements that have the exclusive distribution rights for brands of The Coca-Cola Company in Iraq and Syria. CCI offers a wide range of beverages, including sparkling beverages as well as an expanding portfolio of still beverages (juices, waters, sports drinks, iced tea and hot tea). The core brands in all markets are Coca-Cola, Coca-Cola Light, Fanta and Sprite.

Defining the Problem

CCI needed a profitability system with channel, brand, customer and SKU reporting that was accurate, scalable and had fast turnaround. All managerial levels needed the right information to make good decisions quickly.

For Example:

- **Marketing** wanted to see net profitability by channel, brand, and SKU so they could focus marketing efforts and budget direct marketing expenses accordingly.

- **Sales** wanted to analyze net profitability by channel and SKU to segment customers based on growth potential, size of business, and profitability.

- **Supply Chain** wanted accurate costing information for each SKU regarding warehouse and delivery expenses.

- **Executive Management** wanted to track net profitability at various dimensions to set company strategy.

Goals for an Innovative Solution

- Make net profitability for customers, channels, SKUs and brands more transparent, standard, and easy to access.

- Facilitate growth through market segmentation and enable CCI to institutionalize revenue growth management.

- Identify profitable and unprofitable customers, channels, SKUs, brands etc. and understand the drivers of profitability.

- Help create sales and promotion strategies by channel and product based on net profitability.

- Track actual customer net profitability and compare it with estimated contract profitability.

- Provide support to channel-based marketing decisions (i.e. direct marketing expense).

- Make it easier to drill down profitability information through reporting layers (channel à customer à SKU or brand à SKU à customer).

Business Value Realized

As a result of the profitability system implemented with Acorn and Batuman Consulting, CCI has accurate information they did not have before.

Outlet Profitability

For the first time, CCI can see the net profitability for each outlet (i.e. customer sales location) under each Area Sales Manager.

Each ASM can now see the top and bottom 20 outlets in their area and act on that information. They can understand the impact of promotions and discounts on the profitability of each outlet by SKU and direct the sales developers under their responsibility to push for profitable SKU sales via the right mix and amount of promotions and discounts.

Product Profitability

Previously, CCI regional finance teams had to perform independent, manual analysis to generate SKU profitability. That analysis took days, was not very accurate and it was difficult to compare SKU profitability across regions and sales centers. In addition, they could not analyze SKU profitability by trade channels. The Acorn solution allows all departments of CCI to use one model that provides very accurate information overnight, using minimal resources. CCI can also analyze SKU profitability by trade channels.

Analysis of net SKU profitability by trade channels for each region and sales center provides tremendous benefit and some surprises. For example, the same SKU for the same channel can be profitable in one region or sales center but unprofitable in another due to local ways of doing business. CCI can now capture these differences within regions and sales centers and take action to improve profitability. Pricing decisions are managed through promotions and discounts by trade channel and SKU. Prior to implementing Acorn, the sales team did this manually, at a high level and with no trade channel detail available. CCI can now produce very accurate and detailed information, enabling more accurate pricing decisions.

CCI has analyzed the net profitability of SKUs and package sizes by channel and brand. For instance, the profitability of Pet 2 liter vs. Pet 2.5 liter has historically been a point of discussion within the CCI management team. CCI can now compare the profitability of these package sizes within any dimension such as trade channel (i.e. traditional, on-premise and modern channels) and brand (i.e. Coca-Cola, Fanta, Sprite, etc.) within each region and sales center.

Customer Profitability

CCI has a system called Customer Investment Analysis (CIA) to measure the value of a customer at the time of signing the contract. The system is widely used internally and is created based on contract terms. CCI now has the capability to compare CIA and Acorn results side by side so that they can track whether the customer is generating the value CCI anticipated before signing the contract. The finance team has completed the profitability analysis of National Key Accounts and National Cold Drink customers, and the results have been shared with the sales team. CCI also plans to analyze the profitability of customers by Area Sales Manager and grow additional relationships by understanding profitable customer profiles. Customer profiles show NET profitability and can be created based on segment, sub-trade channel, income level, SKU mix, etc.

Operating results used to create these profiles include:

- Gross revenue per unit case
- Number of unit cases sold
- Mix and amount of promotions and discounts applied
- Level of sales and marketing organization support
- Direct marketing expenses
- Delivery and warehouse expenses

Adapted from http://www.acornsys.com/Portals/76901/docs/coca-cola-case-study.pdf

Exam-style questions

1. Define the following terms:

   (a) Revenue   [2 marks]

   (b) Net profit   [2 marks]

2. Examine how the new data could help CCI increase its profitability (per outlet, per customer, per product).   [10 marks]

Revision checklist

✓ Ratio analysis is a financial analysis tool that assesses a firm's financial statements and aids its decision making by making meaningful historical and inter-firm comparisons through analysing past ratios and ratios of other businesses in the same or different industries.

✓ Profitability ratios that assess a firm's ability to generate profit include gross profit margin (GPM) and net profit margin (NPM).

✓ An example of an efficiency ratio that assesses how well a firm internally utilizes its assets and liabilities is return on capital employed (ROCE).

✓ Liquidity ratios measure the ability of a firm to pay off its short term debt obligations with two examples being current ratio and acid test (quick) ratio.

Practice question

Woolman Windows (WW)

Woolman Windows (*WW*) manufactures windows for houses. The windows are sold to suppliers of building materials in Canada. *WW's* windows have two pieces of glass sealed in a wooden frame with a special glue that prevents any air from passing through. The windows are energy-efficient. In addition, moisture never appears between the two pieces of glass, a problem common to many other energy-efficient windows. The *WW* brand is widely recognized in the residential construction industry in Canada.

Because of the housing crisis in North America, *WW* has seen its sales fall and its financial position deteriorate.

WW manufactures only standard-sized windows using flow production. *WW* offers trade credit* with payment in 30 days. However, *WW* is considering taking "special orders", that is, to manufacture windows that are not standard-sized. Doing so might be profitable if the number of windows per special order were a minimum of 100 windows (break-even point). *WW* would manufacture special orders using batch production. For special orders, the buyer would pay 50% upon placing the order and the remainder upon delivery. The disadvantage is that an additional employee would have to be employed to plan the production process for each special order. *WW* is uncertain if special-order sales will be sufficient to cover the cost of the recruitment and training of the new employee.

a) Define the following terms:

(i) *share capital* [*2 marks*]

(ii) *debtors* [*2 marks*]

b) (i) Using the information in **Table 1**, construct a balance sheet for *WW* as at 31 May 2009 and calculate the loan capital (figure X). [*5 marks*]

(ii) Using relevant information from **Table 1**, calculate the acid test (quick) ratio (*show all your working*). [*2 marks*]

(iii) Using relevant information from **Table 1**, calculate the gearing ratio. [*1 mark*]

(iv) Using the information in **Table 2**, calculate the net profit before interest and tax (*show all your working*). [*2 marks*]

(v) Using relevant information from **Table 2**, calculate the gross profit margin. [*1 mark*]

c) Using financial and non-financial information, examine *WW's* decision to start producing special-order windows. [*5 marks*]

IB, Nov, 2012

Table 1. selected items from *WW's* balance sheet as at 31 May 2009 (all figures in $ thousands)

Cash	150
Creditors	515
Debtors	850
Loan capital	X
Short-term borrowing	285
Retained profit	1300
Share capital	300
Stock	400
Total (net fixed assets)	1800

Table 2. selected items from *WW's* profit and loss account for the year ended 31 May 2009 (all figures in $ thousands)

Cost of goods sold	4700
Expenses	2150
Gross profit	2195
Sales revenue	6895

---

* trade credit: credit extended to a business from its suppliers. Trade credit is usually listed on the balance sheet of a business as "creditors" or, in some countries, "accounts payable".

> **By the end of this chapter, you should be able to:**
> → calculate and interpret the efficiency ratios: **stock (inventory) turnover, debtor (trade receivable) days, creditor days** and **gearing ratio**
> → evaluate possible strategies to **improve the above ratio.**

Efficiency ratios

As indicated in section 3.5, these ratios assess the utilization of a firm's resources in terms of its assets and liabilities. In this section further efficiency ratios will be explored, namely, **stock turnover, debtor days, creditor days** and **gearing ratio**.

Stock turnover ratio

This ratio measures how quickly a firm's stock is sold and replaced over a given period. It considers the number of times stock is sold and replenished. It can be calculated using two approaches.

One approach looks at how many times in a given period (usually a year) a firm sells its stock. The formula is:

$$\text{Stock turnover ratio (number of times)} = \frac{\text{cost of goods sold}}{\text{average stock}}$$

Average stock is calculated by finding the average value of the stock at the beginning of the year and at the end of the year:

$$\text{Average stock} = \frac{(\text{opening stock} + \text{closing stock})}{2}$$

Example: Supposing a firm has a cost of sales totalling $400,000. It started the year with goods worth $150,000, and closed the year with $50,000 worth of goods. Calculate its stock turnover ratio.

Average stock is first calculated:

$$\text{Average stock} = \frac{\$150,000 + \$50,000}{2} = \frac{\$200,000}{2} = \$100,000$$

$$\text{Stock turnover ratio} = \frac{\$400,000}{\$100,000} = 4 \text{ times}$$

Another approach in calculating stock turnover is to consider the number of days it takes to sell the stock. The following formula can be used:

$$\text{Stock turnover ratio (number of days)} = \frac{\text{average stock}}{\text{cost of goods sold}} \times 365$$

Using the above example, stock turnover ratio in the number of days is calculated as:

$$\text{Stock turnover ratio} = \frac{\$100,000}{\$400,000} \times 365$$

$$= 91.25 \text{ days}$$

A supermarket has a high stock turnover ratio

The above business turns over its stock four times a year, or every 91 days, on average. Higher stock turnover (number of times) is preferred – or lower figures for stock turnover ratio (number of days). In considering the first approach to stock turnover (number of times), a high stock turnover ratio means that the firm sells stock quickly, thereby earning more profit from its sales. This also means that goods do not become obsolete quickly and perishable goods do not expire, showing that the firm has good control over its purchasing decisions. It is important to note, though, that stock turnover differs significantly between different industries. For example, manufacturing companies such as luxury car producers may have on average lower stock turnover times than retail businesses such as supermarkets. This ratio is not very relevant to service industries that do not quite hold "tangible" products as their stock.

The stock level is an important item of working capital in a business and therefore the stock turnover ratio is a good instrument for assessing the effectiveness of working capital management. Generally, the faster a business turns over its stocks the better; however, it is important that this is done profitably, rather than selling stocks at low gross profit margins or worse still at a loss.

This luxury car dealer is likely to have a low stock turnover ratio

Possible strategies to improve stock turnover ratio

- Slow-moving or obsolete goods should be disposed of. This will help reduce the firm's level of stock. The downside is that it could lead to losses due to lost sales revenue that these goods could have generated.

- Firms with a wide range of products will need to offer a narrower, better-selling range of products. The disadvantage is that this may minimize the variety of products offered to consumers.

- Keeping low levels of stock has the added benefit of reducing the costs of holding stock. However, during sudden increases in demand for goods by customers, businesses with low levels of stock may not have sufficient amounts to sustain the market.

- Some firms are able to adopt the **just-in-time** (JIT) production method, where stocks of raw materials are ordered only when they are needed (see section 5.3). The major drawback is that if there are any delays in the delivery of the raw materials to producers it could negatively affect production and eventually sales.

Debtor days

This ratio measures the number of days it takes on average for a firm to collect its debts from customers it has sold goods to on credit. These customers who owe the business money are known as debtors and the ratio is also referred to as the **debt collection period**. It assesses how efficient a business is in its credit control systems. It is calculated using the following formula:

$$\textbf{Debtor days ratio (number of days)} = \frac{\textbf{debtors}}{\textbf{total sales revenue}} \times \textbf{365}$$

Example: A firm's total sales revenue amounts to US$16 million while the total number of debtors equals US$2 million. What is its debtor days ratio?

$$\text{Debtor days ratio} = \frac{\text{US\$2 million}}{\text{US\$16 million}} \times 365 = 45.625 \text{ days}$$

It therefore takes the business an average of 46 days to collect debts. The shorter the debtor days the better it is for the business. This is because the business will have working capital to run its day-to-day operations and can also invest this money in other projects. The credit period given to customers varies from business to business and could range from 30 to as many as 120 days. However, allowing too long a credit period could land a business into serious cash-flow problems leading to a liquidity crisis.

Possible strategies to improve debtor days ratio

- A firm can provide discounts or other incentives to encourage debtors to pay their debts earlier. The drawback here is that the business receives less income from these customers than was originally agreed.

- A firm might impose stiff penalties for late payers such as fines. This may, however, chase away long-time loyal customers.

- A firm might stop any further transactions with overdue debtors until payment is finalized. This still does not guarantee payment, though, with some debtors opting to seek alternative suppliers for their goods.

- A business may have to resort to legal means such as court action for consistently late payers. This may harm the reputation a business has in dealing with customers.

Creditor days

This ratio measures the average number of days a firm takes to pay its creditors. It assess how quickly, usually within a year, a firm is able to pay its suppliers, for example. The ratio is calculated using the following formula:

$$\text{Creditor days ratio (number of days)} = \frac{\text{creditors}}{\text{cost of goods sold}} \times 365$$

Example: A business owes its creditors US$700,000 with a cost of sales of US$7 million. Calculate its creditor days ratio.

$$\text{Creditor days ratio} = \frac{\text{US\$700,000}}{\text{US\$7 million}} \times 365 = 36.5 \text{ days}$$

This means that the firm has about 37 days to pay its creditors. A high creditor days ratio enables the firm to use available cash to fulfil its short-term obligations. However, allowing this period to extend too long may strain the firm's relations with, for example, its suppliers, leading to future financial problems. In addition, other stakeholders such as investors may perceive this as a firm in financial trouble and may reconsider investing in it. The creditor days period will vary according to a firm's relationship with its suppliers or other creditors.

Possible strategies to improve creditor days ratio

- Having good relationships with creditors such as suppliers may enable a firm to negotiate for an extended credit period. However, some suppliers could object to the extension and refuse to support the business in future – when it might be in dire need of assistance.

- Effective credit control will improve creditor days ratio. Managers will need to assess the risks of paying creditors early versus how long they should delay in making their payment. This may not be an easy task and will depend on the cash-flow position and needs of the business at that time.

Gearing ratio

This measures the extent to which the capital employed by a firm is financed from loan capital. Loan capital is a long-term liability in the business while capital employed includes loan capital, share capital and retained profits. The commonly used gearing ratio formula is:

$$\text{Gearing ratio} = \frac{\text{loan capital}}{\text{capital employed}} \times 100$$

Example: A business has a loan of US$10 million with a capital employed of US$25 million. What is its gearing ratio?

$$\text{Gearing ratio} = \frac{\text{US\$10 million}}{\text{\$25 million}} \times 100 = 40\%$$

The business has a gearing ratio of 40 per cent, which means that two fifths of the capital requirements of the business come from long-term loans. A gearing ratio can help assess the level of debt a business is burdened with. A business is seen as high geared if it has a gearing ratio of above 50 per cent and low geared if below this figure. A high gearing ratio could be viewed as risky by financiers, who may be reluctant to lend to businesses in such a situation due to the large debt burden. Shareholders and potential investors will be concerned about high-geared businesses because they may not foresee any future dividend payments because of these firms' main obligation to pay their long-term loans. In addition, any sudden interest rate increases will worsen the loan repayment position of such businesses. On the other hand, low-geared businesses that might be viewed as "safe" may in fact not be borrowing enough to fund future growth and expansion initiatives. Shareholders may therefore see low-geared businesses as offering minimal returns and may even prefer high-geared businesses with good growth strategies promising higher future returns on investment.

Possible strategies to improve gearing ratio

Businesses that are very highly geared can generally place themselves in a difficult financial position. This ratio could be reduced using the following measures:

- A business may seek alternative sources of funding that are not "loan related", for example preferring to issue more shares. The drawbacks are that the issuing of shares may take a long time and go against the objective of any existing shareholders who do not want to lose ownership of the business.

- A firm might decrease or not declare and issue dividends to shareholders so as to increase the amount of retained profit. This may however, lead to resentment among shareholders, especially if the reasons for doing so are not well explained.

Key terms

Stock turnover ratio

measures how quickly a firm's stock is sold and replaced over a given period

Debtor days ratio

measures on average, the number of days it takes for a firm to collect its debts

Creditor days ratio

measures the average number of days a firm takes to pay its creditors

Gearing ratio

measures the extent to which the capital employed by a firm is financed from loan capital

TOK discussion

What role does today's financial evidence play in making judgments about an organization's future performance?

Student workpoint 3.15

Be a thinker

1. Referring to Tables 3.4.1 and 3.4.2 in section 3.4, calculate and interpret the following ratios:

    a) stock turnover

    b) debtor days

    c) creditor days

    d) gearing ratio.

2. Which of the ratios from (a) to (d) are in need of further improvement? Evaluate possible strategies to improve each of these ratios.

Revision checklist

✓ Other efficiency ratios that assess how firm's utilize their resources in terms of assets and liabilities include stock turnover ratio, debtor days, creditor days and gearing ratios

✓ Stock turnover ratio measures how fast a firm's stock is sold and replenished over a given period. It can be measured in two ways. Firstly, it assesses how many times in a given period a firm sells its stock and secondly, it considers the number of days it takes for a firm to sell its stock.

✓ Debtor days measures the average number of days it takes for a firm to collect money from its debtors. It is also known as *debt collection period*.

✓ Creditor days assesses how fast in number of days within a year a firm is able to pay its creditors.

✓ Gearing ratio measures the percentage to which the capital employed by a firm is financed from loan capital to establish whether it is high geared or low geared.

Practice question

CU Ltd

CU Ltd started up in business seven years ago producing web cameras for computers. It has developed a reputation amongst its customers for high quality and reliability. At first the company grew rapidly. As a result of an initial injection of venture capital *CU Ltd* was valued at $75 million at the height of the technology boom. Unlike many other firms, it survived the technology crash at the start of the century. However, despite slow but consistent sales growth it has faced significant financial problems since. In recent months *CU Ltd* has even had to negotiate with staff to delay salary payments by up to two weeks to help with cash flow. The financial director has been looking at a range of solutions and is suggesting the flotation of the company on the Stock Exchange to inject new capital.

The profit and loss account and balance sheet for 2003 and 2004 are given below:

Balance sheet as at 31 December

$000		2003		2004
Fixed assets		1500		1400
Current assets				
Stock	910		1220	
Debtors	550		650	
Cash	10		5	
Total current assets		1470		1875
Current liabilities				
Creditors	300		250	
Overdraft	350		475	
Total current liabilities		650		725
Net assets		2320		2550
Share capital		250		250
Profit and loss account		320		350
Loan capital		1750		1950
Capital employed		2320		2550

Profit and loss account for the year ended 31 December

$000	2003	2004
Turnover	5750	6100
Cost of goods sold	4175	4750
Gross profit	1575	1350
Marketing and admin expenses	1250	1300
Net profit before interest and tax	325	50
Interest	175	225
Taxation	100	10
Profit after interest and tax	50	(185)
Dividends	20	0
Retained profits	30	(185)

a) Calculate the level of working capital for 2003 and 2004. *[2 marks]*

b) Assess the likely impact on *CU Ltd* of increasing worldwide Internet access. *[4 marks]*

c) Examine the value of these accounts to the board of directors of *CU Ltd*. *[4 marks]*

d) Using appropriate liquidity, efficiency and profitability ratios analyse the financial position of *CU Ltd* from the perspective of a potential investor. *[10 marks]*

IB, Nov 2005

3.7 Cash flow

By the end of this chapter, you should be able to:

→ distinguish between **profit** and **cash flow**

→ explain the **working capital cycle**

→ construct and interpret **cash-flow forecasts**

→ comment on the relationship between **investment, profit**, and **cash flow**

→ evaluate possible strategies for dealing with **cash-flow problems**.

The difference between profit and cash flow

Cash is money that gets into the business through either the sale of its goods or services, borrowing from financial institutions, or investment by shareholders. It is the most liquid asset in a business and is found under current assets in the balance sheet. This cash is essential to the smooth running of any business and a lack of it could result in business failure or bankruptcy. **Cash flow** is the money that flows in and out of a business over a given period of time. **Cash inflows** are the monies received by a business while **cash outflows** are the monies paid out by a business over a period of time. Cash flow is a key indicator of a firm's ability to meet its financial obligations. A positive cash flow (where cash inflows exceed cash outflows) will enable businesses to meet their day-to-day running costs.

Cash is generated by selling goods or services

Profit is obtained by subtracting total costs from total revenue. It is profit if the difference is positive and a loss if it is negative. Profit is a great indicator of the financial success of a firm's core operations.

Profit and cash flow are different. When buying goods or services, customers can either use cash or buy on credit. If either of the two methods are used, this will still count as part of the sales revenue of a business. Moreover, if the sales revenue exceeds the total costs, a business will be said to have earned a profit. However, if most of the purchases were credit purchases then the cash-flow position at that point in time for the business will differ with its profitability.

Example: During a particular month a business sold $10,000 worth of goods, incurring a total cost of $4,000. The business offered customers one month's credit of 50 per cent of sales. What was the profit and cash flow for that month?

> **Profit = sales revenue – total costs**

Profit = $10,000 − $4,000 = $6,000

> **Net cash flow = cash inflow – cash outflow**

Net cash flow = (50% of 10,000) − $4,000 = $1,000

From the above example we can see during the month that the business incurred a profit of $6,000 but a positive cash flow of only $1,000, clearly bringing out the difference between the two concepts. The cash-flow figure is lower than the profit figure because even though the goods were sold, 50 per cent of the money was not received in that month. However, the sold goods counted as sales revenue for the month.

Two possibilities can arise in differentiating between profit and cash flow.

a) A business can be profitable but have little or no cash. This is known as **insolvency** and it may be brought about by:

- poor collection of funds, possibly by allowing customers a very long credit period
- paying suppliers too early and leaving little or no cash for operations
- purchasing capital equipment or many non-current assets at the same time
- overtrading – purchasing too much stock with cash that is eventually tied up in the business
- servicing loans with cash.

b) A business can have a positive cash flow but be unprofitable. It can achieve a positive cash flow in the following ways. Cash could be:

- sourced from bank loans
- gained from the sale of a firm's fixed assets
- obtained from shareholders' funds.

Key terms

Cash flow

money that flows in and out of a business over a given period of time

Profit

the positive difference between sales revenue and total costs

Insolvency

a situation where a business runs out of cash but may still be profitable

3 Finance and Accounts

The working capital cycle

Working capital is the money needed to pay for the day-to-day running costs of a business. These costs could include paying wages, purchasing raw materials, and paying for electricity and gas, among others. Working capital, also known as the **net current assets** of a business, is calculated by subtracting current liabilities from current assets:

> **Working capital = current assets – current liabilities**

Current assets are the liquid assets of the business and include cash, debtors, and stock. Current liabilities are the monies the business owes that need to be paid in the short term, such as creditors and bank overdrafts. To have sufficient working capital, businesses need to ensure that their current assets exceed their current liabilities. If the opposite is the case, the business could run into working capital problems and face insolvency or a serious liquidity crisis. An **illiquid** business (one that is not able to pay its short-term debts) could also eventually be **liquidated** (when all a firm's assets are sold off to pay any funds owing – leading to its closure).

Working capital management is an assessment of the way the current assets and current liabilities are being administered. It is important for businesses to manage working capital effectively so as to maximize the gains from the net current assets by maintaining optimal levels of these assets.

A **working capital cycle** is the period of time between payment for goods supplied to a business and the business receiving cash from their sale. It shows movements of cash and other liquid assets in and out of the business. It is usually desirable to keep the cycle as short as possible in order to maximize on the working capital. However, in many cases there are delays or time lags that occur between purchasing stocks of raw materials and receiving cash from debtors after selling finished goods (see Figure 3.7.1). The longer this interval is, the greater are the working capital needs of the business. For example, extending the credit period to customers lengthens the working capital cycle, while suppliers asking for later payments (suppliers extending credit to businesses) help to shorten the working capital cycle.

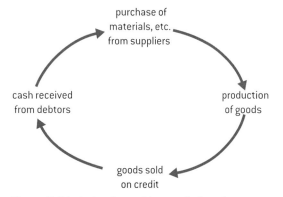

Figure 3.7.1. A simple working capital cycle

Therefore businesses need to control their working capital well by having enough to run their daily operations. On the other hand, high levels of working capital could mean that funds are tied up in current assets providing no returns, creating great opportunity costs.

Key terms

Working capital

the difference between current assets and current liabilities

Liquidation

a situation where all a firm's assets are sold off to pay any funds owing

Working capital cycle

the period of time between payment for goods supplied to a business and the business receiving cash from their sale

Cash-flow forecasts

These are future predictions of a firm's cash inflows and outflows over a given period of time. This is in the form of a financial document that shows expected month-by-month receipts and payments of a business that have not yet occurred. Examples of likely cash inflows include cash sales from selling goods or business assets, payments from debtors, cash investments from shareholders, and borrowing from banks. Cash outflows include purchasing materials or fixed assets for cash, cash expenses such as rent, wages and salaries, paying creditors, repaying loans, and making dividend payments to shareholders.

Constructing cash-flow forecasts

In constructing a cash-flow forecast, knowledge of the following terms is important:

- **Opening cash balance** – this is the cash that a business starts with every month. It is the cash held by a business at the start of a trading year.

- **Total cash inflows** – this is a summation of all cash inflows during a particular month.

- **Total cash outflows** – this is a summation of all the cash outflows during a particular month.

- **Net cash flow** – this is the difference between the total cash inflows and the total cash outflows.

- **Closing cash balance** – this is the estimated cash available at the end of the month. It is found by adding the net cash flow of one month to the opening balance of the same month.

Table 3.7.1 shows how the above terms are applied.

Table 3.7.1. Cash-flow forecast for XYZ Ltd company for the first five months of trading

All figures in $	January	February	March	April	May
Opening balance	2,000	4,500	5,600	4,650	3,250
Cash inflows					
Cash sales revenue	10,000	9,000	8,000	9,500	7,500
Payment from debtors	6,000	5,000	4,500	4,000	4,750
Rental income	4,000	4,000	4,000	4,000	4,000
Total cash inflows	20,000	18,000	16,500	17,500	16,250
Cash outflows					
Electricity	1,500	1,800	1,750	2,000	1,900
Raw materials	5,000	4,000	4,500	5,500	6,000
Rent	3,000	3,000	3,000	3,000	3,000
Wages	5,000	5,000	5,000	5,000	5,000
Telephone	500	600	700	900	450
Loan repayments	2,500	2,500	2,500	2,500	2,500
Total cash outflows	17,500	16,900	17,450	18,900	18,850
Net cash flow	2,500	1,100	(950)	(1,400)	(2,600)
Closing balance	4,500	5,600	4,650	3,250	650

In the above example, XYZ Ltd shows a positive closing balance at the end of May, but this amount has been on a decline from March. This can be attributed to the negative net cash flows in March, April and May. Can you identify the specific reasons for this? Assuming the cash sales revenue in December of the previous year was $12 000, what does this tell you about the credit period offered to customers?

It is important to note that cash-flow forecasts are based on estimates, and accuracy of the figures depends on how well the business is able to predict its future cash inflows and outflows.

Benefits of cash-flow forecasts

Some of the advantages of cash-flow forecasts are as follows:

- A cash-flow forecast is a useful planning document for anyone wishing to start a business. This is because it helps to clarify the purpose of the business and provides estimated projections for future performance.

- Cash-flow forecasts provide a good support base for businesses intending to apply for funding from financial institutions. This is because they enable the banks to check on the solvency and creditworthiness of the business.

- Predicting cash flow can help managers identify in advance periods where the business may need cash and therefore plan accordingly to source it.

- A cash-flow forecast can assist in monitoring and managing cash flow. By making comparisons between the estimated cash flow figures and its actual figures, a business should be able to assess where the problem lies and seek the respective solutions to solve it.

The relationship between investment, profit, and cash flow

Investment generally refers to the act or state of investing. In finance or business, investing is spending money on purchasing an asset with the expectation of future earnings. Investing involves wealth creation, including hoping that the bought asset appreciates in value over time. Examples of financial investments include buying bonds, stocks, or property. All forms of investment come with risks, especially risks brought about by unexpected changes in the market conditions in an economy. The relationship between investment, profit, and cash flow can be linked to the different stages of growth in a business. This is noted in Table 3.7.2.

Table 3.7.2. The relationship between investment, profit, and cash flow, using various stages in a business

Business stage	Investment (owner's funds)	Profit	Cash flow
Start-up	This involves very high investment due to the purchase of initial assets or set-up costs	There is no profit because costs are not yet met	Cash flow is negative – cash outflow is significantly higher than cash inflow
Growing	Investment could still be high because the business is not yet fully established	There is a small profit, as more revenue starts to be generated to cover costs	Cash flow may be positive (i.e. cash inflow is higher than cash outflow) but low until cash inflows increase especially from sales revenue
Established – thriving	Investment may be minimal as the business can plough back profits	High profit is achieved	Cash flow is positive – cash inflow is higher than cash outflow

> **Key term**
>
> **Cash flow forecast**
> the future prediction of a firm's cash inflows and outflows over a given period of time

Table 3.7.2 provides a simplified model of how investment in terms of the owner's injection of capital into the business relates to profit and cash flow. However, it is important to note that the above features could be affected by qualitative attributes that are beyond the control of the business. (A more detailed explanation of the difference between profit and cash flow has been covered earlier.

Key term

Investment
the act of spending money on purchasing an asset with the expectation of future earnings

Strategies to deal with cash-flow problems

As noted earlier, a business can be profitable yet insolvent, which means it is said to be facing a liquidity crisis and is facing difficulties in sustaining its working capital to run its day-to-day operations. We have already seen that there can be various causes of cash-flow problems in a business. The major causes are lack of effective planning and poor credit control. The following strategies can be used to deal with these problems.

Reducing cash outflow

The following methods aim to decrease the amount of cash leaving a business:

- A business will negotiate with suppliers or creditors so as to delay payment. This helps the business to have working capital for its short-term needs. The drawbacks with this are that negotiations may be time consuming and delaying payment to suppliers could affect future relationships, including their refusal to supply in future.

- Purchases of fixed assets can be delayed. Assets such as machinery and equipment may take up a lot of cash for the business and delaying purchases of them helps to avail cash in the business. However, if the machines or equipment are becoming obsolete or outdated, a lack of purchasing replacements may lead to decreased efficiency and higher costs in the long term.

- A business may decrease specific expenses such as advertising costs that will not affect production capacity. If not well checked, though, this may reduce future demand of a business's products.

- It might be possible to source cheaper suppliers. This will help reduce costs on materials or essential stock, decreasing the outflow of funds. A possible danger of this is that the quality of the finished product may be compromised, affecting future customer relationships.

Improving cash inflows

- A business may insist that customers pay cash only for goods purchased. This avoids the problem of delayed payments from debtors, which tie down cash. The disadvantage is that the business may lose customers who prefer to buy goods on credit.

- Offering discounts or incentives can encourage debtors to pay early. This will reduce the debt burden on debtors as they will pay less than earlier agreed. The limitation here is that, after the discount, businesses will receive less cash than earlier expected.

- A firm may diversify its product offering. This will help avail a variety of goods on offer for sale to customers, potentially increasing sales. It is worth remembering that diversification comes with higher costs and with no clear guarantee of sales.

CHANGE

The cash flow statement will only change if the inflows and outflows impact on cash and cash equivalents. The net change in cash position is the difference between the total amount of money brought in by the business and the total amount that it expended over the reporting period.

The cash flow statement therefore provides information on an organization's liquidity and solvency and its ability to change cash flows in future circumstances. In addition, it provides additional information for evaluating changes in assets, liabilities and equity.

Using the internet, do some research on the various cash flow statements of different organizations. How do the changes in the other financial documents influence their cash flow statements?

Looking for additional finance sources

Reference to these sources is as seen in unit 3.1 and they include the following:

- **Sale of assets** – the focus should be on selling obsolete fixed assets to generate cash. Selling assets that are still needed could lead to reduced production.

- **Arranging a bank overdraft** – this is a short-term loan facility that allows firms to overdraw from their accounts. It greatly helps during times of immediate cash setbacks. However, there are interest payments on the loan which are also usually high.

- **Sale and leaseback** – assets can be sold to generate cash and these assets can be hired back by the business for use in production. The disadvantage is that leasing can prove costly in the long run and this also denies the business the use of the asset as collateral in seeking future loans.

- **Debt factoring** – external debt-collecting companies can purchase the bills owed by customers in a business, thereby providing immediate cash to the business. The major drawback is that the business does not get the full amount owed by its customers, affecting its profitability.

- **Grants and subsidies** – struggling businesses can apply for grants and subsidies from the government to help increase their cash inflows. The drawback is that these sources of finance come with specific conditions that have to be met before money is guaranteed.

Limitations of cash-flow forecasting

Prediction generally characterizes a cash-flow forecast and inaccuracies are bound to occur that limit the forecast's effectiveness. Some of the causes of these inaccuracies could include the following:

- **Unexpected changes in the economy** – for example fluctuating interest rates could affect borrowing by firms and have a negative impact on its cash-flow needs.

- **Poor market research** – improperly done sales forecasts due to poor demand predictions can have a negative effect on future cash sales, thereby affecting cash inflows.

- **Difficulty in predicting competitors' behaviour** – competitors may change their strategies often and make it hard for other businesses to predict their actions and compete with them. This can negatively affect the cash flow of a struggling business.

- **Unforeseen machine or equipment failure** – breakdown of machinery is difficult to predict, and it can drastically affect the cash position in a business.

- **Demotivated employees** – being demotivated can negatively affect the productivity of workers, reducing output or sales and leading to less cash inflow.

Student workpoint 3.16

Be knowledgeable

Juma plans to open a restaurant next year beginning in January. Use the following information to answer the questions that follow:

- He has $4,000 of his own money to inject into the business.

- He has secured a bank loan of $6,000 to add to his capital requirements.

- He estimates the cash sales revenue for the first five months of trading to be as follows; $2,000, $4,000, $5,000, $5,500, $6,000.

- Material expenses are 50% of cash sales revenue per month and paid in cash every month.

- Wages and salaries are a constant figure of $5,000 every month.

- Total advertising costs of $6,000 are paid in two installments, one in February and the other in April.

- A loan repayment is $500 each month.

- Rent is $6,000 every month.

1. Using the format shown in Table 3.7.1, construct a cash-flow forecast for Juma's restaurant business for the first five months of trading.

2. Comment on the cash-flow position faced by Juma's business and recommend a way forward for him.

TOK discussion

Is it morally right for businesses to insist on early payments from debtors while they delay payments to creditors?

Revision checklist

✓ Profit is the positive difference between total revenue and total costs when both cash and credit transactions are considered. Cash flow on the other hand is the flow of money in and out of the business and only considers cash transactions.

✓ The working capital cycle is the time interval between payment for goods supplied to a business and finally receiving cash from their sale. In order to effectively maximise on the working capital it is usually desirable to keep the cycle as short as possible.

✓ Cash flow forecast is a financial document that shows the expected month by month cash receipts (cash inflows) and payments (cash outflows) of a business that have not yet occurred. Cash inflows include; cash sales from selling goods or business assets, payments from debtors and borrowing from banks. Cash outflow examples include; purchasing materials or fixed assets for cash, cash expenses such as rent, wages and salaries and dividend payments to shareholders.

✓ When constructing cash flow forecasts the following need to be included; opening cash balance, total cash inflows, total cash outflows, net cash flows and closing cash balance.

✓ Some strategies to reduce cash outflow include; negotiating with creditors to reduce payment and delaying to purchase fixed assets, while some strategies to improve cash inflow include; insisting on cash purchases and offering incentives to encourage debtors to pay early.

Practice question

New Philanthropy Foundation (NPF)

Steve Dawes founded the *New Philanthropy* Foundation* (*NPF*) in 2005. It was set up with a very generous donation from a retired businessman. It is an online non-profit organization financing educational opportunities for children in developing countries. Steve has been looking at his financial statements with concern. *NPF's* cash reserves are being used up quickly and in the current poor economic climate, *NPF's* main source of finance – online donations – is falling.

In 2010, *NPF* has no debt but also no fixed assets. *NPF's* outgoings are Internet usage fee, maintenance fee for servers and computers as well as a web designer's fee for regularly updating the *NPF* web site.

NPF has volunteers from all over the world running the organization. An online community of social networking web sites connects them with Steve as the chief web site administrator. All funds to finance educational projects are transferred electronically and only e-mail communication is allowed. According to its vision statement, *NPF* aims to become the first paperless charity.

Steve has been asked by a very popular rock band to sponsor a reunion concert, which will be broadcast only over the Internet. The opportunity would generate substantial public relations possibilities, but some volunteers on the *NPF* forums are not convinced. They argue that the money spent sponsoring the concert should be used to provide further educational opportunities for children. They also believe that many people watching the concert may be frustrated if global Internet broadband connections become too slow or fail.

Steve is preparing a cash-flow forecast for the next six months (all figures refer to 2010) based on the following figures:

- Donations are transferred to the educational projects **one month after** the money has been received.

- Educational projects receive 95% of all donations.

a) Define the following terms:

    (i)   *vision statement*   *[2 marks]*

    (ii) *fixed assets*   *[2 marks]*

b) (i)   Using Steve's forecast figures, prepare a cash-flow forecast for *NPF* from June to November 2010, clearly showing the opening and closing monthly cash-flow forecast balances.   *[6 marks]*

    (ii) Comment on your results from part (i).   *[3 marks]*

    (iii) Explain **two** possible solutions to the liquidity problems highlighted in parts (i) and (ii).   *[6 marks]*

c) Analyse the impact of **two** external threats on *NPF's* decision to sponsor the concert.   *[6 marks]*

IB, May 2010

Forecast	Donations (millions of US$)
June	40
July	30
August	30
September	20
October	20
November	10

	Millions of US$
Opening balance in June 2010	1
Donations received in May 2010	50
Internet usage fee	1 to be paid in June and September
Maintenance fee for servers and computers	0.25 per month
Web designer's fee	0.5 per month
Concert sponsoring fee	5 to be paid in November

---

* *Philanthropy*: voluntary action for the public good. An activity performed with the goal of promoting the well-being of fellow man.

3.8 Investment appraisal

By the end of this chapter, you should be able to:

→ calculate and evaluate the **payback period** as an investment appraisal method

→ calculate and examine the **average rate of return** as an investment appraisal method

→ calculate and discuss the **net present value method** as an investment appraisal method **(HL only)**.

Introduction

Investment appraisal refers to the quantitative techniques used in evaluating the viability or attractiveness of an investment proposal. It attempts to assess and justify the capital expenditure allocated to a particular project. It therefore aims to establish whether a particular business venture is worth pursuing and whether it will be profitable. Investment appraisal also assists businesses in comparing different investment projects. In this section we look at three methods of investment appraisal – **payback period, average rate of return**, and **net present value**.

The payback period

This method estimates the length of time required for an investment project to pay back its initial cost outlay. It looks at how long a business will take to recover its principal investment amount from its net cash flows. It can be calculated using the following formula:

$$\text{Payback period} = \frac{\text{initial investment cost}}{\text{annual cash flow from investment}}$$

Example 1: A construction engineer plans on investing $200 000 in a new cement-mixing machine and estimates that it will generate about $50,000 in annual cash flow. Calculate the payback period for the machine.

$$\text{Payback period} = \frac{\$200,000}{\$50,000} = 4 \text{ years}$$

Hence the payback period for the new machine would be four years.

Example 2: Another construction engineer aims to invest $300,000 in a new timber-cutting machine. The machine is expected to generate the following cash flows in the first four years: $60,000, $80,000, $100,000 and $120,000.

Its payback period can be identified by calculating the cumulative cash flows over the four years, as shown in the table below:

Table 3.8.1. Expected cash flows of a new machine

Year	Annual net cash flows ($)	Cumulative cash flows ($)
0	(300,000)	(300,000)
1	60,000	(240,000)
2	80,000	(160,000)
3	100,000	(60,000)
4	120,000	60,000

The initial investment outlay will be paid back sometime in year four – but in which month exactly? This can be calculated using the following formula:

$$\frac{\text{Extra cash inflow required}}{\text{Annual cash flow in year 4}} \times 12 \text{ months}$$

The extra cash inflow shown in Table 3.8.1 is $60,000. This is because in year 3 it has been calculated that only $60,000 needs to be paid in year 4 to pay off the initial investment. The annual cash flow in year 4 is $120,000. Therefore applying this to the formula we get:

$$\frac{\$60,000}{\$120,000} \times 12 \text{ months} = 6 \text{ months}$$

It therefore takes three years and six months to pay back the initial investment of $300,000.

The results in examples 1 and 2 can be compared with results from other projects to aid decision making. As a general rule, the shorter the payback period of the project the better it is for the investing business. The business may also have decided on an internal payback period or "cut-off" that an investment should not go below, for example four years. In example 1 the investment project just meets this criterion while the one in example 2 is better off by six months.

Advantages of the payback period

- It is simple and fast to calculate.

- It is a useful method in rapidly changing industries such as technology. It helps to estimate how fast the initial investment will be recovered before another machine, for example, can be purchased.

- It helps firms with cash-flow problems because they can choose the investment projects that can pay back more quickly than others.

- Since it is a short-term measure of quick returns on investment, it is less prone to the inaccuracies of long-term forecasting.

- Business managers can easily comprehend and use the results obtained.

Disadvantages of the payback period

- It does not consider the cash earned after the payback period which could influence major investment decisions.

- It ignores the overall profitability of an investment project by focusing only on how fast it will pay back.

- The annual cash flows could be affected by unexpected external changes in demand which could negatively affect the payback period.

The average rate of return

This method measures the annual net return on an investment as a percentage of its capital cost. It assesses the profitability per annum generated by a project over a period of time. It is also known as the accounting rate of return. It can be calculated using the following formula:

$$\text{Average rate of return (ARR)} = \frac{\frac{(\text{total returns} - \text{capital cost})}{\text{years of usage}}}{\text{capital cost}} \times 100$$

Example: A business considers purchasing a new commercial photocopier at a cost of $150,000. It expects the following revenue streams for the next five years; $30,000, $50,000, $75,000, $90,000 and $100,000 respectively. Calculate its ARR.

$$\text{Total returns} = \$30,000 + \$50,000 + \$75,000 + \$90,000 + \$100,000$$
$$= \$345,000$$

$$\text{Net return per annum} = \frac{(\$345,000 - \$150,000)}{5} = \$39,000$$

$$\text{ARR} = \frac{\$39,000}{\$150,000} \times 100 = 26\%$$

The business therefore expects an ARR of 26% on its investment. A business can compare this figure with the ARR of other projects and choose the project showing the highest rate. The ARR can also be compared with banks' interest rates on loans, to assess the level of risk. For example, in the above case if banks offer an interest rate of 15%, businesses may find it worthwhile to pursue investment projects with a return of 11% higher than the base lending rate. Other businesses set **criterion rates** or a minimum rate that an investment project should not go below if it is to be selected. For example, if the criterion rate was 20% for the above business, the ARR is 6% above this rate and would still be considered a desirable project to pursue.

Advantages of the ARR

- The ARR shows the profitability of an investment project over a given period of time.

- Unlike the payback period, it makes use of all the cash flows in a business.

- It allows for easy comparisons with other competing projects, for better allocation of investment funds.

- A business can use its own criterion rate and check this with the ARR for a project, to assess the viability of the venture.

Key terms

Investment appraisal

the quantitative techniques used in evaluating the viability or attractiveness of an investment proposal

Payback period

the length of time required for an investment project to pay back its initial cost outlay

Average rate of return (ARR)

measures the annual net return on an investment as a percentage of its capital cost

3 Finance and Accounts

Disadvantages of the ARR

- Since it considers a longer time period or useful life of the project, there are likely to be forecasting errors. Long-term forecasts decrease the accuracy of results.

- It does not consider the timing of cash inflows. Two projects might have the same ARR but one could pay back more quickly despite this.

- The effects on the time value of money are not considered.

Net present value (HL only)

This is defined as the difference in the summation of present values of future cash inflows or returns and the original cost of investment. Present value is today's value of an amount of money available in future. For example, $100 invested at the beginning of the year in a bank account offering 10 per cent interest would be worth $110 at the end of the year:

$$\left(\frac{10}{100} \times \$100\right) + \$100$$

Hence, $110 in one year's time is worth $100 today. In other words, $100 is the present value of $110 in a year's time. If $110 is invested for another year it amounts to $121 and in a further year to $133. What do you observe? If $100 invested in a bank account at 10 per cent over three years grows to $133, then $100 received over a three-year period will be less than a $100 received today, i.e. a fixed amount of money paid in the future is worth less than a fixed amount paid today. How do we get the present value of $100 invested over three years at 10 per cent interest?

To do this we use what is called the **discounted cash-flow method**. This is a technique that considers how interest rates affect the present value of future cash flows. It uses a discount factor that converts these future cash flows to their present value today. This discount factor is usually calculated using interest rates and time.

Table 3.8.2. Discount factors

Years	Discount rate				
	4%	6%	8%	10%	20%
1	0.9615	0.9434	0.9259	0.9091	0.8333
2	0.9246	0.8900	0.8573	0.8264	0.6944
3	0.8890	0.8396	0.7938	0.7513	0.5787
4	0.8548	0.7921	0.7350	0.6830	0.4823
5	0.8219	0.7473	0.6806	0.6209	0.4019
6	0.7903	0.7050	0.6302	0.5645	0.3349
7	0.7599	0.6651	0.5835	0.5132	0.2791
8	0.7307	0.6271	0.5403	0.4665	0.2326
9	0.7026	0.5919	0.5002	0.4241	0.1938
10	0.6756	0.5584	0.4632	0.3855	0.1615

Source: *IB Business management guide* p. 78

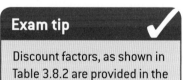

Exam tip ✔

Discount factors, as shown in Table 3.8.2 are provided in the *Business management guide*

To get the present value of future cash flows, the appropriate discount factor is multiplied by the net cash flow in the given year. In the earlier example, the present value of $100 invested over three years at 10 per cent will be:

Present value = 0.7513 (taken from Table 3.8.2) × $100 = $75.13. This means that $100 received in three years' time is worth only $75.13 today.

Example: Consider an investment project that costs $500,000 and produces net cash flows over the next four years as follows:

Year 1: $100,000

Year 2: $200,000

Year 3: $300,000

Year 4: $250,000

Calculate the net present value (NVP) at a discount factor of 8 per cent.

The working is shown in the following table:

Table 3.8.3 Calculating net present value

Year	Net cash flow ($)	Discount factor at 8%	Present value in $
0	(500,000)	1	(500,000)
1	100,000	0.9259	92,590
2	200,000	0.8573	171,460
3	300,000	0.7938	238,140
4	250,000	0.7350	183,750

> **NPV = total present values – original cost**

NPV = $685,940 − $500,000 = $185,940

The NPV in this example is a positive value of $185,940, signifying a viable project that should go ahead. If the value was negative then the viability of the project would be in question and it should not be pursued. An increase in the discount rate reduces the NPV because future cash flows will be worth less when discounted at higher rates.

Advantages of NPV

- The opportunity cost and time value of money is put into consideration in its calculation.

- All cash flows including their timing are included in its computation.

- The discount rate can be changed to suit any expected changes in economic variables such as interest rate variations.

Disadvantages of NPV

- It is more complicated to calculate than the payback period or ARR.

- It can only be used to compare investment projects with the same initial cost outlay.

- The discount rate greatly influences the final NPV result obtained, which may be affected by inaccurate interest rate predictions.

Key terms

Discounted cash flow

uses a discount factor that converts future cash flows to their present value

Net present value (NPV)

the difference in the summation of present values of future returns and the original cost of investment

3 Finance and Accounts

Student workpoint 3.17

Be knowledgeable

A large retail business has the following forecasted net cash flows for a major project:

Year	Net cash flows ($)
0	(40,000)
1	15,000
2	30,000
3	10,000
4	5,000

1. Calculate the payback period.

2. Calculate the ARR.

3. Calculate the NPV at a discount rate of 6 per cent (use the discount factors in Table 3.8.2). **[HL only]**

Revision checklist

✓ Investment appraisal is the quantitative assessment of the viability of an investment proposal. It establishes whether a particular business venture is worth pursuing or profitable as well as assisting businesses in making comparisons with other different investment projects. Investment appraisal techniques include payback period, average rate of return and net present value.

✓ Payback period looks at how long a business will take to recover its principal investment or initial cash outlay from its net cash flows. It is simple to calculate and a useful method in rapid changing industries. However, it does not consider the cash earned after the payback period and ignores the overall profitability of an investment project.

✓ Average rate of return assesses the profitability per annum generated by a project over a period of time and is also known as *accounting rate of return*. It makes use of all the cash flows in a business and shows the profitability of an investment project over a given period of time. However, it does not consider the timing of cash inflows and effects on the time value of money.

✓ Net present value is the difference in the summation of present values of future cash inflows or returns and the original cost of investment. It makes use of the *discounted cash flow method* in its calculation. It includes all cash flows in its computation as well as the opportunity cost and time value of money. However, it is more complex to calculate and can only be used to compare investment projects with the same initial cost outlay. **(HL only)**

Practice question

Easy E Booking (EEB)

Easy E Booking (*EEB*) is a small, well-known, reputable and financially stable online hotel reservation service. *EEB* employees are highly motivated and take great pride in their work. *EEB* has received recognition for their high quality customer service. Due to an increase in global demand, greater competition and changes in technology, the finance director, Maia, has decided to upgrade *EEB's* computers and/or software.

Maia has two options:

Option A: purchase only a new software called "Book-Fast" from a local software designer.

Option B: purchase new computers with installed software called "Global Reach" from a manufacturer abroad.

	Option A	Option B
Cost	$20,000	$40,000
Technical support	24 hours onsite at *EEB*	24 hours online
Further payments payable:		
Employees	No change	At the end of their contract 15% of employees to be made redundant, cost: $15,000 in year 2
Training cost	On-the-job: free	Intensive: $12,000 in year 1
Maintenance cost	Free	$1000 per year
Insurance cost	$500 per year	$1000 per year

The average rate of return (ARR) of Option A is 46.25%.

Maia is considering using a straight line method of depreciation.

EEB employees favour Option A, even though some of their competitors using "Book-Fast" have reported problems with the software, including security issues. However, Maia has chosen Option B, which will provide more up-to-date, sophisticated and secure reservation system software. It will also give *EEB* a competitive advantage and an ability to handle a large global volume of hotel reservations.

The estimated return/total revenue in $ per year is shown below:

	Option A	Option B
Year 1	10,000	14,000
Year 2	12,000	16,800
Year 3	17,000	23,800
Year 4	20,000	28,000

a) Describe **one** strength and **one** weakness of *EEB* using a straight line method of depreciation. [4 marks]

b) Calculate the payback period for Option A (*show all your working*). [2 marks]

c) Calculate the average rate of return (ARR) for Option B (*show all your working*). [4 marks]

d) For **both** Option A **and** Option B, calculate the net present value (NPV) using a discount rate of 4% (*show all your working*). [5 marks]

e) Explain **one** advantage and **one** disadvantage for *EEB* of using the NPV method of investment appraisal. [4 marks]

f) Examine Maia's choice of Option B. [6 marks]

IB, Nov 2012

3.9 Budgets (HL only)

By the end of this chapter, you should be able to:
→ explain the **importance of budgets** for organizations
→ state the **difference between cost centres and profit centres**
→ analyse the **role of cost centres and profit centres**
→ calculate and interpret **variances**
→ analyse the **role of budgets and variances in strategic planning**.

Introduction

A **budget** is a quantitative financial plan that estimates revenue and expenditure over a specified future time period. Budgets can be prepared for individuals, for the government, or for any type of organization. Budgets help in setting targets and are aligned with the main objectives of the organization. They enable the efficient allocation of resources within the specified time period. The person involved in the formulation and achievement of a budget is known as the budget holder. The **budget holder** is responsible for ensuring that the specified budget allocations are being met. Commonly used budgets are sales revenue budgets and cost budgets.

The importance of budgets for organizations

- **Planning:** by setting targets, managers ensure that budgets help to provide a sense of direction or purpose for organizations. A budget as a planning document should also assist in anticipating future problems and devising possible solutions.

- **Motivation:** budget holders who are responsible for **budgetary control** (modalities taken that ensure that the budgeted performance is in line with actual performance) feel empowered and trusted, which boosts their morale. In addition, staff who are involved and participate in the budgetary process feel recognized as part of the organizational team, which could even lead to increased productivity.

- **Resource allocation:** budgets help to prioritize how resources will be used in the organization. Since the demands for financial resources could be very high, budgets set certain boundaries that ensure that available resources are not overstretched but used for specified purposes based on designated needs.

- **Coordination:** budgets help to bring people from different departments together to work for a common purpose. Coordination helps all departments to reach uniform budget agreements for more effective achievement of the set targets.

- **Control:** budgets act as monitoring and evaluation tools to check how funds are being spent in each department. Budget holders need to ensure that they are within the budget in their spending patterns and especially ensure that they do not exceed the budget as this could lead to serious financial debt problems in the organization.

Cost and profit centres

To be able to account for the revenues generated and costs incurred, different parts of a business are divided into **cost centres** or **profit centres**.

Cost centres

This is a part or section of a business where costs are incurred and recorded. Cost centres can help managers to collect and use cost data effectively. Examples of costs collected and recorded in these sections include electricity, wages, advertising, and insurance, among others. Businesses can be divided into cost centres in some of the following ways:

- **By department** – examples include finance, production, marketing, and HR, where each department is a specific cost centre.

- **By product** – a business producing several products could ensure that each product is a cost centre. For example, Samsung produces mobile phones, televisions, computers, and many more products. Each of these products could be cost centres because costs are measured in their production.

- **By geographical location** – businesses such as the McDonald's Corporation or Coca-Cola Company are located in different parts of the world and each of the areas they are located in could be treated as cost centres.

Profit centres

This is a part or section of a business where both costs and revenues are identified and recorded. These sections allow businesses to calculate how much profit each centre makes. Profit centres enable comparisons to be made to judge the performance in the various sections of the business. For example, Toyota can identify the most profitable car models in the market by comparing the profit each product makes or by comparing which geographical location is most profitable. Therefore, just as in cost centres, profit centres can be divided according to product, department or geographical location as long as, in addition to cost, revenue is also generated.

The role of cost and profit centres

- **Aiding decision making:** cost and profit centres help in providing managers with financial information about the different parts of a business and this information can assist them in deciding whether to continue or discontinue producing a particular product. Production of high-cost and the least profitable products will be stopped to pave the way for new products.

Key terms

Budget

a quantitative financial plan that estimates the revenue and expenditure over a specified future time period

Budget holder

a person involved in the formulation and achievement of a budget

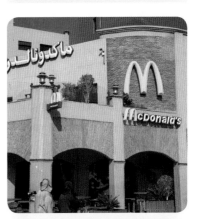

McDonald's has outlets all over the world – each geographical area could be treated as a cost centre

Key terms

Cost centre

a section of a business where costs are incurred and recorded

Profit centre

a section of a business where both costs and revenues are identified and recorded

- **Better accountability:** cost and profit centres help to hold specific business sections accountable. For example, managers who perform poorly in their department can be identified and held accountable for their inefficiency.

- **Tracking problem areas:** cost and profit centres enable particular problem areas in a business to be detected. For example, if in one store there are a lot of customer complaints resulting in a high number of costly product replacements, this can be checked by the use of a cost centre, leading to quick solutions being sought.

- **Increasing motivation:** providing departmental managers and staff with incentives such as promotion or bonuses to enable them to achieve set targets helps to increase their morale within cost and profit centres. Empowering staff and delegating control to managers in charge of these centres also helps in improving motivation.

- **Benchmarking:** comparing the performances in the various cost and profit centres in a business can help to check areas of most or least efficiency. This monitoring of individual parts of a business can help improve overall efficiency in the business.

Problems of cost and profit centres

- **Indirect cost allocation:** indirect costs such as advertising, rent or insurance are difficult to allocate specifically to particular cost centres. They may be allocated unfairly, distorting the overall business performance.

- **External factors:** Factors beyond the control of the business such as competition may affect specific cost and profit centres differently. Competition in one centre may be higher than in another, thereby negatively influencing the performance of the centres there.

- **Centre conflicts:** staff and managers may consider the performance in their own centres to be superior to the overall performance of the organization. This could lead to unhealthy competition between the centres for a firm's resources and a lack of sharing of vital information.

- **Staff stress:** the pressure of managing a cost and profit centre may be very high for some staff, especially if they lack the right skills. This could lead to staff demotivation.

Variance analysis

In budgeting, a **variance** is the difference between the budgeted figure and the actual figure. This variance is usually calculated at the end of a budget period once the actual amounts are determined. Variance analysis is a budgetary control process of assessing the differences between the budgeted amount and the actual amount. This analysis can be done for both cost and sales revenue budgets. Variances can either be **favourable** or **adverse**.

A **favourable variance** is when the difference between the budgeted and actual figure is financially beneficial to the firm. For example, if the budgeted sales revenue in one month was $30 000 and the actual sales revenue was $40 000, then the firm has a favourable variance of $10 000.

If the budgeted marketing costs were $80,000 in a month and turned out to be $65,000, then the firm has a favourable variance of $15,000.

An **adverse variance** occurs when the difference between the budgeted and actual amounts is financially costly to the firm. For example, if the actual sales revenue amount was lower than the budgeted figure or the actual costs were higher than the budgeted costs, then the firm has an adverse or unfavourable variance.

Example: Table 3.9.1 shows some of the budgeted and actual amounts taken from Mr Kamau's business.

Required

Complete the missing figures and state the nature of the variance obtained – write (F) for favourable or (A) for adverse.

Table 3.9.1 Calculating variance

Particulars	Budgeted figure ($)	Actual figure ($)	Variance
Sales of televisions	10,000	12,500	
Cost of materials	4,000	3,800	
Sales of laptops	15,000	13,900	
Cost of labour	5,000	5,700	
Cost of rent	3,000	3,000	

Solution:

Particulars	Budgeted figure ($)	Actual figure ($)	Variance ($)
Sales of televisions	10,000	12,500	2,500 (F)
Cost of materials	4,000	3,800	200 (F)
Sales of laptops	15,000	13,900	1,100 (A)
Cost of labour	5,000	5,700	700 (A)
Cost of rent	3,000	3,000	0

From the above example it can be noted that:

- Favourable variances were experienced in the sale of televisions and cost of materials. Here, both presented a financial benefit to the business, one with a higher actual sales figure than expected of $2,500 and the other with reduced actual costs of $200 respectively.

- Adverse variances were experienced in the sales of laptops and the cost of labour, which proved financially costly to the firm. Expected laptop sales declined by $1,100, while the cost of labour increased by $700.

The role of budgets and variances in strategic planning

Strategic planning is an organization's systematic process of defining its future direction and deciding on how to allocate its resources

3 Finance and Accounts

accordingly, to fulfill this vision. In defining its future position, it first needs to know its current position and the available opportunities there are before pursuing its desired course of action. The course of action involves formulating key goals or objectives derived from the vision and putting in place a series of steps to achieve them. Budgeting and carrying out variance analysis is one of those steps and both play an important role in strategic planning. This role is further explored in the following points:

Advantages of using budgets and variances in strategic planning

- Budgets help to control revenue and expenditure by regulating how money is spent to minimize losses and wastage of resources.

- Budgets provide realistic targets that are clearly understood by all internal stakeholders to aid in the attainment of an organization's goals.

- Budgets help in the coordination of the various business departments, improving the flow of communication and ensuring a sense of people working together.

- Budgets should be set based on the SMART criteria – being specific, measurable, agreed, realistic and time-bound – and all in line with the organization's objectives.

- Variance analysis aims to compare actual performance to budgeted performance, thereby helping to assess organizational performance.

- Variance analysis assists in detecting the causes of any deviations in the budget so that corrective measures can be taken to rectify them.

- Variance analysis provides an objective way of appraising budget holders responsible for their various departments.

However, in an attempt to fulfil the strategic objectives of an organization, budgeting brings with it some of the following limitations.

Limitations of budgets in strategic planning

- Inflexible budgets that do not consider any unforeseen changes in the external environment, such as increases in raw material costs, may be too difficult to stay within and therefore be unrealistic.

- Significant differences between the budgeted and actual results could make the budget lose its importance as a planning tool.

- Since most budgets are based on the short term, long-term future gains such as increased sales potential due to unexpected increases in demand could be lost by looking only at the current budgeted amount.

- Highly underspent budgets towards the end of the year could result in unjustified wasteful expenditure by managers.

- Setting budgets without involving some people could result in their resentment and affect their motivation levels.

Despite the above limitations, budgets do play an important role in strategic planning. They are vital financial planning documents that help to monitor and control income and expenditure so that the specified organizational objectives are attained.

Student workpoint 3.18

Be a thinker

The following information refers to XAV Ltd:

Particulars	Budgeted figure ($)	Actual figure ($)	Variance
Material costs	12,000	18,500	
Direct labour costs	9,000	7,800	
Sales of radios	25,000	25,600	
Sales of the Apple iPod®	15,000	12,750	
Advertising costs	6,000	7,100	

1. Calculate the missing figures from the table above and note whether the variance is favourable (F) or adverse (A).

2. Interpret the material costs variance and suggest possible reasons for your answer.

3. What do the overall variance figures tell you about the business?

Revision checklist

✓ A budget is a financial plan that helps in target setting by estimating the revenue and expenditure of a business over a specified future time period.

✓ Budgets are important for planning, motivation, resource allocation, coordination and control.

✓ Cost centres are sections of a business where costs are incurred and recorded and help to collect and effectively use cost data, while profit centres are sections of a business where both costs and revenues are identified and recorded, which allow businesses to calculate how much profit each centre makes.

✓ Cost and profit centres are important in aiding decision making, improving accountability, tracking problem areas, increasing motivation and benchmarking. However, some challenges faced include difficulties in allocating indirect costs to particular cost centres and external factors beyond the firm's control.

✓ Variance analysis is a budgetary control process of assessing the differences between the budgeted amount and the actual amount. If the difference between the budgeted figure and actual figure is beneficial to the firm it is known as a *favourable variance*. On the other hand if the difference between the budgeted and actual figure are financially costly it is known as an *adverse variance*.

3 Finance and Accounts

TOK discussion

Accounting practices such as budgeting vary from country to country. Is this necessary or could we have the same accounting practices everywhere?

Practice question

KJC Ltd

KJC Ltd specialises in making pots of all sizes and shapes. Over the years it has developed a good reputation for high quality products. They have a well-developed distribution network both nationally and overseas. For the first half of this year they have experienced significant growth in the sales of their products. However, for the second half of the year their sales have slowed down drastically. Some stakeholders attribute this to the recession that the country is experiencing while others feel that increased competition is the cause. The company's budget holder Mr John Juma has been tasked with carrying out a variance analysis so as to ascertain how the company performed over the year. He may have to carry out strict budgetary controls and monitor each cost centre and profit centre closely. The table below shows the budgeted figures and actual figures for KJC Ltd for this year.

$000	Budgeted figures	Actual figures	Variance
Sales revenue	500	400	
Direct labour costs	50	45	
Direct material costs	80	90	
Gross profit	370	265	
Overheads	100	95	
Net profit	270	170	

a) Define the following terms

   (i) Budget holder   *[2 marks]*

   (ii) Variance analysis   *[2 marks]*

b) Explain the importance of budgets to *KJC Ltd*   *[4 marks]*

c) Complete the variance column in the table above and establish whether the results obtained are adverse or favourable   *[6 marks]*

d) Comment on the performance of *KJC Ltd* using the variance results   *[4 marks]*

e) Evaluate the role of cost and profit centres to *KJC Ltd*   *[7 marks]*

4 MARKETING

4.1 The role of marketing

By the end of this chapter, you should be able to:

→ define marketing and understand its relationship with other business functions

→ explain the difference between the marketing of goods and the marketing of services

→ distinguish between **market orientation** and **product orientation**

→ explain the difference between **commercial marketing, social marketing** and **social media marketing**

→ describe the elements that characterize the market in which an organization operates

→ calculate **market share**

→ discuss the importance of market share and **market leadership**

→ compare and contrast the marketing objectives of for-profit organizations and non-profit organizations

→ evaluate how marketing strategies evolve as a response to changes in customer preferences

→ examine how the concepts of **innovation**, **ethics** and **culture** influence marketing practices and strategies.

Marketing is essential to the success of any business. However, marketing is not just about selling or advertising, as many people think. It is much more than that: it is more of a business philosophy of how best to think about satisfying consumer needs or demands. There are many globally acceptable definitions of marketing. Some common ones include the following.

"Marketing is the management process involved in identifying, anticipating and satisfying consumer needs profitably."

The Chartered Institute of Marketing

"Marketing is the activity, set of institutions, and processes for creating, communicating, delivering, and exchanging offerings that have value for customers, clients, partners, and society at large."

American Marketing Association

Kotler (1994) summarized it well when he said "Marketing is meeting the needs of your customer at a profit."[1] Ultimately, marketing is about getting the right product to the right customers at the right price at the right time. This means that marketing involves a number of activities that every marketing department should aim to satisfy, all centred on the consumer. However, all marketing decisions, whether related to products, pricing, distribution, or promotion, are affected by other business functions.

Finance and marketing

Since marketing costs money, the marketing and finance department have to work together in setting the appropriate budgets. The marketing department may want to spend more than is in its budget to meet the requirements of a demanding marketing plan, but the finance department may advise that it sticks to its given budgetary allocations. This will cause a departmental conflict.

Human resource management (HRM) and marketing

Marketing information can enable more effective workforce planning in the HRM department. This can influence the demand and supply of labour in an organization. For example, an increase in the demand for a product as a result of improved marketing may require the recruitment of extra staff from the sales and production departments in order to meet this demand. Ensuring that the right quality of salespeople are hired – those with innovative minds and a competitive spirit – will also aid in meeting the marketing department's objectives.

Operations management and marketing

The production and marketing departments will need to work together to ensure that the products developed meet the specifications of the customers. Market research will help the marketers in determining the needs and wants of the consumers. However, both departments need to balance the time needed to test, develop, and launch products, to avoid any loss in sales or reputation and any arousal of potential stakeholder conflict.

The marketing of goods and services

In deciding how to market their products, businesses first need to distinguish between goods, such as cars, and services, such as insurance. This is because goods and services differ in a number of ways.

Key terms

Marketing

the management process of getting the right product to the right customer at the right price to the right place and time

Marketing of goods

the use of the 4 Ps of product, price, place, and promotion in the marketing mix

Marketing of services

the use of the 7Ps of product, price, place, promotion, process, people, and physical evidence in the marketing mix

---

[1]   Kotler, P. 1994. *Marketing Management: Analysis, planning, implementation and control.* Englewood Cliffs, NJ, Prentice Hall.

Table 4.1.1. Differences between goods and services

Goods	Services
are tangible, i.e. can be touched	are intangible, i.e. cannot be touched
can be returned if you did not like what you bought	cannot be taken back, e.g. a bad haircut
can be stored and consumed later, e.g. yoghurt.	cannot be stored and will need to be consumed immediately, e.g. your consultant's time.
There is ownership of the product.	There is no ownership of the product.
Goods are easier to compare because of the similar nature of some products, e.g. one TV can easily be compared to another.	Services are more difficult to compare because of different experiences a customer may get from a given service, e.g. a hotel may treat a customer differently each time he or she visits.

In selling goods, businesses can focus on specific characteristics that appeal to the consumer. In buying a new cellphone, customers can choose one over another based on the elaborate features one may have over the other, such as the number of applications. Managers in a service-providing company such as a hotel may talk about the number and type of rooms it has, but their marketing angle is mostly about offering good customer service to ensure that the customer returns.

To remain globally competitive, multinational companies today are outsourcing their goods to countries producing at lower costs. For example, a clothing company based in the USA can manufacture a specific clothing line in Asia and ship it to customers living in Europe. However, service businesses need to be closer to their customers; for example, it may be very difficult for many people to travel from country to country on a day-to-day basis sampling varied country cuisines, from the popular Indian curry to the sumptuous Kenyan nyama choma (roast meat). Therefore different cafés or restaurants (mostly franchises) are increasingly drawing closer to customers in their localities to sell their cultural foods. In addition, organizations offering services must always guard their reputation by having well-trained and approachable employees who will help in enhancing their product quality and image. For example, an airline industry with well-groomed and smiling staff greeting passengers at the entrance of the plane can help in further marketing the airline.

Essentially, the marketing of goods is based on the four "Ps" of the **marketing mix** – namely *price, product, promotion,* and *place.* The marketing of services includes the three additional aspects of *people, processes,* and *physical evidence.* These aspects will be explored later in this unit. It is important to note that many products now have both goods and service elements to them. For example, a customer may buy an iPad as a physical product but may receive after-sales service in the form of a warranty or free maintenance for a year.

Market orientation verses product orientation

There are two distinct approaches that businesses can use to market their products. They can either use a **product-orientated approach** or a **market-orientated approach**. These two approaches are shown in the table below.

Table 4.1.2. Differences between a product-orientated approach and a market-orientated approach

Product-orientated approach	Market-orientated approach
inward looking and focused on making the product first and then trying to sell it	outward looking and focused on carrying out market research first and then making products that can sell
product-led and assuming that supply creates its own demand (Say's law). Here businesses produce innovative products and tempt the customers to buy them	market-led and focused on establishing consumer demand so as to supply products that meet consumers' needs and wants

Organizations that have adopted a product-orientated approach to their products include Microsoft, Ferrari, Dyson, and Apple. Many organizations are now market-orientated businesses, including Ford, Sony, Samsung, and Nokia.

These are the benefits to a business of being market-orientated:

- As a result of market research, firms have increased confidence that their products will sell, therefore reducing the risk of failure.

- Access to market information means that firms can respond more quickly to changes in the market and are also able to anticipate market changes.

- Firms will be in a strong position to meet the challenge of new competitors entering the market as a result of regular feedback from consumers brought about by market research.

However, market orientation does have some limitations:

- Conducting market research can be costly and therefore weigh heavily on a firm's budget.

- Due to frequently changing consumer tastes, firms may find it difficult to meet every consumer's needs with its available resources.

- Uncertainty about the future could also have a negative influence on market-planning strategy.

Product-orientated businesses put a lot of emphasis on the production process rather than on their potential customers. A product-orientated business will have these advantages:

- It is associated with the production of high-quality products such as luxury sports cars and safety products such as crash helmets.

- It can succeed in industries where the speed of change is slow and the firm has already built a good reputation.

- It has control over its activities, with a strong belief that consumers will purchase its products.

However, the major limitations such a firm faces include the following:

- Since the firm ignores the needs of the market, it takes risks that may lead to eventual business failure or closure.

- Spending money on research and development without considering consumer needs could be costly and not yield any promising results.

Dyson takes a product-orientated approach to marketing

Key terms

Product orientation

a business approach that focuses on making the product first before attempting to sell it

Market orientation

a business approach of first establishing consumer demand through market research before producing and selling a product

Commercial marketing

This involves creating, developing, and exchanging goods or services that customers need and want. In this case, market research is carried out to establish consumer demand and businesses will supply what is demanded. Commercial marketing is value-free and does not involve making moral judgments on the buying habits of customers. Once the specific product is identified, appropriate strategies need to be put in place to market the product. The strategies used in commercial marketing need to be tailored specifically to the type of product the commercial is selling. These strategies may include a traditional focus (using billboards, television advertisements, or local print media) or an online marketing campaign (using Google Ad Sense or emails). There is also the option of either adopting a mass-marketing campaign, to get the product into the minds of as many consumers as possible, or to use targeted advertisements aimed at specific demographics.

Social marketing

This involves the use of marketing approaches that help bring about changes in behaviour that ultimately benefit society. The Social Marketing Institute (SMI) defines it as:

"the use of commercial marketing concepts and tools in programmes designed to influence individuals' behaviour to improve their well-being and that of society."

Social marketing is a wide concept involving other stakeholders. It ensures that businesses make good marketing decisions based not only on consumers' wants and the firm's requirements but also on consumers' and society's long-term interests and welfare. Examples of social marketing include public health campaigns, for example anti-smoking campaigns centred on reducing smoking, providing information on the dangers of drink-driving, and educating the public on the benefits of eating healthy food to discourage overeating or poor dietary habits. Social marketing programmes also include environmental campaigns to promote recycling, clean air, and water as well as other measures of conservation. Today social marketing also looks into areas such as human rights and family planning.

Some advantages of social marketing include the following:

- It gives firms a competitive advantage as consumers may perceive such firms to be socially responsible and therefore buy products from them.

- Firms can charge premium prices for providing goods that society is deriving benefits from.

However, getting people to change their habitual behaviour poses a major challenge to social marketers. As a result, a number of non-profit organizations (NPOs) have set up in an effort to help people change their behaviour, for example Alcoholic Anonymous (AA).

The Social Marketing Institute encourages the use of a wide range of marketing tools by going beyond just "Promotion" in the marketing

4 Marketing

Key terms

Commercial marketing

marketing activities that determine consumer needs and wants before using appropriate strategies to market the product

Social marketing

a marketing approach aimed at influencing a positive change in individual behaviour and improvements in societal well-being mix and fully incorporating the other elements of the marketing mix as well in the effort to bring social change. (See more on promotion in the marketing mix in sections 4.2 and 4.5)

Social media marketing (SMM)

SMM is a marketing approach adopted by businesses that uses social networking websites from the Internet to market its products. SMM is a marketing tool that incorporates the use of technological concepts and techniques with the aim of growing a business through different media.

SMM has increased in popularity with the development of websites such as Facebook, Twitter, LinkedIn, and YouTube.

These are the benefits of SMM:

- It enables a firm to get direct feedback from its customers while still appealing to them personally, through its interactive sections that provide customers with the opportunity to ask questions and voice their complaints. This is known as social customer relationship management.

- It provides a low-cost way for firms to reach a large target audience. For example, the number of users of Facebook stood at 1.11 billion in April 2013.

- It can enhance a firm's brand. Since many social networking websites already have large established online communities, firms can gain exposure by simply joining these websites.

However, while SMM is a very useful marketing tool, most businesses will use it as a supplement to other marketing methods and not as a replacement for them. Since it is easy for any business to join a social networking website, it can be difficult for a business to stand out from the crowd, hence the need also to rely on other marketing techniques.

Social media can be a powerful way to reach lots of customers very quickly

TOK discussion

In marketing, what role does language play in the different areas of knowledge?

Student workpoint 4.1

Be a thinker

1. Distinguish between marketing a good and marketing a service.

2. Using specific organizational examples, comment on the benefits of market orientation.

3. Explain how social marketing differs from SMM.

Key terms

Social media marketing

the use of the Internet through social networking websites to market a firm's product or service

Characteristics of the market in which an organization operates

A market is an arrangement where buyers and sellers exchange goods and services. It includes actual as well as potential buyers or customers of a product whose needs or wants are satisfied by sellers or suppliers in the exchange process.

The elements that characterize the market in which an organization operates are as follows:

- Market size – this represents the total sales of all businesses in a given market. It is measured in two ways:

  - **By volume** – this measures the number of goods bought by customers. It is a quantitative measure of the units sold by businesses, for example bags of maize.

  - **By value** – this measures the amount spent by customers on the total number of goods sold by businesses. It is the total revenue expressed in monetary terms, e.g. Kenyan shillings (Kshs), US dollars (US$), or South African rands (ZAR).

Knowledge of market size assists firms in identifying their market growth and in calculating market share.

- **Market growth** – this is the percentage change in the market size over a given period of time, usually a year. This can be based on the market value or volume. For example, an increase in sales revenue resulting from the sale of televisions from US$50 million to US$80 million indicates a 60-per-cent growth in the market. Sales of smartphones are on the rise globally, with many consumers finding multiple uses for the gadget. This has attracted many suppliers of the product because of the high profit potential. However, this growth is influenced by several external factors, such as economic growth patterns, technological changes, changes in consumer tastes, and income, among others.

Student workpoint 4.2

Be a thinker

Coca-Cola published 2013 highlights on its website: http://www.coca-colacompany.com

The company announced that volume sales of its sparkling drinks were up by 3%, whilst still drinks had increased by 6%.

As well as providing financial information for investors and stakeholders, do you think that publishing sales figures in this way can be a marketing tool for businesses?

- **Market share** – this is the percentage of one firm's share of the total sales in the market. It is calculated by using the following formula:

$$\text{Market share } \% = \frac{\text{firm's sales}}{\text{total sales in the market}} \times 100$$

Market share can be measured by value (revenue) or volume (units), just like market size. An increase in market share could mean that a business is successful against its competitors and has adopted effective marketing strategies as a result. This could be associated with increased profits and result in the business being the key player in the industry.

Measuring market share is important because it could indicate that the firm is a market leader. A market leader can influence other businesses or competitors to follow it. Its status as market leader can also affect its future strategy and objectives.

The benefits of being a market leader include the following:

- The market leader will have increased sales, translating to higher profits.

- The business will be able to gain economies of scale, (i.e. a decrease in the average costs of production as a result of increasing its scale of operation).

- Since the market leader could also be the brand leader (providing the product with the highest market share), the leading brand can act as a good promotional tool for consumers who would like to associate with popular brands.

However, when interpreting the market share, careful thought is needed:

- Since market share can be measured in different ways, by value and volume, different results may be obtained in the same time period.

- Changes in the time period and market can influence market share results.

- The type of products included may also influence the calculation of market share.

Key terms

Market size

the total sales of all firms in a market

Market growth

the percentage change in the total market size over a period of time

Market share

the percentage of one firm's share of the total sales in the market

Market leader

a firm with the highest market share in a given market

Student workpoint 4.3

Be knowledgeable

Table 4.1.3. Different sales volumes and values from different companies

Company	XYZ		ABC		PQR	
Year	2011	2012	2011	2012	2011	2012
Sales of toys (million units)	550	580	700	740	620	650
Sales of toys ($ million)	25	28	45	48	32	30

Use Table 4.1.3 above to calculate the following:

a) Market share of XYZ Company by volume in 2011

b) Market share of ABC Company by value in 2012

c) Market share of PQR Company by volume in 2011

d) Market growth for the whole industry by value from 2011 to 2012

Marketing objectives of for-profit organizations and non-profit organizations (NPOs)

Marketing objectives are the goals or targets that businesses aim to achieve through their marketing department, which are in line with the organization's overall strategic objectives. As earlier noted, many marketing definitions include the notion that businesses should aim to satisfy consumer needs and wants **profitably**. Therefore the sole marketing objective of for-profit organizations is to identify, design and develop marketing strategies that will ultimately be profitable to the business. This will involve appropriately applying the elements of the marketing mix to achieve this objective. For-profit organizations use a market-led approach, where their focus is purely on the needs and wants of consumers. They are very responsive to the needs and wants of consumers and use market research as a way of identifying those needs.

NPOs such as churches, charities, and some schools engage in marketing activities more for social marketing reasons. In such cases, social marketers would run campaigns to encourage the public to donate money or support a certain cause, for example campaigns aimed at helping orphaned and vulnerable children with food and clothing. Increasingly, NPOs are using more complex marketing strategies to achieve their aims, which include enhancing their image and reputation. They are also using marketing to inform and influence certain behavioural change. For example, a government may seek to educate the public on the dangers of smoking and adopting responsible drinking habits.

A major drawback of most NPOs is limited financing, which seriously affects their marketing budgets. A number therefore seek to raise funds through fundraising events, seminars and endorsements, in an effort to be heard and to improve their public relations. This funding is also linked to their ability to attract potential "customers" and therefore receive sponsorships or donations, such as in the case of public sector colleges. As a result, they are able to gain competitive advantages over their rivals in the private sector.

Internet marketing, which includes social media marketing, is also increasing in popularity among a number of NPOs. With the growing number of global Internet users, a number of charities have raised a lot of money from online donations made using PayPal, for example. Other NPOs, such as Sandra Lee children's home in Swaziland, have increased the number of retail outlets that they seek to raise money from, by having money collection containers at the till in most supermarkets.

NPOs have to be ethical at all times and practise a high degree of social responsibility if they are to continue benefiting from free publicity from other organizations as well as maintaining public interest in their causes.

How marketing strategies evolve as a response to changes in customer preferences

Due to a variety of factors, customers' preferences have changed significantly over the past two decades and businesses have responded in various ways to meet these new demands. The ways in which marketing strategies have been adapted to suit these new preferences are discussed

BMW's marketing strategy

BMW operates across the globe in a highly competitive industry – the automotive industry. As a result, BMW invests heavily in its marketing mix to maintain its customer base and brand loyalty. However, competitors Mercedes-Benz and Jaguar are similarly well invested in marketing campaigns to increase their market shares while maintaining their brand loyalties. Previously, BMW used its unique selling point or proposition (USP) of building high-performance, high-quality sports cars with unique handling characteristics to gain customers' attention and loyalty. Slogans such as "Pure driving pleasure" and "Perfection perfected" punctuated BMW's marketing campaign around the world. Whereas BMW, in the context of the Ansoff's Matrix (see Unit 1.3 on Organizational objectives), had begun with a market-extension strategy into markets such as China and India, it later switched to product development as its key strategy.

This shift in marketing strategies came about because a market segment became the largest single market in which BMW operated. Customers have developed a new preference in the last two decades that continues to grow in strength and popularity – high fuel efficiency. Due to dramatic increases in oil prices, in all but the OPEC nations (a PEST factor), customers have sought out vehicles that use less fuel to travel further. For example, the Toyota Prius and Tesla car company have thrived because of their environmentally friendly, low fuel consumption features – a result of focused differentiation. In response to this development, BMW instituted a raft of changes to its marketing strategy.

First, as part of product changes in the marketing mix, BMW began designing and showcasing "vision" concept cars at the largest automotive expos in the world. None was more definitive than the BMW i8, which was branded the "efficient dynamics" concept car. Essentially, it showcased BMW's latest fuel-efficiency technology to the world's media and immediately positioned BMW towards consumers' new preferences. BMW also changed many of its promotion techniques to fit this new brand image. Below-the-line methods including slogans such as "Exhilaration without excess" became BMW's new focus and efficient dynamics became its USP and major product-differentiation tool. The institution of new products in BMW's marketing strategy was paired with new promotion strategies. BMW began to emphasize the fuel efficiency of its existing models (which it had

М. МОЩЬ ОДНОЙ БУКВЫ.

previously neglected to publicize) and products such as the BMW X-series cars were rebranded by taking part in the gruelling Dakar rally. Considered a race that requires participants to have vehicles with extraordinary fuel efficiencies, the Dakar rally also allowed BMW to challenge one of its main competitors in the luxury SUV market – Volkswagen.

However, BMW's shift in market strategy has not been a complete success. In an attempt to please the majority of customers who desire fuel-efficient cars, BMW has lost some of its most loyal customers to competitors. This has largely been a result of changes to the product element of its marketing mix. In order to increase fuel efficiency and to lower carbon emissions, BMW ceased using V10 engines in its M-Power 5 Series cars in favour of twin-turbo charged V8 engines that use less fuel. As a result, BMW lost many loyal, high-income customers who preferred the more powerful V10. In short, BMW's pivot towards a new customer preference caused its profitability to be damaged to some extent. However, with increased market shares in Africa, North America, and Asia, BMW's medium-risk strategy appears to have paid off.

Exam-style questions

1. Define the following terms:

   (a) Marketing mix   [2 marks]

   (b) Market share   [2 marks]

2. Analyse how BMW can be customer-focused.   [4 marks]

3. Evaluate the success of BMW's marketing strategy.   [10 marks]

below in the **context** of two firms and industries: first, BMW and the automotive industry and second, the Multichoice Group and the television broadcasting industry. Each of these businesses has adapted its marketing strategy to improve its profitability by rebranding and penetrating new markets, or by diversifying.

Case study

Multichoice's marketing strategy

The Multichoice Group has also shifted its marketing mix and strategy to meet customers' preferences. In particular, the arrival of high-definition (HD) technology in a variety of fields, ranging from cellphones to cameras and televisions, has drawn a great deal of the customers' attention. However, unlike BMW, it is apparent that Multichoice does not operate in a highly competitive market. In fact, DSTV (owned by the Multichoice Group) could be considered a monopoly as it benefited heavily from the first mover advantage. However, Multichoice has still changed to meet customer preferences to ensure that there is no market gap for new entrants to exploit.

Multichoice's marketing mix has refocused in terms of techniques to reach customers rather than using a shift in focus like BMW's. For example, DSTV's premium subscribers (those who pay the highest rates) form part of the demographic in Southern Africa that has the highest income. As a result, they are the most technologically aware demographic in Southern Africa and because of this DSTV has placed a greater emphasis on online advertising on social media and unique websites. DSTV now has Twitter and Facebook pages for customers to follow and prospective customers to view that provide the latest information on new products brought to market. For example, the arrival of HD channels such as HD Discovery Showcase and M-Net HD were first promoted online to their premium customers (those most likely to purchase these products) before reaching other customers via television advertisements (a result of market segmentation).

However, the implementation of this strategy has not come without some drawbacks – the largest of which is the increased cost to customers. As a result of expensive technological upgrades to DSTV's broadcasting system to support HD television, customers have suffered a price increase to pay for both the new systems and the marketing campaign to promote it. This increase in price also priced out prospective customers who could have increased DSTV's market share. This demonstrates how responding to customer preferences can have negative effects on the customers themselves.

Exam-style questions

1. Describe two forms of market segmentation relevant for Multichoice. [4 marks]

2. Analyse how effectively Mulitichoice's marketing strategy has responded to customer preferences. [6 marks]

3. With reference to Multichoice and to one other organisation that you have studied, discuss the impact of changing technology on promotional strategies. [10 marks]

When compared with BMW's complete change in marketing strategy, Multichoice's shift in marketing methods seems inconsequential. However, both companies' shift in marketing strategy was vital in maintaining their market share and positions. Each shift was a direct response to a change in what the customer wanted. Failure to respond to these needs has dire consequences and certain other companies, for example Ford and Chevrolet, failed to make the necessary changes, and have seen huge drops in market share over the past five years.

In conclusion, marketing strategies, much like all business strategies, must adapt to remain relevant. Failure to adapt can result in a loss of profitability or even total failure, as in the case of Hummer. BMW and DSTV are just some of the many businesses around the world that have changed their marketing strategies because of changing customer preferences. Whether it is a change in marketing methods, or reconfiguration of the marketing mix, marketing strategies can and must adapt to changing customer preferences.

How innovation, ethical considerations and cultural differences influence marketing

In an increasingly globalized world, where the world's economies and markets are integrating, innovation, ethics and culture now affect marketing strategies more than ever before. Using specific companies, an assessment of how these factors have influenced and continue to influence global marketing practices and strategy will be explored, including the firms' responses to changes in these factors. The companies in question include Nokia, Chevron, British Petroleum, Apple, and Rolls-Royce.

Innovation

First, it is important to consider the responses by businesses to changes in innovation in terms of their marketing strategies for their products. There is no industry more exposed to innovation than the highly competitive technology industry. The technology industry is one with a great threat of new entrants and fierce competition, making Apple's achievements all the more impressive.

For the last six years, Apple has dominated the technology market with products such as the iPod®, iPad®, and iPhone®. Within the framework of Ansoff's Matrix (see Unit 1.3 on Organizational objectives), Apple has mostly focused on strategies involving market penetration and product development to out-compete its main rivals Nokia and Samsung. Apple has mostly branded its products as tools for a young, dynamic demographic in need of the newest and most innovative technology. However, Apple's dominance is increasingly being challenged, in part because of the new marketing strategies of its main competitors.

Nokia has adopted a new global marketing strategy to reinvigorate its market share. This shift has occurred on two levels: the marketing mix and the channels through which Nokia markets itself. Nokia's new slogan, "#Switch" best sums up these two elements. First, in terms of its products, Nokia has introduced a new range of cellphones built to beat Apple called Lumia®. The Lumia® range has a physical design similar to the iPhone®, yet more styled than the iPhone®. It is sold in a variety of vibrant colours to suit different tastes, unlike the uniform iPhone®. In terms of performance, the Lumia® range has higher processing speeds and more vivid HD touchscreens than the iPhone®. In short, the Lumia® phones are designed to be superior versions of the iPhone®. This is mirrored by the promotional campaign for the Lumia® range. #Switch is the slogan Nokia uses to motivate consumers to purchase its cellphones instead of Apple's.

Furthermore, #Switch is a Twitter address for customers around the world to follow to receive real-time updates about new Nokia products. When customers use the hashtag on Twitter it automatically spreads the message to all their followers – indirectly advertising Nokia's Lumia® range. Along with a greater emphasis on social networking, Nokia has used YouTube to brand itself as the new innovative business in the market. In terms of place, Nokia has also mimicked iStores by hiring young, energetic employees to operate its stores and interact with customers. Samsung has also tried to rebrand itself as a highly innovative business with state-of-the-art products such as the Samsung Galaxy™ range of cellphones. Its advertising campaign centres on showcasing the unique features of its products rather than selling a brand like Apple.

However, the shift to online advertising has come at a great cost to Nokia – the loss of customers in developing nations. Nokia and many other companies, such as Sony and Microsoft, have failed to respond to the large customer base that has either no Internet access or access at poor speeds. Markets in China, Sub-Saharan Africa and Latin America have been left largely untapped as a result of this. Compared with the Coca-Cola Company and PepsiCo, these companies are lagging behind in terms of major market penetration. As a result, the capacity for growth is immense; however, Nokia is failing to exploit it. In turn, revenues and profits are not being maximized.

Ethical considerations

Ethical considerations have also had a major impact on the way businesses brand themselves and their products. The energy and resource exploitation industry provides a clear example of this.

Two major events have reshaped the consumer's perception of oil companies in the last 40 years. These are the Exxon Valdes oil spill in 1989 and the BP Deep Water Horizon spill in 2010. Each incident caused a great deal of damage to the corporate images of not only BP and Exxon but all oil companies around the world. As a result, most have rebranded themselves to enhance their corporate images and improve their stakeholder relations –without which they could not be profitable. For example, Chevron (formerly Texaco) now has "protecting the environment" as one of its core values and "sustainability" as one of its visions. In terms of its marketing mix, particularly promotional techniques, Chevron has branded itself as a socially responsible organization interested in the well-being of ordinary people and innovating energy technologies to solve social issues such as poverty. BP has similarly rebranded by promoting its compensation efforts after the oil spill on Twitter and other social media. It has also promoted its new safety regulations and policies online to reach as many customers as possible to avoid major losses.

This shift in marketing techniques paid off. A year after reporting a loss, BP declared a US$3.3 billion net profit in 2012 and has recorded strong results in the first quarter of 2013. Similarly, Nike has dropped many of its sponsorship deals with athletes who have fallen from grace in the public's eye. Lance Armstrong and Oscar Pistorius were once among Nike's strongest representatives but have been dropped because of their transgressions. In short, Nike, BP, and Chevron all recognize the value of their corporate image and have attempted to ensure that their image is not damaged by incidents and sponsorship deals alike. If consumers dislike an organization, they often boycott that organization, causing it to lose profitability and possibly even causing it to close down.

ETHICS

The primary concern of most businesses is to make a profit. A business' marketing strategy is therefore designed to make the service or product on offer seem as attractive as possible.

However, businesses should consider their ethical responsibility to promote their products accurately. Many countries have a regulating body to monitor advertising (such as the Advertising Standards Authority in the UK and South Africa). Ethical advertising is not only a a moral choice but also a pragmatic business decision – the reputation and sales of a business can be severely affected if advertising methods are found to be misleading or offensive.

In 2011, the Coco-Cola company was forced to amend an advert which claimed that it's Vitaminwater drink was 'delicious and nutritious'. A number of people complained on the basis that the drink contained high levels of sugar and so was not 'nutritious'.

Examples such as this can be rectified fairly easily and, for a company the size of Coca Cola, at relatively little cost. For a smaller company, or where the advertising decision has more significant implications, the effects of unethical or misleading advertising can be extremely damaging.

Do some internet research to find examples of unethical advertising. Can you find wide-spread press coverage? What sort of criticisms are made, and how might these affect the reputation of the businesses?

TOK discussion

To what extent are marketing practices a reflection of the values of a given time and culture?

However, many of the oil companies' shifts in marketing practices and strategies have resulted in more fierce opposition from the public and other stakeholders. Companies such as Royal Dutch Shell and Chevron have been accused of "double standards" by pressure groups such as Greenpeace because, while they market themselves as socially responsible, they continue to damage the environment in extraction processes. This causes regular fluctuations in their share prices. In addition, shareholders are uncertain about their long-term profitability because of fear of new legislation that would enormously increase the costs of production. However, the adoption of new marketing strategies has largely helped to mitigate the effects of such market uncertainties.

Cultural differences

Finally, cultural differences also have a heavy impact on marketing strategies used by businesses around the world. Rolls-Royce and Aston Martin are two luxury vehicle manufacturers that have benefited from an understanding of cultural differences.

For example, China has seen massive economic growth and large increases in income for a relatively young consumer base. This has led to an increase in demand for European brands such as Aston Martin and Rolls-Royce, which are seen as more modern and desirable among young Chinese. As a result, Aston Martin changed its marketing strategy in China by targeting younger customers than in Europe and North America. Sponsorship deals with the James Bond franchise and the Gotham City car club are all aimed at enticing new young customers to its products. Furthermore, both Aston Martin and Rolls-Royce have Facebook pages to showcase their latest products that were initially designed for Chinese markets.

In the fast-food sector, McDonald's and KFC have introduced Halal foods to cater for customers of the Muslim faith. This has led to increased revenues as more market gaps have been filled and exploited.

Overall, innovation, ethical considerations, and cultural differences have had huge impacts on marketing strategies and practices around the world. The most common change in marketing practices appears to be the increased use of social media to interact directly with customers on a regular basis. Similarly, a large change in marketing strategies has been to target the youth market more directly, as in the cases of Aston Martin and Rolls-Royce in China and Nokia, Apple, and Samsung across the globe. The businesses discussed above are but a few examples of the many competing firms globally; however, they do provide grounding for one overall conclusion: businesses must adapt their marketing practices and strategies to meet changes as a result of innovation, ethics, and culture if they are to maximize revenues and profits on a global scale.

Revision checklist

✓ Marketing is essentially about getting the right product to the right customers at the right price at the right time. It involves working with other business functions to satisfy the needs to the customer.

✓ Marketing of goods concerns the 4 Ps of the marketing mix while marketing of services involves 3 additional Ps of the marketing mix

✓ Product orientation focuses on producing the product first before selling it while market orientation involves carrying out market research before producing and selling the product.

✓ Commercial marketing activities determine consumer needs and wants before using appropriate strategies to market the product. Social marketing aims at influencing a positive change in individual behaviour and improvement in societal well-being. Social media marketing focuses on the use of the internet through social networking websites to market a firm's product.

✓ Market size looks at the total sales of all firms in a market while Market share is the percentage of one firm's share of the total sales in the market.

✓ The main marketing objective of for-profit organizations is to identify, design and develop marketing strategies that are profitable to the business. On the other hand, the marketing objective for Not for profit organisations (NPOs) is mostly for social marketing reasons.

Practice question

Bajaj

In India, the market leader in motorbike manufacturing is *Bajaj*, with a 34% market share. There are many market segments for motorbikes. For some target markets, price is the most important factor. Other target markets are willing to pay more for extra features, such as better styling*. *Bajaj* is market orientated and offers 12 different models to satisfy the needs of various consumer profiles.

Bajaj has an extensive distribution network even in remote areas. Twice a year, *Bajaj* carries out primary market research through surveys, focus groups and interviews with their customers about the quality, reliability and safety of the *Bajaj* motorbikes. This is particularly important in remote areas where there are few garages to either service or repair them.

In the last 10 years the company has also gained a significant share of other markets, including the Philippines, Colombia and Tajikistan. This was done through strategic alliances. One of the company's long-term objectives is this continued penetration in international markets.

For its international markets as in India, *Bajaj* is determined to make sure that each model of motorbike satisfies local needs and preferences. One proposal is to use social media marketing to first appeal to international markets.

[Source: adapted from *Globality: Competing With Everyone From Everywhere For Everything New York and Boston: Business Plus*, 2008]

a) Outline briefly the difference between market orientation and product orientation. [2 *marks*]

b) Comment on the importance of market share and market leadership for *Bajaj*. [6 *marks*]

c) Analyse the usefulness of social media marketing for *Bajaj*. [5 *marks*]

d) Evaluate how *Bajaj* might have to change its marketing strategies in response to customer preferences [7 *marks*]

IB, May 2010

---

* styling: the various features of style or design that consumers may prefer

4.2 Marketing planning (including introduction to the four "Ps")

4 Marketing

By the end of this chapter, you should be able to:

→ state the elements of a **marketing plan**

→ explain the role of market planning

→ comment on the **four Ps of the marketing mix**

→ prepare and analyse an appropriate marketing mix for a particular product or business

→ discuss the effectiveness of a marketing mix in achieving marketing objectives

→ distinguish between **target markets** and **market segments**

→ identify possible target markets and market segments in a given situation

→ distinguish between **niche market** and **mass market**

→ analyse how organizations target and segment their market and create consumer profiles

→ draw a **product position map/perception map** and comment on it

→ explain the importance of having a unique selling point/proposition (**USP**)

→ evaluate how organizations can differentiate themselves and their products from competitors.

The elements of a marketing plan

A marketing plan is a detailed document about the marketing strategies that are developed in order to achieve an organization's marketing objectives. Marketing departments need adequately to plan and prepare themselves in order to face the competition in the market. The marketing plan is likely to include some of the following components:

- **marketing objectives** that are SMART (specific, measurable, achievable, relevant or realistic, and time-specific),for example increasing sales by 6 per cent in the next year

- **key strategic plans**, which are steps that provide an overview of how the marketing objectives will be achieved, for example plans on how to sell new products in existing markets

- **detailed marketing actions** providing information on the specific marketing activities that are to be carried out, for example which pricing strategies will be used and how the products will be distributed

- **the marketing budget**, including the finance required to fund the overall marketing strategy.

The role of marketing planning

Essentially, marketing planning is a process that involves an organization's decision about which marketing strategies would be effective in attaining its overall corporate or strategic objectives. To facilitate this, a detailed marketing plan is drawn up.

The benefits of marketing planning

- Marketing planning helps a firm in identifying potential problems and seeking solutions to them.

- Setting SMART objectives improves the chances of success of a firm's marketing strategy.

- Sharing the marketing plan with other business departments improves coordination and provides the whole organization with a clearer picture or sense of where it is heading.

- Devising a marketing budget ensures that resources are not wasted on unprofitable activities.

- A clearly spelled-out plan could improve employees' motivation and inspire confidence in them about the organization's future.

The limitations of marketing planning

- Marketing plans may become outdated if organizations are not quick to consider changes in market conditions.

- The process may consume considerable resources in terms of time, expertise, and money in designing the plans.

- Failure to prioritize marketing objectives may make it difficult for firms to tell whether they are meeting them.

To be effective, marketing planning needs to be a reflective exercise where organizations constantly review and evaluate their marketing policies. They need to do this if they are to survive in today's competitive business environment.

The four "Ps" of the marketing mix

Central to market planning is the development of a firm's **marketing mix**. This is a collective term that includes the key elements that ensure the successful marketing of a product. These elements are referred to as the **four "Ps"** of the marketing mix, namely: **product, price, promotion**, and **place**. These are explained briefly below.

- **Product** – this is the good or service that is offered in the market. A good such as a television is tangible while a service such as health insurance is intangible. Products should aim to satisfy the needs and wants of consumers. So, whether providing a new or existing product, firms need to ensure that the consumer's interests are taken into consideration if they are to create a unique selling point or proposition (USP).

- **Price** – this is the amount consumers are charged for a product. It indicates the value consumers perceive the product to have. For example, when the Apple iPad 1® was first introduced, consumers paid a high price for it because of its perceived good quality. On

Key term

Marketing planning
the process of formulating marketing objectives and devising appropriate marketing strategies to meet those objectives

Key term

Marketing mix
the key elements of a marketing strategy that ensure the successful marketing of a product

the other hand, second-hand clothes are priced lower than brand-new ones because they are seen as having a lower value. Setting an appropriate price can be difficult for businesses because of the sensitive nature of consumer purchasing behaviour and the various internal and external factors that influence these behaviours.

- **Promotion** – this refers to the various ways in which consumers are informed about and persuaded to purchase a product. The communication methods used to attract the consumer to buy the product are very important here. A firm may use above-the-line promotion such as television advertising or below-the-line promotion such as sales promotions, or a combination of both, in order to convince consumers to buy the product.

- **Place** – this refers to a product's location or channels of distribution used to get the product to the consumer. Products can be purchased in shops or over the Internet. Intermediaries, who include wholesalers, retailers, and agents, are also used to get products to where consumers need them. For example, large supermarkets such as Shoprite or Nakumatt have a number of retail outlets distributed countrywide to ensure that their products are available to as many consumers as possible.

An appropriate marketing mix

An appropriate marketing mix ensures that consumers' needs and wants are adequately met. This requires businesses to produce the right product, charged at the right price, available at the right place and communicated through the right promotion channels. If the message of the marketing mix is not clear and focused, a firm could risk potential loss in sales, which will affect its long-term profitability. Consumers may not identify with the product and therefore will not buy it. Examples of inappropriate marketing mixes include:

- advertising an expensive car in a colourful children's magazine
- selling an exclusive perfume in a stall where second-hand clothes are sold
- a real-estate agent attempting to sell houses in a vegetable market.

To be effective and in order to achieve its marketing objectives, an appropriate marketing mix for a business will need to:

- be well coordinated so that the elements consistently complement each other
- be clear, focused, and not abstract or ambiguous
- consider the market it is aiming to sell the product to
- look into the degree of competition that its product faces
- target the right consumer.

Student workpoint 4.4

Be a thinker

1. Using an organization of your choice, discuss the elements in the marketing mix that you think your organization would prioritize as most important.

2. Explain the factors that limit an organization's ability to achieve its desired marketing objectives.

Market segmentation, targeting and consumer profiles

Market segmentation

A segment refers to a sub-group of consumers with similar characteristics in a given market. Market segmentation is the process of dividing the market into smaller or distinct groups of consumers in an effort specifically to meet their desired needs and wants.

Markets may be segmented in the following ways:

- **Demographic segmentation** – this considers the varying characteristics of the human population in a market, which include:

  - age – babies will need diapers while teenagers will want cellphones

  - gender – there is a higher demand for personal care products for women compared to men

  - religion – businesses will find it difficult to sell pork products in a country dominated by Muslims

  - family characteristics – here, some businesses have used creative acronyms to segment their markets; for example, OINK (one income, no kids) targets young singles while DINKY (double income, no kids yet) targets young married couples

  - ethnic grouping – radio stations in many African countries broadcast in languages that are geared towards a particular tribe.

- **Geographic segmentation** – this is where the market is divided into different geographical sectors and may consider factors including:

  - regions in a country where consumers reside – for example, businesses could segment products differently to urban and rural consumers in the same country

  - climatic conditions – for example, heavy sweaters will be in high demand in Tibet compared to Botswana, which is usually quite hot throughout the year.

- **Psychographic segmentation** – this divides the market based on people's lifestyle choices or personality characteristics, such as:

  - social and economic status – some high-income-earning individuals belong to particular luxury clubs that exclude people not of a certain wealth status

  - values – people's morals and beliefs need to be considered here, for example customer values regarding recycling of products or animal testing.

The advantages of segmentation

- Segmentation helps businesses identify existing gaps and new opportunities in domestic as well as international markets.

- Designing products for a specific group of consumers can increase sales and, through this, profitability.

- Segmentation minimizes waste of resources by businesses through identifying the right consumers for their products.

- By differentiating their products, businesses could diversify and spread their risks in the market and so increase market share.

However, market segmentation can be expensive in terms of research and development, production, and promotion as a firm attempts to reach a large segment of actual and potential consumers.

Targeting

After segmenting its market, a firm must now decide on its target market. A **target market** consists of a group of consumers with common needs or wants that a business decides to serve or sell to. Targeting is therefore the process of marketing to a specific market segment. Targeting can be carried out using the following strategies:

- Undifferentiated marketing – also known as **mass marketing**, in this strategy a firm ignores the differences in the specific market segments and targets the entire market. Here businesses consider the common needs or wants of consumers in the market and aim to sell their products to a large number of customers in order to maximize their sales. Examples of companies that do this are Samsung, Nokia, LG, Dell, HP, and Coca Cola.

- Differentiated marketing – a differentiated or **segmented marketing** strategy targets several market segments and develops appropriate marketing mixes for each of these segments. For example, Toyota designs cars for the different socio-economic status of people in the world. With segmented marketing, firms hope to gain a stronger position in each of their segments and so increase their sales and the market share of their brands.

- Concentrated marketing or **niche marketing** – this is a strategy that appeals to smaller and more specific market segments. It is a good strategy for smaller firms that may have limited resources. These firms may serve market niches where there are few competitors and take advantage of opportunities that may have been overlooked by larger firms. Products provided by businesses that operate in niche markets include Apple's iTunes® and Rolls-Royce cars. Businesses using this strategy can market their products more efficiently and effectively by targeting consumers it can serve best and most profitably.

Consumer profiles

Consumer profiles consist of information provided about the characteristics of consumers of a particular product in different markets. These characteristics include gender, age, social status, and income levels. Consumer profiles may also consist of details of the spending patterns in terms of the number and frequency of products bought by consumers. For segmentation and targeting to be successful, it is very important that firms have good knowledge of who their consumers are. This will enable them to target their products effectively to the right consumers, using appropriate marketing strategies. In addition, a firm aware of its target market has a cost-effective method of selling its products as it will make savings on promotion costs.

Key terms

Market segment

a sub-group of consumers with similar characteristics in a given market

Market segmentation

the process of dividing the market into distinct groups of consumers so as to meet their desired needs and wants

Target market

a group of consumers with common needs or wants that a business decides to serve or sell to

Targeting

the process of marketing to a specific market segment

Niche market

a narrow, smaller or more specific market segment

Mass market

a large or broad market that ignores specific market segments

Consumer profile

the characteristics of consumers of a particular product in different markets based on their gender, age, and income levels, among other characteristics

4 Marketing

Niche Marketing – Toyota

Toyota, a huge company with a global focus on the auto business, is an excellent niche marketer. They were one of the first companies to realize there was a group of car buyers who would be very interested in environmentally friendly cars. Toyota answered this need with development of the legendary Prius, the first mass production hybrid car. Where other car manufacturers saw Toyota taking a huge risk, Toyota saw it as an opportunity to identify a new niche and establish its brand in that niche. In marketing, it is often the first brand to market, if executed successfully, that can own the niche market with their brand.

Once Toyota took the plunge, it pursued an effective niche marketing plan. It didn't promote the Prius in just any media. It focused on media outlets that were watched, read or listened to by people concerned about the environment. For example, it heavily promoted the car through environmental groups and their publications. As the only game in town at that time, Toyota not only dominated the niche – it was the niche. Today, with increased competition in this niche market, the Toyota Prius is still highly regarded as the niche leading brand.

Simply identifying holes in the market and filling them, is, often times not enough. It takes extensive research, careful planning, execution and extreme adversion to risk to successfully develop, introduce, execute and dominate a niche market with a specific product or service.

Adapted from http://www.smartmarketingllc.com/2012/05/07/successful-niche-marketing/

Exam-style questions

1. Define the term "niche market". [2 marks]

2. Explain the statement "Toyota not only dominated the niche – it was the niche". [4 marks]

3. Discuss the likely reasons for the success of the Toyota Prius. [10 marks]

Student workpoint 4.5

Be a thinker

Suggest the possible consumer profile for someone who buys the following:

a) Louis Vuitton handbag

b) Yamaha motorbike

c) Nintendo Wii game console.

Case study

PepsiCo targeting mass marketing will cater to different segments of consumers

Beverage and snacks maker PepsiCo India is gunning for the bottom-of-the-pyramid consumer for the first time in the country, as its chairman, Manu Anand, drives the New York-based $60 billion parent's target to reach the 'next one billion' consumers in the value segment.

In his first media interaction since he succeeded Sanjeev Chadha in January this year, Anand tells ET that PepsiCo is creating verticals to cater to different segments of consumers, across functions like sales, operations, distribution and marketing.

PepsiCo's low-priced products will be aimed at 330 million consumers graduating from the bottom-of-pyramid to the socio-economic B and C classes.

The move is in line with global chairman Indra Nooyi's target to generate $30 billion in revenues from 'healthier' products-internally called better-for-you and good-for-you products-by 2020, up from the existing $10 billion. India will be the first country in the PepsiCo system to target the value segment with multiple products.

"It's a big transformation for us; we are targeting the next tier of consumers. We are looking at everything differently and doing this in a very structured way. But it's not as if we are under-investing in our core business; it's more about creating new consumption spaces," says Anand, who has been with PepsiCo for the past 17 years.

VERTICAL MOVEMENT

NourishCo, PepsiCo's vertical in partnership with Tata Global Beverages, has just rolled out its first product, a lemon-flavoured glucose-based drink, called Gluco Plus, in Maharashtra. It is priced at 5.

Lehar Foods, another vertical, is a separate operating entity, which will launch value snacks priced at 5 and lower. Its other two businesses are core aerated drinks and snacks.

An innovation vertical has launched biscuits and snacks priced at 2 under the Lehar Iron Chusti brand in Andhra Pradesh initially. This line-up of healthy foods is targeted at women under 'Project Asha', PepsiCo's codename for Nooyi-commissioned plan to develop low-priced nutritional foods for the poor.

Anand, back in India after '07 when he was heading the foods division, says what has changed most at the firm in the past four years is its "sheer scale of operations".

While separate operations, sales and marketing teams have been set up for the verticals, PepsiCo has further split its go-to-market (distribution) model into three divisions. There's a premium arm for distributing Tropicana juices, Gatorade sports drinks and Quaker oats; a mid-rung one for aerated drinks like Pepsi and Slice and snacks like Kurkure and Lays; and a division catering to mass products like Lehar Iron Chusti.

"Had we put, for example, Iron Chusti in the Kurkure system, it would have been another product, hence the decision to set up dedicated sales teams. Communication and marketing for these products will be different too," says Anand. Lehar Chusti packs, for example, are labelled in Telugu. "We need to act like local players, but offer products that don't compromise on taste or quality."

CHEAPER PRICE POINTS

Low-margin products like Iron Chusti will obviously not be profitable in the beginning, but PepsiCo is hoping that the products will achieve scale in about 24 months.

Anand says even in PepsiCo's core business of snacks, such as Kurkure and Cheetos, the firm is stepping up focus on 5 and 3 packs. These packs are growing the fastest among PepsiCo's foods arm and contribute 45-50% to the division's foods sales. While in aerated drinks, selling bottles and cartons for 5 amounts to sacrificing profitability, PepsiCo will look at products at 5 through its joint venture with Tata Global Beverages.

Anand says three-fourths of PepsiCo consumers are common to foods and beverages. But beverages are more asset intensive while the foods business is more systems-driven.

This new strategy comes at a time when food inflation is running high. Anand says he's using all global and local resources to minimise costs, including stepping up conversion efficiencies, using cheaper sources of energy and better commodity procurement.

Adapted from http://articles.economictimes.indiatimes.com/2011-06-06/news/29625847_1_sanjeev-chadha-manu-anand-pepsico-india

Exam-style questions

1. Describe two forms of market segmentation relevant for Pepsico in India. [4 marks]

2. Analyse how PepsiCo caters for different segments of consumers in India. [6 marks]

3. Justify PepsiCo's new strategy in India. [8 marks]

4 Marketing

Positioning

Product positioning involves analysing how consumers define or perceive a product compared to other products in the market. As consumers are sometimes faced with an overload of information, in an effort to simplify their purchasing process they categorize products and position them accordingly. With this in mind, marketers must therefore plan positions that will give their products a competitive advantage in the market. An effective tool they could use in planning their positioning strategies is a **position** or **perception map**. This is a visual representation of how consumers perceive a product in relation to other competing products. The first step in positioning requires marketers to identify product aspects that consumers find important, for example quality, price, and image. Second, the firm will need to choose the key features on which to develop its positioning strategy. Finally, the firm should communicate its desired position to its target customers with the support of its marketing mix.

The importance of a position map

- A position map could help a firm to establish which are its close competitors or threats in the market.
- It also helps identify important gaps or opportunities in the market that the firm could fill by creating or offering new products.
- It is a simple and quick way of presenting usually sophisticated research data.
- It helps a firm in targeting specific market segments to best satisfy consumer needs and wants.

The unique selling point or proposition (USP)

This is a feature of a product that differentiates it from other competing products in the market. The differentiating factor is what makes a product unique and helps to explain why consumers choose one product over another.

The importance of having a USP

A USP:

- helps to establish a firm's competitive advantage in its product offering and, as a result, helps to attract more customers
- leads to customer loyalty as customers can identify something special about the product in comparison to rival products, resulting in increased sales.

By appropriately using the elements of the marketing mix, businesses can effectively differentiate themselves and their products from competitors. Here are some examples:

- Product: Apple is world renowned for its unique product quality in its iPad®, iPod®, and Mac® computer products.

- Price: Cellphone subscriber Safaricom has always managed to offer affordable prices to its consumers in the Kenyan market despite the

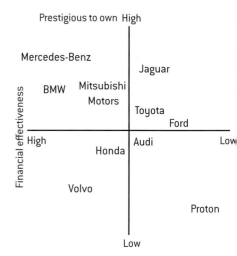

Figure 4.2.1. A position map for cars

Source: http://www.12manage.com

existing competition, and the company has still managed to post very high after-tax profits.

- Place: Coca Cola has managed to differentiate itself well globally by having a wide range of retail outlets providing its product close to its consumers.

- Promotion: Nike's "Just do it" slogan is a powerful promotional tool for the company because it emphasizes the action element, which is an effective strategy in encouraging customers to go ahead and buy Nike's products.

Case studies

Unique selling points- some examples

Successful businesses usually have a unique feature which differentiate them from their competitors. Here are three examples of businesses which have thought creatively about their USPs:

1. Love With Food (LoveWithFood.com)

Love with Food sells organic snack-boxes which are delivered directly to customers for $10 a month. For every box sold, the company donates a meal to a food bank to feed hungry children. This creates a unique buying experience for their customers that they wouldn't get anywhere else. Love with Food offers something different, while still selling exactly what their customers want.

2. Flinja (Flinja.com)

Flinja aims to solve a huge problem that college students and alumni have; finding a job. Their unique selling proposition is clear, and most importantly, benefit-driven. "Flinja helps college students and alumni find jobs." They have defined their target market and stated how they're going to help them solve a problem.

3. Hear and Play

Many websites and businesses help people learn music. Hear and Play focusses specifically on learning to play the piano by ear, making it ideal for people who don't want to or can't read sheet music.

Exam-style questions

1. With reference to Hear & Play, describe two aspects of a USP (Unique Selling Point). [4 marks]

2. With reference to Flinja, explain the link between target market and USP. [4 marks]

3. Discuss whether Love With Food's USP is entirely ethical. [8 marks]

4 Marketing

Student workpoint 4.6

Be an inquirer

1. Draw a position map of an industry of your choice and identify the products or brands on offer.

2. Using the information in question 1, why is it important for the organizations offering those products and brands to have a USP?

Revision checklist

✓ A marketing plan is an essential document that concerns the development of marketing strategies that aid in achieving an organization's marketing objectives.

✓ The four Ps of the marketing mix are product, price, promotion and place.

✓ An appropriate marketing mix for a business ensures that consumers' needs and wants are sufficiently met by producing the right product, charged at the right price, available at the right place and communicated through the right promotion channels.

✓ A target market is a group of consumers with common needs or wants that a business decides to sell to while a market segment is a sub-group of consumers with similar characteristics in a given market.

✓ A mass market is a broad market that ignores specific market segments while a niche market focuses on a narrow market segment

✓ The primary focus of product positioning is to analyse how consumers perceive a firm's product compared to other products in the market in an effort for these firms to gain a competitive advantage in the market.

TOK discussion

To what extent does marketing respond to, or change, the perceptions of individuals and societies?

Practice question

Marketing in a new technological environment, *Second Life*

Second Life is an online, virtual (computer generated) world that exists only on the Internet. Using a 3D virtual character, subscribers lead a second life, mimicking everything from visiting a nightclub to a career in real estate. Millions of dollars change hands daily online as residents create, buy and sell virtual products and services, which may include designer clothes, vehicles, or casinos. *Second Life* registered its one millionth resident in late 2006 with one user making more than US$1 million buying, selling, and renting virtual property.

Many companies such as Dell, IBM, and Kmart use *Second Life* to market products or services to a niche audience and to target younger customers and technologically aware market segments. Dell, for instance, has an "in-world island" with a virtual replica of the Dell factory and a retail store where customers order PCs to be delivered to their virtual homes. On the island, customers pay in Linden dollars, the official *Second Life* currency. The Linden can be converted into US dollars and vice versa. Rates fluctuate, but over the last few years have remained fairly stable as 250 Linden dollars (L$) to the US dollar. Customers can also order a real *Dell* computer that can be delivered to their real home and pay in US dollars. IBM recently purchased 12 islands within *Second Life* for virtual business training and simulations. Musicians and news organizations, including the BBC and the Reuters news agency, have a presence within *Second Life*. The BBC, which is frequently an early adopter, uses the island to debut new bands at virtual rock festivals.

According to *Business Week,* the biggest *Second Life* design shops charge corporate clients between US$10,000 and US$200,000 to establish a virtual world presence.

[Source: adapted from http://secondlife.reuters.com and http://whatis.techtarget.com]

a) Define the term *niche market*.   *[2 marks]*

b) Explain the advantages to major corporations, like *Dell* and *IBM*, of market segmentation and consumer targeting.   *[8 marks]*

c) Discuss how firms may adapt their marketing strategies *and* marketing mixes to changes in technology such as the growth of *Second Life*.   *[10 marks]*

IB, May 2008

4.3 Sales forecasting (HL only)

By the end of this chapter, you should be able to:

→ calculate up to a four-part **moving average**

→ plot the sales **trend lines** and explain the relationship between the trend and the actual sales revenue figures

→ prepare a forecast (including seasonal, cyclical and random variation) using given data

→ examine the benefits and limitations of sales forecasting.

Sales forecasting is the process of predicting what a firm's future sales will be. It uses quantitative methods to estimate the future sales levels and trends over a specified period of time. Accurately predicting the future reduces uncertainty, helps in management of stock and cash flow, and ensures better planning for growth. Businesses need sales forecasting information to assist them in making intelligent business decisions. However, making accurate predictions is a complex process and may be affected by numerous external factors.

Time series analysis

This is a quantitative sales forecasting method that predicts future sales levels from past sales data. It relies on time series data, which is sales information that businesses have kept over a given period since it occurred. The businesses then rely on this past data in an attempt to predict the future. There are certain aspects that need to be identified in time series data:

- **The trend** – this is a visible pattern noted after inputting the past sales data. This may indicate the rise and fall of sales over a given period.

- **Seasonal fluctuations** – these are changes in demand because of the varying seasons in the year. An example of seasonal variation is when a business experiences an increase in sales of clothing at the beginning of a new year but experiences a decline in sales in the middle of the year. Seasonal variations are usually repeated and occur within one year or less.

- **Cyclical fluctuations** – these are variations tied to the business cycle in an economy. For example, sales could be on the rise during the growth phase but declining during a recession. Cyclical variations can extend for more than one year.

- **Random fluctuations** – these are notable changes or fluctuations that stand out from a given trend. For example, there may be a sudden increase in the demand for ice-cream during a rare warm day in winter. Random variations are unpredictable and can occur at any time.

Moving averages

This is a useful indicator in sales forecasting for identifying and emphasizing the direction of a trend. It is a more accurate and complex method than simply predicting future sales from actual sales data. This is because it helps to smooth out any fluctuations from sales data.

Table 4.3.1. Yearly sales of a calculator manufacturer

Year	1	2	3	4	5	6	7	8
Sales (US$000)	400	600	800	650	700	850	950	1,200

Calculating a three-year moving average

Using table 4.3.1, the following steps can be used to calculate the three-year moving average:

1. Calculate the mean sales for the first three years. For example, the mean from years 1, 2 and 3 is US$ $\frac{(400,000 + 600,000 + 800,000)}{3} = 600,000$.

2. Do the same for the next three sets of data:
   US$ $\frac{(600,000 + 800,000 + 650,000)}{3} = 683,333$ for years 2, 3 and 4.

3. The same process should be used for the following sets of threes:

   3, 4, 5: US$ $\frac{(800,000 + 650,000 + 700,000)}{3} = 716,667$

   4, 5, 6: US$ $\frac{(650,000 + 700,000 + 850,000)}{3} = 733,333$

   6, 7, 8: US$ $\frac{(850,000 + 950,000 + 1\,200,000)}{3} = 1,000,000$

The above data is summarized in table 4.3.2 and figure 4.3.1.

Table 4.3.2. Sales revenue with three-year moving average (trend)

Year	1	2	3	4	5	6	7	8
Sales (US$000)	400	600	800	650	700	850	950	1,200
Trend (three-year moving average) (US$000)		600	683.333	716.667	733.333	1,000		

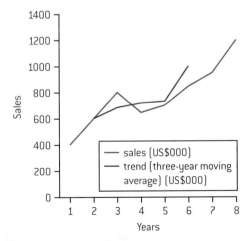

Figure 4.3.1. Actual sales and the three-year moving average trend for the calculator manufacturer

Key terms

Sales forecasting

the process of predicting the future sales of a firm

Time series analysis

a quantitative sales forecasting method that predicts future sales levels from past sales data

4 Marketing

Calculating a four-year moving average

Calculating the four-year moving average is a bit more complex than calculating the three-year moving average. In this case, it makes use of **centring**. This involves the use of a four-year and an eight-year moving total to establish a mid-point. For example, the calculation of the first four-year moving total is as follows:

(i) Summation of sales of years 1, 2, 3 and 4 (US$): 400,000 + 600,000 + 800,000 + 650,000) = 2,450,000

Calculation of the next four-year moving total is:

(ii) Summation of sales in years 2, 3, 4 and 5 (US$): (600,000 + 800,000 + 650,000 + 700,000) = 2,750,000

Calculating the first eight-year moving total involves adding the summations in (i) and (ii) (US$): 2,450,000 + 2,750,000 = 5,200,000

To get the first four-year centred moving average, the eight-year moving total is divided by 8 as follows (US$): $\frac{5,200,000}{8}$ = 650,000. It is important to note where this value is placed in the table. It will be placed in the line where year 3 is positioned.

Using the same approach as above, the next eight-year moving totals and four-year moving averages are summarized in table 4.3.3 and figure 4.3.2.

Table 4.3.3. Sales revenue with four-year moving average (trend)

Year	1	2	3	4	5	6	7	8
Sales ($000)	400	600	800	650	700	850	950	1,200
Eight-year moving total ($000)			5,200	5,750	6,150	6,850		
Trend (four-year moving average) ($000)			650	718.75	768.75	856.25		

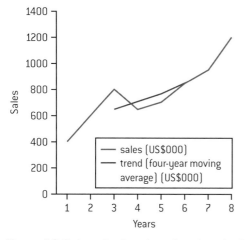

Figure 4.3.2. Actual sales plotted against the four-year moving average (trend)

Extrapolation

Once the trend line has been drawn, this line can be extended using a "line of best fit", shown by a dotted line, to predict future sales. This is known as **extrapolation**. The trend lines from figures 4.3.1 and 4.3.2 can be extrapolated to provide an estimated sales value for future years.

Figure 4.3.3 shows how a trend line can be extrapolated.

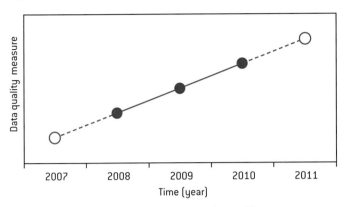

Figure 4.3.3. Example of an extrapolated trend line

Source: ops.fhwa.dot.gov

Key terms

Moving average

sales forecasting method that identifies and emphasizes the direction of a trend

Extrapolation

an extension of a trend line to predict future sales

Variation

difference between actual sales and trend values

Calculating variations

Variation is calculated by getting the difference between actual sales and the trend values. This is shown in table 4.3.4.

Table 4.3.4. Sales revenue with variations in each year

Year	1	2	3	4	5	6	7	8
Sales (US$000)	400	600	800	650	700	850	950	1,200
Trend (four-year moving average) (US$000)			650	718.75	768.75	856.25		
Variation in each year (US$000)			150	−68.75	−68.75	−6.25		

The average cyclical variation using the above table can be calculated as the sum of variations over the period divided by the number of years within the period:

$$\frac{(\text{US\$: } 150{,}000 - 68{,}750 - 68{,}750 - 6{,}250)}{4} = 1{,}562.5$$

If, for example, the extrapolated trend value (in US$) was 1,400,000 for year 9, then adding 1562.5 gives a more accurate predicted future value of 1,401,562.5 for year 9.

Seasonal variations can also give a more accurate prediction by calculating the average seasonal variation in each quarter (three-month period). For example, if in the first quarter of year 5 the variation was −25,500 and the variation in the first quarter of year 6 was −40,300, then the average seasonal variation for the first quarter in those two years is calculated as follows:

$$\frac{(-25{,}500 - 40{,}300)}{2} = -32{,}900$$

4 Marketing

Assuming that the predicted sales revenue for year 7 in its first quarter was US$350 000, then subtracting 32,900 from 350,000 gives a more accurate sales prediction figure of 317,100 for the first quarter of year 7.

The benefits of sales forecasting

- Better cash flow management – by taking into consideration cyclical and seasonal variation factors, financial managers can better plan to improve the liquidity position of a business.

- Increased efficiency – sales forecasting greatly assists the production department in knowing the number of goods to produce and in planning for the amount of stock required in the future.

- Better workforce planning – accurate sales forecasting can help the human resources department in succession planning regarding the number of staff required in the future.

- Improved marketing planning – marketers will gain greater awareness of future trends and be able to adjust their marketing strategies accordingly in an effort to increase their market share.

The limitations of sales forecasting

- Sales forecasting is time-consuming – it takes a long time to calculate because of its complex nature, especially when considering the calculation of average seasonal variations in each quarter over a number of years.

- Sales forecasting ignores qualitative external factors. A number of political, social, and economic factors can influence the accuracy of sales forecast predictions, for example political instability, changes in consumer tastes and preferences, and exchange rate fluctuations.

> **TOK discussion**
>
> To what extent does knowing assist us in predicting? How do we know that our predictions are reliable?

Student workpoint 4.7

Be knowledgeable

Table 4.3.5 shows the yearly sales figures of a paper manufacturer over a period of eight years.

Table 4.3.5. Paper manufacturer's sales 2004–11

Year	2004	2005	2006	2007	2008	2009	2010	2011
Sales revenue (US$000)	200	350	400	600	500	750	900	1,000

a) Calculate the three-year and four-year moving averages.

b) Plot both trend lines and the actual sales revenue on graph paper.

c) Comment on the relationships between the actual sales revenue and the trends noted.

d) Extrapolate the four-year moving trend line and predict the likely sales revenue for 2012.

e) Calculate the average cyclical variation over the period.

Revision checklist

✓ Sales forecasting is a quantitative process of estimating a firm's future sales levels and trends over a specified period of time.

✓ Seasonal variations are caused by changes in demand due the varying seasons in the year. Cyclical variations on the other hand are tied to the business cycle in an economy while random variations are notable changes that stand out from a given trend.

✓ Moving averages greatly assist in developing trend lines that help to smooth out any fluctuations from sales data.

✓ Centring is a more complex method of calculating moving averages that involves the use of a four-year and an eight-year moving total to establish a mid-point when calculating four year moving averages.

✓ Extrapolation is the use of a line of best fit drawn to predict future sales.

Practice question

Fun-Games

Fun-Games is a well known national private limited company, which prides itself on its innovative computer games and dedicated workforce. A recession is predicted for the coming three years in the domestic economy, so the managers of *Fun-Games* are considering expansion into overseas markets. The preferred option is expansion into nearby countries that are also members of a Free Trade Area*, although research showed that the exchange rate had fluctuated significantly in the last few years.

While accepting the need for a growth strategy, the marketing director is worried about *Fun-Games'* lack of experience of operating in overseas markets; cultural, linguistic and social difficulties may be encountered. The financial director is worried about lack of funds for expansion. The managers of *Fun-Games* are considering the best option for external expansion and intend to use sales trend data from the previous seven years, to help make a decision.

Fun-Games computer games sales record: 200–2007

Financial year	Sales
2001	5000 units
2002	5500 units
2003	4500 units
2004	8600 units
2005	9100 units
2006	9300 units
2007	11 000 units

a) Define the term "private limited company" [*2 marks*]

b) Using three years moving average:

   (i) Calculate the sales trend, the yearly variation and the cyclical variation. *(Show all your working)* [*5 marks*]

   (ii) Construct a graph using the sales trend figures from (i) and use it to forecast the sales trend figure for 2009. *(Show all your working)* [*3 marks*]

c) Discuss the benefits and limitations to *Fun-Games* of using sales forecasting in aiding their decision to expand overseas [*10 marks*]

IB, Nov 2008

---

* Free Trade Area: a group of countries that have eliminated tarrif restrictions in order to trade together more easily.

4.4 Market research

By the end of this chapter, you should be able to:

→ explain why and how organizations carry out market research

→ analyse the **primary market research methods**

→ comment on the **secondary market research methods**

→ discuss the **ethical considerations** of market research

→ distinguish between **qualitative** and **quantitative research**

→ explain the various **sampling methods**

→ interpret results from given data.

Market research is the process of collecting, analysing, and reporting data related to a particular market, including data on consumption of goods and services and on competitors' behaviour. Importantly, businesses use market research information to make decisions.

The purposes of market research

- To identify consumer needs and wants as well as aim to understand consumers' satisfaction levels and patterns in purchase behaviour. For example, a beverage company may want to find out the type of customers buying their sodas and the sales trends over a given period.

- To assist a business in predicting what is likely to happen in future. For example, an upcoming recession may signal firms to be prepared for decreases in overall spending patterns because of a possible decline in consumer income levels.

- To reduce the risk of product failure (especially of new products) by effectively carrying out market research that establishes the likes and dislikes of consumers.

- To measure the effectiveness of a marketing strategy. This can be done by assessing or evaluating how a firm implements the activities required by its marketing mix in specific market segments.

- To provide current or the latest information regarding activity in the market. For example, most large technological companies have huge research and development budgets so that they keep up to date in offering first-mover advantages.

Market research methods

Market research can broadly be carried out in two ways: primary and secondary research.

Primary market research

This is also known as field research and involves the collection of first-hand information from the market. Most organizations will conduct this research to find out specific buying patterns of consumers and attempt to anticipate any changes in their spending behaviour over a given period of time. Firms may decide to carry out this research themselves or seek the help of a market research agency. A key advantage of primary research is that the organization that collects the data will be the first to access it, which gives it an advantage over its rivals. For example, a hotel may discover through primary research that a particular airline is prone to flight cancellations. It can use this information to attract customers who may be waiting for many hours and possibly days for their connecting flights. However, field research is expensive because the research process takes time and requires specialized researchers.

Secondary market research

This is the collection of second-hand information from the market. Also known as desk research, it involves analysing data that already exists in some form. Organizations should first carry out secondary research to get an overall background picture and then conduct primary research as a gap-filling measure. Desk research is a quicker and cheaper method than field research and most of the information involved is readily available. However, the information collected may be out of date and have been collected for purposes other than the specific needs of the researching organization. In some cases the source of data may not be reliable.

Primary market research methods and techniques

Surveys

These are questionnaires sent out to a particular target audience to enable the researcher to gather useful information. The questionnaire may contain different types of question, for example those needing "yes" or "no" answers, multiple choice, or open-ended questions. A consumer survey may focus on getting specific information from consumers by seeking their opinion on a particular product or issue. Surveys can be implemented in a number of different ways.

Some of the most common ways to administer surveys include:

- by mail – an example would be an alumni survey distributed via direct mail by the development office in a school seeking the opinions from past students about an issue

- by telephone – an example would be a researcher calling consumers to elicit their opinion on using a certain product or service

- online – for example, workshop leaders may use online surveys as an evaluation tool to seek participants' opinions of the workshop.

Advantages	Disadvantages
• They enable researchers to collect a large amount of data in a relatively short period of time. • If designed well, surveys can be administered and completed easily by the respondents. • Surveys can be used to collect information on a wide range of aspects including attitudes, preferences, and opinions.	• Surveys that are poorly constructed and administered can undermine otherwise well-intended research. • The answers provided by respondents on a survey may not be an accurate reflection of how they truly feel, with some results also being biased. • As large samples are usually used, surveys can prove to be costly and use up a lot of time in their construction and administration. While random sampling is generally used to select participants, response rates can bias the results of a survey.

Interviews

An interview is a conversation during which the interviewer asks the interviewee questions in order to gain information. Interviews can be conducted one on one, face to face or by telephone.

Advantages	Disadvantages
• They can provide detailed information about the perceptions and opinions of consumers through in-depth questioning. • They usually achieve a high response rate because of the one-on-one attention provided. Precise wording can be tailored to the respondent and the precise meaning of questions clarified during the interview process.	• The whole process can be very time-consuming as it involves setting up the interview, carrying it out, analysing responses, gathering feedback, and reporting. • Some interviewers may be biased, therefore influencing interviewees' responses.

TOK discussion

How does the language used in questionnaires influence consumers and businesses' conclusions when doing market research?

Focus groups

Focus groups consist of a small number of people brought together to discuss a specific product or idea. The group comprises individuals who are representative of the customers of the business or of a specific segment of customers. In the discussion, participants respond to questions prepared by market researchers. Participants freely share their opinions, ideas, and reactions. They may also be asked to try a new product. Usually, all their responses are viewed and studied to help researchers predict the reaction of the larger market population.

4 Marketing

Advantages	Disadvantages
• As focus groups consist of a small group of individuals, using them is a cheap and easy way of gathering market research. • They can be used to measure the reaction of customers to a firm's new product or to the firm's strategies. • They help identify key product requirements as well as other needs not addressed by the business and its competitors. • They provide insights on the current position of the firm's competitors in the mind of the customer.	• The business may seek information about the entire market or segment and it could be that the opinions of a small number of individuals do not reflect it. • There is the possibility that some members of the group may not express their honest and personal opinions on the discussion topic. They may be hesitant to express their own views, especially when their opinions oppose those of another participant. • Focus groups are more costly to carry out than surveys as each participant usually has to be compensated in cash or in kind.

Observation

Observation is a fundamental and basic method of getting information by carefully watching and trying to understand certain things or people's behaviour. Some observations are scientific in nature; however, not all follow this trend. Observation can be used by supermarkets to check how quickly consumers notice their displays or how long they may spend queuing as they wait to pay. It can also be used by a government's traffic department to observe the flow of traffic in certain areas and help provide recommendations for improvement.

Advantages	Disadvantages
• It is a direct method of collecting data or information when studying actual human behaviour, as the researcher can see exactly how people behave in a given situation. • A large number of individuals can be surveyed in a short space of time. • Observation is usually a cost-effective way of gathering data.	• Complete answers to any problem or issue cannot be obtained by observation alone, so market researchers need to combine this with other methods such as issuing questionanaires. • Observation cannot be used to study attitudes or opinions of individuals because this usually requires a verbal response from the participant.

Secondary market research methods or techniques

Academic journals

These are publications of scholarly articles written by experts. The articles should be well referenced to provide the exact source of the information given. The experts will usually include professors, graduate students, or others with first-hand experience in a particular subject. Academic journals are written for the sole purpose of providing and distributing knowledge and not as a money-making opportunity.

Advantages	Disadvantages
• Academic journals undergo a peer-review process where they are checked by academics and other experts. This increases the reliability of the information. • Most academic journals include reports, reviews of current research, and topic-specific information. They are therefore good sources when a firm is in need of original research on a topic. • They take less time to publish than books.	• Since they contain information of very specific academic interest, they may not be the best source for general-interest topics. • The peer-review process can be time-consuming, which may also affect the provision of the latest or current event information.

Media articles

These include newspapers and magazines.

A newspaper is a printed publication containing news, feature articles, advertisements, and correspondence. Once viewed as the dominant means of communicating world events, newspapers have declined in readership since the rise of television and the Internet.

Advantages	Disadvantages
• Communicating via a newspaper is cheaper than communicating via television. • Most serious newspaper articles have been well researched, written with reliable sources, and edited for accuracy, which is not the case for some Internet resources. • They are widely available and can be found in many retail stores.	• It is difficult to communicate events in real-time. As the process of producing content, printing, and distributing the finished paper is time-consuming, articles that were written may be out of date by the time they are delivered to the customer. • Newspapers can be biased, depending on the type of organization that owns them. • The process of producing newspapers could be considered a waste of paper and energy resources.

Government publications

These are articles produced by the government on a wide variety of topics. They could provide businesses with useful information on the population census in a country, statistics on social trends, or even surveys on consumer expenditure patterns.

Market analyses

These include commercial publications or market intelligence reports that gather data about particular markets. The highly detailed reports are usually carried out by specialist market research agents. They can be sourced at various local business libraries, but they are quite costly. Organizations that provide such reports include Dun, Mintel and Verdict.

ETHICS

Marketing research has experienced a resurgence with the widespread use of the Internet and the popularity of social networking. It is easier than ever before for companies to connect directly with customers and collect individual information. The way a company conducts its market research these days can have serious ethical repercussions, impacting the lives of consumers in ways that have yet to be fully understood. Further, companies can be faced with a public backlash if its market research practices are perceived as unethical.

Deceptive practices

The ease with which a company can access and gather data about its customers can lead to deceptive practices and dishonesty in the company's research methods. The type of ethical problems could range from not telling customers that information is being collected when they visit a website to misrepresenting research numbers by changing database numbers. Any action that uses lies and deception to find out or establish information about consumers falls under this category.

Invasion of privacy

One of the most serious ethical considerations involved in market research is invasion of privacy. Companies have an unprecedented ability to collect, store and match information relating to customers that can infringe on a customer's right to privacy. In many instances, the customer does not know or understand the extent of the company's infiltration into his [or her] life. The company uses this information to reach the customer with targeted advertising, but the process of targeting can have a chilling effect on personal freedom.

Breaches of confidentiality

Another significant ethical consideration involved in market research involves breaches of confidentiality. Companies regularly share information about customers with partners and affiliates, requiring the customer to opt-out of the sharing if he [or she] doesn't want to be involved. Some companies sell information they have gathered on customers to outside companies. Ethically, any unauthorized disclosure of customer information is problematic.

Objectivity

Marketing and advertising have a significant impact on public perceptions. Market researchers have an ethical obligation to conduct research objectively, so data is available that allows for the development of the varying issues noted. Researchers who allow their own opinions to bias their work tend to contribute to the continuation of stereotypes in advertising. For example, a market researcher with a one-dimensional view of minorities could do a fair amount of harm if allowed to shape an advertising campaign based on biased data collection.

Source: http://smallbusiness.chron.com/ethical-considerations-marketing-research-43621.html

Exam-style questions

1. Describe two forms of marketing research. [4 marks]

2. Discuss how and why ethics and globalisation impact upon marketing research. [10 marks]

The differences between qualitative and quantitative research

Primary research or secondary research can be either qualitative or quantitative in nature.

Table 4.4.1 shows the differences between qualitative and quantitative research.

Table 4.4.1. Differences between qualitative and quantitative research

Qualitative research	Quantitative research
This involves the collection of data about opinions, attitudes or beliefs.	This involves the collection of numerical data or data that can be measured.
Information is open to a high degree of interpretation.	Information is open to less interpretation.
It is subjective.	It is objective.
Key research questions would include "Why?"	Key research questions would include "How many?"
The researcher is part of the process.	The researcher is separate.
It provides multiple realities, i.e. the focus is complex and broad.	It provides one reality, i.e. the focus is concise and narrow.

Generally, qualitative research is collecting, analysing, and interpreting data by observing what people do and say. Whereas quantitative research refers to counts and measures of things, qualitative research refers to the meanings, definitions, characteristics, and descriptions of things. Common methods used in collecting qualitative data include the use of focus groups and in-depth interviews. Surveys and government publications are methods usually used to collect quantitative data. Quantitative research may seek answers to the question: How many customers bought the company's sports shoes in the month of May 2013? Qualitative research may seek answers to the question: Why do customers like the company's sports shoes?

Sampling methods

In reality there is simply not enough time, energy, money, labour, or equipment to carry out a survey of the whole population. The population comprises all potential consumers in a market. However, in an effort to gather adequate primary research and still have a clear idea of consumers' views, taking a **sample** of the population is required. A sample is a small group of people selected to represent the population or target market under research. For example, a small group of consumers could be selected out of a large number of potential buyers of a product. **Sampling** is simply the process of selecting the appropriate sample.

Below are a number of commonly used sampling methods and the advantages and disadvantages of each.

Quota sampling

This involves segmenting a given population into a number of groups that share certain characteristics (mutually exclusive sub-groups) such as age or gender. Targets are then set for the number of people who must be interviewed in each segment. For example, in a school of 500 students offering the IB diploma programme, a researcher may target 15 males and 20 females to interview regarding their perception of the programme.

Advantages	Disadvantages
• This is a quick and cost-effective sampling method, especially where the proportions of the different groups in the population are known. • Findings obtained are usually more reliable than those of random sampling.	• Results obtained are not always statistically representative of the population as random sampling (see below) is not done; this also leads to statistical errors. • The interviewer may be biased in the selection of interviewees and choose those who will cooperate most in the process.

Random sampling

In this case every member in the population has an equal chance of being selected as part of the sample. The sample of respondents is selected randomly. With technology, a list of random numbers can be generated from a target population by the use of a computer. An example of selecting a random sample may be choosing any 50 people from a telephone directory containing the names of 1,000 peo

Advantages	Disadvantages
• Random sampling reduces bias as everyone has an equal chance of being chosen. • It is a relatively easy way of obtaining a sample.	• The sample chosen may be too small and/or it may not consist of the target population: a larger, more representative sample may have to be selected.

Stratified sampling

In this method the target population is made up of many different groups who are subdivided into segments or strata that share similar characteristics. Members are then chosen from each stratum to form a representative sample. For example, a secondary school may be deciding to introduce a new school uniform. It may divide the school population based on the different forms, from Form 1 to Form 5. A random sample is then chosen from each of these forms, ensuring that the same proportions of the sample in each category is maintained. As in the above example, for a sample size of 50 people whose names appear in a telephone directory, 10 students from each form (10×5) would be randomly selected to make up the required sample.

Advantages	Disadvantages
The sample selected is more representative of a particular target population.	It is not easy to select relevant strata from a population of very similar characteristics.

Cluster sampling

This is an appropriate method to use when the population is geographically dispersed. This will involve selecting a group from each region (cluster) and then taking a random sample from the clusters. For example, a multinational wishing to set up a plant in a certain town may carry out research on just a few geographical areas around the location and the opinions of the clusters selected will be assumed to represent the whole population.

Advantage	Disadvantage
• It is a quick and cheap method of carrying out research from widely geographically dispersed populations.	• Results obtained may not be representative of the whole population and may be biased, especially if the cluster sample is obtained from areas where people share similar characteristics.

CHANGE

Technological innovation has transformed the way market research is done.

Social media has expanded the landscape is transforming it in exciting new ways. Social media allows unfiltered feedback abut requires new researching skills.

With new technology, researchers can be much more targeted in what they measure and who they target. Using the most recent social media and online survey products, businesses are able to collect data about all sorts of things. They can do it faster, better and cheaper than ever.

What do you think are some of the major drawbacks inherent in conducting market research using the recent changes in technology? How do you think these drawbacks can be addressed?

Snowballing

This is a process of sampling that involves surveying the first group or individual who then suggests other groups or individuals who could participate, and so on. Members of the initial group use their contacts to refer to other people that they know, hence the snowball effect. It may be used when conducting quite sensitive research, for example a survey done on the use of ARVs among HIV-positive individuals. It is also used when researching expensive sophisticated products where the range of potential customers is limited.

Advantage	Disadvantage
• It is a cost-effective method of obtaining information through referrals.	• There is potential for getting a biased sample, since friends sharing similar lifestyles may refer each other and be part of the same sample.

Convenience sampling

This is a sampling technique where groups are selected based on their easy access and proximity to the researcher. For example, a teacher doing research on the school canteen could conduct a study by being physically present and directly interviewing students purchasing items from the canteen at break time or lunchtime. Another example would be when conducting research in a hospital, when the researcher may use the first ten names in the patient list to select a sample.

Advantage	Disadvantage
• It is a fast, easy and cheap method of sampling because the research groups are readily available.	• The sample may be biased and not be representative of the entire population.

Results from data collection

Businesses are interested in the range of results they get from carrying out research. It is therefore of prime importance that they ensure that their data collection methods are appropriate and offer a high degree of accuracy. Whether using either quantitative or qualitative data, or a combination of both, it is essential to maintain integrity in the research process. Selecting the appropriate data collection instruments and providing clear instructions for their correct use reduces the likelihood of sampling errors occurring.

Benefits of properly collected data include:

• the ability of research to answer accurately the research questions posed

• the ability to repeat and validate a particular study where needed

• increased accuracy of findings resulting in efficient use of resources

• good opportunities for other researchers to pursue areas needing further investigation.

Exam tip

In determining the best sampling method to use, it is important to analyse the strengths and weaknesses of each method. A key consideration is the level of bias in the sample and how cost-effective the method is. This could also be influenced by factors such as financial resources, business size, and rationale of the research.

4 Marketing

Key terms

Quantitative research

the collection, analysis and interpretation of numerical data or data that can be measured

Qualitative research

the collection, analysis, and interpretation of data about consumer opinions, attitudes, or beliefs

Sample

a group of people selected to represent the population or target market under research

Sampling

the process of selecting an appropriate sample

The heart of research is gathering reliable information about an issue or intervention and analysing it to determine the significance of the sample results. Collecting and analysing quantitative data can help highlight connections (correlations) among variables and also address other factors the researcher may not have considered. Collecting and analysing qualitative data can provide insight into the varying participant experiences, including what may need to be improved or changed. On gaining the required knowledge from the research information provided, a researcher should continue evaluating the whole process in an effort to obtain even better results in the next research round.

TOK discussion

To what extent is market research information reliable?

Case study

Marketing research – A case study of Safaricom

Safaricom is the leading telecommunications company operating in Kenya. It provides a host of products and services for telephony, GPRS, 3G, EDGE and data and fax.

It has been faced with a number of problems with time, one of which is the entry of many other telecommunication companies into the market over the years. The companies include, Telkom Orange, Yu and Zain. So far the main rival is Zain. The problem caused by the entry of other companies is that they bring about unwanted competition (decrease in market share). This problem can be solved by conducting marketing research.

The first step in the marketing research process is identifying and defining your problem. Defining the problem would mean expanding on it and explaining why it should be seen as a problem. In this case Safaricom has identified a number of competitors as the threat of losing customers and reducing the market share, which will lead to lower profit margins and growth at the end of the year is contrary to what they want.

Step two is to develop your approach, generally speaking the approach should be developed almost exclusively around a defined set of objectives. Clearer objectives developed in step one will lend them to a better approach development. Developing your approach should consist of an honest assessment of your team's market research skills, establishing a budget, understanding your environment and its influencing factors and formulating hypotheses.

Safaricom has to find an approach to counter the problem they are facing, which is competition. A chosen team at Safaricom came up with a number of possible solutions and chose one that was effective. The first solution would be to introduce lower call rates for subscribers and introduce a competition which only

Safaricom subscribers can participate. The second solution Safaricom can have a charity event were the money they make goes to a special cause for example food aid, tree planting etc this would affect the market socially. And the final solution would be Supremacy to control the telephony industry by outmatching other operators to be the first to launch Apple's iPhone 3G. To do all this they have to carry out extensive research to help in a decision.

Safaricom decided to be the first to launch the Apple's iPhone 3G increasing the competitor advantage. The third step would be to market research to enable the firm to make an appropriate decision on all the elements of the marketing mix as well as reduce the risk of investing in an unprofitable marketing venture. Since Safaricom is a long established firm and has a network running across Kenya they decided to launch the product in a limited geographical area where demand is observed. The price was high as it was a unique product to capture non price sensitive consumers who see new products as a novelty and as the product would grow older the price is reduced to capture the more price sensitive consumer. It will be launched in Westland's Nairobi next to two shopping malls and excessive advertisements will be done to ensure consumers receive information about the new and exciting product.

Step four is called data collection or survey fielding. Generally data analysis is concerned with editing, coding and presenting collected raw materials into a form suitable for solving the research problem and making decisions. The data collected from the test marketing research would include diagrams, sales, etc this would enable us to evaluate it and make the decision on whether to launch the product officially in the whole of Kenya.

Step five is the analysis of the collected information. Data presentations methods chosen should allow for easy interpretation of the research findings by the analyst. Use of charts and diagrams make this possible as they can plot the data to show trends and relationships between variables. Test marketing provides first hand information about the market and also revenues are collected during collection of data. For example the analyst can use a graph that shows the trend of the sales to help in making decisions.

Step six involves the market research report. The report must provide the readers (sponsor) with the information they require in a format they are able to understand and appreciate. Vocabulary, presentations, analysis methods used should match the readers levels and demands. Also the report should contain threats of launching the product. In this case Safaricom launched the iphone 3G as their research in this area was positive, however this was a test on a small group that may not effectively represent the whole market behaviors.

Adapted from http://www.123helpme.com/marketing-research--view.asp?id=166275

Exam-style questions

1. Outline two challenges that companies such as Safaricom may face when carrying out market research. [4 marks]

2. Evaluate Safaricom's strategies to overcome competition. [8 marks]

Student workpoint 4.8

Be an inquirer

Carry out an investigation on any organization of your choice that carries out market research. In the process, consider the following:

1. What are the primary and secondary research methods it uses?

2. Does it use qualitative or quantitative research, or both?

3. Comment on the sampling method or methods it uses.

Revision checklist

✓ Market research aids in business decision making by collecting, analysing and reporting data related to a particular market.

✓ Primary research (field research) and secondary research (desk research) are the two ways in which market research can be carried out.

✓ Primary research methods include surveys, interviews, focus groups and observations.

✓ Secondary research methods include academic journals, media articles, government publications and market analyses.

✓ Quantitative research concerns the collection, analysis and interpretation of numerical data as compared to qualitative research that collects, analyses and interprets data about consumer opinions, attitudes or beliefs.

✓ In conducting market research it is important that the data collection methods businesses use are appropriate and offer a high degree of accuracy while maintaining integrity in the research process.

4 Marketing

Practice question

Global Brand Values

In 1984, Professor Leavitt argued that technology had created a world in which consumer tastes were converging and that successful businesses should market globally standardized products. It is no accident that the companies with the biggest increase in brand value in 2005 operate as single brands everywhere in the world to create a consistent impact. The global bank *HSBC*, for example, increased brand value by 20% by using the same advertising message worldwide.

The traditional approach of building brands through the mass media is over. TV networks have split into hundreds of cable channels, and specialist magazines aimed at smaller groups have replaced mass-market publications. Today, brands increasingly use traditional advertising as just one tool in an overall marketing plan. New generation brands, including *Amazon* and *e-Bay*, have gained huge global value with little traditional advertising. Even older brands, such as *Coca-Cola*, and *McDonalds*, are decreasing traditional spending. *McDonalds* cut TV advertising from 80% to 50% of its marketing budget in 2004.

Promotion has shifted to online advertising and into video games and films, often aimed at children. The Korean electronics manufacturer, *Samsung*, the biggest gainer in brand value in 2005, promoted its brand through entertainment and sponsored the movie, "The Fantastic Four", in which a variety of *Samsung* gadgets played a part.

[Source: adapted from *Global Brands Business Week*, July 2005 and *Should Global Brands Trash Local Favourites?* brandchannel.com]

a) Examine the advantages **and** disadvantages of firms like the bank *HSBC* operating as a single brand around the world.   [*6marks*]

b) Evaluate possible primary **and** secondary market research that companies, like *Coca-Cola* and *McDonalds*, can conduct to ensure new promotional approaches are effective in targeting existing and potential customers.   [*8 marks*]

c) Using examples, explain the impact of new technologies and advertising media on the marketing objectives and promotional strategies of large corporations.   [*6 marks*]

IB, May 2007

4.5 The four Ps (product, price, promotion, place)

By the end of this chapter, you should be able to:

→ draw a product life cycle and identify its various stages

→ analyse the relationship between the **product life cycle** and the **marketing mix**

→ examine and recommend various **extension strategies** that could be used by firms

→ comment on the relationship between the product life cycle, investment, profit and cash flow

→ evaluate an organization's products using the Boston Consulting Group (BCG) Matrix.

→ explain aspects of **branding**

→ discuss the importance of branding

→ examine the importance of **packaging**

→ justify the appropriateness of using particular **pricing strategies**

→ evaluate the impact of new technology on **promotional strategies**

→ discuss **guerrilla marketing** and its effectiveness as an innovative promotional method

→ comment on the importance of **place** in the marketing mix

→ examine the effectiveness of different types of **distribution channel**.

A **product** is any good (tangible item) or service (intangible offering) that is offered to the market with the aim of satisfying consumer needs or wants.

The product life cycle

A **product life cycle** shows the course that a product takes from its development to its decline in the market. Most products go through six stages in their life cycle: development, introduction, growth, maturity, saturation, and decline.

Stage 1: Development

In this stage the product is designed, following this series of steps:

1. **Generating ideas** – this is a brainstorming session where a number of stakeholders are consulted to come up with anything that may help satisfy consumer needs and wants. These stakeholders may include employees, department managers, and customers, among others. Conducting market research also helps in identifying any potential gaps that may exist in the market.

2. **Screening ideas** – this involves deciding which ideas to leave out (poor ideas) and which ones to research further (good ideas). Some product ideas may not be practical or sell well while others may be too expensive to produce.

3. **Creating a prototype** – a prototype is a first or trial form of a product from which others are developed. It allows for visualization or physical examination of the product, especially by the production department. A select group of customers could also be provided with the prototype so that they could give feedback that would help if any alterations are necessary.

4. **Carrying out test marketing** – after making the necessary changes to the product, samples of the developed product are launched in a small but representative part of the market to assess the potential demand or sales of the product. At this stage, if the product does not sell well, it can be changed or removed without costing the firm too much.

5. **Commercialization** – after a successful test marketing, a full launch of the product to the market takes place. This will involve the use of all the elements of the marketing mix.

At this stage the research and development costs are very high as a lot of time, money, and effort is invested in developing the product. There are no sales yet and therefore no profit is experienced. Cash flow is also negative.

Stage 2: Introduction

This is the launch stage of the product on to the market. Sales are low because most consumers are not yet aware of the product's existence. Costs incurred in the launch are high and it is therefore highly likely that the product is not profitable. Moreover, the cash flow is negative as the cash outflow is still greater than the cash inflow. High prices or **price skimming** may be used for brand-new technological products, for example personal computers or cellphones, especially where there are few or no competitors. Where there are many competitors, penetration pricing might be the strategy, or low prices could be charged long term. In an effort to increase awareness of the product, informative advertising is used. Expensive products could be sold in restricted retail outlets targeting high-income consumers.

Stage 3: Growth

Once the product is well received by the market, the sales volumes and so revenues start to increase significantly. This translates to rising profits, especially with the possibility of economies of scale or lowering of unit costs. Cash flow now becomes positive. After a successful launch, prices that were initially low (through **penetration pricing**) can now be increased to maximize profits. On the other hand, products that started at high prices (through price skimming) can have their prices reduced slightly because of increased competition attracted by the profits. Advertising becomes persuasive so as to convince consumers to buy more products and establish brand loyalty. A larger number of distribution

> **Key terms**
>
> **Price skimming**
> setting a high price when introducing a new product to the market
>
> **Penetration pricing**
> setting a low initial price for a product with the aim of attracting a large number of customers quickly and gaining a high market share

outlets are used to push the product to different consumers in various locations. To maintain consumer demand, discussions begin on issues regarding product improvements and developments.

Stage 4: Maturity

At this stage sales continue to rise but they do so slowly. The product is well established, with a stable and significant market share resulting in a positive cash flow. Sales revenue is at its peak and profit is high, but with little growth as competitors have entered the market to take advantage of these profits. Competitive or promotional pricing strategies are preferred to keep competitors at bay. Promotion assumes a reminding role so as to maintain sales growth and emphasize brand loyalty. A very wide range of distribution outlets for the product has been established. Plans on new product developments are at an advanced stage, with some firms introducing extension strategies to extend the life of their products. (This is discussed further below.)

Stage 5: Saturation

Here, many competitors have entered the market and saturated it. Sales are at their highest point and begin to fall. However, cash flow is still positive. Some businesses are forced out of the market as a result of the stiff competition. Prices will have to be reduced, so competitive pricing is used. Many firms use extension strategies to stabilize their market share and also use high levels of promotional activities such as aggressive advertising in an effort to maintain sales. The widest range of geographical distribution outlets has been established to get the products to consumers. Profits are high and mostly stable.

Stage 6: Decline

This stage signifies the steady drop in sales and, through this, the profits of a product. In addition, cash flow begins to fall but is still positive. The product may have lost its appeal in the eyes of consumers because new models of a product have been introduced to replace the old model. If sales become too low, the product is slowly withdrawn from the market. Promotional activities are reduced and kept at a minimum. Prices are lowered in most cases to sell off any existing stock. Distribution outlets that are not profitable are closed.

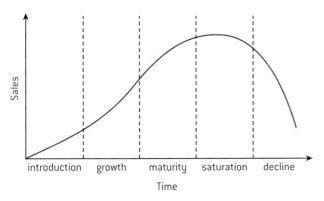

Figure 4.5.1. The product life cycle.

Extension strategies

Extension strategies are an attempt by firms to stop sales from falling by lengthening or extending the product's life cycle. This is done at the maturity or saturation stages of a product's life cycle.

Here are some common methods businesses use to extend their products' life cycles:

- They sell existing products into new markets. They might sell products in other regions within a country and/or export them.

- They find new uses for the product. For example, the cellphone was first introduced as a basic communication device but now the smartphone has a much wider variety of uses, including offering banking and other online services.

- They change the product's packaging. This could include changing the design, appearance, and colour of the package to stimulate consumers' interest and persuade them to buy the product. For example, the washing detergent OMO® has been repackaged many times, which has helped sustain demand for it for a long time.

- They target different market segments. One example is banks having different accounts that customers may open based on their income levels. Some banks have also accommodated customers with various religious beliefs and have special accounts for them – for example in Kenya, Barclays bank opened a "Sheria" account to appeal to customers of the Muslim faith.

- They develop new promotional strategies. For example, firms could create new advertising campaigns to encourage consumers to continue using their products, there by helping to revive demand for their product.

Essentially, extension strategies are important to the long-term success of a business as the market becomes saturated and sales begin to drop. As a result, it would be better to extend the life of a mature product before this decline in sales starts. However, it is not always easy to determine where exactly in its life cycle a product is. Some businesses use sales forecasting to assist in this. However, since forecasting is based on predicting trends, the results obtained may not always be entirely accurate. Moreover, unexpected external factors may have a strong influence on any future sales. For example, a recession may have negative effects on the demand for a firm's existing products as well as new products that it may have introduced as part of its extension strategy. In this situation it would therefore be critical for the firm to know where its products lie in the life cycle for more efficient management of its resources. Spending money on a terminally declining product is a mere waste of resources – one example would be spending money on marketing videotape recorders today.

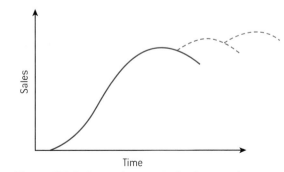

Figure 4.5.2. Extension strategies in a product life cycle

Table 4.5.1. Summary of the relationship between the product life cycle and marketing mix strategies

Strategies	Introduction	Growth	Maturity	Saturation	Decline
Product	The basic product is marketed.	Product improvements or new product development plans start.	New product development is at an advanced stage. Extension strategies are introduced in some cases.	Extension strategies are critical to maintain sales.	Weak products are withdrawn from the market.
Price	Cost-plus, skimming or penetration pricing is used.	Penetration prices slightly increase.	Competitive or promotional pricing is used.	Competitive pricing is used.	Price cuts are made.
Promotion	Informative advertising is used.	Persuasive advertising is used.	There is extensive advertising to remind customers of the product.	Aggressive advertising is carried out to emphasize the brand's benefits and differences.	Advertising is reduced to a minimum.
Place	Selective or restricted distribution takes place.	Intensive distribution or more distribution outlets are used.	There is more intensive distribution or a wide range of distribution outlets.	The widest range of geographical distribution outlets is used.	There is selective distribution and unprofitable outlets are eliminated.

Table 4.5.2. Summary of the relationship between the product life cycle, investment, profit, and cash flow

Product life cycle stage	Development	Introduction	Growth	Maturity	Saturation	Decline
Investment level	High research and development costs	High costs on promotion	Average to high costs on promotion	Lower costs on promotion	Cost focus is on extension strategies	Very low costs on promotion
Profit	None	None or negative	Some profit and rising	High profit; reaches its peak	High and mostly stable profit	Decreasing profit
Cash flow	Negative	Negative but improves with sales	Positive	Positive	Positive	Positive but decreasing cash flow

The Boston Consulting Group (BCG) Matrix

Product portfolio analysis is a process that evaluates the products making up a business. A business will want to invest more resources into its profitable products and phase out the weaker ones. A very common product portfolio analysis method was developed by the management consulting firm Boston Consulting Group, known as the **Boston Matrix** or the **Boston Consulting Group (BCG) Matrix**. The BCG Matrix is a growth–share matrix that measures the market growth rate on the vertical axis and relative market share on the horizontal axis. Market growth rate shows how attractive a product is in the market, while relative market share looks at how much of the market a product has captured – its strength in the market. This growth–share matrix is classified into the following four categories:

- **Stars.** These are products with high market growth and high market share. They are successful products in the market and generate high amounts of income for the business. However, they need high levels of investment to sustain their rapid growth and status in the market, especially in a fast-growing market where competing firms can easily gain market share by attracting new customers. With time, as these products mature and their market growth slows down, they eventually turn into cash cows.

- **Cash cows.** These are products that have low market growth and high market share. They comprise well-established products in a mature market and, as a result, businesses will invest less to hold on to their market share. The product sales are high and very profitable so they generate a good amount of cash for the business. As the products have a strong presence in the market, businesses can even charge slightly higher prices to increase their profit margins.

- **Problem children or question marks.** These are products with high market growth and low market share. They are a concern to businesses because of the large amount of money needed to increase their share in the market. Moreover, the high market growth could mean that the products are operating in a fiercely competitive market and need a good marketing strategy if they are to succeed. Businesses should think hard and be very selective about which problem children they should develop into stars and which ones should be eliminated.

- **Dogs.** These are products that have low market share and low market growth. They operate in markets that are not growing or in declining markets and therefore generate little income for the business. They offer low future prospects for the firm and may need to be replaced. Businesses with many of these products may be faced with cash-flow problems if they continue sustaining them.

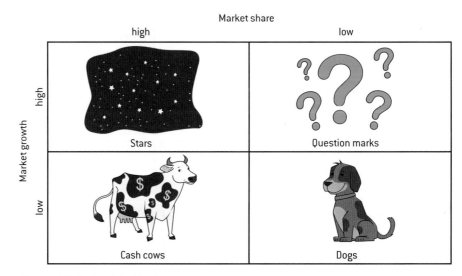

Figure 4.5.3. The BCG Matrix

BCG Matrix strategies

In an effort to support the stars, cash cows, problem children, and dogs, the following strategies could be used:

- **Holding strategy** – the focus here is on products with a high market share, to ensure that they maintain their current position in the market. Some investment will be needed to ensure sustained consumer demand.

- **Building strategy** – this centres on turning problem children into stars. Money from the cash cows could be invested in promoting or distributing the product so as to increase market share.

- **Harvesting strategy** – the focus here is on milking the benefits of products with a positive cash flow. These products provide the necessary finance, which could be used in investing in the other portfolio products.

- **Divesting strategy** – this is where the poor-performing dogs are phased out or sold off. The resources freed up from this will need to be used well in boosting the performance of the other products in the portfolio.

A product portfolio that has a good number of stars and cash cows (finance generators) will effectively be able to invest in the other (high market growth) products, for example problem children. However, a relatively large number of dogs and problem children can seriously drain any positive cash flow from the business if this is not well checked.

The limitations of the Boston Matrix

- It focuses on the current market position of the firm's products, with little advice or information for future planning.

- It may be a time-consuming and complex exercise for businesses to define or classify their products according to market share and market growth.

- High market share does not necessarily equate to high profits. This is because sales revenue could be gained using competitive pricing that may have a downward effect on a firm's profitability.

Student workpoint 4.9

Be a thinker

1. Draw the product life cycle and explain each of its stages.

2. Why are extension strategies important to a business?

3. Discuss the significance of the varying product portfolio in the BCG Matrix for a large business.

Key terms

Product

any good or service that is offered to the market with the aim of satisfying consumer needs or wants

Product life cycle

the course a product passes from its development to its decline in the market

Extension strategies

plans by firms to stop sales from falling by lengthening the product's life cycle

Boston Consulting Group Matrix

an analysis method of a firm's product portfolio regarding its market share and market growth

4 Marketing

Branding

A **brand** may be defined as a name, symbol, sign, or design that differentiates a firm's product from its competitors. **Branding** is the process of distinguishing one business's product from another and can add great value to a product. Branding can have a strong influence on how consumers view or perceive a product. Examples of well-known global brands include Nike, Samsung, Coca-Cola, Google, and KFC, among many others.

Aspects of branding

Brand awareness

This refers to the ability of consumers to recognize the existence and availability of a firm's good or service. To effectively promote a product, creating brand awareness is a major step businesses should take. In addition, it is important when promoting related products because there is usually very little difference between one firm's product and its competitors' products. As a result, the product with the greatest brand awareness will sell more than its competitors' products. For example, in the beverage industry there are very many soft drinks available in the market. However, the name Coca-Cola® is easily recognized by most consumers, clearly showing the image it portrays in their minds. A high level of brand awareness often leads to higher sales and can serve as a strong indicator to competitors of the amount of market share a product commands.

Brand development

This is any plan to improve or strengthen the image of a product in the market. It is a way of enhancing the brand awareness of a product by increasing the power of its name, symbol, or sign, ultimately leading to higher sales and market share. Businesses may have to invest more in promotional campaigns such as sales promotions and advertising to persuade consumers to purchase their products and therefore further develop their brands. Offering free samples is a common way businesses producing consumables, such as Cadbury's, use to provide an opportunity for consumers to taste or try their products in an effort to woo them to buy their brands.

Brand loyalty

This is when consumers become committed to a firm's brand and are willing to make repeat purchases over time. Brand loyalty is a result of **brand preference**, where consumers prefer one brand over another. Customers with brand loyalty will consistently purchase products from their preferred brands, despite the high prices of some products, because they feel the added value the brand carries justifies its price. Successful businesses will often employ a variety of marketing strategies to cultivate loyal customers. In so doing, these businesses develop **brand ambassadors**. These are consumers who will market a particular brand by talking positively about it among their colleagues, friends, or relatives. They help provide free marketing by word of mouth, which is very effective in enhancing the image and reputation of a business. Samsung is a name that is establishing strong brand loyalty in the electronics industry and benefiting significantly from consumer recommendations or marketing by word of mouth.

Key terms

Brand

a name, symbol, sign, or design that differentiates a firm's product from its competitors,

Branding

the process of distinguishing one firm's product from another

Brand awareness

the ability of consumers to recognize the existence and availability of a firm's good or service

Brand loyalty

when consumers become committed to a firm's brand and are willing to make repeat purchases over time

Brand value

This refers to how much a brand is worth in terms of its reputation, potential income, and market value. Brand value is the extra money a business can make from its products because of its brand name. Brands that have a high value are regarded as considerable assets to a business. This is because consumers are willing to pay a high price to obtain such brands. One example would be a consumer purchasing a higher-priced coffee at Starbucks instead of a coffee at another café. Such brands also increase the overall value of a business. Brand values are an expression of a brand's "personality" and act as a code by which a particular brand lives. Brand values are also those things that cause customers to buy a firm's product rather than its competitor's product. They help in differentiating a business and making it seem in some way special and better than its competitors. Emphasizing a firm's brand value is therefore at the heart of successful branding.

The values associated with Starbucks keep many customers coming back, even though cheaper alternatives are available

The importance of branding

Branding is one of the most important tasks of marketers. Despite the heavy initial investment required in ensuring that a brand is widely known and recognized, it is an essential factor for any type of business – from the start-up to the large, well-established companies.

For start-ups, branding is about giving customers a clear image with which they can associate the business. As the business grows, it can work on customer perceptions of its image, and try to establish its brand so that it can be recognized immediately. Initially, it is critical that the brand complements the market and meets the expectations of the target audience. Branding that does not meet the expectations of its target audience is bound to result in decreased sales.

Businesses with well-known brands can use price skimming or charge high prices for their products because of the image the brand has in the minds of consumers. Consumers will associate such brands with consistently high quality, enabling the businesses to make good sales and earn high profit margins on a regular basis. For example, Mercedes Benz and BMW have consistently provided good-quality cars to the global market and their brands have been viewed as representing good quality by most consumers.

Moreover, customers make judgments about certain products and services based on the way they are presented to them. Something as simple as choosing the right colour for a firm's brand can have a massive impact on the way it is perceived by the general public. For example, men may not particularly like their gym being painted pink.

A firm's brand name can provide legal protection to a product's specific features to prevent the product being copied by competitors. Branding provides the product with a unique name that makes it different from its competitors, therefore enabling the business to have a sense of ownership of its products. For example, companies such as Nike, Nestlé, and Toyota have been able to distinguish themselves well in their respective industries.

> **Key term**
>
> **Brand value**
>
> how much a brand is worth in terms of its reputation, potential income, and market value

Effective branding can enable a sense of personal identification and emotional connection among consumers. The key is the impression that branding leaves on potential customers. If the impression is positive, the chances of having repeat customers are high. Good brands communicate messages that ensure that their target customers respond positively. There is a saying: "The first impression is the lasting impression." Therefore, to succeed, businesses need to use enough resources to build a good brand reputation.

The importance of packaging

Packaging refers to the designing and production of the physical container or wrapper of a product. Packaging plays a significant role in marketing and can help in distinguishing one product from an other. Together with getting the other elements of the marketing mix right, getting the right packaging is critical. Packaging has the following important functions in marketing:

- **It provides physical protection.** Packaging protects a product from getting spoilt or damaged, especially during transportation. It must also provide a good cover against dust, direct light, or high temperatures.

- **It offers convenience**. A good package should make it easy for consumers and distributors to handle the product. This could include the ability to reuse, recycle, and easily dispose of the product.

- **It provides information**. The labels on packages can be used to relay important information to the consumer. Food containers may provide information on the particular ingredients a product contains. Technological products may contain information on how to use the item. It may be a legal requirement for companies producing cigarettes and alcohol to provide warnings on their packages regarding the consumption of these products.

- **It can help reduce security risks**, especially during transportation. Packages designed with tamper-proof features can help deter intentional tampering with the product. These features can also help reduce the risks of product pilferage.

- **It aids promotion**. The package should be eye-catching and appeal to the consumer. The colour and shape of the package is key in reinforcing and projecting the brand image of the product. This can also help in differentiating a firm's product from its competitors'. Packages with attractive graphic designs can encourage impulse buying or unplanned purchases by potential buyers of a product. This is especially important in supermarkets that stock a wide variety of consumables, where good packaging can create instant recognition of a firm's product.

Considering the important role packaging plays today, it is not surprising that a great deal of time and money is spent by firms on researching the best way of designing and producing a package that will attract the majority of the consumers to their products. Firms should also consider the impact their packages have on the environment and heed growing

TOK discussion

Is it possible to measure brand loyalty?

Key term

Packaging

concerns the design and production of the physical container or wrapper of a product

Packaging fulfils a variety of roles. Here it not only protects the product, but also provides nutritional information

environmental concerns. For example, in many countries supermarkets are under pressure to reduce the use of plastic bags when packing goods for consumers and instead go "green" by using environmentally responsible packaging.

Price

Price plays a significant role in the marketing mix because it is the only "P" that generates revenue for a business. In essence, the other aspects of the marketing mix are associated with costs. Price refers to the money customers pay or give up for having or using a good or service. In an effort to meet their marketing objectives, businesses need to set the appropriate pricing strategies for new and existing products.

Cost-plus pricing (mark-up pricing)

Cost-plus pricing (mark-up pricing) refers to adding a mark-up to the average cost of producing a product. The mark-up is a percentage of the profit a firm wishes to gain for every product that it sells. The average cost is the cost per unit or the total cost divided by the number of products produced. For example, if the total cost of producing 10,000 packets of biscuits is US$20,000, and the business wants to calculate how much it would sell each packet for and get a 50-per-cent mark-up on each packet, it would use the following cost-plus pricing method. First, it would calculate the average cost, which is US$2 (20,000/10,000). Second, it would work out the mark-up profit, which is $1 (50 per cent of US$2). Finally, it would add the average cost to the mark-up to get US$3 as the selling price.

Advantages	Disadvantages
• It is a simple and quick method of calculating the selling price of a product.	• It fails to consider market needs or customer value when setting prices.
• It is a good way to ensure that a business covers its costs and makes a profit.	• Since competitors' prices are not considered, a firm could lose sales if it sets a selling price that is higher than its competitors'.

Penetration pricing

Setting a low initial price for a product with the aim of attracting a large number of customers quickly and gaining a high market share is known as **penetration pricing**. This could be used by businesses either introducing a new product in an existing market or entering new markets with existing products. This is a strategy used in mass marketing. As a firm gains market share it also can start to raise its price slowly. For example, IKEA is known to have entered the Chinese market by using this strategy.

Key term

Cost-plus pricing
refers to adding a mark-up to the average cost of producing a product

Advantages	Disadvantages
• As the prices are low, consumers are encouraged to buy the products and this leads to high sales volume and market share for the business. • The high sales volume can lead to decreases in the costs of production and increases in stock turnover.	• Gaining high sales volume does not necessarily mean achieving high profits, especially where the prices are too low. • Customers may perceive the product to be of low quality if the price is kept too low. • Penetration pricing is only suitable for use in markets that are very price sensitive. Therefore, as businesses increase their prices over time they risk losing potential customers, who may seek lower-priced products from rival firms.

Price skimming

Price skimming is when firms set high prices when introducing new products to the market. This strategy is usually used for a limited period with the objective of gaining as a high profit as possible. These high prices are usually aimed at various market segments where the firm can obtain short-run profits so as to recoup its high research and development costs. Technological companies that produce and sell phones and computers, such as Apple, are known to use price skimming when initially introducing their products in the market, before lowering their prices over time.

Advantages	Disadvantage
• Consumers associate the high price with a high-value or high-quality product and an enhanced brand image. • Firms are able to obtain initial high revenues that help in recovering their research and development costs.	• The high prices may discourage some consumers from buying the product.

Psychological pricing

Psychological pricing refers to when firms consider how pricing affects consumers' perception of the value of their products. It considers the psychological effect of pricing on consumers. Consumers may associate a high-priced product with high quality, for example designer clothing. On the other hand, firms may reduce their prices slightly to persuade consumers who may be looking for value for money. For example, they may charge US$9.95 instead of US$10 for a given product – a strategy common in most supermarkets that sell frequently purchased products.

> **Key terms**
>
> **Psychological pricing**
> when firms consider how pricing affects consumers' perception of the value of their products
>
> **Loss leader**
> charging a low price for a product, usually below its average cost, to attract consumers to buy other higher-priced products
>
> **Price discrimination**
> charging different prices to different groups of consumers for the same product

Advantages and disadvantage of psychological pricing

Advantages	Disadvantages
• The psychological effect of selling at a slightly lower price can obtain large revenues for a firm selling in large quantities. • Since it looks at consumers' perceptions, it is a strategy that can be suitably applied in many market segments.	• Using prices such as US$199 or US$9.99 may be inconvenient for some businesses that require whole numbers in their transactions, for example transport businesses.

The loss leader

Businesses that charge a low price for a product, usually below its average cost, refer to that product as a **loss leader**. The aim of this strategy is to attract many customers. Large supermarkets use this strategy by selling some products at a loss with the view that customers will also buy the other higher-priced (profitable) products and therefore compensate for any losses made.

Advantages	Disadvantages
• Businesses selling a large number of frequently purchased products may attract many customers and benefit from higher overall profits. • Businesses may use loss leaders as a promotional strategy to encourage consumers to switch to their brand instead of buying the competitors' brands.	• Firms using this strategy may be accused by competitors of undercutting them by using unfair business practices.

Price discrimination

Charging different prices to different groups of consumers for the same product is referred to as **price discrimination**. For effective price discrimination certain conditions have to be satisfied. First, the business has to have price-setting ability. This means that a firm can vary its prices to charge higher prices in a market that is not very competitive. Second, the consumers should have different price sensitivities or elasticities of demand. This is a measure of how consumers respond in their buying patterns as a result of changes in the price of a product. If the change in price leads to a greater than proportional change in the quantity demanded, we say that consumers have price elastic demand, i.e. they are very sensitive to changes in price. On the other hand, if a change in price leads to a less than proportional change in demand, we say that consumers have price inelastic demand, i.e. they are less sensitive to changes in price. For example, sellers will lower the prices of their products if the demand is elastic as there is a possibility of getting higher total revenue. Finally, the markets should be separated to ensure that the product is not easily traded. For example, the prices for children's and adults' tickets may differ for the same music concert.

Key terms

Competitive pricing
charging a price that is in line with or just below the competitors' prices

Advantages	Disadvantages
• Time-based price discrimination can be of benefit to either consumers or producers. During peak times businesses such as phone companies charge high prices and so generate higher revenues, while during off-peak times consumers benefit from the lower prices charged.	• Businesses need to be certain about the type of elasticity of demand of their consumers. For example, charging higher prices in a market with elastic demand could lead to lower sales revenue. In addition, if firms were still to charge a lower price in the elastic market, they should ensure that the extra cost of producing and selling more products does not exceed the extra revenue.

Competitive pricing

Competitive pricing is a pricing strategy that takes into consideration what competitors are charging for their product. It involves charging a price that is in line with or just below the competitors' prices. It is mostly applicable to businesses selling similar products. Charging prices lower than the competitors with the aim of driving them out of the market is known as **predatory pricing**, also known as **destroyer pricing** because it aims to eliminate any opposition, and could include firms charging prices lower than their average costs of production. If successful, businesses can subsequently dominate the market and charge higher prices. This strategy is commonly used in highly competitive markets where the products are in the maturity or saturation stages in the product life cycle.

Advantages	Disadvantages
• Consumers benefit from the low prices, especially in very competitive markets. • After using destroyer pricing, remaining dominant firms could gain higher sales revenue as a result of the higher prices charged.	• Predatory or destroyer pricing is a form of anti-competitive behaviour and is illegal in many countries because it is used to restrict competition.

Student workpoint 4.10

Be knowledgeable

1. Analyse the importance of branding for a start-up business.

2. Examine the most appropriate pricing strategies needed when introducing a new product to the market.

Promotion

Promotion is concerned with communicating information about a firm's products to consumers. The main aim of promotion is to obtain new customers or to retain existing ones. Promotional activities should be communicated clearly to consumers and provide useful information to enable them to purchase a firm's product.

Some promotional objectives include:

- creating awareness or informing consumers of a new or improved product in the market

- convincing or persuading consumers to purchase a firm's products instead of its competitors' products

- reminding consumers of the existence of a product in order to retain existing customers or gain new customers for a product

- enhancing the brand image of the product as well as the corporate image of the business.

Promotion can be categorized into two forms: above-the-line promotion and below-the-line promotion.

Above-the-line promotion

This is a paid form of communication that uses independent mass media to promote a firm's products. It includes advertising through the television, radio, or newspapers so as to reach a wide target audience. In this case the control or responsibility of advertising is passed on to another organization.

Advertising

Advertising plays a central role globally in passing on information about a product to a particular target audience. Choosing the right media for advertising is important in ensuring a successful promotional campaign. Advertising can be categorized as follows:

- **Informative advertising** – the focus here is to provide information about a product's features, price, or other specifications to consumers. It increases consumers' awareness of a firm's product so as to enable them to make rational decisions about what to buy. It is useful when businesses want to introduce a new product to the market. Examples of informative advertising include classified advertisements in newspapers and government campaigns to discourage drink-driving.

- **Persuasive advertising** – this aims at convincing customers to buy one firm's product instead of a competitor's product. It persuades consumers to think that they really need the product and should buy it. It makes consumers make unplanned purchases for a product – an act known as **impulse buying**. It helps in enhancing a product's brand image. For example, when advertising a slimming product, firms may use pictures of how people looked before they took the product and how they look after they consumed the product – in this case they show the picture of a very fit individual based on the idea that most people would want to look like that.

- **Reassuring advertising** – the focus is on existing customers, to remind them that they made the right purchasing decisions when they chose to buy the firm's product and that they should continue purchasing it. Coca-Cola's promotional campaigns are well-known examples of this strategy.

The main forms of advertising media include television, newspapers, magazines, cinema, radio, posters, billboards, and the Internet.

Below-the-line promotion

This is a form of communication where the business has direct control over its promotional activities. Unlike above-the-line promotion, it does not depend on the use of independent media. Below-the-line promotion can focus the promotional activities on consumers they know or on those who are interested in their products.

Forms of below-the-line promotion include:

- **Direct marketing** – this ensures that the product is aimed directly at the consumers. It eliminates the use of intermediaries and therefore can save the business money. Direct mail, which is a form of direct marketing, refers to sending information about a product through the post or via email. Businesses that commonly use this method include restaurants sending out their menus or property developers sending out their catalogues. A limitation of this method is that most consumers can regard the information as junk and not pay any particular attention to it.

- **Personal selling** – this involves the sale of a firm's product through personal contact. It makes use of sales representatives and can be done face to face or over the telephone. It is commonly used when selling expensive products such as cars or technically complex products such as specialized machinery. In these cases, customers will need to be reassured that they are making the right purchasing decision. They can then be given personal and individualized attention. A major disadvantage of this method may be the cost involved as it may be expensive to retain a sales representative team for this type of selling, especially if they are also paid by commission.

- **Public relations** – these are promotional activities aimed at enhancing the image of the business and its products. It includes the use of publicity or sponsorships. For publicity purposes a

TOK discussion

Many advertisements use scientific knowledge. Why do they do this and what does this tell us about the hierarchy of different areas of knowledge?

Key terms

Above-the-line promotion

a paid form of communication that uses independent mass media to promote a firm's products

Below-the-line promotion

a form of communication that gives a business direct control over its promotional activities so that it is not dependent on the use of independent media

Promotional mix

a balance of both above-the-line and below-the-line methods used by a firm to support its marketing goals business could hold a press conference where it invites the media and provides information about a social responsibility project it would like to launch. In the process, the business could showcase its products and gain free publicity for them. Through sponsorship, a business may provide financial support to an organization, team or event. Examples include Samsung sponsoring Chelsea football club in the UK and Kenya Airways sponsoring the Kenya national rugby team.

- **Sales promotions** – these are short-term incentives provided by a business with the aim of increasing or boosting its sales. Examples include the following:

  - Money-off coupons – discounts provided to customers when a product is purchased. The coupons are often found in newspapers, leaflets, or magazines.

  - Point-of-sale displays can be used for attractive arrangement or display of products at the location where the business sells the items. The main objective is to draw the attention of consumers and encourage impulse buying. It is commonly used by supermarkets when selling confectionary products such as sweets, chocolates, and other snacks.

  - Free offers or free gifts can be offered to customers such as a free charger when buying a cellphone. Giving free samples such as through food taste sessions outside supermarkets and offering free sachets for particular products can also help encourage sales.

  - Competitions – after purchasing a product, customers can enter a draw where they stand a chance to win a prize in the competition. This method is commonly used during festive seasons to attract a large number of customers.

  - "BOGOF" (buy one get one free) is a promotional strategy that can be used to attract new customers or assist in eliminating excess stock. It is often used in the maturity or saturation stages of a product's life cycle.

The promotional mix

A successful promotional mix will involve a good balance of both above-the-line and below-the-line promotional methods. This could involve using an appropriate mix of advertising, sales promotions, personal selling, direct marketing, and public relations when communicating the advantages of a product to customers or supporting a firm's marketing goals. However, certain factors will need to be considered for an effective promotional mix:

- **Cost:** Does the marketing budget support the use of a particular promotional method?

- **Legal framework:** Has the law been taken into account when deciding on the various promotional methods to use?

- **Target market:** What specific segment of the market is the product aimed at?

- **Stage in the product life cycle:** Which promotional methods will be most appropriate at the different product life cycle stages?

- **Type of product:** Has the promotional method considered the nature of the product and how it would be successfully sold to customers?

Businesses will therefore need to consider the above questions carefully when designing and developing their promotional mix. Moreover, they will need to be flexible and where necessary tweak the promotional mix to succeed in achieving their marketing objectives.

The impact of new technology on promotional strategies

In the marketing context, technology is defined as the information or tools required to sell a firm's good or service. Over the last decade, technology has changed rapidly and marketers are increasingly incorporating it in their marketing strategy. Important technological terminologies being used today include social networking, social media marketing (SMM), and viral marketing. The impact of these on promotion will be explored below.

Social media is defined as the technology that connects people. It is any medium where content is shared or where individuals chat.

Social networks are the places where social interactions happen, which include sharing, discovering, or advertising information. Examples of social networks include Facebook, Twitter, LinkedIn, and MySpace.

A **social networking service** is a platform to build social networks or social relations among people who, for example, share interests, activities, backgrounds, or real-life connections. A social network service consists of a representation of each user (often a profile), his or her social links, and a variety of additional services. Most social network services are web-based and provide means for users to interact over the Internet.

Social media marketing (SMM) refers to the way technology is used to build relationships, drive repeat business, and attract new customers through individuals sharing with other individuals. SMM is the process of gaining website traffic or attention through social media sites. SMM programs usually centre on efforts to create content that attracts attention and encourages readers to share it with their social networks. A corporate message spreads from user to user and presumably resonates because it appears to come from a trusted, third-party source, as opposed to the brand or company itself. Basically, SMM is promotion through word of mouth powered by technology.

Viral marketing is a form of peer-to-peer communication where individuals are encouraged to pass on promotional messages within their social networks. Not so long ago, advertisements were mostly seen in newspapers, magazines, or television. However, with the advent of the Internet things have changed. Today, advertisements appear as banners, pop-up advertisements, social media, and YouTube videos.

Key terms

Social media marketing

the use of technology to build relationships, drive repeat business, and attract new customers by individuals sharing with other individuals

Viral marketing

a form of peer-to-peer communication where individuals are encouraged to pass on promotional messages within their social networks

Advertisements in the form of YouTube videos are often called "viral ads", especially when they gather millions of views, and are part of what is known as a viral marketing campaign.

The main objective of viral marketing is to increase brand awareness through replicating a viral-like process, like the spread of a virus in computers. Often, viral videos are spread through sharing by viewers, which is more like promotion through word of mouth. Viral marketing therefore often comes in the form of videos, but also in games, software, images, or messages.

Another key goal of viral marketing is to create infectious, viral messages that appeal to their target market with high social networking potential that can easily spread through individuals.

The benefits of new technology on promotional strategies

The general advantages of using social networking, SMM, and viral marketing are as follows:

- **Wide reach** – the Internet has enabled firms to reach out to more consumers at a more personal and interactive level. A large percentage of the Internet's total population uses social networking sites such as Facebook, Twitter, and YouTube, where time spent in social media far exceeds time spent on email.

- **Engagement** – in most cases, customers and other key stakeholders are participants rather than passive viewers. This also means that a firm can find out what challenges customers are facing and what they like and do not like about the firm's product offerings. Engaging in ongoing dialogue can be more valuable than any kind of paid market research and it helps to create a sense of community.

- **Market information** – social networking, SMM, and viral marketing provide useful and valuable measurable data on trends, consumer interaction, feedback, public opinion, brand activity, and customers' buying habits.

- **Cost savings** – using social networking, SMM and viral marketing is relatively less expensive than using traditional methods such as television advertising.

- **Brand recognition** – the sharing and spreading of information, especially due to repeat exposure, can increase consumers' awareness of particular brands, leading to brand loyalty and an enhanced brand image.

- **Speed** – coupled with high Internet speed, advertisements can reach a wide audience in a short space of time.

The limitations of new technology on promotional strategies

Despite their benefits, social networking, SMM, and viral marketing have the following general drawbacks:

- **Accessibility problems** – regions with no computers or Internet, areas with poor Internet connectivity, will miss out on any ongoing promotional campaign that uses these tools.

4 Marketing

- **Distraction** – the use of pop-ups in advertising can be viewed as time-wasting and annoying by customers who want to focus on other issues.

- **Lurkers** – these are individuals who just sit tight and absorb information. According to TopRank Online Marketing Blog, 34 per cent of social media users are lurkers, while others are newcomers who have not quite honed their online social skills. These are individuals who may not be active in helping a firm promote its product.

Despite these negative effects of social networking, SMM, and viral marketing, the benefits in many ways outweigh the drawbacks and, most importantly, these technologies provide great ways to drive repeat business and attract new customers.

Guerrilla marketing

Levinson and Lautenslager (2009) define guerrilla marketing as a marketing form which involves the use of "untraditional" activities that help companies weaken their rivals and stay successfully on the market, even with limited resources. Guerrilla marketing therefore uses unconventional marketing strategies that have an innovative and significant promotional effect at half the budget spent on "traditional" marketing strategies for the same objective.

The term guerrilla marketing is coined from military and warfare-related terminology. It adapts the "hit and run" guerrilla warfare tactics used by Mao-Tse Tung, where you hit if you can win but run if you cannot. Guerrilla marketing activities are eye-catching and surprising and so highly efficient in capturing customers' attention.

The differences between traditional and guerrilla marketing are summarized in table 4.5.3.

Table 4.5.3. Differences between traditional and guerrilla marketing

Traditional marketing	Guerilla marketing
The primary investment is money.	The primary investments are time, effort, and creativity.
It forms a model for big businesses.	It focuses on small businesses.
Success is measured by sales.	Success is measured by profits.
What can I take from the customer?	What can I give to the customer?
Mass media (direct mail, radio, television, newspapers) are used.	Marketing weapons are numerous and most are free.
Advertising works.	Types of non-traditional marketing succeed.
How much money do you have at the end?	How many relationships do you have at the end?

Source: Based on Levinson, J.C. and Lautenslager, A. (2009) *Guerilla Marketing in 30 Days*, second edition. Entrepreneur Press. Irvine, CA.

Principles of guerrilla marketing

The following principles characterize guerrilla marketing. They can be remembered using the acronym "APENS".

- **Activity** – firms need to have an awareness of the available opportunities that exist to make their products known and they should seek ways of doing this when an opportunity presents itself.

- **Presence** – firms should look for ways to make their business known to the market. This could be through email, forums, discussion boards, radio, magazine, street posters, graffiti, and so on.

- **Energy** – businesses need to note that every contact and every day is an opportunity to market their company. This is known as 360-degrees marketing.

- **Networks** – businesses should be on the lookout for new contacts and focus on building relationships.

- **Smart** – firms should ensure that they do not offend customers. However, some businesses have deliberately offended customers and used the controversy to create awareness.

Methods used in guerrilla marketing

- Peer marketing – bringing people with similar interests or ages together to build up interest in the product

- Product give-aways including free demonstrations and consultations

- SMS texting and video messaging

- Roach baiting and buzz marketing – where actors are used to behave as normal customers to create interest, controversy, or curiosity in a product or service

- Intrigue – the process of generating mystery to engage customers

- Live commercials – using people to do live commercials in key places such as clubs and pubs

- Bill stickers – an approach used to promote DJs and club events

The benefits of guerrilla marketing

- **Low cost** – the types of activities involved do not require large financial outlay, so it is a very low-cost way of marketing.

- **Flexibility** – it can be changed easily because it is small scale. As a result, the campaign can respond to changing conditions and circumstances quickly.

- **Simplicity** – many guerrilla marketing methods are simple and easy to implement.

- **Identified target market** – activities can be targeted at the market that is most likely to buy the product or service. This improves the efficiency of the marketing campaign and improves returns.

- **Communication tool** – it provides new ways of communicating with customers. For example, Nike sought to communicate with consumers through instant messaging. In a competition called "Speed Mob", pairs of participants were sent questions about new Nike products via instant messages; the first participant to answer the questions correctly progressed to the final round.

- **Interaction opportunity** – it can be used as a platform to interact with the audience. In 2005, Burger King implemented a guerrilla marketing campaign to increase sales in Asian countries. The campaign, designed by Ogilvy RedCard, aimed to attract more consumers into Burger King's restaurants. For example, the company printed "I™BK" on T-shirts and placed them on statues of Ronald McDonald, it placed large footprints from McDonald's to Burger King, and it put signs on empty benches that said "Gone to BK – Ronald".

- **Accessibility** – most guerrilla marketing activities aim to be as accessible to customers as possible, therefore increasing the customer base. For example, to promote its "Orange" online banking solutions, ING Direct initiated guerrilla marketing campaigns in the metropolitan regions of Boston, San Francisco, and Washington DC.

The negative effects of guerilla marketing

- **Denting the brand image** – if guerrilla marketing strategies are directed to the wrong group of people or not executed properly, they can seriously hurt the company's brand image.

- **High negative attitudes** – since the main goal of some advertisements is to evoke a range of negative emotions, such as fear and anger, guerilla marketing campaigns may lead to highly negative attitudes towards the brand or the whole company. Overuse of fear-related marketing campaigns may cause the overall effectiveness of the promotion to decline.

- **Negative impact on social life** – for example, billboards placed in the middle of a highway or in places with high traffic congestion may cause traffic accidents.

- **Ethical issues** – for example, in the USA, in an advertisement used to promote the *Kill Bill* movie, a shocking image was used in the restroom of a movie theatre, seen from outside the toilet cabin. It was a realistic image of blood leaking from under the door of the cabin. However, when the door was opened, it became clear that the image was just a sticker giving the release date of the movie. Such an advertisement does not necessarily threaten the psychology of an adult, but it may cause problems to children, which may result in their inability to use the toilet alone.

Other common pitfalls of guerrilla marketing are trespassing on private property, defacing private or public property, and not getting permission from property owners when required. For example, in Singapore, placing Burger King stickers on bus schedules to indicate store locations is considered an act of vandalism. In addition to getting permission from private owners, some irregular action held in public places should also be approved by local government.

Despite their drawbacks, the key characteristics of being untraditional, creative, surprising, and efficient make guerrilla marketing strategies one of the most innovative and effective promotional methods businesses can use. Instead of the traditional method that concentrates on "me" marketing and talking only about the business, through guerrilla marketing a business encourages customers to consent willingly to interact with it and aims for this interaction to continue over a period of time. Gallagher (2004) summarizes it well by saying: "What matters in

TOK discussion

What role do logic and emotion play in marketing? Is there room for both?

guerrilla marketing is what the firm does to differentiate itself from its rivals and its success in reaching a broader customer potential".[1]

Student workpoint 4.11

Be a thinker

1. Distinguish between above-the-line and below-the-line promotional strategies.

2. Using a business of your choice, evaluate how new technologies are having an impact on its promotional strategies.

Place

Place is about how the product reaches consumers. It is concerned with how the product is distributed to make it available to consumers. The distribution system includes getting the right product to the right place at the right time. Distribution is a crucial element in the marketing mix for businesses of any size.

Place is important in the marketing mix for the following reasons:

- It refers not only to the location of the business but also to the location of the customers. Businesses should therefore develop strategies to get goods from their present location to the location of consumers.

- It enables businesses to come up with the best ways to distribute their products efficiently and effectively to consumers.

- The use of intermediaries such as wholesalers and retailers helps businesses to store and market their products and enhance their brand image.

- The growing global use of the Internet is making it easier for businesses to reach a wide range of consumers directly with their products.

Types of distribution channel

A distribution channel or channel of distribution is the path taken by a product from the producer to the consumer. Some distribution channels make use of intermediaries. These are middle people such as wholesalers, agents, and retailers that lie in the product's path from the producer to the consumer. The common distribution channels are described below.

Zero intermediary channel

This is where a product is sold directly from the producer to the consumer. For example, agricultural products can be sold through this method. Other examples include the use of mail order catalogues and e-commerce. In the service sector, airline ticket bookings can also be made via this method.

---

[1] Gallagher, B. (2004) *Guerilla marketing and branding*. CA: Marketing Turkiye Press.
Hamel, G. and Prahalad, C.K. (1996) *Competing for the future*. Harvard Business School Press.

One intermediary channel

This involves the use of one intermediary such as a retailer or an agent to sell the products from the producer to the consumer. In most cases it is used where the retailer is operating on a large scale or where the products are expensive. Examples include selling expensive furniture or jewellery through retailers. In addition, using large supermarket chains such as Nakumatt to sell various household products, and the use of travel agents such as Harvey World for flight bookings, are also common in this distribution channel.

Two intermediaries channel

In this case two intermediaries, which usually include wholesalers and retailers, are used by producers to sell the product to the consumer. The wholesalers are important in this channel and act as an additional intermediary between the producer and the consumer. This channel is particularly useful when selling goods over long geographical distances.

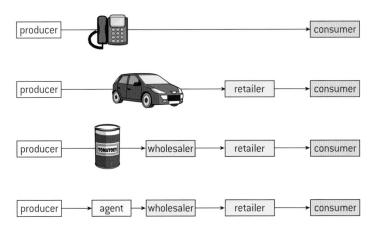

Figure 4.5.4. Channels of distribution

Table 4.5.4. Advantages and disadvantages of different distribution channels

Distribution channel	Advantages	Disadvantages
Zero intermediary channel	It is low cost. It is fast. It is ideal for perishable products. The producer is the key decision-maker in the distribution process.	Promotion is done by the producer, which could be time-consuming and expensive. The producer incurs all storage and delivery costs.
One intermediary channel	Promotion and customer service are done by the retailer. The costs of holding stock are incurred by the retailer. The retailer assists in selling the product at convenient places to consumers.	As the retailer's profit mark-up is included in the selling price, the product may be expensive for consumers. The producer may not be aware of the promotional strategy used by the retailer.
Two intermediaries channel	The wholesaler incurs storage costs, therefore reducing these costs for the producer. The wholesaler breaks the bulk for the retailer by providing large quantities in smaller batches. This is an appropriate channel when selling over long distances.	Two profit mark-ups could lead to a more expensive product offered to consumers. This channel further reduces the producer's responsibility for promoting products.

Student workpoint 4.12

Be an inquirer

Examine which distribution channels are likely to be most effective for each of these industries:

- clothing
- jewellery
- bakery.

Explain your answer.

Key term

Channel of distribution
the path taken by a product from the producer or manufacturer to the final consumer

Revision checklist

✓ A product life cycle illustrates the six life cycle stages that a product passes from its development, introduction, growth, maturity, saturation and decline in the market.

✓ Extension strategies are implemented at the maturity or saturation stages of a product's life cycle in an effort to stop a firm's sales from falling by lengthening the product's life cycle.

✓ The Boston Consulting Group (BCG) Matrix is a growth-share matrix that measures the market growth rate and relative market share of a firm's product portfolio by classifying the products as stars, problem children, cash cows or dogs.

✓ BCG Matrix strategies include harvesting, holding, building and divesting.

✓ Branding is concerned with distinguishing one business's product from another and has a strong influence on how consumers perceive a product.

✓ Packaging is vital in the marketing mix to differentiate one product from another by designing and producing the physical container or wrapper of a product.

✓ Price as one of the marketing mix elements is essential in generating revenue for a business and refers to the money customers give up for using a good or service.

✓ Appropriate pricing strategies include cost plus pricing, penetration pricing, competitive pricing, price skimming, psychological pricing and price discrimination.

✓ Promotion's main aim is to obtain new customers or retain existing ones by communicating information about a firm's products to consumers. It can be categorized as either above the line or below the line.

✓ Above the line promotion uses independent mass media to promote a firm's products including advertising through the television, radio or newspapers.

✓ Below the line promotion does not depend on the use of independent media and firm's focus their direct control on promotional activities to consumers who they know or those who are interested in their products e.g. direct marketing, personal selling, public relations and sales promotions.

✓ Marketers are increasingly incorporating technology in their marketing strategy. These strategies include Social media marketing which is a way of building relationships, driving repeat business and attracting new customers through social media sites. In addition, viral marketing uses peer-to-peer communication where people pass on promotional messages within their social networks.

✓ Guerrilla marketing is a low cost unconventional marketing strategy that has a great innovative and significant promotional effect on a business.

✓ Place is about how a firm's product is distributed to make it available to consumers by getting the right product at the right place at the right time.

✓ Distribution channels include zero intermediary channel, one intermediary channel and two intermediaries channel.

Practice question

The Q-Drum: "A Revolution in Thinking and Innovation"

The problem is obvious. Millions of women and children worldwide endure backbreaking labour carrying open, unstable, heavy water containers for long distances.

The solution: the Q-Drum, invented by brothers Hans and Piet Hendriske. The brothers have obtained a patent (intellectual property rights) for producing the Q-Drum.

Even a child can pull up to 50 litres of water in the doughnut-shaped plastic drum as it rolls along the ground. In a recent test, one family of 13 used the Q-Drum daily, travelling 12 000 km in 20 months, providing 120 000 litres of transportable water.

"The Q-Drum represents a revolution in thinking and innovation", claimed Dr Paul Polak, who runs an organization helping poor farmers become entrepreneurs. He added, "A billion customers in the world need a US$2 pair of eyeglasses, a US$10 solar light and a US$100 house. Why do innovators and designers only research and develop products that target the needs of the planet's richest 10 per cent?".

However, despite its simplicity and life-saving innovation, the Q-Drum has only sold several hundred so far. At US$50 the price is too high for those who need it most. Until it can be manufactured more cheaply and appropriate distribution channels can be found, sales will remain low. A non-government organization (NGO) sponsored by the United Nations has offered to help with the market development of the Q-Drum, but the brothers know that significant marketing issues still remain.

a) Define the following terms:

   (i) innovation   *[2 marks]*

   (ii) distribution channels.   *[2 marks]*

b) Explain the role and importance of obtaining a patent (intellectual property rights) for the Hendriske brothers in producing the Q-Drum.   *[6 marks]*

c) Analyse *two* reasons why "innovators and designers only research and develop products that target the needs of the planet's richest 10 per cent".   *[6 marks]*

d) Discuss an appropriate marketing mix to increase sales of the Q-Drum.   *[9 marks]*

IB, May 2010

Source: http://ecoscraps.com/files/2008/09/qdrum1.jpg, 20 October 2008

4 Marketing

4.6 The extended marketing mix of seven Ps (HL only)

By the end of this chapter, you should be able to:

→ discuss the importance of employee–customer **relationships** in the marketing mix of a service and the **cultural** variation in these relationships

→ evaluate the importance of **delivery processes** in the marketing mix of a service and **changes** in these processes

→ examine the importance of tangible **physical evidence** in the marketing mix of a service

→ apply the seven Ps model in a service-based market.

People

Interestingly, many businesses work very hard on the other elements of the marketing mix and pay little attention to the people in the businesses who essentially are involved in decision-making on a regular basis. A firm's ability to select, recruit, hire, and retain the best people, with the right skills and abilities to do the job, is a crucial aspect of any business. Collins (2001) found that an important factor present in the best companies was that they first "got the right people, on the bus and the wrong people off the bus". After hiring the right people they then "got the right people in the right seats on the bus". Successful businesses think in terms of getting the right people to carry out specific tasks and responsibilities.[1]

People are the most important element of any service business. Services are produced and consumed at the same moment, and the specific customer experience can be changed to meet the needs of the person consuming it. People usually buy from people they like, so businesses should ensure that their staff have the right attitude, skills, and appearance at all times. For example, restaurants should encourage their waiters to dress appropriately, to be courteous, and to smile when serving customers. Offering customers an opportunity to feed back to staff can also help to assess how effective customer service is. Examples include banks providing brief questionnaires asking customers if they waited too long to be served or questioning cinema goers on the service experience as they queue to book a ticket. People have an important role to play in service delivery and maintaining good customer relationships. Behind key events such as hosting soccer's World Cup there are many

---

1 Collins, J. (2001) *Good to Great: Why Some Companies Make the Leap ... and Others Don't.* HarperBusiness. London.

people, for example managers, engineers, chefs, and security guards, who ensure that the service is appropriately delivered to the customers.

Another important factor is that people form a transactional link between the organization and its customers. For example, people deliver the service and they collect money, i.e. they get paid on behalf of the organization for the service. When you go to a restaurant, in most cases there will be a waiter who greets you on arrival, he or she then takes your order and serves you what you requested. After that you pay the waiter money for what you consumed, completing the contractual transaction. Therefore, the people's role in the customer relationship between the business and the consumer is vital. Customer relationship management (CRM), which ensures that staff are trained to deliver good customer service, is important in developing a long-term employee–customer relationship.

However, organizations need to deal with the various cultural settings they are faced with. Culture includes the way employees perceive or behave in the organization. Undoubtedly, some cultures may dominate others in the same organization, with groups of employees having differing beliefs and opinions, leading to the formation of a cultural gap. It is the organization's responsibility to close this gap and foster a sense of unity among its employees. This will help in improving teamworking and will motivate employees to work to achieve the organization's goals. Consequently, a motivated workforce can also be seen in how the employees treat the customers, further strengthening the employee–customer relationship. In addition, marketers need to learn and understand the cultural dimensions of customers to be able to satisfy the customers' needs fully.

Processes

This refers to the procedures and policies pertaining to how an organization's product is provided and delivered. It should inform customers on "how easy it is to do business" with a particular organization. Call centre staff who do not answer customers' questions and products in supermarkets with barcodes that are not recognized when customers are ready to pay are examples of processes that are not functioning well and need urgent attention. The more intangible the product, the more important it is to get the process right.

Process also involves how the product is delivered to the consumer. DHL, for example, is known for its fast and efficient delivery of parcels or documents and prides itself on having the right systems or processes to facilitate this. It also ensures that utmost care is taken by doing a security check on documents before they are sent to the recipient. This also ensures that the product is delivered in its exact state and form as required by the sender, maintaining optimal quality standards throughout. In addition, the sender receives a tracking number they can use for tracking the document's path and enquiring about any delay in delivery if necessary.

At the outset, businesses need to define clearly the shape their processes will take so that all stakeholders are fully aware of what to

Key terms

People

the human capital in terms of skills, attitudes, and abilities necessary in the production of goods or the provision of services

Processes

the procedures and policies pertaining to how an organization's product is provided and delivered

Physical evidence

the tangible or visible touch points that are observable to customers in a business do. For marketing to be effective, there are a number of processes that businesses need to consider, including processes for identifying customer requirements, handling customer complaints, and handling orders, among others. If these are tackled well they can go a long way towards developing customer loyalty and ensuring repeat customers.

These are some of the ways a business can improve on its processes:

- Any measure taken to speed up the delivery of products to customers is of prime importance.

- A business needs to provide easy and varied payment methods for customers such as paying over the Internet, paying cash, or paying on credit.

- Provision of after-sales services such as technical support reduces the time a customer has to spend solving problems when using a product.

- Informing customers how long their meal will take to be prepared in a restaurant adds to customer service.

However, ensuring that the right process is in place may be time-consuming, complex, and expensive, especially for start-up businesses, which may lack the experience and capital that larger businesses may have.

Physical evidence

This refers to all the tangible or visible touch points that are observable to customers in a business. Unlike businesses offering tangible products where consumers can try, touch, or smell the product before purchasing it, service businesses usually depend on customers' recommendations or testimonials, which are usually based on trust. As a result, businesses need to ensure that they are providing adequate evidence of quality throughout. Examples of good-quality evidence include well-groomed and well-dressed staff, a well-organized reception area, ambient lighting with pleasant music in a restaurant and offices located in a clean and prime location. To create a good customer experience, tangible aspects must therefore be delivered with the service.

Physical evidence is an important differentiator in service marketing. For example, managers of a private school may pay more attention to providing well-designed and equipped classrooms and spacious offices for their teaching staff than managers in public schools, clearly bringing out the differentiating element of physical evidence.

The intangible nature of products with a service element, however, makes it difficult for consumers to evaluate the service being offered, especially regarding the quality and value for money, before deciding to buy. In addition, it is difficult for a business to position new products with a service element because of their intangible nature. Effectively focusing on the tangible aspects of the service offering will enable the business to remain competitive in the market.

Physical evidence should therefore enable customers to "see" what is on offer, prior to purchasing the service offering. Businesses should also ensure that the testimonials customers pass on to others about their product are good and lead to an enhanced image and increased sales.

The seven Ps model in a service-based market

Figure 4.6.1. Summary of the seven Ps relevant to a business in the service sector providing intangible products

Student workpoint 4.13

Be an inquirer

Choose a service-based industry of your choice. Evaluate how important people, processes and physical evidence are in its marketing strategy.

TOK discussion

The four Ps and seven Ps frameworks suggest that marketing has four or seven aspects, all of which can be described with a word that starts with a "P". How helpful are such analytical frameworks to you as a knowledge-seeker?

4 Marketing

Revision checklist

✓ People comprise an essential element of any service business so businesses should ensure that their employees have the right attitude, skills and appearance at all times as they are the face of the organisation. These people also form a transactional link between the organization and its customers due to their vital role in the long term customer relationship between the business and the consumer.

✓ Processes are the procedures and policies pertaining to how an organization's product is provided and delivered to the consumer. They inform customers on the ease of doing business with a particular organization.

✓ Physical evidence includes the visible touch points that are observable to customers in a business and is an important differentiator in service marketing.

Practice question

Fast Eater

Fast Eater, a fast food restaurant company went public in 1975 and until 2000 had always made a profit. From 2000, sales in Europe (the company's biggest market) started to decline. The following table gives information on *Fast Eater's* current portfolio:

Date of launch	Product	Market information	Other information
1975	burger rolls	high market share but beginning to fall, very low sales growth	very profitable, core product but profitability is beginning to fall
1975	fried potatoes	high market share but beginning to fall, very low sales growth	very profitable, core product but profitability is falling rapidly
1995	toasted bacon sandwich	high market share, low market growth	very successful product
2002	chicken roll	falling sales, low market share in a low growth market	not a commercial success
2002	cheese and tomato pizza	falling sales, low market share in a low growth market	not a commercial success

During the 1990s, *Fast Eater* opened stores worldwide at the rate of 250 a year. However, by 2004

Fast Eater was closing restaurants and concentrating on attracting more customers into existing outlets. Industry analysts suggest that the trend towards healthier food is affecting the popularity of the chain and so *Fast Eater* is proposing the introduction of a new product to cater for the market. Newly established health-food stores are becoming major competitors. *Fast Eater* is caught in a marketing war with aggressive rivals. In addition, economic downturn in its major markets is affecting demand.

a) Explain what is meant by the "company went public in 1975". [2 marks]

b) (i) Use the Ansoff Matrix to identify and explain *Fast Eater's* past and current growth strategies. [4 marks]

(ii) Use the Boston Consulting Group Matrix to analyse *Fast Eater's* product portfolio. [6 marks]

c) Suggest a new product for *Fast Eater* and devise a marketing mix (7Ps) to support your chosen product. [8 marks]

IB, Nov 2005

4.7 International marketing (HL only)

By the end of this chapter, you should be able to:

→ explain the methods of entry into international markets

→ examine the **opportunities and threats** posed by entry into international markets

→ discuss the **strategic and operational implications** of international marketing

→ evaluate the role of **cultural differences** in international marketing

→ discuss the implications of **globalization** for international marketing.

International marketing refers to the marketing of goods and services across national boundaries: products from one country are marketed to another country. Unlike global marketing, where firms use a standardized approach to market their products in other countries, in international marketing firms have the flexibility to differ in their marketing approach to other countries. Increasing worldwide competition, also known as **globalization**, is the main cause of the rise in international marketing.

Methods of entry into international markets

A method or mode of entry into an international market is a channel through which a business gains entry into an international market. Firms can employ various strategies to enter international markets. Some are considered below:

- **The Internet** – many businesses are increasingly using the Internet to market their products because of its global reach. New Internet businesses are increasingly being set up to take advantage of the low costs involved in marketing their products abroad. Existing businesses are using the Internet as an additional channel to enhance their current marketing methods. Trading over the Internet, also known as **e-commerce**, will be explored further in this unit.

- **Exporting** – this can be done both directly and indirectly. In direct exporting a country commits to market its product abroad on its own behalf. The main advantage here is that the business has control over its products and operations abroad. Indirect exporting, on the other hand, involves hiring an export intermediary or agent in the home country to market the domestic firm's product abroad. A common form of indirect exporting is **piggybacking**, where already existing distribution channels of one domestic business are used by another home country business trying to sell a new product overseas.

- **Direct investment** – which is also known as foreign direct investment, where a business sets up production plants abroad. One benefit of investing in production plants in a foreign country is that a business gains access to the local market, making products easily available to customers. It also becomes well versed in local market knowledge and is able to adapt its products accordingly to suit consumer needs and wants. Many companies have followed this route, including Coca-Cola, Nike, Samsung, and Toyota.

- **Joint venture** – this is a business arrangement where two or more parties agree to invest in a particular business project. These parties share their resources, with each being responsible for the costs, profits, and losses incurred. However, the participants have their independent business interests separate from the newly formed joint venture. For example, in the effort to enter international markets, the joint venture Virgin Mobile India Limited, which is a cellphone service provider company, was formed from Tata Tele service and Richard Branson's Service Group. The company (joint venture) makes use of Tata's CDMA network to offer its services under the Virgin Mobile brand name.

- **International franchising** – this is a business arrangement where the franchisor (a business in one country) grants the franchisee (a business in another country) permission to use its brand, trademark, concepts, and expertise in exchange for a franchise fee and a percentage of the sales revenue as royalty. Examples of businesses that have used this as an international marketing strategy include Ocean Basket, Steers, Wimpy and Nandos. See unit 1 for more on franchising.

Opportunities of entry into international markets

International marketing offers many potential opportunities or benefits for the business owner. These include the following:

- **A larger market** – introducing a company's products to a new market provides a greater reach for its products, which increases the customer base. This enables the business to gain higher sales and profitability. This is also an effective extension strategy when an existing product is in the saturation stage of its product life cycle in the home country but enters a new market to begin its life cycle afresh.

- **Diversification** – this provides an opportunity for businesses to spread their risks by investing in other countries. Diversification reduces dependence on gaining sales revenue from just the home market in case of key risks such an economic downturn.

- **Enhanced brand image** – the global reach brought about by international marketing means that the businesses involved can be perceived to be more "successful" than those that operate only in the domestic market. This creates greater brand prestige that can drive brand loyalty.

- **Gaining economies of scale** – a business can increase its scale of operations through international marketing by selling more products abroad. As a result, this may reduce the average costs of production and

Key terms

International marketing

the marketing of goods and services across national boundaries

Globalization

the increasing worldwide competition leading to a rise in international marketing

Piggybacking

the use of the existing distribution channels of one domestic business by another home country business trying to sell a new product overseas

4 Marketing

327

so make the business more competitive. The business can then take advantage by increasing its profit mark-up and gaining higher profits.

- **Forming new business relationships** – marketing overseas can enable a business to make new contacts with various stakeholders, such as suppliers who may provide good prices for inputs, for example raw materials, compared to suppliers in the home market. These contacts can therefore provide opportunities for increased efficiency and profitability for home businesses.

Threats posed by entry into international markets

There are a number of external environmental factors that can be a source of major challenges for businesses engaging in international marketing:

- **Economic challenges** – the inequitable distribution of income in many countries can pose a major problem for countries wanting to market overseas. Many developing countries have very low per-capita incomes or purchasing power and therefore may lack the income to buy the products being marketed. Fluctuating exchange rates and differing interest rates also pose planning problems for businesses willing to market abroad.

- **Political challenges** – unstable political regimes pose a great threat to domestic businesses willing to operate in foreign markets, due to the volatile nature of the political arena. The easy tendency for governments to change regulations also increases the political risk of doing international business. The increased threats of global terrorism and civil unrest have also heightened awareness of which countries businesses should trade with. The instability of the Middle East and the invasions of Afghanistan and Somalia are some examples.

- **Legal challenges** – different countries have different laws that businesses need to abide by if they are to market overseas. For example, the EU is known for its strict policies on anti-competitive behaviour, advertising and product standards. International marketers must also adhere to the various consumer protection laws and intellectual property rights that exist in other countries.

- **Social challenges** – differences in the demographic or population structures of different countries should be a key consideration for international marketers. In a number of countries in Europe there is an increasing older population, while in many African countries there is a growing younger population. Marketers need to be aware of this disparity and segment the markets accordingly if they are to reap any benefits. The composition of the population in a country in terms of gender or number of immigrants present is also a vital social factor to consider.

- **Technological challenges** – the growing use of the Internet has increased the speed in the way businesses operate on a global scale. However, access to this vital resource is still lacking in a number of developing countries. This, coupled with limited infrastructure and poor communication systems, can have a drastic impact on how businesses operate.

The strategic and operational implications for international marketing

A well-defined strategic and operational plan is crucial for a business deciding to operate in international markets. All staff need to be clear on the vision, mission, values, and objectives that are laid down by the organization they are working in. This will keep them motivated and inspired to work towards fulfilling that dream. However, in some cases long-term strategic plans are very rigid and cannot survive major changes in the external environment such as economic and political changes. Conflict between internal stakeholders may arise. For example, there may be conflict between managers regarding the difference between a strategic issue and an operational tactic. A senior manager operating in a foreign subsidiary company may consider increasing market share as a strategic issue while another manager in the home country headquarters may view it as an operational issue, which would clearly result in a clash in their priorities.

A firm's ability to pursue a given international marketing strategy effectively depends to a large extent on the aims and expectations of its stakeholders. These stakeholders play an important role in providing the necessary support and resources needed for strategy implementation. Successful firms carefully identify the various stakeholder groups and focus on understanding their key expectations and evaluating their power and influence so as to get a broader picture of how to more effectively operate their businesses.

Hamel and Prahalad (1996) suggest that, for firms to succeed in their global operations, they have to perceive the changes in the international environment and develop strategies that will enable them to respond accordingly.[1] In addition, they argue that early identification of changes in the markets and respective industries, together with a thorough analysis of the external international marketing environment, is important for global survival. For a sustainable competitive advantage, businesses need to have management foresight and emphasize organizational learning. Firms also need to understand that international markets are dynamic and need constant monitoring and evaluation. Therefore, as markets change so should marketing strategies and tactics. Innovation as a result is an important competitive variable, not only in terms of developing and improving goods or services but also as a driver of better international marketing strategies. The challenge posed to international marketers is to have the discipline to conduct thorough market research continuously and have a clear understanding of what is required in order to remain competitive.

For firms wanting to be successful in international markets, Doole (2000) suggested three key aspects that firms should incorporate in to their strategies.[2] First, they should have a clear international competitive focus achieved through a thorough knowledge of the international markets, a strong competitive positioning, and a strategic perspective

---

[1] Hamel, G and Prahalad, CK (1996) Competing for the Future. Harvard Business School Press. Boston, MA.

[2] Doole, I. (2000) 'How SMEs Learn to Compete Effectively on International Markets', Ph.D.

4 Marketing

that is truly international. Second, they should incorporate an effective relationship strategy achieved through strong customer relations, a commitment to quality products and service and a dedication to customer service throughout international markets. Last but not least, a well-managed organization should continuously emphasize a culture of learning. Firms that are innovative and willing to learn showed high levels of energy and commitment to international markets and had effective monitoring and control procedures for all their international markets.

The global business environment is becoming more and more competitive and only organizations that can adapt to the changes in external factors will remain competitive and continue taking advantage of the opportunities that arise in international markets.

The role of cultural differences in international marketing

Culture plays a significant role in international marketing. Businesses that recognize the varying cultural differences globally in marketing their products stand a better chance of gaining a competitive advantage than businesses that do not.

Language is a key component of culture globally and understanding the meanings of words in different contexts should be a major priority for international marketers. This is because, in the process of translation, some words are given totally different meanings from the original and in some cases the translated words are confusing or even offensive to the audience. For example, in China Coca-Cola initially sounded like "Kooke Koula" which means "a thirsty mouthful of candle wax" after translation. Coca-Cola Company later had to work on the pronunciation to sound like "Kee Kou Keele" which means "joyful tastes and happiness". Pepsi Cola's campaign "Come Alive with Pepsi" failed in Germany because translated it meant "Come Alive out of the Grave." "Silver Mist" was a model car manufactured by Rolls-Royce; however, "mist" translated into German means "dung". General Motors' brand name "Nova" was unsuccessful in Spain because "nova" in Spanish means "no go".

The differing roles of men and women in society should also be considered. In Europe and the USA it is common to use female models wearing bikinis to advertise summer wear. However, this would be against the culture of more conservative countries. For example, in the United Arab Emirates women are expected to cover their bodies completely. An advertisement by Camay soap in France showing a husband washing his wife's back was successful in France but failed in Japan as women saw this as an invasion of privacy.

Local tastes and preferences are another important cultural consideration. In India, McDonalds had to change their beef burgers to chicken burgers because the Hindu religion does not allow people to consume beef. In Kenya, the Maasai are keen beef consumers. Serving a Maasai household with fish would be considered inappropriate and might even be offensive.

The 'Silver Mist' was renamed 'Silver Shadow' to avoid an awkward translation!

Ethics and culture also go hand in hand. For example, chewing gum is banned in Singapore and is viewed as unethical; however, it is allowed in many other countries. Smoking in public is allowed in some countries but banned in others. Alcohol consumption is only allowed for adults aged 21 and above in the USA; however, in many African countries anyone aged 18 years and above can consume alcohol.

There are many other significant cultural issues that businesses must consider, including symbols and colours used, that have a great impact on how they penetrate international markets. Awareness of all these cultural elements is vital for success in international marketing.

The implications of globalization for international marketing

Globalization, mostly brought about by the growing importance of international trade and the growth of multinational companies, has necessitated the increased use of international marketing. Businesses will need to consider the following implications of globalization while conducting international marketing:

- **Competition** – globalization has led to many foreign businesses getting access to domestic markets, so firms in the local markets have had to use aggressive marketing campaigns to compete with the larger foreign multinationals. Deregulation or the liberalization of markets has also increased global competition. Firms that once enjoyed monopoly power in the domestic market, such as Safaricom (a mobile telecommunications provider) in Kenya, have had to face it off with major cellphone subscriber giants such as Orange, Yu, and Airtel. However, in some cases foreign firms have used anti-competitive measures that have driven local businesses out of the country, causing unrest among members of the public there.

- **Changing consumer tastes and expectations** – the influx of cultural exports, which are the beliefs, values, and ideas transferred from one country to another, are changing how businesses are operating today. Indian curry is very popular in the UK, while the US burger is consumed widely in South Africa. While travelling, many consumers expect to see their cultural dish available in many countries. Businesses have therefore had to adapt so as to provide a variety of food products to meet this growing consumer demand. On the other hand, traditional foods in some countries are disappearing and being replaced by the more westernized dishes.

- **Location decisions** – choosing an appropriate global location in which to produce or operate can have significant international marketing advantages. Many clothing and shoe companies, for example Nike and Adidas, have located to India and China to take advantage of the low cost of labour. As a result of their cost savings they can use the extra money to market their products and reach a wider customer base. However, some of these companies have been accused of acting unethically, especially towards their workers and mostly with regard to overexploitation.

CULTURE

When businesses market their products and services across international boundaries, they need to understand each local market individually.

Carry out more research on how culture influences international marketing. Which cultural factors do you think have the strongest influence on international marketing? Why?

4 Marketing

- **Economies of scale** – in the process of overseas expansion, businesses have been able to spread their fixed costs over an increased output. This has lowered their average costs of production and increased the possibility of gaining higher profits. They have also gained better negotiation power with suppliers in their countries of operation. However, some of the foreign firms have grown so large in the domestic context that they are even able to influence the government to set policies that act in their favour.

Undoubtedly, globalization has played a major role in international marketing. A consideration of the above factors, including their costs and benefits, will assist firms in making better overseas marketing decisions.

TOK discussion

To what extent does the Internet provide true value to the customer?

Student workpoint 4.14

Be a thinker

1. Evaluate the benefits and problems of overseas expansion.

2. Discuss how culture has influenced current international marketing.

Revision checklist

✓ International marketing is the marketing of goods and services from one country to another. It provides businesses with the flexibility to differ in their marketing approach to other countries. Globalization is the main causal factor to the rise in international marketing.

✓ Modes of entry into international markets include the internet, exporting, direct investment, joint ventures and international franchising.

✓ The opportunities of international marketing include a larger market share, diversification, enhanced brand image, economies of scale and the formation of new business relationships

✓ The threats of international marketing include political, economic, social, legal and technological challenges.

✓ Due to the global business environment becoming more competitive, businesses that can adapt their strategies to suit the changes in external factors will remain competitive and continue to take advantage of the opportunities that arise in international markets.

✓ As a result of the significant role culture plays in international marketing, businesses that recognize the varying cultural differences globally in marketing their products stand a better chance of gaining a competitive advantage than businesses that do not.

✓ Implications of globalisation that businesses will need to consider in international marketing include competition, changes in consumer tastes and expectations, location decisions and economies of scale.

Practice question

Pacific Blue

In 2007, the low cost airline *Pacific Blue* entered the New Zealand market with an initial offer to sell 70 000 tickets at low prices on flights between Auckland, Christchurch and Wellington. Almost half of the $29 tickets were booked online within hours. Chief executive Brett Godfrey expressed his surprise: "It almost caused our website to crash".

Air New Zealand and *QANTAS*, the established market leaders were quick to respond to the new competitor by cutting prices to $49. A director of *Air New Zealand* doubted whether *Pacific Blue* could sustain these prices as part of its long-run strategy to enter the New Zealand market. She also questioned whether the company could satisfy demand with only 2 planes for 11 scheduled flights per day between Auckland and Wellington, the most popular route. By contrast, *Air New Zealand* uses 7 planes on the same route. A *QANTAS* director has commented that *Pacific Blue* could face significant capacity utilization problems.

Brett Godfrey accepted that *Pacific Blue* might run at a loss initially, but he was also confident about penetration pricing: "we have done this before in Australia and we have money in the bank to survive and hope to offer more routes, subject to government approval and the support of the New Zealand public."

Air New Zealand and *QANTAS* promised to remain competitive.

[Source: adapted from *The Age*, 4 September 2007]

a) Define the following terms:

    (i) *market leader*   [2 marks]

    (ii) *penetration pricing.*   [2 marks]

b) Explain **two** other marketing strategies that *Pacific Blue* could have used.   [6marks]

c) Examine **two** problems that *Pacific Blue* could face when using penetration pricing.   [6marks]

d) Evaluate **two** potential opportunities and **two** potential threats which *Pacific Blue* could face when entering into a new international market.   [9 marks]

IB, May 2009

4 Marketing

4.8 E-commerce

> **By the end of this chapter, you should be able to:**
> → describe the features of e-commerce
> → analyse the effects of changing technology and e-commerce on the marketing mix
> → distinguish between the three types of e-commerce
> → discuss the costs and benefits of e-commerce to firms and consumers.

E-commerce involves the buying and selling of goods and services through electronic networks, commonly via the Internet.

The features of e-commerce

- **Ubiquity** – the Internet is widely available at any time. It can be accessible at home, at work, or in hotels for 24 hours each day, 7 days a week.

- **Customization** – individuals can personalize their messages and decide how they will be delivered to other individuals or groups.

- **Global reach** – also known as the worldwide web, the Internet traverses many national boundaries.

- **Integration** – the Internet allows the combined use of audio, video, and text messages to deliver a marketing message.

- **Universal standards** – there is only one set of Internet standards globally.

The effects of changing technology and e-commerce on the marketing mix

Technological advancements such as the increased use of iPads®, smartphones, and laptops, and the growing use of e-commerce today in business transactions have had a great impact on the marketing mix:

- **Product.** With e-commerce, businesses such as Amazon can sell to a wider customer base than ever before. This also allows them to stock a wide range of products to meet demand, which could lead to higher sales and profitability. Interactive websites such as Dell online allow customers to view and customize a product to suit their own specifications. This can lead to greater customer satisfaction as the product is delivered according to the individual needs of the consumer.

- **Price.** Consumers can now make easy price comparisons using websites such as "Google product search" that can search for price information for them. They can therefore get access to the most competitive global prices leading to good savings. E-commerce has also led to the increased use of a direct selling approach from manufacturer to consumer, which has helped reduce distribution costs for producers and made affordable products available to consumers.

- **Promotion.** E-commerce has provided an additional medium for businesses using traditional promotion. Many businesses are now supplementing their current promotional methods with online advertising. The increased use of pop-up advertisements, banners, and viral marketing has led to a faster and more cost-effective spread of promotional material than ever before. E-commerce, with the help of technological tools, provides multiple ways for businesses to promote their products. For example, through a combined use of audio, video, text messages, or picture images, a promotional campaign is bound to be more effective in the eyes of the consumer. Feedback from consumers through online surveys can further help businesses to tailor products to their customers' specific needs.

- **Place.** E-commerce has definitely reduced the need for intermediaries in the chain of distribution. This has led to cost savings for manufacturers of various products. However, the role of these intermediaries in the marketing process should not be disregarded. For example, the personal appeal retailers provide to consumers is lost by trading over the Internet, which is impersonal. On the other hand, the Internet has made it more convenient for consumers to buy products – they no longer have to visit the retail outlets. Customers searching for products from various global locations will benefit from the many language translation applications available on websites, which they can download to their technological tools to aid them in their purchasing decisions.

Amazon is currently the largest online retailer in the world

Types of e-commerce

E-commerce can be categorized into the following types.

Business-to-business (B2B) is a type of e-commerce where a business trades with another business. Goods and services are bought and sold from one organization to another. This could involve producers transacting with wholesalers or wholesalers with retailers in a chain of distribution. The volume of transactions involved in B2B businesses is usually large. Automobile manufacturers are an example of how B2B is used. In most cases, vehicle component parts such as batteries, tyres, and windows will be sourced and purchased separately from other dealers by the main auto manufacturer.

Business to consumer (B2C) is e-commerce carried out from a business to a particular end user who is usually the customer or consumer. These transactions are more visible to the public compared to B2B transactions. Successful B2C businesses include Amazon, eBay, Priceline, and Google.

Consumer to consumer (C2C) refers to e-commerce that allows for transactions from one customer to another. C2C businesses provide opportunities for individuals to interact and exchange with one another in addition to selling or buying products to or from each other. Examples of businesses that fit well into these criteria are eBay and Craigslist.

The benefits of e-commerce to firms

- Firms can reach a wide target market in an effort to market and sell their products, resulting in an increased customer base.

- It is a more cost-effective method to use in advertising a firm's product compared to other means such as television advertising.

- Social networking companies such as Facebook have benefited from high advertising revenue by selling their high-valued space.

- Reduced wastage on paper is noted by firms that insist that consumers view instructions, news, or information on the web instead of waiting to be sent relatively expensive brochures or newspapers. This helps to cut costs for businesses.

The benefits of e-commerce to consumers

- It is convenient for consumers because they can trade on the Internet in the comfort of their location without having to visit a shop physically.

- Increased choice is also a key advantage for consumers. They can easily make comparisons of the various products on offer before deciding to make a purchase.

- Good online customer service increases customers' satisfaction and makes them happy. For example, delivery companies such as Fedex that deliver documents provide tracking numbers to customers to use online to check the whereabouts of their documents.

The costs of e-commerce to firms

- Concerns by consumers about Internet security regarding the payment process may lower the sales and growth potential for firms.

- Businesses spend significant sums trying to find measures to curb online fraud by Internet criminals trying to gain access to customers' accounts.

- Firms may be vulnerable to competitors who can gain access to their product details and business information.

- Setting up and maintaining a website can prove to be expensive for many businesses, especially start-ups, and may turn out to be a high-risk venture.

The costs of e-commerce to consumers

- Consumers may not have the ability to try or feel certain products before buying them. For example, many consumers would like to sit on a chair before buying it.

- Online pop-up advertisements and advertising spam are considered major distractions and time-wasters by consumers.

Key terms

E-commerce
the buying and selling of goods and services through the internet.

Business to business (B2B)
a type of e-commerce where a business trades with another business.

Business to consumer (B2C)
a type of e-commerce carried out from a business to a particular end user who is usually the customer or consumer.

Consumer to consumer (C2C)
a type of e-commerce that allows for transactions from one customer or consumer to another.

- In some countries, consumers may lack tools such as computers or smartphones to access the Internet. Poor Internet connectivity is also a problem experienced by consumers in some locations.

- When looking for information using a search engine, consumers are sometimes faced with too much information (information overload) and so they resort to using other means of getting the product.

Student workpoint 4.15

Be an inquirer

Examine how e-commerce is currently influencing the marketing strategies of businesses.

Revision checklist

✓ E-commerce is the buying and selling of goods and services via the internet.

✓ Common features of e-commerce include ubiquity, customisation, global reach, integration and universal standards.

✓ E-commerce due to advancements in technology has had a great impact on the marketing mix elements of product, price, promotion and place in businesses.

✓ The categories of e-commerce include; Business to business (B2B) where a business trades with another business, Business to consumer (B2C) which is carried from a business to a customer or consumer and Consumer to consumer (C2C) which allows transactions from one consumer or customer to another.

✓ Benefits of e-commerce include a wider market reach, cost effectiveness and convenience while costs of e-commerce are internet security concerns, increased competition and a lack of ability to try out product before purchasing it.

Practice question

Peace Frogs (PF)

Peace Frogs (PF) is an American company selling clothes and accessories that are branded by a frog making the "peace sign". PF specializes in teenage and young-adult clothing.

The company started operations in 1985 with the sale of multi-coloured shorts designed after various national flags from around the world. Founder Catesby Jones chose the name Peace Frogs because the frog is a Native American (American Indian) symbol for peace and, in some cultures, a symbol for good luck. As the shorts reached maturity in the product life cycle, the company shifted to selling other items, always branded with the image of the "peace frog".

PF products include T-shirts, sweatshirts, hats, swimsuits, stickers, and other items. In 2007 the company introduced organic cotton T-shirts to its branded product line. The cotton meets rigorous organic certification standards. The T-shirts are made without using chemicals harmful to the environment. The company refuses to purchase clothing from manufacturers that employ children or that do not maintain rigorous safety standards.

PF uses e-commerce and has its own retail stores in 11 American states. Since 1998 the company has had multi-coloured vans that drive to shopping centres, concerts and theme parks around the country. Drivers then sell PF-branded products, using the van as a retail store.

A concern among environmentalists is the decline in the number of species of frogs worldwide. At present, several species of frogs face extinction. The destruction of their natural habitat is the main threat for them. PF makes financial contributions to several organizations committed to environmental protection, which strengthens PF's brand.

a) Identify *two* features of e-commerce. [*2 marks*]

b) Explain *two* ways PF practices ethical behaviour. [*6 marks*]

c) Analyse the benefits of *two* methods of distribution of PF's product. [*5 marks*]

d) Discuss the importance and role of branding for PF. [*7 marks*]

IB, May 2012

5 OPERATIONS MANAGEMENT

5.1 The role of operations management

By the end of this chapter, you should be able to:

→ define operations and describe their relationship with other business functions

→ comment on operations management in organizations producing goods and/or services

→ discuss operations management strategies and practices for ecological, social (human resource), and economic sustainability.

What are "operations"?

Operations refer to the fundamental activities of organizations: what they do and what they deliver, i.e. how they produce the goods and services that meet consumers' needs and wants. Every organization is a producer of something. When we think of production processes, we tend to imagine a large factory with long lines of sophisticated machines, but production can take a variety of forms. There are the large-scale capital-intensive production lines such as oil refineries or car plants, but a small bakery, a restaurant, and a school are also all organizations with an end product. The art of managing production to get the best end product is called operations management.

The first factory

In ancient China, imperial and private workshops, mills and small manufactories had been employed since the Eastern Zhou Dynasty (771–221 BC), as noted in the historical text of the *Zhou Li*. In Europe, large mills and manufactories were established in ancient Rome. The Venice Arsenal provides one of the first examples of a factory in the modern sense of the word. Founded in 1104 in Venice, Italy, several hundred years before the Industrial Revolution, it mass-produced ships on assembly lines using manufactured parts. The Venice Arsenal apparently produced nearly one ship every day and, at its height, employed 16 000 people.

Operations may be easier to understand in the case of the secondary sector, with the image of a large factory with long lines of sophisticated machines; however, operations are found in all sectors, for example:

- in the primary sector, mining or harvesting

- in the secondary sector, industrial manufacturing

- in the tertiary sector, open-heart surgery

- in the quaternary sector, business consultancy.

Student workpoint 5.1

Be a thinker

1. List ten organizations that you know. Try to cover a range of types (e.g. sole trader, charity) and sectors (e.g. primary and quaternary), as studied in unit 1.2.

2. Identify the main operations of those organizations. Are they always straightforward? Why is that?

The study of operations provides the opportunity to investigate how products are made – at a very concrete level. Look around you – at this book, your computer, your clothes, the furniture in your school and in your house, your parents' car. They are all manufactured, using raw materials (such as cellulose pulp extracted from wood for your book) that go through a process of transformation. A simple input–output model can represent how operations are the result of a transformational process (see Figure 5.1.1). The finished product can then be packaged, transported, maybe exported or imported, and then commercialized and sold or bought.

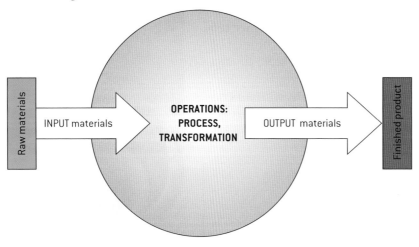

Figure 5.1.1. Input–output model

Student workpoint 5.2

Be a thinker

1. Apply the input–output model to an organization that you have studied, for example the organization you chose for your IA. How useful is that model?

2. Apply the input–output model to your school; what corresponds to "the input", "the process" and "the output"? What conclusions can you draw from this?

Operations and the other business functions

Operations can be described as the "how to" of business management. Operations are closely linked to the other functions:

- Operations deliver the "what" question of an organization's objectives (see Unit 1), for example manufacturing cars or cutting someone's hair.

- Operations are done by people (see Unit 2), directly in the case of the hairdresser, or indirectly in the case of the car factory worker who controls and programmes the manufacturer's machines.

- Operations need funding (see Unit 3) and all financial aspects must be carefully budgeted and monitored, for example to pay the car factory worker's salary or to ensure that the hairdresser breaks even.

- Operations produce goods and services that must be marketed (see Unit 4), promoted and sold at the right price to the right audience, so that both the hairdressing salon and the car manufacturer are successful.

In the hairdressing salon, operations are carried out directly by employees

The relationship between operations and the other business functions is easy to understand: all business functions depend on one another. As a consequence, the operations manager of a large company is in a good position to work with the other departments and make valuable recommendations. Here are some examples:

- The operations manager has direct experience of the economies of scale or diseconomies of scale that may take place on the factory floor (Unit 1.6), or may help identify some of the strengths and weaknesses of the organization (Unit 1.3) that other departments would not necessarily know about, for example machinery obsolescence or likely costs of maintenance in the foreseeable future.

- The operations manager can suggest which forms of non-financial rewards (such as job rotation or teamwork) may be suitable (or not) for the organization (Unit 2.4): the HR manager may not appreciate the fact that some forms of motivation may be very good in theory, but not in practice.

- The operations manager may know which production costs (such as some semi-variable energy costs) could be cut (Unit 3.2), which would in turn have an impact on the break-even point and the organization's margin of safety (Unit 3.2).

- The operations manager can advise on which product extension strategies (Unit 4.5) may be easily implemented (or not). The marketing manager may have interesting ideas that would, however, result in diseconomies of scale.

As a consequence, it is important that you understand that operations is not just about "doing and delivering" (despite the negative image that operations may sometimes have): operations management is an integral part of the organization and its decision-making process.

Student workpoint 5.3

Be a thinker

1. Find an organizational chart of an organization showing the relationships between workers, with levels of hierarchy and chains of command.

2. On that organizational chart, identify the department and the workers responsible for operations. How are they linked to the workers in the other business functions? What can you conclude?

Operations and the production of goods or services

Production is usually defined as the creation of physical products (goods) or non-physical products (services). Earlier units (such as 1.1 and 4.1) have used this distinction between goods and services, but in terms of production it may not be as fundamental and clear-cut. Although some products can be either goods or services, there is also a range of products between the two extreme types, and there can be an overlap in definitions, as shown in Table 5.1.1.

Table 5.1.1. Range of goods and services

Goods	High physical content but with some services	High service content but with some physical products	Services
Mobile phone, smartphone	Cosmetic surgery	Airline travel	Music concert
Consumer gets the product but there may also be after-sales service (for example in cases of malfunction or when updates are needed)	Consumer gets the "new" nose, breasts or wrinkle-free face but there is extensive treatment before and after the operation	Customers travel from A to B but they may have a meal and watch a film, all part of the experience that the airline offers	Assuming that consumers don't buy the T-shirt or the CD or even the sponsor's soft drink, they only pay for the pleasure of the music

This may also be represented through a continuum, as shown in Figure 5.1.2:

Pure goods   Combination of goods and services   Pure services

←——————————————————————————————————————→

Figure 5.1.2. Continuum of goods and services.

Student workpoint 5.4

Be a thinker

1. Consider the continuum between "pure goods" and "pure services". Locate some examples of products on this continuum.

2. How useful do you find this visual representation between the two extremes? Can you apply it to other areas of business management? And maybe even to other areas of knowledge?

There could not be a business without some form of operations, even if in the tertiary and quaternary sector it is not always easy to identify exactly where the operations take place. Think of a book author, for example (such as the author of the book you are reading). Where did the operations take place? In his mind, as he thought about the text? On his computer, as he wrote the sentences? In his home office? Or when he was walking his dog, thinking about the chapters he would write? Or what if he was travelling: in the plane or the troposphere? And ultimately, does it matter? For goods and services alike, operations are essential, but the notion must be adapted to the situation. The secondary sector and the manufacturing of goods still provide the best contexts in which to examine the operations of a business.

Operations management and sustainability

In our typical example of a large factory, operations management is about planning, organizing, and controlling the different elements and stages of the production process, from choosing the most appropriate raw materials and equipment, to ensuring that the finished product is of the standard required. The input–output model (Figure 5.1.1) reminds us of the responsibilities of an operations manager. If the finished product is not of the standard required (for example, it is defective), the operations manager will need to identify where in the process an error occurred. The role of the operations manager, however, is wider than just ensuring that production is correctly planned and executed; operations managers also have to take several other factors into account. These factors fall into three categories:

- economic factors

- social factors

- ecological (also called "environmental") factors.

Economic factors refer to the fact that budgets must be respected; wastage must be kept to a minimum and, whenever possible, further savings should be made, for example through greater efficiency. This is usually measured in monetary terms. For example, in some cases it may possible to cut some unnecessary costs, such as energy costs. The aim is to use the available resources and raw materials to their best advantage – ultimately ensuring profitability over the long term (as a profitable organization is more likely to continue to operate from one year to the next). This is also called **economic sustainability**.

Social factors refer to the fact that more and more organizations are becoming aware of their responsibility towards their workers, as internal stakeholders, and towards local communities, as external stakeholders. As a consequence, they seek to ensure that all employees are fairly treated, that their working conditions are acceptable, and that the quality of life for local people is not negatively affected by the decisions taken by the organization (for example in the case of expansion or relocation). This is also called **social sustainability**.

Ecological (or "environmental") factors refer to the fact that more and more managers understand the negative impact that their organization may have on the natural environment, especially different forms of pollution, such as air pollution (from carbon monoxide and CFCs), water pollution (industrial waste near factories, mills, and mines), or noise pollution (industrial noise that can also affect the workers themselves, for example in a noisy environment such as ship building). This is also called **ecological sustainability** (or **environmental sustainability**).

Economic sustainability, social sustainability and ecological sustainability are also called "the three pillars of sustainable development". Their combination is called the "triple bottom line". It is often represented in a Venn diagram, as shown in Figure 5.1.3.

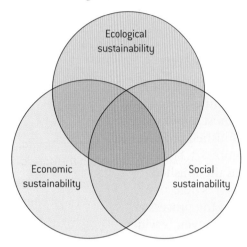

Figure 5.1.3. The triple bottom line

This "triple bottom line" stresses the fact that business decisions should not only consider financial aspects (i.e. breaking even and making money for shareholders), but also the well-being of local communities and the natural environment. Although this is relevant for all business functions, it is particularly relevant for operations, as manufacturing activities may have more negative impacts than marketing campaigns or financial transactions. In many cases, though, the "triple bottom line" remains an ideal rather than a reality, as economic aspects largely drive most commercial organizations.

Student workpoint 5.5

Be a thinker

1. How can you link "sustainability" and the "triple bottom line" to notions that you have studied in Unit 1, such as corporate social responsibility (CSR) and social enterprise?

2. Consider one organization that you have studied. How important is the "triple bottom line" in the decisions made by senior managers? Why?

3. Can you think of examples of situations of conflict between different types of sustainability (economic, social, and ecological)?

This is an example of one small business organization and its strategies and practices for economic, social, and ecological sustainability.

Key terms

Economic sustainability

the need to use available resources and raw materials to their best advantage, ultimately ensuring profitability and financial performance

Social sustainability

the need to take human factors into account, both internally (e.g. workers) and externally (e.g. local communities), when making business decisions

Ecological sustainability

the need to take ecological factors into account when making business decisions (especially about nature and ecosystems)

Triple bottom line

the need to take economic, social, and ecological factors into account when making business decisions

The Casa Blanca Eco-lodge

The word "eco-lodge" is used to describe a type of accommodation (lodge) that is environmentally friendly (eco-friendly). Eco-lodges aim to minimize their negative impacts on the environment and they make this very clear in all their promotional materials. They often receive official certificates confirming that they fulfill the criteria of sustainable development.

The Casa Blanca Eco-lodge is located in the Mayan mountains of Belize in Central America. It targets three types of visitor: rich tourists and jet-setters who seek an exotic, nature-based holiday experience; young backpackers keen to see non-coastal parts of Belize; and environmental scientists working on research or conservation projects.

The rainforest around the eco-lodge offers many opportunities for exploration and adventure. Visitors can go horseriding or hiking up the many canyon trails with a local guide, or they may prefer to canoe down the nearby rivers. The abundant bio-diversity of fauna and flora contributes to the tourist appeal of the area, from its butterflies to its jaguars, from its iguanas to its toucans, not to mention the rare black orchids unique to that environment.

Luis Morillo Medina opened The Casa Blanca Eco-lodge in 2006. Here is an extract from an interview with Luis that was published in the magazine *Eco-tourism Today* in 2012:

- Luis, why did you set up this business venture?

- *Of course I realized that there was a market opportunity, but I also wanted to do something for the local community. You see, I grew up here before I moved to Belize City where I worked in the hospitality industry. I am very attached to this area which has so much to offer. With the eco-lodge, we want to give tourists the chance to discover the beauty of the area, yet without destroying what we have. We are totally embracing the principles of eco-tourism and sustainable development.*

- Luis, can you give us some concrete examples of what that means?

- *For example, all our electricity is produced from solar power, and all our water is supplied by a nearby mountain spring. We make sure that we stay in harmony with the natural environment.*

- So the eco-lodge is all about integrating the accommodation in its environment, is that correct?

- *Yes, this is true, although we go further than that. We are fully integrated in the local economy; for example we only employ local people and we only use food produced from local suppliers.*

Questions

1. Which strategies and practices for economic, social, and ecological sustainability can you identify?

2. Can you suggest to Luis Morillo Medina other strategies and practices to ensure the economic, social, and ecological sustainability of the Casa Blanca Eco-lodge?

Revision checklist

✓ Operations are the fundamental activities of organizations.

✓ Operations are done by people – human resources.

✓ Operations need to be funded – accounts and finance.

✓ Operations produce goods and services which need to be promoted and sold at the right price – marketing and sales.

✓ Operations management is influenced by economic, social and environmental factors. Operations should aim to be sustainable in all three areas.

TOK discussion

- Is operations management an art or a science?

- In terms of operations and production, is there a difference between goods and services?

- Are "good working conditions" universally the same all over the world, or could they vary by country or by culture?

By the end of this chapter, you should be able to:

→ define and explain the following production methods:
- job or customized production
- batch production
- mass production
- flow, line, or process production
- cellular manufacturing

→ recommend the most appropriate method of production for a given situation.

A business organization, such as a factory manufacturing cars or cakes, may use a range of production methods. The main methods of production are defined in Table 5.2.1, which also provides some typical examples for large, complex products (cars) and smaller, simpler ones (cakes or cookies).

Table 5.2.1. The main methods of production

Type	Definition	Example
Job (customized) production	Production of a special "one-off" product made to a specific order (for one individual customer).	Custom-made cars with individualized accessories. A personalized wedding cake following the bride and groom's own design, favourite colours and required size.
Batch production	Production of a group of identical products (the word "batch" refers to the fact that the items in each group go together from one stage of production to the next).	Car models with differing features for each model. A series of cookies in different flavours: chocolate chip, peanut, and coconut.
Mass production	Production of a high volume (hence the word "mass") of identical, standardized products. Flow production, process production, and line production are alternative terms that stress one particular aspect of the mass-production process.	Cars that are made to a standard design. Identical, undifferentiated cookies produced for a mass market.
Cellular production	Cellular manufacturing (also called "cell production") is a form of mass production in which the flow is broken up by teams of workers who are responsible for certain parts of the line.	

Job production

Job production is a production method normally associated with the highest end of the market, where the emphasis is on quality and originality, and the producer can charge premium prices. Production is market-oriented, with the client deciding precisely what the product should be. This is also called "customized production", which means that the order is made for a specific customer.

Job production requires clear objectives and careful planning, which means there may be a longer development phase of the product life cycle. The client may require – and expect – greater consultation during the process and even after the product has been created. It is likely that the same format would be inappropriate another time. This can add to the time taken to produce the product, as there may not be a successful "blueprint" to use.

Advantages

- The mark-up is likely to be high.

- Clients get exactly what they want.

- This production method is likely to motivate skilled workers working on individual projects.

- It can be a flexible production method.

Disadvantages

- This production method can be expensive, requiring skilled workers and non-standardized materials.

- It is likely to be time consuming, as there is much more consultation with the client than when using other production methods.

- There is a possibility that the product might fail because of the lack of knowledge of the client. This may reflect badly on the business.

- This method can be very labour intensive and reliant on skilled workers.

Batch production

Batch production is normally associated with the middle of the market, where the emphasis is on quality and affordability. Products are still market-oriented; customers are offered customized products, but using a range of standardized options. This method of production requires careful planning, as the components for the products need to be interchangeable. Some consultation will need to be made with customers, as their needs have to be taken into account, although the exact options may be limited. Market research can replace that consultation.

Advantages

- Businesses can achieve economies of scale (for example when a small manufacturer makes savings on its budget by bulk buying, or a group of operators pools resources).

- Batch production allows customers more choice – and so captures more market share.

- Batch production may be useful for trialling products, especially through smaller quantities.

- Batch production may help deal with unexpected orders.

Disadvantages

- Businesses may lose production time as machines are recalibrated and/or retooled (this is known as "down time").

- Businesses may need to hold large stocks of work (in case of unexpected orders).

- The sizes of batches are dependent on the capacity of the machinery (or of labour) allocated to them.

It should be recognized, however, that increasingly sophisticated automation is now allowing greater customization, even in a mass-production environment.

Mass production

As it names indicates, mass production is all about quantity: mass production refers to the production of a high volume of standardized products, typically by using a continuous flow of raw materials along an assembly line. Labour is usually unskilled; its main role may be one of quality control or robotic functions, so there is a good argument for the automization of this method of production (as machines do not need regular breaks and can be relied on to produce to the same standard every time they are set). Mass production, however, requires careful planning in order to synchronize all the stages of the production process. For the process to be viable, the production must rely on large, reliable orders for the final product. There is likely to be a large "sunk cost" in setting up this method and this investment must be recouped by selling a high volume of the standardized products. The product is therefore sold at the low end of the market and in large quantities.

In mass production, most process are automated. In this factory, bottles are transported from one machine to another

The term "flow production" is sometimes used as a synonym for "mass production"; this term stresses the fact that the business uses a continuous flow of materials along an assembly line (this is the common image of a Taylorist factory with long conveyor belts routing the product through the different stages of production without any pause). Likewise, the terms "line production" and "process production" are used, too, stressing the idea of a line (where the end product is gradually created, step by step) and of a process (i.e. a progression through different stages in a particular order).

Advantages

- Once set up, the system needs little maintenance.

- The business can cater for large orders, thereby achieving considerable economies of scale.

- Labour costs may be low as the jobs required are relatively unskilled and with a fully automated process they are even replaceable.

- The business can respond to an increase in orders very quickly, as the process has already been set up.

Disadvantages

- Set-up costs will be high.

- Breakdowns are costly, as the whole assembly line may have to stop.

- The business is very dependent on a steady demand from a large segment of the market.

- The system is inflexible: if there are sudden changes in demand, the business may well be left holding large stocks of unwanted products.

- The production process can be demotivating for workers doing robotic activities.

Comparison of the main production methods

The three main methods of production may be compared according to different criteria (such as set-up time), as shown in Table 5.2.2.

Table 5.2.2. Comparison of the three production methods

	Job production	**Batch production**	**Mass production**
Set-up time	There is a long set-up time as there is a new set-up for every new job.	As set-up is usually a modification of an existing process, set-up time can be reasonably fast. Otherwise it is as for mass production.	There is a very long set-up as it takes time to synchronize the whole process.
Cost per unit	High	Medium	Low
Capital (machinery)	This can be flexible as it depends on specific use.	A mixture of machines is used, but this method is based on general-purpose machines.	This can involve large numbers of general-purpose machines designed for a specific function.
Labour	Highly skilled workers are needed – and may be craft workers.	Workers are semi-skilled and need to be flexible.	Workers are unskilled and need minimum training.
Production time	This is likely to be long.	Once set up, production can be swift.	Production is swift.
Stock	This involves low quantities of raw materials and finished stock but a high amount of work in progress.	High quantities of raw materials are needed (buffer stocks). There will be medium amounts of work in progress and finished stock.	There will be high quantities of raw materials and finished stock and a low amount of work in progress.

Cellular manufacturing

Also called "cell production", cellular manufacturing is a form of mass production in which the flow is broken up by teams of workers who are responsible for certain parts of the line. This is a more recent attempt to improve mass-production techniques by allowing teams of workers to operate as self-contained units (called "cells" or sometimes "pods") with more autonomy and responsibility, in order to motivate them more.

5 Operations Management

Student workpoint 5.6

Be a thinker

1. Can you link "cellular manufacturing" with other elements that you have studied, such as teamwork and empowerment (Unit 2.4) or project-based organizational structures (Unit 2.2)?

2. Can you link "cellular manufacturing" to some motivation theories (Unit 2.4)?

3. Can you identify and explain the disadvantages of cellular manufacturing, compared with other methods of production?

Many traditional manufacturing businesses have been drawn to this method, as well as many of the newer industries in the quaternary sector. It is believed that cell production can lead to a greater competitive advantage for many manufacturers, as they can achieve the three aims of improving quality, increasing productivity, and reducing costs of production. Quality improvements will come from the cooperative nature of the production, with members of the team being directly responsible for their own quality checking. This should lead to less wastage and lower rejection rates. It is also easier to halt production in a cell compared with an assembly line, so if there is a quality problem it can be dealt with quickly and without affecting other parts of the production process. Besides, by working as part of a close-knit team, each worker is given greater responsibility compared with the robotic and repetitive nature of working on an assembly line.

Changing production method

Once a business has chosen and implemented a particular production method, it can be difficult and costly to change. At the very least, this may involve retooling machines, redeploying human resources and refinancing the new system. At its most drastic, a business could decide to re-engineer itself: this means that the company completely reworks itself, not only by changing the production process, but also the entire organization of the business. Business re-engineering was a fashionable management tool in the 1990s, but not so much now.

Changing production method would have implications for all the business functions.

These are some of the implications for **HR**:

*   Some workers may have to be redeployed, retrained, or even let go, so human resources would need to be carefully managed.

*   Refining the roles and responsibilities of workers and middle managers would require careful planning.

These are some of the implications for **marketing**:

*   Production runs can reflect the orientation of a business as well as the choice of product available to the consumer, so the image or perception of the business may be altered.

- Distribution channels may be affected, which may lead to differing response times.

- Changes in costs of production could be passed on to the consumer through changes in price (which are likely to mean an increase, at least in a short term, to pay for the transition costs).

These are some of the implications for **finance**:

- Changing production method will have an impact on stock control, which affects costs.

- Changes may take time and could interrupt current production, causing delays in the working capital cycle.

- Any change will need financing, whether it is short term or for significant developments that may require major long-term funding.

What is the most appropriate method of production for a given situation?

The most appropriate method will vary from business to business – there is no one correct method. Factors affecting the decision include:

- the target market – for example, the business may be producing a high volumes of a low-cost product for a very large market with little disposable income

- the state of existing technology – this can limit how flexible production can be

- the availability of resources – fixed capital, working capital, and human capital

- government regulations– for example, a business may have to meet certain targets for recycling or waste emissions.

Once a business has a particular production method in place, it is not easy to change it, because of the opportunity costs involved. However, it may be possible and suitable to combine different methods. Combining production methods, when appropriate, may result in integrating the advantages of each different model and making the business more productively efficient. For example, a Thai restaurant might have a continuous supply of a staple food such as green curry, but would produce batches of a less popular dish, for example Tom Yam soup, and would even be able to make a special order on demand. Likewise, Apple might mass-produce its most famous iPhones and iPads, but could also have limited editions of luxury gold-plated $30 000 models. In this way, the business can achieve economies of scale from the mass-produced products, while satisfying the need for changes in demand for more customized and higher-market products. There is no single recipe suggesting that a particular business should adopt a particular production method: there are always advantages and disadvantages to be compared and contrasted before a recommendation can be made.

Key terms

Job or customized production

production of a special "one-off" product made to a specific order (for one individual customer)

Batch production

production of a group of identical products (the word "batch" refers to the fact that the items in each group go together from one stage of production to the next)

Mass production

production of a high volume (hence the word "mass") of identical, standardized products

Flow, line or process production

alternative terms that stress one particular aspect of the mass-production process

Cellular manufacturing

a form of mass production in which the flow is broken up by teams of workers who are responsible for certain parts of the line

5 Operations Management

Revision checklist

✓ Job (or customized) production is market-oriented, meaning that the customer or client decides what the product should be. This is often production of a special, one-off product.

✓ Batch production creates a group of identical products, which can be customized.

✓ Mass production creates a high volume of identical, standardized products.

✓ Flow, line or process production is an aspect of mass production, wherein a business has a constant flow of materials in the production process.

✓ Cellular manufacturing is a form of manufacturing in which teams of workers are responsible for certain parts of the production process.

TOK discussion

- Is there always an ideal production method? Or does that depend on who decides?

- What evidence and whose experiences should business leaders consider when deciding on the production method?

By the end of this chapter, you should be able to:

→ outline the following features of lean production:

- less waste
- greater efficiency

→ distinguish between the following methods of lean production:

- continuous improvement (*kaizen*)
- just-in-time (JIT)
- *kanban*
- *andon*

→ explain the features of cradle-to-cradle design and manufacturing

→ outline the features of quality control and quality assurance

→ explain the following methods of managing quality:

- quality circle
- benchmarking
- total quality management (TQM)

→ examine the impact of lean production and TQM on an organization

→ explain the importance of national and international quality standards.

What is "lean production?"

"Lean production" (also called "lean manufacturing" or just "lean") is an approach to operations management that focuses on cutting all types of waste in the production process (such as waste of time) with one aim: greater efficiency. Lean production is of Japanese origin (it was first developed by the automobile manufacturer Toyota) and became popular in other countries in the 1990s. Literally, the word "lean" refers to the fact that, as with a healthy piece of lean meat without much fat (if you are a meat eater), the production process gets rid of all the elements that do not directly add value. This is not a new idea: Taylorist manufacturing in the early 20th century was already based on the idea of cutting waste, with assembly lines and factory workers specialized in one task (see Unit 2.4). It was only in the late 20th century that management researchers started writing books conceptualizing lean production and studying how this approach might be applied in other companies, in other industries, and in other sectors. The principles of lean production have now spread all around the world, especially in the automobile industry; but they can also be adopted and applied to other industries, too, from logistics to distribution and from construction to retail. Even some government agencies and services such as education and health care now use the principles of lean production.

The starting point for lean production consists in identifying the values desired by the customer (for example long battery life, possibilty for customization, or easy after-sales service connection), then all the stages of the production process that do not add value are eliminated. This elimination of waste is a key goal of lean manufacturing – the word "waste" must be interpreted in a broad sense, which can include waste of:

- time (for example waiting for the next stage of production, or waiting for some elements to arrive from a different location)

- transportation (for example the movement of half-constructed cars in a factory may not add anything to the production process itself)

- products (for example defects that need to be reworked or scrapped)

- space (for example when too much stock is being produced and stored; this is called "overproduction")

- inventory (for example with a much too high quantity of raw materials being purchased and stored, before they are used)

- energy (for example by under-utilization of some machines, which at full capacity would not proportionally require more power)

- talents (for example not optimally using workers' skills and knowledge).

In the context of lean production, the meaning of "waste" is very broad: it is not just about the disposal of substances or objects such as scrap metal or papers, but about all other aspects of the production process.

Cutting waste is directly linked to greater efficiency: with less waste, the organization's resources (such as physical resources, human resources, and financial resources) will be better used, employed, and deployed:

- Physical resources can be used more efficiently, especially without space for storage (which is doubly expensive, because of both the unused stock and the storage space itself, such as rent, lighting, and heating of a warehouse).

- Human resources can be deployed more efficiently, for example reducing unproductive travel times between venues (which is also expensive and not environmentally friendly).

- Financial resources can be used more efficiently, too as, for example, holding stock ties up working capital (which means that this money cannot be used elsewhere in the organization).

Student workpoint 5.7

Be a thinker

Can you link lean production to several lessons from other parts of the course?

1. The starting point of lean production consists in identifying the values desired by the customer. How can this refer to a marketing orientation that you have studied (Unit 4.1)?

2. What are the best methods of market research to identify the values desired by the customer (Unit 4.4.)?

3. How can a fishbone diagram (Unit 1.6) help identify areas of waste in a production process?

4. Lean production aims at greater efficiency; how can this appear in ratios that you have studied, such as the acid test (Unit 3.5) and stock turnover ratio (Unit 3.6)?

Methods of lean production

Over the years, several methods of lean production have been defined and implemented. If the managers of an organization decide to adopt lean production, they will choose the method that suits best their context. The following four methods are particularly important:

- continuous improvement (*kaizen*)
- just-in-time (JIT)
- *kanban*
- *andon*.

Continuous improvement (*kaizen*)

The word "*kaizen*" (which means "continuous improvement") is a Japanese term commonly used, as this method originates from Japan: like lean production as a whole, the idea of *kaizen* was developed by Toyota. The emphasis is on continuous change, as opposed to just occasional changes. In its simplest form, this process may involve suggestion boxes or competitions to find suitable areas for improvements, as often the workers themselves may have very good ideas, based on what they observe or experience directly on the shop floor. *Kaizen*, however, can be more sophisticated, requiring certain key principles:

- It must be inclusive of all levels of the hierarchy (i.e. the whole organization must adopt that management philosophy, not just a group of managers or one department only).

- There should be no blame attached to any problem or issues raised (otherwise some employees may hesitate to make suggestions).

- Systemic thinking is needed in order to consider the whole production process, and not just some parts of it.

- *Kaizen* focuses on the process, and not on the end product.

The main difficulty with *kaizen* is the fact that it is difficult to maintain the necessary momentum over a long period of time. To do so would require high levels of commitment and a sense of loyalty by the employees. The culture of the organization may influence this, and so will the leadership style: *kaizen* is unlikely to work under an autocratic leadership or bureaucratic corporate culture.

Just-in-time (JIT)

A business may hold stock (inventory) for many reasons, for example to ensure that it can reply to any sudden, unexpected demand (this called "**buffer stock**"), or to take advantage of bulk purchasing of raw materials. Holding stock, however, may incur several costs: not only storage costs, but also insurance costs and even the payroll costs of staff who look after the stocks. Controlling stock levels is very important for a business: this function is called **stock control**. Stock control is based on a balance between:

- JIC, which means "just-in-case": holding reserves of both raw materials and finished products in case of a sudden increase in demand (or of a problem in production or in the supply chain)

- JIT: avoiding stock by being able to get supplies only when necessary, and to produce only when ordered.

The difference between JIT and JIC and the factors affecting stock control and optimal stock levels will be further explored in unit 5.5.

JIC is the traditional method of stock control; however, in terms of lean production, JIT means that the company will not hold buffer stock, which contributes to the two pillars of less waste (there is no waste of space in storage facilities) and greater efficiency (not having money tied up in stock).

Kanban

"*Kanban*" is another Japanese word, as the idea also originates from the Japanese company Toyota. *Kanban* refers to one of the systems that supports JIT. Imagine a large table with coloured stickers and sticky notes that may be moved around, from one place to the other. At a very basic level, this is what *kanban* is about. A *kanban* card is a message, telling the factory workers what to do next, for example move to the next stage of production or reorder some stock. In terms of operations management, consider now how such coloured labels could be fixed on groups of items, boxes, or shipments: the aim is to ensure a regular and steady flow, without any waste of time or resources. The rate of demand is used to control the rate of production. *Kanban* is not a tool of stock control, but a tool to facilitate lean production.

Modern *kanban* cards are all computerized, with electronic code bars that are directly read and interpreted. This is a good example of an innovation used directly in a factory, to help the production process of other products (which may also be innovative in their own right). Although *kanban* originates from the automotive industry and works best in similar manufacturing contexts, the basic principle can be transferred to other areas – for example emails sent to salespeople to tell them that products are available are a form of *kanban*; the expression "ekanban" is increasingly used, too.

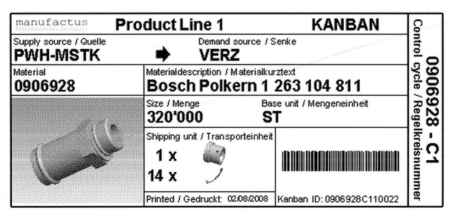

A *kanban* card

Andon

Another Japanese term, *andon*, refers to a signal (usually visual and electric or electronic) which informs workers (supervisors, maintenance staff, even managers) of a problem (typically a quality problem or some

delay in a process at a workstation). Like *kaizen* and *kanban*, the *andon* system was developed in Toyota factories.

When a problem occurs (for example a product defect or an anomaly with the machinery), the worker triggers the alert system – and a team of co-workers come and help immediately. This means that the problem will be resolved as quickly as possible, again in the spirit of lean production: less waste of time when dealing with a problem. The problem will then be logged in a database – should it occur again (at the same workstation or another one) the workers will promptly retrieve information about the causes and the solution.

Andon has other advantages:

- Workers on a production chain are immediately notified (workers at all levels of the chain of command, including engineers).

- Supervisors do not need to spend time monitoring production: their time is instead spent problem solving.

- Feedback can be provided to all teams (even the ones that did not get involved in that specific incident).

- The whole organization learns from its problems and mistakes, which enables *kaizen* (continuous improvement).

Originally, *andon* alerts were simple (such a red signal meaning "problem here"); however, modern systems can include other forms of displays, such as text or symbols, with audio alarms too.

An *andon* signal

Cradle-to-cradle design and manufacturing

Cradle-to-cradle design and manufacturing refers to a recent approach to design and manufacturing based on principles of sustainable development, especially recycling.

The term "cradle" refers to the production phase, i.e. the creation of a product such as a book or a car. The term "cradle to cradle" comes from the expression "cradle to grave": it suggests that products, once they have been used, should be entirely recycled to create the same new products again. At the moment, this is only the case for a small number of products from a small number of companies, for example some clothes or office furniture – but the current socio-cultural momentum towards environmental sustainability will put pressure on companies to design and manufacture more and more products that are partly, if not entirely, recycled.

To receive the official "cradle to cradle (C2C) certification", products need to fulfil several criteria, for example regarding:

- the reutilization of the material itself (recycling, strictly speaking)
- the amount of energy necessary for the recycling process, ideally renewable energy
- the amount of water needed as part of the recycling process
- the corporate social responsibility (CSR) of the company, for instance about fair labour practices.

The topic of cradle-to-cradle design and manufacturing is still in its infancy: the independent non-profit organization called The Cradle to Cradle Products Innovation Institute was launched in 2012. This means that the criteria and features will become more defined and refined over time. As part of their research and development, many companies are exploring what it could mean in practice. For example, Ford has proposed a concept car called "Ford Model U", a car for the 21st century based on recycling and eco-friendliness, using sunflower-seed engine oil and soy-based seat foam – however, the Ford U only exists as a prototype and as a theoretical example of what cradle to cradle could do.

Student workpoint 5.8

Be a thinker

How can you link cradle-to-cradle design and manufacturing to other parts of the course? Consider:

- Unit 5.1 about the three types of sustainability
- Unit 1.3 about CSR
- Unit 1.4 about STEEPLE analysis.

Quality control and quality assurance

A key component of operations management is the issue of quality. In the past this was very much a matter of **quality control** but, thanks to the **quality revolution** that has sprung from Japan since 1945, there has been a move towards **quality assurance**. This change in quality management came about largely due to the work of one man: the US management theorist W. Edwards Deming, whose ideas about how to produce quality products are still influential today.

Quality is important for a producer as it can lead to:

- increased sales
- repeat customers (brand loyalty)
- reduced costs
- premium pricing.

W. Edwards Deming

From a marketing viewpoint, a product need not be a high-quality product to bring all of these rewards, but as long as the consumer perception is one of quality, then that can often be enough. So league tables showing "top" business schools, airlines, or MP3 players can be hugely important for businesses, even if the product voted "the best" is not actually so!

The term **quality** suggests that a product is:

- reliable – it is not going to break down

- safe – it is not going to fail

- durable – it is going to last

- innovative – it is leading the way in terms of functionality or design

- value for money – you get what you pay for.

The quality revolution showed that even businesses not at the top end of the range could benefit from producing good-quality products. While a Honda car may not have the same brand image as a BMW, there is still a huge amount to be gained by producing good-quality, cheaper cars. This is a fact that GM and Ford are only just starting to realize, and Rover and British Leyland never did work out.

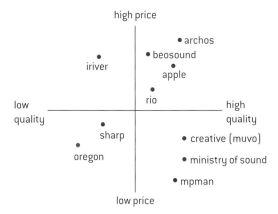

Figure 5.3.4. A way of mapping products based on scales of quality and price

Student workpoint 5.9

Be an inquirer

An IB class did some research to find the best-quality MP3 player. They initially did a survey of all the students, then used the website of a professional magazine for an external, reliable judgment. They then created a product positioning map, with the two axes of price and quality. They concluded that quality is not always reflected in the price.

Why not try the same exercise for a product of your choice?

The move from "quality control" to "quality assurance" can be summarized as in Table 5.3.1, which shows the major difference between the two systems.

Table 5.3.1. Quality control versus quality assurance

	Quality control	Quality assurance
Concept	• Quality is "controlled" by one person (the manager) by inspection after the production run has been completed	• Quality is "assured" because no one person is in overall control of quality; the whole business is focused on ensuring quality production
Costs	• A certain % reject rate is set, for example 2% of products are allowed to fail • Wasteful production	• Zero rejects are expected – every product is expected to pass inspection • Lean production
Processes	• It is rare to halt production as it is costly to do so • Associated with assembly line, flow production • Quality stops with the job; the focus is only on the job at hand	• The company expects to halt production to fix errors • Associated with cellular or modular production • Quality includes suppliers and after-sales servicing
People	• Quality is the responsibility of one person – a quality inspector • "Role culture" • Autocratic leadership • Top-down, one-way communication	• Quality is the responsibility of the team – quality circles • Total quality culture • Democratic consultative leadership • 360-degree communication

In order for quality assurance to work effectively, the whole business has to embrace a total quality cultural shift; as with a *kaizen* approach, this is difficult and costly to achieve in the short term, but it may well prove beneficial to the business in the long run. Several methods are possible to manage quality; the following three are particularly important:

• quality circle

• benchmarking

• total quality management (TQM).

Quality circles

A quality circle can be defined as a formal group of volunteers (employees from different departments and from all levels of hierarchy) who meet regularly to discuss and suggest ways of improving quality. The meetings are facilitated by a team leader (who needs to be trained in leadership and group facilitation). This is comparable to a focus group for market research, although a focus group would not necessarily meet several times, whereas a quality circle, to be successful, needs continuity. Quality circles may operate in different ways: they could choose any topic they want to discuss, or they may be working on specific issues. The underlying principle is the idea that, coming from a range of perspectives on the company, the members of the quality circle will be able to improve the overall quality of the company; for example, when discussing an issue of staff turnover, the members of the quality circle may present different views, thereby enabling the company, as a learning organization, to understand the problem (such as staff turnover) and to come up with solutions (such as reducing safety

hazards and giving workers more flexibility). This is not the same as managers doing a consultation exercise: the focus here is on generating solutions that are about quality.

As a tool of quality enhancement, quality circles were first established in Japan in 1962. This illustrates again how the quality revolution came from Japan after the Second World War. Quality circles are now very common in some countries (such as Japan and China), though less so in Anglo-Saxon countries and Western Europe, where the method did not spread and did not prove that successful.

Student workpoint 5.10

Be a thinker

1. What skills may facilitators of quality circles need? What could their training require?

2. Quality circles are very common in some regions of the world (such as South East Asia) but not others (such as Europe). Why could that be?

Benchmarking

Benchmarking is about comparing yourself to your competitors. Benchmarking is a tool that many businesses use. As a point of reference, some benchmarks are established – and the businesses can then compare their practices and standards with those of their competitors. A well-known example of benchmarking is the number of stars used to classify hotels: a five-star hotel is of a different quality standard from a three-star hotel. This is useful for consumers, who know what they can expect – but it is also very useful for business managers, as the benchmarks help them identify how they could improve the quality of their products and services, should they wish to do.

Businesses take the best players or the market leader in their industry and follow those organizations' "best practices". It is not so much about copying the rivals' products as understanding their practices and processes in order to improve quality. Benchmarking can be done in several ways. Some companies may use the benchmarks already existing in their industry (such as hotel standards); a company may have a specific quality issue (for example about communicating on quality and innovation) and may then study another company that they identify as the model they want to follow and emulate. Benchmarking can also be done in a collaborative way, with competing businesses acting together to keep up to date.

In all cases, the success of benchmarking relies on the business's readiness to "think outside the box", trying to introduce something new and not to carry on as it always has. Besides, what works for one organization may not necessarily work for another, so benchmarking, too, has its limits.

Total quality management (TQM)

As indicated by its name, TQM is an approach to quality enhancement that permeates the whole organization.

TQM can include quality circles and benchmarking, as well as *kaizen, kanban,* and *andon*. All these quality tools are not mutually exclusive; they may be combined and integrated in a wider framework of TQM.

Some other possible features of TQM are outlined in Table 5.3.2.

Table 5.3.2. Other features of TQM

Feature	Purpose
Quality chain	As the quality of a business depends on the quality of its suppliers and after-sales service, all stages of the production process must have concern for quality. A possible way to consider this is by imagining that the next part of the chain is the final customer.
Statistical process control (SPC)	All stages of production are monitored and information is given to all parties, usually in the form of easy-to-understand diagrams, charts, and messages.
Mobilized workforce	All employees (at all levels of seniority and in all departments, even the ones not directly in contact with products or customers) are expected to embrace TQM. Everyone is encouraged to feel pride in their work, given responsibilities and recognition, for example through employee of the month schemes – so everyone is included in the quality decision-making process.
Market-oriented production	By focusing on what the customer wants, the business can make sure that it is innovating and continually reinventing its products. This can lead to improved sales and brand loyalty.

Student workpoint 5.11

Be knowledgeable

Read the text below and answer the questions that follow.

Mattel in China

Mattel has recalled more than 18 million toys worldwide, the second such recall in two weeks.

Chinese-made Sarge die-cast toys from the Pixar film *Cars* have been recalled because their paint contains lead. Mattel has also recalled toys containing small magnets that can come loose, including Polly Pocket, Batman Magna, Doggie Daycare and One Piece playsets. Previously the company had recalled Dora The Explorer dolls' houses.

The Consumer Products Safety Commission (CPSC) said it had no reports of any injuries from the recalled products.

1. Outline the possible costs to Mattel of recalling its toys. (2 marks)

2. Explain what may be the costs of not recalling the toys. (4 marks)

3. To what extent would a system of TQM help Mattel overcome this type of problem in future? (8 marks)

Key terms

Lean production

a Japanese approach to operations management focusing on less waste and greater efficiency

Kaizen

a method of lean production based on continuous improvement

JIT

"just-in-time": a method of stock control which means avoiding holding stock by being able to get supplies only when necessary and to produce just when ordered

JIC

"just-in-case": holding reserve of both raw materials and finished products in case of a sudden increase in demand (or of a problem in production or in the supply chain)

Kanban

a system of messages (written or electronic) to help manage production flows and JIT delivery

Andon

a system of signals and alerts informing workers of a problem that requires immediate attention

Cradle-to-cradle design and manufacturing

a recent approach to design and manufacturing based on principles of sustainable development, especially recycling

Lean production and TQM are closely linked. Lean production focuses on less waste and greater efficiency, TQM focuses on quality assurance and quality enhancement. For a company, implementing lean production and TQM has many advantages:

- It can create closer working relationships with all stakeholders (including suppliers and customers).

- It can motivate the workers.

- It can reduce costs (especially long-term costs).

- It can improve the design and production of quality products.

- It can enhance the reputation of the company.

However, implementing lean production and TQM has some disadvantages too:

- It is costly (especially in the short term).

- Staff may need significant training.

- It may take time to change a corporate culture.

- It can create a lot of stress on formal relationships in the business.

- It is difficult to maintain over a long period of time.

TQM and lean production are more commonly used by businesses that are new or looking to make significant changes to retain their competitive advantage. However, many long-established businesses now also understand that their traditional approaches to operations (including production and quality control) may be too costly, and that they need to make changes to ensure their economic sustainability.

National and international quality standards

An excellent way for businesses to assure the consumer of the quality of their products is by gaining certification for recognized quality standards. At national or, even better, international level, a certificate is a mark of assurance that the product has met certain minimum requirements. International standards are set by organizations such as the IOS (International Organization for Standardization) or the EU (European Union). The most common standards published by the IOS are the ISO9000 family, which certifies quality management systems in organizations (for example ISO9001).

The problem of national versus international certification is a complex one. For example, in 2007 a Chinese producer manufacturing toothpaste for an international brand satisfied national regulations but failed international safety standards, as the toothpaste was found to contain chemicals not accepted by the international standards.

Meeting recognized standards can be very favourable to a business because it can:

- enable exports (market development abroad)

- give a competitive edge

- save on the costs of withdrawing products

5 Operations Management

- act as an insurance
- bring better profit margins.

Revision checklist

✓ Lean production is an approach to operations management which aims to cut waste and promote maximum efficiency.

✓ The continuous improvement method of lean production involves continuous change, as opposed to occasional changes. This approach must include all levels of hierarchy and focusses on the process rather than the end product.

✓ The just-in-time method (JIT) reduces the amount of stock held by ensuring products are made only when ordered.

✓ *Kanban* is a system which supports JIT. It aims to ensure a steady flow of production, without any waste.

✓ *Andon* refers to a signal which will inform workers of a problems in the production process. It allows problems to be identified and resolved as quickly as possible.

✓ Cradle-to-cradle design and manufacturing is the concept the once products are used, they should be entirely recycled to create the same product again.

✓ Quality control and quality assurance should ensure that products and services are reliable, safe, durable, innovative and offer value for money.

✓ Quality control involves inspecting finished products to check they meet the desired level of quality.

✓ Quality assurance is a system of setting and monitoring quality standards across the whole production process.

✓ A quality circle is usually a group of volunteers who meet to discuss ways of improving quality.

✓ Benchmarking involves comparing products or services against the products or services of competitors.

✓ Total quality management (TQM) is an overarching approach to improving quality. It can include a combination of different quality tools.

Location of production

One of the most important decisions a business has to make is where it will locate or, as the business grows, where it should **relocate** to. Organizations must consider several factors when deciding where to start up or where to move to.

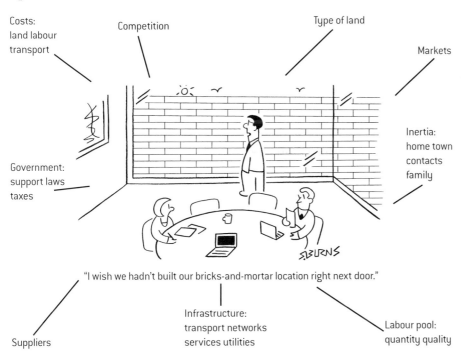

Figure 5.4.1 Factors to consider when starting up or relocating a business

Factors in locating a business

There is a distinction between setting up a business for the first time and moving the business to a new location. However, many of the same factors have a bearing in both cases. The main difference involves the objectives of the company at that particular time. Setting up may be simply to get started, but relocation can be for a number of reasons,

5 Operations Management

such as expanding or following the market; the business might also go through a merger and need a new, larger premises.

Costs

Costs will be a key determining factor and will largely depend on the type of business being started or relocated. Costs may well arise from the following, for example:

- **Land** – if the business is a large manufacturer, it may need a large, flat surface area, whereas a small home-based office may only require a spare room.

- **Labour** – if the business is a technical one (such as a laboratory) requiring skilled workers, the biggest cost may be labour.

- **Transport** – if the business is producing large quantities of a physical product, transport costs could be crucial. Two options are possible:

  - If the business is **bulk increasing** (i.e. buying in many components and building something bigger, such as televisions or cars), it may make sense to set up the business close to the market, as transporting the finished bigger items would be more expensive than bringing in lots of small components.

  - If the business is **bulk decreasing** (i.e. buying in large quantities of raw materials and turning them into smaller end products, such as happens at paper mills or slaughterhouses), it may make sense to set up the business close to the source of the raw materials.

Competition

Where are competitors located? A balance needs to be made between finding a gap in the market and setting up not far from the direct competitors. Retail outlets, theatres, law firms, and many more businesses often set up close to their rivals, as the chances of getting passing trade increase if the area becomes known for a particular product. Sometimes, some companies (such as chains of coffee shops) adopt a system called **cannibalistic marketing** whereby they set up more than one branch in a location (such as shopping mall); they may keep on opening more branches in the same sector, even though each new branch eats up some of the profits of the existing outlets (hence the word "cannibalistic"), until eventually there are so many outlets that there is no more possible extra trade to be generated.

Type of land

Different types of land will not only incur different costs, but will also vary in their suitability for the business in question. For example, some ski resorts may have been popular and successful in the 20th century, but with the onset of climate change and global warming, those locations might not be appropriate any more, if there is not enough snow for skiers. Importing artificial snow could be an alternative, though skiers (consumers) may prefer to go elsewhere.

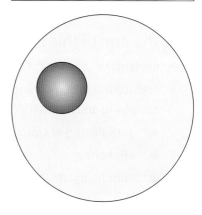

The outer circle is a city. The small circle is the first franchise and its sphere of influence (where its customers come from).

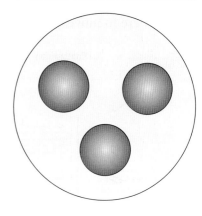

So another outlet is opened and as yet there is no problem—so another outlet is opened…

… until eventually although the franchisor (for instance, Starbucks) is doing OK—the company is covering lots of the market—the individual franchisee find themselves losing custom.

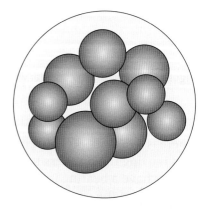

Figure 5.4.2. Cannibalistic marketing

Markets

In the past, for centuries, many businesses had to set up close to their customers. There were even sometimes special markets set up for special products, or general marketplaces (such as the great bazaars in North Africa and the Middle East, for example Damascus, Marrakesh, Aleppo, and Istanbul). With e-commerce, the need for a physical marketplace has changed, which may bring considerable advantages to start-up Internet companies. Rather than depending on a physical market, they may require only an efficient distribution system.

The Grand Bazaar, Istanbul – one of the largest and oldest markets in the world

Familiarity with the area

Often, new businesses are set up in the place that the owners are familiar with. This sense of inertia has advantages and disadvantages. On the one hand, it means that the business owners may already have some knowledge of the local networks (for example possible suppliers and customers, on whom they may have done some research). On the other hand, it means that they may let pass a more appropriate venue in another area (for example with better access to suppliers or distribution networks). Setting up in your garage may cut down on costs, but it will also restrict your ability to expand.

Labour pool

Critical to any business are its workers. Whether the business requires university graduates or school leavers, most businesses need to take account of the type of workers available and balance this with the skills and qualifications needed for all the business operations. In a more strategic perspective, demographic change could make considerable differences to the type of workers available – not only in the present but also in years to come. For example, the increasing number of women in the workplace – and higher up in the workplace – means that more and more businesses have to adapt to part-time working, job sharing, flexitime and the provision of crèche facilities. Linked to the labour pool, another point to consider is the level of unemployment in the area, as this may be a good indicator of possible savings on salaries: a higher unemployment level could mean that more people may want to become employed, even on a low salary.

Infrastructure

Infrastructure refers not only to the existing transport networks for people and products, but also to electronic networks (for example telephones, computers, Internet, and all forms of digital communication). In a broader sense, other factors and facilities may need to be taken into consideration, for example regarding the provision of services such as education, housing, health care, and police, as well as utilities such as power and water. Access to services is important for the business, as this may affect the welfare and motivation of staff. If staff have to be relocated, this could become a major issue. Besides, as many people become more environmentally conscious, the extent of a company's carbon footprint may also have to be weighed against ease of distribution.

Suppliers

The availability of a range of good, reliable local suppliers may also be very important for the business, especially if it is using the JIT system of stock control (Unit 5.3), which implies a greater degree of coordination than otherwise.

Government

The role of both local and national government can be crucial for a business, especially for a new business or one that is considering locating in a deprived area: in many cases, governments may offer some support (resulting in significant savings). This could be through grants (non-returnable, one-time only funds) or subsidies (funds to be offset against the cost of production), soft loans (loans at preferential rates of interest), or even tax rebates (a cut in the tax to be paid).

- **Laws** – from labour laws and health and safety regulations, to rules on advertising, and restrictions on sales, laws are crucial for businesses. Businesses have to be careful because laws do change. Even if there is no regime change, there may well be a change in government policy. Even minor local changes (for example to traffic rules or hours of delivery) could have a major impact on a business (especially with a JIT method of stock control, if delivery is only possible at some restricted hours).

- **Taxes** – the amount of money a business is liable to pay in tax will have a major effect on where a business may wish to locate. Businesses are more highly taxed in some countries (especially developed countries) than in others, with different types of taxes. They include national corporation tax and local council taxes for the business itself, income tax for the employees, capital gains tax for the owners, and even variable taxes and duties payable by the customers. All of these will have a major impact not only on the amount of business the company can conduct, but also on how much profit can be retained and reinvested – and that, too, may be taxed.

National, regional, or international

The progress in communications over the past 100 years has led to major changes in where businesses set up. In the past, businesses were initially local, serving their immediate vicinity. However, as it has become easier to communicate and transport large volumes of materials, many businesses, when locating or relocating, do not only think first in terms of their own locality. There may well be regional differences which still ensure that domestic businesses can locate within a certain area, but the distinction between local, domestic, regional, and even international is changing. Besides, the increasing importance of regional trading blocs (such as the EU, Mercosur and NAFTA) has had a major impact on location decisions. For example, Nissan built a car factory in the north of England to circumvent the EU import duties. A final factor is the growth of trading hubs such as Hong Kong, Singapore, and Dubai, as these can seem good options for a business wanting to set up a regional base or to access global transport networks.

The impact of globalization on location

The impact of globalization on location decisions is best analysed in terms of "push factors" and "pull factors", affecting the four areas of:

- operations management
- marketing
- HR
- finance.

Pull factors

Setting up or relocating abroad is an attractive option for many businesses for the following reasons, presented in terms of pull factors:

- improved communications
- dismantling of trade barriers
- deregulation of the world's financial markets
- increasing size of multinational companies.

Improved communications

Nowadays, it is far easier not only to transport products around the world, but also to communicate with suppliers, customers, or co-workers, irrespective of their own locations and time zones.

Dismantling of trade barriers

More than three-quarters of the world's countries are signatories to the World Trade Organization (WTO). The WTO has a commitment to reducing trade barriers, which makes it far easier for trade to take place across borders. China became a member of the WTO in 2000 and since then it has exploded on to the world stage, with US and European companies setting up in China. With the money earned, China is now starting to acquire foreign banks and manufacturers, and it is even sponsoring football teams; so are other countries, such as Qatar, which has a reputation that will keep growing.

Deregulation of the world's financial markets

The deregulation of the world's financial markets has made the transfer of vast sums of money very easy, which has facilitated quicker start-ups for many businesses. Again, the rise in Internet banking has made it much easier to keep track of company finance and, allied to the digitization of the world's financial markets, it is much more common for investors to cross borders. This, again, helps to build up collaboration such as forming joint ventures and strategic alliances, or working with venture capitalists.

Increasing size of multinational companies

The size, and consequently the influence, of the world's biggest companies (conglomerates) makes it easier for them to persuade countries to allow them to set up. The enormous power and influence of multinational companies can create momentum for other businesses in the same field. For example, the impressive growth of the Chinese influence in Africa may have been driven by the need for raw materials, but itself has generated interests in other areas.

Push factors

As well as these external factors, there are a number of internal factors that may help push companies (especially companies that are already multinational) to operate overseas. They may be able to:

- reduce costs
- increase market share
- use extension strategies
- use defensive strategies.

Reduce costs

By setting up production facilities abroad, businesses may be able to reduce costs by moving closer to the raw materials or using cheaper labour, so they may be able to achieve **productive economies of scale**. They may also be able to take account of more favourable tax regimes, and so achieve **financial economies of scale** as well.

Increase market share

By opening up business in a new country, many organizations hope to tap into a new market (market development in the Ansoff matrix – see Unit 1.3); there are, however, some risks and disadvantages to bear in mind, such as:

- language barriers
- different cultural practices and etiquette
- historical tensions between countries
- lack of knowledge of local or regional networks
- local law and politics, especially labour law
- time differences and the challenges of working across many time zones
- possible challenges in finding reliable, trustworthy partners.

The rewards can, however, be extremely high, especially if the business has **first mover advantage** in a large market. This partly explains the rush by many big-name companies to China and India, with over 1 billion potential customers in each country.

Use extension strategies

Some businesses may have even reached the saturation point for their product and may be looking to extend the **life cycle** of their product. McDonald's, one of the leading players in the US fast-food industry, has found increasing competition not only from other burger outlets, but from pizza suppliers, sandwich bars, and Mexican and other fast-food outlets. This increased competition has had a major impact on McDonald's profits and, being a **market leader**, McDonald's has also

been one of the hardest hit by bad publicity and by increasing awareness of obesity and the dangers of overindulging in fast food. To counter this, McDonald's has made major strategic changes. The company has introduced healthy food options, diversified into coffee, published its nutritional values, and reduced the fat and salt content in its foods. Besides these general strategies, McDonald's has also targeted areas where people are more likely to appreciate the service it provides. Of the 35 000 McDonald's restaurants worldwide, more than two-thirds are now outside the United States.

Use defensive strategies

Many businesses make the decision to move overseas, not so much because they need to, but because they do not want their competitors to do it first. Growth and expansion are key drivers for businesses, and the fear that rivals might steal a lead can act as a catalyst for locating overseas. The rush for oil companies to set up in Central Asia to secure oil and gas reserves is a recent example, and so is the emergence of China as a big player in Africa, as China has felt the need to secure the supply of raw materials to feed its growing industries.

Outsourcing (sucontracting) and offshoring

Outsourcing (subcontracting) refers to the practice of using another business (as a third party) to complete part of the work (literally, subcontracting refers to the idea of contracting out work). This can enable the organization to focus on its core activity, by employing another business. A school, for example, would regard teaching as its core activity – and it could then outsource other services, such as:

- catering
- transport
- administrative duties and examination invigilation
- excursions, visits, and expeditions
- staff recruitment and training
- security
- cleaning and maintenance.

Student workpoint 5.12

Be an inquirer

Does your school outsource (subcontract) some of its services? You may not even realize it! What are the advantages and disadvantages for your school?

Outsourcing can help a business cut costs (and consequently lower prices) in order to earn a competitive advantage. Traditionally, a business may have had a number of activities happening on a day-to-day basis, many of which may not have been part of the core business skill sets, so they become transferable and thus a saving for the business. By buying in these peripheral services from producers (who can achieve economies

Key terms

Outsourcing or subcontracting

the practice of employing another business (as a third party) to perform some peripheral activities (this enables the organization to focus on its core activity)

Offshoring

the practice of subcontracting overseas, i.e. outsourcing outside the home country

5 Operations Management

of scale because they are specialists in that particular service), the main business can reduce costs.

Figure 5.4.3 provides a visual representation of the link between core and peripheral activities, particularly their costs. The peripheral activities could be provided at a lower cost by an external provider – and possibly with a better result, as that third party would be a specialist.

We have already seen (in Unit 2.3 in the context of the HR plan) examples of activities that are commonly outsourced:

- in **marketing** – using an advertising agency
- in **production** – for example, licensing a producer to make your product
- in **HR** – employing an agency to "headhunt" potential staff
- in **finance** – hiring accountants to run an external audit.

Outsourcing can bring many advantages:

- It can reduce costs by losing employees and other assets.
- It can allow the business to focus on its core activities.
- The quality of the core products or activities should improve, as the business may now focus on them.
- It can lead to improved capacity utilization.
- Delivery time can be reduced.
- It can lead to transfer of expertise.

Outsourcing, however, also has disadvantages:

- The business becomes more dependent on the supplier (reliability, for example for deliveries, could be an issue: what if the transporters go on strike?).
- The business has less control of the final product (what if a key component is not at the expected standard?).
- Dilution of the brand could be a problem (if the consumer realizes that product "x" is not produced by company "y").

Offshoring is an extension of outsourcing: in the case of offshoring, a business outsources outside the home country (this is the meaning of "offshore"). With improved global communication, this has been a growth area in the modern business environment. India, for example, has seen a massive growth in IT offshore contracts, such as call centres and help desks signed up with Western businesses.

All the advantages and disadvantages of outsourcing apply – but the international aspect usually intensifies them, in particular as follows:

- There may be cultural differences between the companies, both in terms of national cultures and corporate cultures.
- Communication could sometimes be difficult (especially when people have to deal with different languages and time zones).
- There may be issues of quality and ethics (for example use of sweatshops).

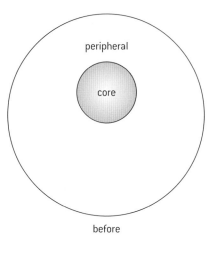

before

after

Figure 5.4.3. Core and peripheral elements

In-housing and reshoring

A recent trend can be observed in the business world: some companies have now started to reverse outsourcing, to stop this approach and to start performing peripheral activities internally again. This is the opposite of outsourcing: it is called in-housing (or insourcing, literally meaning "in the house", "at source"). This is the opposite of outsourcing (subcontracting). The business decision to stop outsourcing may be motivated by the desire to regain full control, or to reduce costs of taxes, labour, and transportation.

The word "reshoring" (or "backshoring") refers to the practice of taking back jobs lost to subcontracting overseas, in order to refocus on the quality end of the market. This is the opposite of offshoring. This is a new trend in the international business world and it is too early to evaluate the extent to which reshoring will fully affect manufacturers.

Revision checklist

✓ Locating a business will depend on multiple factors including costs, competition, type of land, labour pool, infrastructure, government, proximity to suppliers.

✓ Outsourcing is the practice of using another business to complete part of the work.

✓ Offshoring is an extension of outsourcing, which involves contracting with a business in another country.

✓ In-housing is the reverse of outsourcing. It is when organizations choose to bring outsourced activities back into the main business.

✓ Reshoring is the opposite of offshoring. Activities may still be outsources, but they are outsourced in the home country, rather than overseas.

TOK discussion

- What ways of deciding where to locate their production do business leaders use?

- Can business leaders always anticipate the impacts of decisions to relocate?

- Do you think the recent shifts to insourcing and reshoring were predictable?

5 Operations Management

By the end of this chapter, you should be able to:

→ comment on the supply chain process

→ distinguish between just-in-time (JIT) and just-in-case (JIC)

→ interpret a stock control chart (especially the buffer stock, reorder level, reorder quantity, and lead time)

→ calculate a capacity utilization rate

→ interpret productivity rates

→ distinguish between cost to buy (CBT) and cost to make (CTM).

The supply chain process

The supply chain refers to the wide system of connected organizations (for example suppliers), information (such as orders), resources (for example raw materials), and operations (for example transport) that a business needs to produce goods and provide services to its customers.

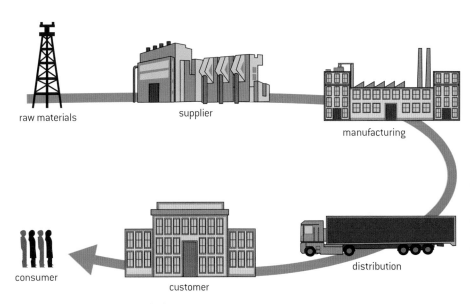

Figure 5.5.1. The supply chain process

In terms of operations, two flows have to be managed:

1. The flow from raw materials to the finished product purchased by the end customer, via the different stages of manufacturing.

2. The flow of information (from consumer to supplier, especially orders with specifications).

So the supply chain has two dimensions:

1. Logistics (the "hardware" of the supply chain: this is well illustrated by the trucks transporting raw materials to a factory, or the shipments ready to leave the warehouse).

2. Information and communication (the "software" of the supply chain: this is well illustrated by the database and spreadsheets used by the administrative staff of the organization).

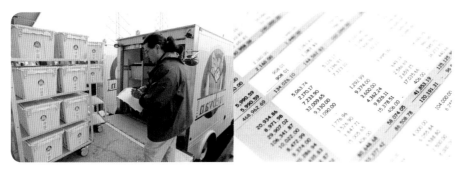

Two flows of the supply chain

Supply chains are often presented through networks or flowcharts, linking together the organizations involved, as illustrated by Figure 5.5.3 where some distribution channels have been included as well (a wholesaler and a retailer, as studied in Unit 4.3).

Key terms

Supply chain

the system of connected organizations, information, resources, and operations that a business needs to produce goods and provide services to its customers

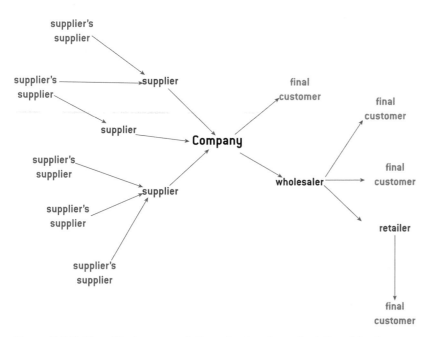

Figure 5.5.3. Simplified representation of networks and relationships in a supply chain

Figure 5.5.3 is a simplified representation of the complexity of networks and relationships involved. If the supplier of a supplier is not able to deliver its product, it may block the entire chain. The final customer

5 Operations Management

may be left waiting for the spare part of a good (for example the door seal of a washing machine or the metal blade of a lawnmower), being increasingly dissatisfied with the manufacturer of the washing machine or the lawnmower – and yet the responsibility lies elsewhere, as the manufacturer might well be dependent upon its own supplier, or its supplier's supplier. When considering the whole supply chain process, stock control becomes particularly important: when businesses start operating the just-in-time (JIT) method of stock control, they are unlikely to have the necessary buffer stock to deliver, which may create problems in the supply chain.

Just-in-time (JIT) and just-in-case (JIC)

Unit 5.3 introduced JIT as a modern method of stock control in the perspective of lean production, and its traditional counterpart JIC.

Reminder of definitions

JIC ("just-in-case") is the traditional method of stock control which means holding reserve of both raw materials and finished products in case of a sudden increase in demand (or of a problem in the supply chain).

JIT ("just-in-time") is a modern method of stock control which means avoiding holding stock by being able to get supplies only when necessary and to produce just when ordered.

There are arguments in favour of each method but the current trend is in favour of JIT methods. Table 5.5.1 shows the main differences between JIT and JIC.

Table 5.5.1. The main differences between JIT and JIC

JIT	JIC
Stock is only brought in from suppliers as and when required. The aim is to hold low (even zero) levels of stock.	Stock is brought in and stored with a reserve (the buffer stock) and kept back from daily use just in case of need.
JIT is beneficial for the working capital – the business can use more of its money for its day-to-day activities.	JIC reduces pressure on the cash flow.
JIT reduces costs (storage and wastage).	JIC reduces costs (by buying in bulk).
JIT reduces the chance of holding stock that cannot be sold (for example obsolescent stock).	JIC means that you can meet sudden changes in demand.
JIT means less chance of damaged or ruined stock.	JIC provides spare parts too.
JIT creates more space for alternative production plans.	JIC means that all stock is stored – ready to use. There is a delivery issue and no waiting for customers.
JIT creates a closer relationship with suppliers (they may need to run JIT too).	JIC has the advantage that suppliers will not charge a premium price.

Key terms

JIT

"Just-in-time": a method of stock control which means avoiding holding stock by being able to get supplies only when necessary and to produce just when ordered

JIC

"Just-in-case": a method of stock control which means holding reserve of both raw materials and finished products in case of a sudden increase in demand (or of a problem in the supply chain)

Student workpoint 5.13

Be reflective

Building a Boeing 747

The manufacturing of a Boeing 747 is done in seven stages, which take on average six months to complete in total. The engines are bought from a supplier (Rolls Royce) for the sixth stage, as buying them and storing inventories for five months would be expensive. The engines cost approximately US$10 million each.

Generally, Boeing can sell a 747 for US$200 million.

Question:

Does Boeing use JIT or JIC? Why?

Figure 5.5.4.

Stock control

The question of holding stock raises two issues in terms of cost:

- on the one hand, the cost of not having stock when required (for example the cost of lost orders and expensive emergency deliveries)

- on the other hand, the cost of holding too much stock (especially the cost of storage and damage).

We can combine these two sets of costs in Figure 5.5.5.

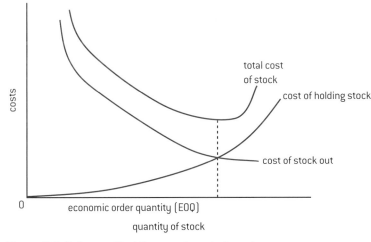

Figure 5.5.5. Costs of holding stock and of stock out

- Cost of holding stock – if we do not have any stock, there is no cost, but then the cost rises as we store more and more units.

- Cost of stock out – if we have a small amount of stock, then the cost of having a sudden surge in demand could be substantial, but this will go down as more stock is ordered and bought in.

- Total cost – by combining the two sets of costs, we can see the minimum point of the total cost. This is called the "**economic order quantity**" (EOQ); it is the amount that should be ordered for a given time period. The EOQ is one of the oldest calculations in the area of operations management and stock control.

5 Operations Management

The following seven elements of stock control are important yet easy to understand and remember:

- **The initial order**: the first amount of stock delivered, for example at the start of the year.

- **The usage pattern**: how much stock is used over a given time period. Is usage pattern regular or not? Are there some predictable highs and lows (for example for Christmas, Chinese New Year, school holidays)? In general, the stock is depleted over time and so is shown by a line with a negative slope.

- **The maximum stock level**: the maximum amount of stock held at any one time.

- **The minimum stock level**: the amount of stock that is kept back as a reserve, also called the **buffer stock**. The amount of stock should never go lower than this level (otherwise production of finished goods may not be possible, and customer orders cannot be fulfilled).

- **The reorder level**: the level at which stock has to be reordered (this is always a bit higher than the minimum stock level) as a form of trigger or signal.

- **The reorder quantity**: the amount of stock that is ordered.

- **The lead time**: the amount of time it takes between ordering new stock and receiving it.

A typical stock control diagram will look like Figure 5.5.6.

Key terms

Buffer stock

the minimum amount of stock that should be held (to ensure that production is still possible and customers' orders may still be fulfilled)

Reorder level

the level at which stock has to be reordered (a form of trigger or signal)

Reorder quantity

the amount of stock that is reordered

Lead time

the amount of time it takes between ordering new stock and receiving it

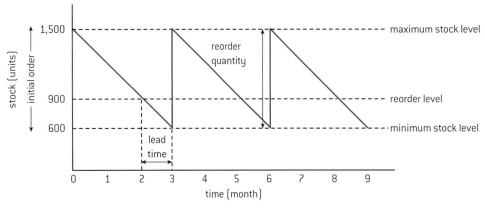

Figure 5.5.6. Stock control diagram

Imagine that the example shown in Figure 5.5.6 is a company selling smartphones on the Internet. The company may always want to keep a reserve of 600 smartphones just in case. The manager has calculated that, assuming no unforeseen changes in demand, he will run through 900 phones over a three-month period. After two months, he knows that stock will go down to 900 phones, which is his reorder level, when he decides to arrange for a new delivery of phones to be made from the company's suppliers. It takes one month for that reorder quantity of 900 phones to arrive and when they do the whole cycle is continued. This simple example assumes no unforeseen changes in demand, but usage patterns may be forecasted to take account of seasonal differences and occasional surges in demand. Businesses will often have software

to make those calculations and to establish the optimum reorder level and reorder quantity, but the basic diagram remains as shown in Figure 5.5.6. It is a very useful tool for managers to see where the stress points are likely to be and how to resolve them.

Optimal stock levels

In order for a business to calculate the optimal level of stock, several factors must be taken into account:

- **The market** – Is it growing? Is the business increasing sales? Are there any new organizations (competitors) coming into the market? Is the market share likely to shrink?

- **The final product** – What type of product is it? Is it a cheap, single-use, fast-moving, high-volume product or is it the opposite? Is it a complex product requiring many individual components? Does its production depend on many suppliers?

- **The stock** – Is it perishable? Is it likely to be out of date? How big is it? Will it take up much storage space?

- **The infrastructure** – Is it reliable, or is there a need to stockpile? Could the weather or other factors influence the ability of suppliers to meet demand?

- **The finance** – Does the business have the required money at the right time? What possibilities for credit do the suppliers allow? Are there going to be significant savings from buying in bulk?

- **The human resources** – What are the implications for resourcing changes in stock holdings?

Using the EOQ and stock control charts and diagrams, businesses may get some idea of the correct amount of stock to order and when, but overall it is difficult to judge precisely. Businesses should be aware that many factors can change, which creates more pressure, depending on the system that they are using. This partly explains why the JIT method of stock control requires greater coordination and cooperation with suppliers than the JIC system.

Capacity utilization rate

Production managers often want to know how efficient the facility is. Is it being used to its maximum capacity? For example, a hotel may want to know what the occupancy rate of its rooms is, a factory may want to know how often a machine breakdown affects the work done, or a school principal may want to know whether there is a chance to use the school's facilities more at weekends and holidays by renting the site out. It would be theoretically possible for a hotel to be full all year round, or a factory to work at full capacity (24 hours a day, 365 days a year), or a school to house a day school and a night school in the same buildings. In reality, though, there will be times when it is neither desirable nor suitable, for example for maintenance purposes: the hotel may need some slack time to refurbish the rooms, the factory may need time to upgrade the machines, the school may need to close on some holidays when no student would be willing to come. These simple examples show that it is usually impossible to achieve 100 per cent capacity utilization, though businesses will often aim to get as close as possible to this figure.

Capacity utilization can be calculated using the following equation:

$$\text{Capacity utilization rate} = \frac{\text{actual output}}{\text{productive capacity}} \times 100$$

For example, if a hotel has 100 beds, and on average 80 are filled, the capacity utilization is 80 per cent. Similarly, a factory might be able to produce a maximum of 100,000 pairs of shoes in a year, but it only has orders for 40,000. Its capacity utilization is 40 per cent. Finally, a school with sufficient space for 3,000 students but that has only 2,900 students has a 96.6 per cent capacity utilization.

Businesses that should aim for a high capacity utilization will be ones where profit margins are low, for example budget airlines or fast-food outlets. These businesses cannot afford to lose any opportunity to sell their product and so will need to market it accordingly. At the other end of the range, business-class travel or five-star restaurants will not need and may not wish to aim for high-volume sales.

Productivity rate

The productivity rate is another ratio that a manager would be interested in. It is a measure of the efficiency of production. In unit 5.1, Figure 5.1.1 showed the input–output model: the productivity rate is the ratio of output to input in production; it refers to the added value of the business.

$$\text{Productivity rate} = \frac{\text{total output}}{\text{total input}} \times 100$$

On its own, the productivity rate is very crude data; it needs to be contextualized, particularly in connection to the industry in which a business operates – ideally by establishing comparisons and benchmarks with competitors. For example, knowing that its productivity rate is 65 per cent would not help a factory manager much: is this low, is this high? Only when comparing it with the industry averages would the factory manager be able to make a judgment and possibly take action.

- If the productivity rate is (much) lower than the industry average, the manager should take remedial action; adopting a lean strategy could enable the factory to cut down on waste and to increase efficiency. Several factors and variables would have to be studied closely: maybe the input is too high, with too many inventory items that lose their value, cannot be used, and are eventually discarded. Maybe the output is too low, because of too many defects.

- If the productivity rate is higher than the industry average, the manager will be pleased with the efficiency of the company's operations. Nonetheless, the manager could decide to investigate how the factory could be even more productive, using its resources (raw materials, human resources, machines, energy) in a more efficient way.

Cost to buy (CBT) and cost to make (CTM)

One business decision is whether to buy or to make.

In unit 5.4 we discussed the decision to outsource (or even offshore) or not. A key factor, as always in business decisions, is costs: it may be cheaper for a business to buy a product made elsewhere, by specialists, rather than making it directly (and this applies to services too). The decision can be supported by using the costs and revenues formulae in unit 3.3 (costs and revenues) to create cost to buy (CTB) and cost to make (CTM) equations:

$$CTB = P \times Q$$
$$CTM = (VC \times Q)$$

For example, imagine that a small international school in South East Asia has to decide whether to subcontract the transport of students by bus, or to provide the service itself. If the school requires 20 buses and a company called School Run charges $10,000 per bus for the year, according to the formula

$$CTB = P \times Q$$

this service would cost the school:

$$\$20 \times \$10,000 = \$200,000$$

If, however, the school decides to buy the 20 buses from Dodgy Dealers Inc for $100 000 but faces variable costs of $10 000 per bus for fuel and the driver's wages over the year, then the cost to make the service using the equation

$$CTM = FC + (VC \times Q)$$

would be:

$$\$100,000 + (\$10,000 \times 20) = \$300,000$$

In this case CTB < CTM, so the school should outsource.

This simple example ignores some of the factors that may have a bearing on the supply chain. For example, how reliable is the company School Run? And how reliable are the buses bought from Dodgy Dealers? What are the implications of the school employing drivers as opposed to someone else doing so? Are there some legal issues involved? When deciding on what action to take, a business would also take qualitative factors such as these into account.

Supply chains should be kept on a short leash

Simon Caulkin, the Observer, 27 April 2008

The big business idea of the last 20 years is going rancid. Last week, Boeing's embarrassed chief executive announced the third major delay to its much-hyped 787 Dreamliner project.

Unbelievably, although nearly 900 of the aircraft have been sold, its profitability is in question as the firm's global **supply chain** cracks up. At the heart of the problem is the "Dell model" (after the computer manufacturer), applied to the project's funding and management. Industry researchers say that Boeing's attempt to minimise financial risks by maximising the number of development partners has had the opposite effect: outsourcing on this scale (80 per cent, including large and complicated components) has actually increased the risk of project and management failure.

Boeing should have paid heed to the experience of Dell, which posted a powerful warning on the dangers of paying more attention to the supply than the demand chain: being good at giving customers what they get is not the same thing as being good at giving them what they want.

But it's not only computer and aerospace companies that are learning these lessons. One automotive component maker was shocked to discover that parts arriving for final assembly in the US had spent up to two years shuttling between 21 plants on four continents—when it had only actually taken 200 minutes to make them. Much of the work was done in China to benefit from lower labour costs, but any advantage was more than offset by the costs of managing and scheduling inventory in the tortuous supply line. With hindsight, the China move was rated "a disaster".

Yet undeterred, service industries are now making exactly the same mistakes. In theory, since there is nothing physical to make or transport, services are ideal candidates for disembodied processing and reassembly by low-cost labour in foreign parts. But state-of-the-art call centres and distant graduates are quite often the wrong answer to the wrong question. A friend [in the UK] trying to get to Norwich [from the north of England] over Christmas spent ages on the phone to India working out how to do it without taking 24 hours [because of delays and cancellations]. When

he got to Liverpool Street the man on the spot told him: "Go to King's Cross, mate: trains to Cambridge aren't affected, then change for Norwich." Similarly, when your cable broadband is down, you don't need someone thousands of miles away reading from a script, but a spotty youth around the corner who will sort it out for £60 and a supply of cola or coffee.

Why do companies—and public-sector organisations—continue to get this so wrong, pursuing the will-o'-the-wisp of cost reduction with measures that end up increasing them? Aided and abetted by consultants and computer firms that should know better, they are prey to three management myths.

- One is **economies of scale**. Manufacturers and service outfits alike think they can cut costs by mass producing processes in vast specialist factories. They can't, because of all the unanticipated costs noted earlier: carrying and transport costs (for physical inventory) ramifying the possibility and consequences of mistakes, re-work (mopping up complaints about things not being done or being done wrongly), knock-on costs up and downstream, and finally the management costs of sorting it all out.

- The second myth is that there's no alternative because **quality costs more**. Yet quality—in the sense of giving customers what they want, no more, no less—costs less, not more. This is because if you do just that, a) you don't incur the cost of giving them what they don't want, and b) indirect costs fall too, since there are fewer mistakes to rectify.

- Third, companies habitually overestimate the coordinating power of markets (and thus the attractiveness of short-term outsourcing to India and China) and underestimate the role of organisation. But while the internet can undeniably cut the cost of some market coordination, for any complex task a good organisation can still out-compete what can be supplied unaided by the market—which is why we still have organisations in the first place.

For both products and services, the principles are the same. Supply chains should be as short as possible in both time and distance; small and local, from police stations and GPs' surgeries to banks and computer firms' call centres, almost always beats large and

remote. Expertise should be upfront, whether on the production line or the phone, where it can respond immediately to the customer. The title of a report from the Cambridge Institute for Manufacturing, "Making the Right Things in the Right Places", says it all: in a globalised, virtual world, location and supply-chain decisions are more critical, not less.

Exam-style questions

1. Define the terms in bold. [6 marks]

2. Explain how Boeing can "minimise their risk by maximising their development partners". [4 marks]

3. Discuss the costs and benefits to Boeing of outsourcing the 787 plane. [10 marks]

Revision checklist

✓ The supply chain is the system of connected organizations, information, resources and operations that allow a business to fulfil its business activities. It includes suppliers, distributors, retailers and customers.

✓ Just in case (JIC) is a traditional method of stock control which means holding a reserve of raw materials and finished products in case of a sudden increase in demand.

✓ Just in time (JIT) is a modern method of stock control which involves getting supplies only when necessary and producing only when an order is made.

✓ The capacity utilization rate is calculated by (actual output/productive capacity) × 100.

✓ The productivity rate is calculated by (total output/total input) × 100.

TOK discussion

- Is it possible to draw an exhaustive supply chain diagram?

- Are the capacity utilization rate and productivity rate always open to interpretation?

5.6 Research and development (HL only)

By the end of this chapter, you should be able to:

→ evaluate the importance of research and development (R&D) for a business

→ explain the importance of developing goods and services that address customers' unmet needs

→ distinguish between different types of innovation:

- product innovation

- process innovation

- positioning innovation

- paradigm innovation

→ distinguish between **adaptive creativity** and **innovative creativity**

→ examine how pace of change in an industry, organizational culture, and ethical considerations may influence research and development practices and strategies in an organization.

The importance of research and development

Research and development (R&D) is a form of innovation directly associated with the technical development of existing products or processes, or the creation of new ones. Large businesses spend vast sums of money on R&D, typically with a bespoke department specializing in R&D, with engineers and researchers whose creativity is essential for the organization. R&D is important in all industries, from pharmaceuticals to household goods, from electronics to space exploration – and also in sectors that might not be spontaneously associated with R&D, such as agriculture and fashion.

R&D is important as it can help extend the product life cycle by developing new ways to use existing products (such as increasing the functionality of a mobile phone) or by indicating new strategic directions for the company (such as when Apple branched off from PCs to iPods, iPhones, and iPads).

Student workpoint 5.14

Be a thinker

1. Is R&D only important for large businesses? Why?

2. At the start of the course, you studied the Ansoff matrix (Unit 1.3). How can you link R&D and the Ansoff matrix?

3. In the unit on marketing, you studied the BCG matrix (Unit 4.5). How can you link R&D and the BCG matrix?

There is no single best way of conducting R&D, but to be at its most effective R&D requires good planning, teamwork, communication, and leadership. There are a number of stages between thinking of an idea and launching a product. These stages are listed in Figure 5.6.1.

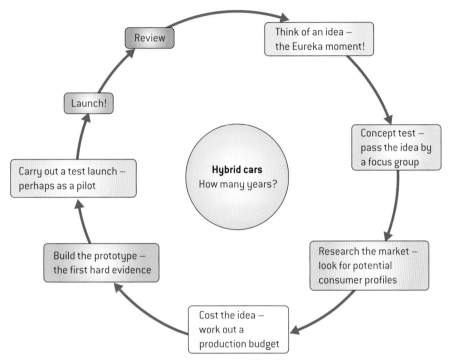

Figure 5.6.1. From thinking of an idea to launching a product

The process can take a very long time: for example up to 15 years for a new drug in the pharmaceutical industry (as different stages of testing and authorization are required). Many brilliant ideas do not get to the production stage because the product is deemed too costly, or the market does not seem large enough to make it viable.

Successful R&D can lead to many advantages for a business. It can:

- give the business a competitive advantage
- extend the life of an existing product
- open up new markets
- enhance the prestige of the company – being a known innovator
- motivate the workforce – designing new products, appearing at the cutting edge of innovation
- lead to improvements in quality
- reduce costs.

However, R&D is not without its problems:

- There may be opportunity costs – what else could the money be spent on?
- R&D may be in the wrong direction – as a new product does not mean there is a market for it.
- R&D is time consuming – the R&D workforce is tied to a project for years, without any ROI (return on investment) for the company during that time.

- R&D can be fiercely competitive – work on Blu-Ray versus HD-DVD, for example.

- R&D can become bureaucratic and non-productive – despite extensive R&D, how many new products do drug companies actually produce, for example?

- There may be ethical issues involved – for example with R&D involving genetically modified crops, stem cell research or animal experiments for cosmetics.

Marketing aspects of R&D

Innovation is essential for any business. Quality can be improved through methods such as *kaizen* or approaches such as TQM, but most businesses do not simply develop a product and then leave it unchanged for ever. Even Coca-Cola has modified its secret formula, for instance. If businesses fail to innovate, they may lose market share against existing competitors who innovate, or against new entrants with refreshing ideas and new products or services. In the BCG matrix of their product portfolio (see Unit 4.5), their "cash cows" may become "dogs".

R&D can also allow the business to find gaps in existing markets, or to open up new markets entirely. It is also important to develop goods and services that address customers' unmet needs, which is why the marketing department and the R&D department should work together. One of the key functions of market research is to identify customers' unmet needs, i.e. to spot business opportunities, for example for a new piece of software, a new book, or a new flavour of ice-cream. This information can then help the R&D department develop the items for which there is a market demand. This is a key premise of market orientation, as opposed to product orientation. The absence of a dialogue between the marketing and R&D departments could have unfortunate, costly consequences.

> **Key term**
>
> **R&D**
>
> a form of innovation directly associated with the technical development of existing products or processes, or the creation of new ones

Student workpoint 5.15

Be a thinker

These products were launched:

- edible deodorant

- canned whole chickens

- children's toothpaste in an aerosol

- tissues impregnated with vitamin C

- smokeless cigarettes

- garlic cake.

They didn't sell. Why do you think they didn't?

Marketing and R&D also overlap on the important issue of intellectual property rights. Those property rights fall into different categories: patents, copyrights, and trademarks. Their ownership by the business constitutes a valuable asset that needs to be protected; without this

protection, the business could lose its edge and the competition may be able to develop identical products.

Patents

When individuals or businesses invent products or production processes, they should take out a patent to protect their idea. Once the patent has been bought, it gives the individuals or businesses undisputed rights to exclude anyone else from making the product exactly to the specifications laid down in the patent, usually for a period of up to 20 years. After that time, the individuals or business can of course renew the patent. A patent on one product does not stop anyone producing similar products, but they must not be exactly the same (they must have different features). For example, Apple had to fight for the right to produce the iPod because Apple was alleged to have used the touch wheel technology from another producer, Quantum Research Group. The patent gives the inventor "first mover advantage". The Apple iPod has become an iconic market leader because of its head start.

Copyright

Copyright is similar to a patent. It originally applied to written material but has now been extended to cover other artistic forms of media presentations such as cartoons, music, and films. Again, the individual or business is protected for a period of time (for example 50 years) from the unlawful copying of the material. In our digital age, this has become a major source of concern for major record companies and film producers, especially with the introduction of file-sharing sites on the Internet.

Trademarks

A final form of intellectual property rights is that of trademarks. These are split into two general forms. Conventional trademarks include logos, slogans, designs, and phrases. The name Coca-Cola, for example, is protected by the symbol ™. There are non-conventional trademarks, which are qualities that are distinctive to the design, for example the Coca-Cola label, including the exact colour, match, and shape of the letters.

All these intellectual property rights help to ensure that the business can:

- have first mover advantage
- increase profit margins
- safeguard continuity of production
- develop brand loyalty
- have time to develop new products
- financially benefit from its creativity, innovation, and R&D.

Types of innovation

Although all innovations, by nature, are different, it is possible to distinguish between types of innovation. The two types of innovation that are the easiest to understand are about the product itself (**"product innovation"**) and about the way the product is made (**"process innovation"**).

- **Product innovation** is a type of innovation where new products are created, or improvements to existing products are made, for example producing flat-screen televisions or new models of smartphones. Product innovation refers to what an organization offers.

- **Process innovation** is a type of innovation where some parts of the manufacturing or service delivery are improved, for example with the JIT system. Just as production innovation refers to the "what" process, innovation refers to the "how".

In the case of services, the notion of "service innovation" may cover aspects pertaining to both "product innovation" and "process innovation", for example in e-commerce the ability for customers to track online the progress and location of an item they have purchased.

There are two further types of innovation. One refers to the use or perception of the product itself and is called **"positioning innovation"** or sometimes just "position innovation". The other refers to the impact the new product or service may have on the whole industry and is called **"paradigm innovation"**.

- **Positioning innovation** refers to the use or perception of a new product or service. The word "positioning" is not geographical: it is in the marketing sense of "in relationship to competitors", as with a product position map. The focus here is on the business environment and the competitive context. The most commonly cited example is that of Lucozade: it used to be a medicinal drink, until the organization producing it(the pharmaceutical giant GlaxoSmithKline) decided to reposition it (and rebrand it) as an energy sports drink in 1983.

- **Paradigm innovation** refers to an innovation so important that it may change the industry itself. The focus is on the impacts, both short-term and long-term, of the new product or service. For example, in the 1990s the advent of no-frills airlines and budget air travel created a massive change in thinking (and in travelling practice) by individuals, airports, and established airlines. It also spawned a whole set of new business opportunities, for instance the practicality of buying property in other countries (because travelling to them is much cheaper than in the past) or the organization of trips for final-year high-school students who travel as a group.

Product innovation, process innovation, positioning innovation, and paradigm innovation are called "the 4 Ps of innovation".

Key terms

Product innovation

a type of innovation where new products are created or improvements to existing products are made

Process innovation

a type of innovation where some parts of the manufacturing or service delivery are improved

Positioning innovation

an innovation in the use or perception of a new product or service

Paradigm innovation

an innovation so important that it may change the industry itself

Student workpoint 5.16

Be a thinker

1. Identify two examples of each type of innovation (product, process, positioning, paradigm).

2. Can you think of some innovations that are not easy to classify in those four categories? What does that show us about innovation – and about the meaning of the word itself?

Forms of creativity

Faced with a new situation or an unknown problem, what do you do? You could apply methods and approaches that you have used before, or you could try new methods and approaches, new ways of thinking. This is the case in mathematics and in science – and this is also the case for R&D. When chemists create new drugs to fight new viruses, when engineers develop an electric car, when marketeers design a new promotional campaign, they have to be creative – and that creativity may be described as **adaptive creativity** or **innovative creativity**.

- **Adaptive creativity** is a form of creativity that transfers and applies existing forms of thinking and problem solving to new scenarios or different situations.

- **Innovative creativity** is a form of creativity that generates new forms of thinking, addressing problems from an unusual perspective.

One form is not better than the other: they are complementary. They correspond to different creative styles: some people tend to display an adaptive style of creativity, and others an innovative style of creativity. The main characteristics of these two styles of creativity are summarized in Table 5.6.1.

Table 5.6.1. Main characteristics of both styles of creativity

Main characteristics of someone with the adaptive style of creativity	Main characteristics of someone with the innovative style of creativity
Takes a disciplinary approach	Takes a interdisciplinary approach
Shows systematic, linear thinking	Shows divergent thinking
Needs more structure	Needs less structure
Prefers incremental changes	Prefers radical changes
Solves problems by adapting, refining, and improving the current paradigm	Solves problems by breaking, modifying, and replacing the current paradigm
Thinks "inside the box"	Thinks "outside the box"

Student workpoint 5.17

Be a thinker

1. Can you think of recent examples when you have been an "adaptive innovator"? Can you think of recent examples when you have been a "creative innovator"?

2. It is sometimes said that adaptive creativity is about doing things better, whereas innovation creativity is about doing things differently. Do you agree? Why?

Factors affecting R&D

Numerous factors may affect the ability of an individual, a team, or a business to innovate successfully – and may influence the R&D practices and strategies of an organization.

- **Organizational culture** – if an organization has a rather low-risk, role-based, bureaucratic, or autocratic culture, innovation may then be very limited, as the fear of failure can outweigh the rewards of success; on the other hand, democratic or collaborative organizational cultures may foster risk taking and view creative input as a valuable resource.

- **Past experience** – a proven track record of innovative practices can help develop the expectations for future change and can act as an archive of "what has worked in the past". This is also called "path dependence"; it may shape and frame the R&D strategy of the organization.

- **Technology** – this can play a leading role in the development of ideas, especially with computer-assisted design (CAD) and the use of the Internet. For example, the collaborative nature of freeware (as "open-source software") has largely resulted from the ease of sharing ideas and practices in a supportive environment – hence the success of Mozilla Firefox and other freeware.

- **The pace of change** – some industries are more responsive to change than others. In high-tech industries, businesses may be less able to stay ahead of the market for long, as the pace of development is so fast. Other markets (for example for local, traditional goods and for services such as organizing weddings and craft fairs) are not affected in the same way.

- **The level of competition** – the more competition there is in a market, the more of an incentive there is for businesses to create the competitive edge brought about by innovation.

- **Finance** – the amount of finance available, and particularly the R&D budget, can limit the amount of innovation a business may be able to achieve.

- **HR** – tied into the availability of finance is the related field of available workers to innovate. The number of workers, their skill sets, and the amount of time allocated to innovation will all have an impact on their ability to innovate.

- **Legal constraints** – whether in the development stage or in the implementation stage of a product, there are many legal concerns that a business must take into account. Taking airlines as an example, whether it is possible for them to reduce the turnaround time of airplanes on the ground is dependent on labour practices. It will also vary from country to country.

- **Ethical concerns** – even when some innovations are possible legally, some stakeholders may have strong ethical concerns, for example about testing new cosmetic products on animals. Some companies such as The Body Shop and LUSH do not do animal testing of any kind. In turn, they use this stance for marketing purposes.

Given all of the above, the possibility for businesses to innovate successfully may be restricted; the number of businesses that come out with radical paradigm-shifting inventions is even more limited.

TOK discussion

What is the role of creativity, imagination, and emotion in a business context?

"Imagination is more important than knowledge." How can Einstein's famous words be reinterpreted in a business context?

Can one make an argument that the more people's needs and wants are met, the more difficult innovation is?

Is R&D a topic of business management, or a topic of science, design, and technology? Why?

However, any business has the capacity to make small-scale adjustments to improve productivity by adopting new techniques and innovative practices, as long as the resistance to change can be addressed.

Revision checklist

✓ Research and development allows organizations to develop new and existing products in an innovative way.

✓ Product innovation exists when new products are created or existing products are improved.

✓ Process innovation improves the manufacturing or service delivery process.

✓ Positioning innovation refers to the use or perception of a new product – where it sits in the market and how it is perceived.

✓ Paradigm innovation is a substantial innovation which could change a whole industry.

✓ Adaptive creativity transfers and applies existing forms of thinking and problem-solving to new scenarios.

✓ Innovative creativity generates new forms of thinking, addressing problems from a new perspective.

By the end of this chapter, you should be able to:

→ distinguish between between crisis management and contingency planning

→ explain the factors that ensure effective crisis management:

- transparency
- communication
- speed
- control

→ comment on the advantages and disadvantages of contingency planning:

- cost
- time
- risks
- safety.

Crisis management

When a major, unpredictable event occurs and threatens to harm an organization and its stakeholders, the organization faces a crisis. Crisis management refers to the systematic steps and efforts by the organization to limit the damage from a sudden crisis. Crises may be triggered by:

- **human activity** (such as the financial crises of 1929 and 2008)

- **industrial accidents** (such as the Bhopal gas tragedy of 1984, the Chernobyl nuclear disaster in 1985 and the BP Gulf of Mexico disaster in 2010)

- **natural disasters** (such as the Sichuan earthquake in China in 2008, the tsunami in north-eastern Japan in 2011 and the floods in Thailand in 2011).

Crises are not all of a global scale: on a small local scale, a crisis may be a sudden power cut (preventing the whole factory or someone's home office operating), a failure of the IT system of a company (or just the printer of the *kanban* cards), the illness of a key member of staff (the only one who knows how to reprogram a machine), an accident on the premises, or a gas leak in a nearby building (with the obligation to evacuate and consequently the impossibility to work on that day). The outcomes of a crisis may be major (such as a plane crash with human

casualties) or minor (such as a delay in delivering extended essays to an IB examiner). Any elements of the supply chain may be affected: a road block or some workers on strike may prevent the delivery of an essential component, thereby stopping the production flow. By nature, crises are unpredictable – and managers must then take action to limit the damage for their stakeholders.

Four related factors affect crisis management:

- **Transparency** – stakeholders will want to be kept informed of what is happening; staff, customers, and local residents will want to be sure, for example, that safety is the priority. Irrespective of its size and share of responsibility in the crisis, the business will need to be honest and tell the truth; this is part of its corporate social responsibility (CSR).

- **Communication** – senior managers will need to communicate in an objective way, despite the temptation to turn this into a media exercise in public relations (PR), with a possible bias and concerns for the reputation of the business rather than for the safety of all involved.

- **Speed** – managers will need to act promptly, both in their actions (for example in the factory or on the field) and in their communications (such as through a press conference or media release). This will be a particular challenge, as analysing the problem and evaluating possible solutions, before implementing one, may require more time than is available. A rushed decision will not always be the best one.

- **Control** – managers need to do their utmost to prevent further damage and keep the situation under control. Depending upon the crisis and its nature, this may be more or less feasible. This is about minimizing further impacts, be they environmental, social, or economic.

Contingency planning

Contingency planning refers to an organization's attempts to put in place procedures to deal with a crisis, anticipating it through scenario planning. Contingency planning is about being prepared, should the crisis occur for real. Although it is not possible to imagine all the possible crises, the most likely ones (for example fire) can be anticipated; set procedures can be written and rehearsed (such as a fire drill with evacuation of the premises). Contingency planning is comparable to a list of "what if…?" scenarios, with simulations and procedures in place.

For contingency planning, four factors are particularly important:

- **Cost** – contingency planning may be costly, both the planning process itself and the need to train staff to deal with a wide range of events and scenarios, from IT failure to accidents at work to terrorist attack. However, contingency planning is much less expensive than dealing with a crisis without it, not to mention the lawsuits that could follow.

- **Time** – just as contingency planning may be costly, it may be time consuming, again both in terms of planning and training. For example, health and safety legislation will vary from country to country; some members of staff may sometimes need, by law, to be trained and retrained in first aid and emergency response.

- **Risks** – contingency planning will have to assess a range of possible risks (to the workers, to the machines, to the company, and to other stakeholders, too, such as suppliers and customers). The degree and level of risks and hazards are also likely to change, so contingency planners will need to review their plans regularly.

- **Safety** – contingency planning hinges on the notion that safety must be the priority, which is why the number one aim of fire drills is to ensure that everyone would keep safe in the case of a real fire.

The key benefit of having people in a crisis management team who have prepared contingency plans is that the plans can be written when working on a theoretical, hypothetical crisis, as opposed to a real one. If a crisis occurs, and there is no contingency plan in place, it is likely that decisions will be made under great stress and urgency. In this situation, there is a chance that the wrong decision may be made. While members of the crisis management team will not be able to anticipate every crisis, the fact that they are a team and have a contingency plan means that they will at least be prepared. If the crisis that occurs is similar to one that has been simulated, the chances of the damage being limited are much greater.

Student workpoint 5.18

Be reflective

Imagine that there is an outbreak of a very virulent virus at your school – potentially fatal! The outbreak is totally unexpected and has occurred during the final IB examinations. All stakeholders want the school to remain open, and for students to attend school and sit their examinations.

Discuss the steps that could be taken to minimize the spread of the virus and enable the school to remain open and students to take examinations.

Key terms

Crisis management

the systematic steps and efforts by an organization to limit the damage from a sudden crisis

Contingency planning

an organization's attempts to put in place procedures to deal with a crisis, anticipating it through scenario planning

---

Case study

You think flying is bad now...

To fully appreciate the impact that soaring oil prices have had on the beleaguered airline industry in the US, consider that carriers spent around $60 billion on jet fuel in 2008—nearly four times what they paid in 2000. Airlines lose roughly $60 on every round-trip passenger, a slow bleed that meant losses of around $7.2 billion in 2008, the largest yearly loss ever.

Consolidation is likely

Experts believe that the crisis could profoundly reshape the industry in coming years. That means not only far fewer carriers than at present, but forcing the survivors to rethink every facet of how they operate, from ticket pricing to the very way they fly. "The problem right now is that no one knows where the

price of oil is going to fall down, says Darryl Jenkins, an aviation expert at Ohio State University. "Your planning becomes 'What do we do to lose the least amount of money?'"

Experts believe that any carrier that falls into Chapter 11 [a form of bankruptcy] will likely have to liquidate. That would probably include one or more of the major airlines. Historically, airlines have attracted sufficient funding to operate while restructuring, and new capital when they exit. It's not clear that current market conditions—high oil prices and credit-squeezed lenders—would allow that. Airlines with the financial muscle to step in—for example Southwest (LUV)—would be interested. Southwest has avoided major acquisitions and considers them a steep risk but clearly recognizes potential opportunity in a bankrupt rival. "It just gives the acquiring carrier a tremendous amount of flexibility to impose change that would otherwise be very difficult," says Southwest CEO Gary Kelly, whose company has remained profitable because of long-term fuel contracts.

European buyers

Analysts say liquidations could well leave an industry consisting of two dominant carriers, most likely the combined Delta (DAL)-Northwest (NWA) and perhaps a combined American (AMR)-Continental (CAL), along with a couple of discount players like Southwest. "I think the industry is going to look more like Europe—a couple of far-flung carriers and then a bunch of little guys," says Roger King, airline analyst for CreditSights, a New York-based institutional research firm.

The oil crisis may eventually prompt Washington policymakers to drop their long-standing resistance to foreign ownership of US carriers, leading to the first generation of truly global carriers. "The US airlines badly need more capital to survive, and the only players with the resources to buy in are the [cash-rich] European carriers. Why would Congress object to that?" asks Robert Mann, an industry consultant in Port Washington, NY.

That could give British Airways the opening for the acquisition of American it has long coveted, and a similar move by Lufthansa on either United Airlines or JetBlue Airways, in which it already owns a 19% stake. For all its aviation woes, the US remains the largest, most lucrative travel market in the world. "Don't you think BA would fall over itself to buy American Airlines for $1.6 billion?" King says. "That's peanuts to them."

Creative pricing

This consolidation will come with a cost. Experts believe that if surviving carriers are to earn a profit it will require hefty fare hikes and a 20–25% cut in capacity. That means fewer routes, fewer flights, and even more crowded planes. The biggest losers would be smaller cities like Cedar Rapids, Iowa, and Baton Rouge, Louisiana, that became accustomed to dozens of daily flights, usually on 50-seat jets. But oil priced near $130 rendered those smaller jets uneconomical, meaning that carriers are likely to fly one much larger plane on marginal routes each day, but no more. "We might keep one flight just to keep Congress off our back," muses one industry executive.

Coast-to-coast flights will change, too. With roughly 30% of the weight of any transcontinental flight consisting of the fuel alone, carriers can be expected to replace many of those longer non-stops with one-stop flights, intended largely for refuelling.

The era of cheap fares will end, too. Since deregulation in 1978, fares have fallen by more than 50% in real, inflation-adjusted terms. Prices will rise, and airlines will become even more creative in how they set fares, and take other steps to wring more cash out of passengers, as American did when it announced plans to charge $15 to check a bag. Even more classes of service will be sold. A premium will be charged, for example, for window or exit-row seats, and for separate check-in, boarding, and baggage-claim service for travellers willing to pay more to save time.

Technical upgrades

The fee changes and higher fares are likely to cull millions of travellers from the ranks of regular fliers, ending an era of $99 cross-country fares and bargain-basement weekend flights. It is also likely that a far larger array of travel products will be sold at airline websites, such as aggressive hotel packages and travel insurance.

But airline executives know that they could get far more significant savings if they could lower the costs of operating their current fleets of fuel-guzzling jets. Engineers working on Boeing's X-48 Blended Wing Project designed a jet that uses nearly 25% less fuel but the design limitations (no easy exit, nor windows for passengers to look out) mean that the planes are likely destined for military use.

Congress is being prodded to fund the long-stalled modernization of the FAA's air traffic control system, which still relies on 1950s-era radar. Replacing it with a GPS-based system could cost the government and industry a collective $47 billion, but airline executives say it could save the industry billions in fuel costs each year. If pilots could fly point to point, that could cut some flight paths by a third.

A lovely bunch of coconuts

Developing a GPS-based system could take a decade or more, and in the meantime airline executives are exploring ways to reduce their reliance on jet fuel, a kerosene-based oil that in mid-2008 cost roughly $4.09 a gallon, up 98% in a 12-month period. But developing an alternative hasn't been easy: jet fuels have to pack enough oomph to power jet engines and at the same time be dense enough not to freeze in the air at −40°C—a temperature that turns most biofuels into solids.s

But progress is coming. The Pentagon, which buys more aviation kerosene than any other group, has successfully tested a jet fuel made from liquefied coal. Airbus, meanwhile, is leading a consortium on a project to replace a third of jet fuel with advanced biofuels extracted from algae and plant oils. The efforts will help lower fuel costs and reduce dependence on crude oil.

In February 2008 Virgin flew the first-ever commercial flight powered by biofuels—a Boeing 747 running on a blend of oils from coconut and Brazilian babassu trees, produced by Seattle-based Imperium Renewables. "Two years ago, we thought this was pie in the sky," says Billy Glover, managing director of environmental strategy for Boeing's commercial division. "But things have evolved very rapidly. Our guess is that in five years we could have commercial biojet fuels on the market." Projected cost: around $2 per gallon, or a third less than current prices for aviation kerosene. Coupled with higher fares, biofuels would be cheap enough for airlines to turn a profit. These days, that'd be enough to make many an airline executive go out and collect the coconuts.

Source: Extracts adapted from: www.businessweek.com

Exam-style questions

1. Define these terms:

   a) crisis management [2 marks]

   b) contingency plan. [2 marks]

2. Describe three crises that you would expect an airline to have contingency plans for. [3 marks]

3. Outline the main contents of a contingency plan that an airline should have in place to deal with a major airplane crash. [8 marks]

4. Explain how rising fuel costs will affect the profit & loss account of an airline. [4 marks]

5. Outline two strategies that an airline could introduce to reduce costs. [4 marks]

6. Outline two strategies to increase revenue. [4 marks]

7. Discuss two strategies that airlines could put in place in anticipation of rising oil costs. [6 marks]

8. Evaluate the strategies that an airline could put in place to cope with rising oil costs. [10 marks]

Revision checklist

✓ Crisis management is a direct response to a specific, unpredictable event.

✓ Crisis management needs to be well-communicated, controlled and prompt (although not rushed).

✓ Contingency planning refers to an organization's efforts to minimise the negative effects of potential crises.

✓ Contingency planners must take account of cots, time, risks and safety.

TOK discussion

- Can a business plan for a crisis?

- Can the hypothetical scenarios of contingency planning be the same as a real crisis?

- Contingency planning uses scenarios (i.e. imagination) – so is there a place for imagination in business management?

6 ASSESSMENT

External Assessment

By the end of this chapter, you will know

→ the basic structure of external assessment in IB Business Management (for first examinations in 2016)

→ the meaning, importance, and definitions of examination command words

→ how to prepare for examination questions

→ how to answer examination questions

→ how IB examinations are marked.

Basic structure

At both Higher Level (HL) and Standard Level (SL), IB Business Management is assessed in three parts.

	HL	Weight	SL	Weight
External assessment	Paper 1 – seen case study	35%	Paper 1 – seen case study	35%
	Paper 2 - data response	40%	Paper 2 – data response	40%
Internal assessment	Research project	25%	Written commentary	25%

As the table above shows, Business Management has two external examinations at both HL and SL. The structure of these exams is shown in more detail here:

Higher Level				
Paper 1	Case Study	2 1/4 hrs	70	Section A—three out of four structured questions (30 marks)
				Section B—One compulsory evaluation question (20 marks)
				Note: Section B uses unseen material based on the case study
				Section C—One compulsory extended response question based primarily on HL extension topics. (20 marks)
				Note: Section C uses unseen material based on the case study.

Paper 2	Data Response	2 ¼ hrs	80	Section A—One out of two structured (numerical) questions (20 marks)
				Section B—Two out of three structured questions (40 marks)
				Section C—Students answer one of three extended questions. This question is based primarily on two concepts that underpin the course (20 marks)
Standard Level				
Paper 1	Case Study	1 ¼ hrs	50	Section A—Three out of four structured questions (30 marks)
				Section B—One compulsory evaluation question (20 marks)
				Note: Section B uses unseen material based on the case study.
Paper 2	Data Response	1 ¾ hrs	60	Section A—One out of two structured (numerical) questions (20 marks)
				Section B—One out of three structured questions (40 marks)
				Section C—One of three extended response questions based primarily on two concepts that underpin the course (20 marks).

Similarities and differences between HL and SL

The similarities between the examinations are more striking than the differences. In Paper 1, HL students have an extra section C, which draws on the HL only material in the syllabus. SL students have proportionately less time to answer the questions than HL students, which is indicated in the table below (this simply shows the time allocated for the paper divided by the marks available, to get minutes per mark.).

	HL	SL
Paper 1	1.92	1.5
Paper 2	1.69	1.31

Marking

The examination is marked holistically and marks are applied in bands. It is important to realize that it is not the number of points you make that determines the mark you get, it is **how** you answer the question.

Command terms

A crucial part of doing well on IB Business Management examinations is to understand the meaning, importance, and definitions of command words. Command words are the verbs in an examination question that indicate how you should approach the question and the depth of treatment you should provide. You can find the command terms in the subject guide. Knowing what the command terms are asking you to do will allow you to provide sufficient depth and prevent you from providing a longer or more detailed answer than is necessary, which may reduce the amount of time you have available to answer other questions.

The command terms used in each question indicate the depth required. These command terms are organized by assessment objective level in the subject guide as follows:

AO1—Demonstrate knowledge and understanding

AO2—Demonstrate application and analysis

AO3—Demonstrate synthesis and evaluation

AO4—Demonstrate a variety of appropriate skills

Levels AO1 to AO3 are of increasing cognitive demand, while the command terms in AO4 are specific to particular skills. Knowing the assessment objective levels and the command terms will allow teachers to know the depth of treatment needed in teaching and allow candidates to know the appropriate depth needed in responses to examination questions.

In the latest guide (for examinations beginning in 2016), the assessment objective levels are specified by AO1, AO2, AO3, and A04 rather than, as in the past, by particular command terms. You should note that:

- Examination questions could include any of the command terms from a particular assessment objective level. For example, if the assessment objective level for a topic is AO2, an examination question could contain any of the command terms for AO2, such as "explain", "distinguish", "interpret" and so forth.

- The examination question could contain a command term from a lower level of cognitive demand. So, if a concept in the syllabus is designated as AO2, a command term from AO1, such as "describe" could be used. However, a more demanding command term, such as "evaluate", from a higher level (AO3 in this case), cannot be used.

The table below, listing the command terms within each assessment objective level, is taken from the subject guide.

	Assessment objective	Key command term	Depth
AO1	Demonstrate knowledge and understanding	Define Describe Outline State	These terms require students to learn and comprehend the meaning of information.
AO2	Demonstrate application and analysis of knowledge and understanding	Analyse Apply Comment Demonstrate Distinguish Explain Interpret Suggest	These terms require students to use their knowledge and skills to break down ideas into simpler parts and to see how the parts relate.

| A03 | Demonstrate synthesis and evaluation | Compare
Compare and contrast
Contrast
Discuss
Evaluate
Examine
Justify
Recommend
To what extent | These terms require students to rearrange component ideas into a new whole and make judgments based on evidence or a set of criteria. |
| A04 | Demonstrate a variety of appropriate skills | Annotate
Calculate
Complete
Construct
Determine
Draw
Identify
Label
Plot
Prepare | These terms require students to demonstrate the selection and use of subject-specific skills and techniques. |

A definition of each term can be found in the "Glossary of command terms" in the appendix to subject guide.

Preparing for exams

To prepare for exams, candidates should learn the material in the syllabus up to the designated assessment objective level specified in the guide. Candidates should study this material in the context of numerous "real world" and, where appropriate, fictitious case studies. For HL and SL paper 2, section C, candidates must answer in response to a real-world business. Since candidates do not know the questions in advance of the exam, and since the examination questions can ask about any of the overarching concepts (see page 404), candidates should have detailed knowledge of several small, medium-sized, and large real-world organizations when they sit the exams.

Candidates should be familiar with the examination format, both the overall format and specific example questions. Teacher Support Material, including specimen papers, is available to IB teachers on the Online Curriculum Centre. In addition, schools may purchase past exam papers to use as practice. One benefit of using past examinations is that students get to practice the use of command terms and can see the markschemes written for the questions.

A common problem is that students sometimes memorize extended responses to certain types of questions (for example, the advantages and disadvantages of franchising). To examiners it appears as though these students regurgitate a memorized response after reading just a few words in the question (they see the word "franchising" and start to produce the memorized response). We strongly caution against this. Candidates need to answer the question they were asked exactly. Often, when students provide memorized responses without looking at the question, they get fewer marks than if they had provided a shorter answer that was properly focused on the question.

A similar caution needs to be made about studying from past exams, although we encourage the use of past exams as practice. Candidates need to be familiar with examinations, both their overall structure and various types of questions so that they know what to expect in terms of format, question type, and command word. However, studying from past examinations can be taken too far. If all candidates do is learn through past exams and practice past exams, they may not be genuinely learning about business but rather learning examination "tricks", strategies, and other methods to get more marks. Tricks and strategies constitute shallow preparation, which invariably comes out in the longer-response questions. Thus, our advice to teachers and students: use exams to know what to expect and to practice, but do not overuse them.

How to answer examination questions

In general, the most important points to remember when answering IB examination questions are:

- Answer the question exactly as asked
- Answer the question to the depth expected
- Do not "over-answer" a question (for example, don't provide an AO3 answer to an AO1 question)
- Structure your answers
- Provide balanced answers to AO2 and AO3 questions
- Know what is meant by evaluation (AO3)

The first three bullet points have already been covered in this chapter. We will now turn to the final three bullet points: structure, balance, and evaluation.

Structure

You will be rewarded for structuring your answers well. Two common, weaker structures which you should avoid are:

Bullet points: Unless the command term used is "identify", a bulleted response rarely helps an answer. Too often, bullet points are just lists that do not explain anything. If you use simple bullets or lists that do not explain your point when the command term asks for depth at AO2 or AO3, you will only score within the level 1 band of marks. A simple descriptive sentence also only scores within this band.

Unstructured response or stream of consciousness: Sometimes, students believe that they must say everything that they know about a subject and just start writing without thinking about (a) what they need to say and (b) how they should organize their ideas. In these circumstances, students tend to repeat themselves, contradict themselves, make digressions, or include irrelevant information. The IB follows "positive marking", which means, in the context of a business exam, they are awarding marks for relevant business knowledge and the understanding that you show. Whilst you are not necessarily penalized for poor English or for composition skills, when a candidate produces an entirely unstructured or stream-of-consciousness response, their writing has less force, meaning and persuasiveness. As a result, the depth of their understanding or knowledge may not be clear.

Aim to use structured paragraphs for your answers. Each new point deserves a new paragraph and every new paragraph builds on the one before it. Candidates should also produce balanced responses for responses to command terms AO2 and AO3.

Balance

What is meant by balance? It can represent several approaches but in general it refers to proving both sides of an answer. For example, balance is often achieved by providing:

- **Positives and negatives to a situation**. For example, a question such as "Analyze the decision of Company X purchasing environmentally-friendly cars?", asks candidates to consider the positive aspects of this decision (helps the environment, the positive public relations benefit of being environmentally friendly, etc.) as well as the negatives (the cars cost more, may have less power, be harder to service, etc.).

- **Two points of view**. Distinguish, when possible, different perspectives on an issue, such as from the perspective of the business owner and of the customer, of the workers and the manager, those employees in favour and those opposed, etc.

- **Providing "the extent to which" and the limits**. In Nov. 2013, on SLP2, one question was "Examine how branding may have contributed to the success of *Zeitim* restaurants." Top-mark answers addressed how branding contributed to the success of Zeitim and how other factors contributed (which, in effect, says that Zeitim's success was not entirely attributable to branding).

Evaluation

All examination papers will have questions that expect you to evaluate a course of action, which will be asked by way of A03 command terms: compare, compare and contrast, contrast, discuss, evaluate, examine, justify, recommend, and to what extent. When you see one of these terms, you should always include a separate concluding paragraph that gives an opinion. Just writing, "In conclusion" or "as we can see there are more advantages than disadvantages…" is not a substantial

evaluation. A substantial evaluation should take at least one of these points into consideration:

- short- versus long-term
- stakeholders
- pros and cons
- priorities

How IB Business Management examinations are marked

Both HL and SL paper 1, sections 1 and 2, will be marked in the same way as they have been in the past. Examiners will consult the markscheme and award marks according to its instructions. For longer response questions, examiners also use markbands, which can be found in the subject guide under "External Assessment." We strongly recommend that teachers and students consult past examinations and the Teacher Support Material, both of which are available from the IB.

What follows is (1) the method for marking HL paper 1, section C, and (2) the method for marking the new type of external assessment question, HL and SL paper 2, section C.

(1) Method for marking HL paper 1, section C

Section C will be marked with assessment criteria (identical conceptually to how internal assessments and extended essays are marked.) For HL paper 1, section C, the five assessment criteria are:

- **Knowledge and understanding of tools, techniques and theories:** This criterion addresses the extent to which the student demonstrates knowledge and understanding of relevant business management tools, techniques and theories as stated and/or implied by the question. This includes using appropriate business management terminology.

- **Application:** This criterion addresses the extent to which the student is able to apply the relevant business management tools, techniques and theories to the case study organization.

- **Reasoned arguments:** This criterion assesses the extent to which the student makes reasoned arguments. This includes making relevant and balanced arguments by, for example, exploring different practices, weighing up their strengths and weaknesses, comparing and contrasting them or considering their implications, depending on the requirements of the question. It also includes justifying the arguments by presenting evidence for the claims made.

- **Structure:** This criterion assesses the extent to which the student organizes his or her ideas with clarity, and presents a structured piece of writing comprised of: an introduction; a body; a conclusion; fit-for-purpose paragraphs.

- **Individual and societies:** This criterion assesses the extent to which the student is able to give balanced consideration to the perspectives of a range of relevant stakeholders, including individuals and groups internal and external to the organization.

A full description of each criterion can be found in the subject guide. Examiners will also receive marking notes in the markscheme for additional guidance on how to apply the assessment criteria.

(2) Method for marking HL and SL paper 2, section C.

This question will also be marked with assessment criteria. Questions in this section will focus on the six major concepts of that are the foundation of Business Management:

- Change

- Culture

- Ethics

- Globalization

- Innovation

- strategy.

Questions in Section C will focus on two of these concepts and students must use relevant content from the syllabus, including the HL extension if appropriate. Key features of this section include:

- Students answer one extended response question from a choice of three.

- No stimulus material is provided, only prompts (questions).

- Answers relate to one "real-world" organization that they have studied.

- In their response, candidates should consider the perspectives of individuals and societies in relation to the real-world organization they choose.

- Candidates may draw from other examples, include real businesses studied in class, IA research, or examples from stimulus in past exams. However, the real-world organization that students use in their response (second bullet point in this list) must not be the case study organization featured in paper 1.

- Each question will use an assessment objective level 3 (AO3) command term.

- Each question is worth 20 marks.

- Section C is worth a total of 20 marks.

For section C, marks are allocated using the following assessment criteria.

- **Knowledge and conceptual understanding:** This criterion addresses the extent to which the student demonstrates knowledge and understanding of the given concepts and relevant business management content (theories, techniques or tools, depending on the requirements of the question).

- **Application:** This criterion addresses the extent to which the student is able to apply the given concepts and the relevant business management content (theories, techniques or tools, depending on the requirements of the question) to his or her chosen real-world organization(s). The real-world organization(s) must not be the organization featured in the prescribed case study for paper 1.

- **Reasoned arguments:** This criterion assesses the extent to which the student makes reasoned arguments. This includes making relevant and balanced arguments by, for example, exploring different practices, weighing up their strengths and weaknesses, comparing and contrasting them or considering their implications, depending on the requirements of the question. It also includes justifying the arguments by presenting reasonable evidence or other support for the claims made.

- **Structure:** This criterion assesses the extent to which students organize their ideas with clarity, and presents a structured piece of writing comprised of: an introduction, a body, a conclusion, fit-for-purpose paragraphs.

- **Individual and societies:** This criterion assesses the extent to which the student is able to give balanced consideration to the perspectives of a range of relevant stakeholders, including individuals and groups internal and external to the organization.

Examiners will receive marking notes with the markscheme which give additional guidance on how to apply the assessment criteria.

Conclusion

The major change in the latest guide involves a new approach to marking HL paper 1, section C and the concept-based question in paper 2 at both HL and SL. Teachers and candidates need to know the command terms and what they mean in terms of expectations for candidates. For examination preparation, we urge mostly the study of the syllabus through a range of real-world examples. We also recommend the use of past examinations, with care. Students need to know how examinations are marked, both with markschemes and markbands and with assessment criteria and they should practice marking their own responses.

Exam tips

- Answer the question exactly as asked. Do not regurgitate a memorized answer to a question that is similar to the one asked.

- Do not use bullets—unless responding to the command term "identify".

- Structure your answer and show all workings.

- Do not "over" answer. Candidates often lose valuable time by providing unnecessarily lengthy responses to AO1 questions.

- Know the difference between "describe" and "explain".

- Provide balance—always think of both sides to a point of view.

- Look out for level AO3 questions—make sure you evaluate

The internal assessment (IA) is an integral and compulsory element of the Business Management programme for both HL and SL students. It accounts for 25% of the final mark for the subject. The IA enables you to demonstrate your business skills and apply your knowledge to a range of real-world business situations.

The IA requirements for SL and HL are different. HL students will complete a research project , whilst SL students prepare a written commentary. Before attempting either, it is important to meet with your teachers and look carefully at the IB Diploma Programme Business Management Guide so that you're familiar with the requirements.

You should refer to the assessment criteria at every stage of your IA project - this is what you will be marked against. Once you've finished your IA, it is a good idea to consider your work in light of the assessment criteria and ask yourself: "Have I met the requirements for the higher levels of each criterion?"

Higher Level research project

The DP Business Management HL internal assessment is a compulsory research project that enables students to pursue their personal interests and demonstrate the application of their skills and knowledge to a real business organization. It is important that the chosen organization is facing a real problem or issue. This integral component accounts for 25% of the final marks. As part of the research project, students are expected to produce a research proposal with a maximum of 500 words and a written report that does not exceed 2000 words.

Choice of research topic and organization

It is important that students choose a topic that they find interesting and motivating. Before the research process begins it is important that the teacher approves the topic to ensure that it complies with the requirements for internal assessment. For confidentiality reasons some organizations may not provide data so students should contact the organizations beforehand to ensure that they will be able to obtain the necessary information from their chosen organization (e.g. being able to carry out interviews with the managers, surveys with staff or access to financial reports among other research methods). The more information that can be obtained from the organization the better, as this should ensure a robust understanding of the business issue under consideration. However, students must be aware of ethical considerations when undertaking any research and be tactful and sensitive to other people and show respect for confidentiality when required.

Choice of a research title

It is crucial that the research title is phrased as a question. This research question should be forward-looking, targeted at an issue or a decision

still relevant for the business organization(s) rather than backward-looking or descriptive of something that has already happened. In addition, the question should be well focused and relate to a specific section of the Business Management syllabus. As a result, students should be able to draw effective conclusions and make recommendations for further action.

Examples of unsuitable backward looking questions include:

* How did Coca Cola promote its products in Kenya following the global recession?

* Why didn't Company X merge with Company Y to increase their market share?

* To what extent did the joint venture between ABC Company Ltd and XYZ Company Ltd lead to increased profitability?

Other unsuitable titles that are not phrased as questions and would turn out to be very descriptive include:

* An analysis of the profitability of M&K Ltd.

* An investigation into the causes of staff turnover at Omondi's restaurant.

Some examples of suitable questions include:

* Should South African Airways change its pricing strategy to gain a higher market share on the Johannesburg to London route?

* How should WNA differentiate itself from other bookstores in Mbabane?

* How can QRS Ltd improve its cash flow position?

* How should RST adjust its promotional strategy to increase market share?

* Should XYZ Motors produce a new model to compete with ABC Motors?

* What would be the most effective way for DFG fashions to promote its new range of luxury clothing?

* Should HIB introduce non-monetary rewards to reduce staff turnover?

The research proposal

The research proposal must be done as the first part of the internal assessment process. It is an important planning document that provides direction on how the research project will be tackled. The word limit for the research proposal is 500 words and moderators will not read beyond these words. The four components that should be present in a research proposal are:

(1) Research question

(2) Proposed methodology, including:

* the rationale for study

- areas of the syllabus to be covered

- possible sources of information

- organizations and individuals to be approached

- methods to be used to collect and analyse data, and the reason for choosing them

- the order of activities and timescale of the project

(3) Anticipated difficulties, such as limited or biased sources

(4) Action plan

The research proposal is criterion A in the assessment criteria (see page 409). Failure to produce a research proposal will lead to a mark of zero.

Written report

Once research has been carried out, the next step is to begin on the written report. This is where the main findings of the research are documented. The required format for the written report is as follows

- Title page: This should give a clear indication of what is contained in the research project, including the name of the student, the title of the project with research question, the intended audience, and the word count of all required sections.

- Acknowledgements: This page should acknowledge any individual and/or organization that has made the production of the report possible.

- Contents page: This should include the major headings in the report, beginning with the executive summary. Page numbers should be clearly indicated.

- Executive summary (abstract): This should be a concise, clear and explicit summary of the document, including the recommendations or conclusions. The research question and executive summary should guide the reader to the substance of the report. The maximum length of the executive summary is **200 words**, and this is not included in the word count.

- Introduction: This should demonstrate some background knowledge about the organization(s) and give a clear outline of the issue or decision under investigation.

- Research question: this page should state the research question as it appears in the title page and research proposal.

- Methodology employed: This section should be a summary of the primary (and, where relevant, secondary) research undertaken and the business tools, techniques and theories applied. It should also include an assessment of the validity and reliability of the data collected (for example, partiality and scope) and the methods employed. Any changes made as the work progressed should be explained.

- Main results and findings: This section should clarify what the raw data has revealed. This should include a summary of the data

Internal Assessment

collected and of the findings made, and should, where appropriate, be supported by tables, graphs and statistics.

- Analysis and discussion: In this section, the results and findings should be analysed with the help of relevant business tools, techniques and theories. They should also be interpreted: what main issues emerge from the research and why and how are they helpful (or not) to answering the research question? An evaluative approach to the discussion of findings should be pursued: for example, what are the strengths and weaknesses of the various positions on the issue or decision under investigation and what are their implications?

- Conclusion(s) and recommendation(s): The conclusions should follow on from the analysis and discussion; new facts or arguments should not be presented. Recommendations should be precise, answer the research question and be practical proposals for action that stem from the conclusions. If the results of the research are inconclusive, further research should be recommended. To be of practical value to management, the report should be forward-looking and support the organization's decision-making process.

- References and bibliography: A standardized referencing and bibliography system should be used that is consistent throughout the research project.

- Appendices: These should contain only information/data that is required in support of the text, and should be clearly referred to at the relevant points. The appendices will typically include examples of photographs, documents, questionnaires, numerical raw data in tables and statistical calculations.

It is important to ensure that the written report does not exceed **2,000 words**. The word count must be clearly shown on the title page. If the word limit is exceeded the teacher will only assess up to the first 2000 words of the report.

HL assessment criteria

The HL research project is marked against nine criteria from Criterion A to I. The maximum attainable mark for the research project is 25. A summary of the marking criteria is shown in the table below:

Criterion	Particulars	Marks available
A	Research proposal	3
B	Sources used and data collected	3
C	Use of tools, techniques and theories	3
D	Analysis and evaluation	6
E	Conclusions	2
F	Recommendations	2
G	Structure	2
H	Presentation	2
I	Reflective thinking	2
	Total	25

For more details on the level descriptors for each criterion, the Business Management guide should be consulted.

SL commentary

The SL commentary is a piece of writing based on three to five supporting documents about a real issue or problem facing a particular organization. The main features are as follows:

- The title of the commentary must be phrased in the form of a question.

- You must select a real and contemporary issue or problem, not a fictional one, focussing on a single business organization.

- The commentary should be based on secondary sources, but primary sources may be used as support.

- The commentary requires analysis and evaluation of the issue or problem, and you must form judgments, and incorporate them into the commentary in light of the question posed in the title.

- The maximum number of words for the written commentary is 1,500. It is important that you stay within this limit as your mark will be based upon the first 1,500 words only.

- It is recommended that 15 hours of your class time should be allocated to the written commentary.

- You must use no less than three but no more than five sources as supporting documents. You may of course consult other sources and these should be referenced in the body of the commentary and included in your bibliography.

The written commentary has no mandatory format, but it should be well-structured, well presented, and written clearly and concisely. A brief introduction should set the scene: briefly demonstrate some background information about the business organization, give a clear outline of the issue or problem under investigation and explain the methodology used to investigate this issue or problem. At the end of the introduction, it is good practice to list the supporting documents on which the commentary is going to be based.

Following the introduction should be a body section of commentary with analysis and discussion. Findings from the supporting documents should be presented and analysed with the help of relevant business tools, techniques and theories. Candidates should also interpret their findings. What main themes emerge from the analysis of the supporting documents, and why and how are they helpful (or not) to answering the commentary question? An evaluative approach to this discussion of findings should be pursued. For example, what are the strengths and weaknesses of the various positions on the issue or problem and what are their implications?

The commentary should end with a conclusion that answers the commentary question explicitly. The conclusion should not introduce new facts or new arguments that have not been discussed in previous sections of the commentary. Rather, it is good practice to include those

aspects of the commentary question that have not been fully answered in the commentary or that might need further investigation in order to be judged more effectively.

A well-presented commentary would include a title page, an accurate table of contents page, appropriate headings and sub-headings, consistent referencing, a complete bibliography and numbered pages. For presentation of references and bibliography, see the information on acknowledging the ideas and work of another person in the "The Diploma Programme" section of the subject guide.

Selecting a topic

Your teacher will be able to offer guidance when you choose your topic. It is important that you choose an issue that:

- engages your interest
- is realistic in terms of resources
- meets the criteria for assessment.

The title question must be clear and focused, allowing you to investigate the topic within the 1,500 word limit.

The following are examples of suitable questions:.

- Is producing a range of clothing for male customers a profitable decision for company X?
- Is an increase in wages an effective way to increase productivity and motivation in company Y?
- Is company Z's decision to increase productive capacity by building a new factory a sound financial decision?
- Can company X, an independent book shop, survive?

Selecting sources

Your supporting documents must be contemporary and written a maximum of three years before the submission of the commentary.

Whilst the commentary must be based on secondary sources, you may also include some primary data.

Examples of secondary sources include:

- articles from the local, regional, national or international press
- financial reports
- business accounts
- business plans
- mission statements
- web-based surveys
- extracts from company websites
- government and other statistics

- academic publications
- transcripts of a relevant audio-visual file.

Examples of primary data include:

- responses to questionnaires (you must include a blank copy of the questionnaire and a summary of your results)
- transcripts of interviews and discussions with focus groups
- results of surveys you have conducted.

You should choose your documents carefully to ensure they present a range of ideas and views that provide balance and objectivity.

SL assessment criteria

Your commentary is assessed against criteria laid out in the subject guide.

Criterion	Particulars	Marks available
A	Supporting documents	4
B	Choice and application of business tools, techniques and theories	5
C	Choice and analysis of data and integration of ideas	5
D	Conclusions	3
E	Evaluation	4
F	Structure	2
G	Presentation	2
	Total	25

For more details on the level descriptors for each criterion, the Business Management guide should be consulted.

INDEX